T0330986

Indian SMEs and Start-Ups

Growth through Innovation and Leadership

ASIA-PACIFIC BUSINESS SERIES   (ISSN: 1793-3137)

Series Editor
Léo-Paul Dana
Professor
Montpellier Business School, France & Dalhousie University, Canada

Published

Vol. 13 *Indian SMEs and Start-Ups: Growth through Innovation and Leadership*
edited by Léo-Paul Dana, Omvir Gautam, Ashish Gupta & Naman Sharma

Vol. 12 *Cooperatives as a Catalyst for Sustainability: Lessons Learned from Asian Models*
edited by Léo-Paul Dana, Naman Sharma, Sneha Kumari, K K Tripathy, B P Pillai & R Jayalakshmi

Vol. 11 *Organising Entrepreneurship and MSMEs Across India*
edited by Léo-Paul Dana, Naman Sharma & Satya Ranjan Acharya

Vol. 10 *Guanxi and Business (Third Edition)*
by Yadong Luo

Vol. 9 *Asian Models of Entrepreneurship: From the Indian Union and Nepal to the Japanese Archipelago: Context, Policy and Practice (Second Edition)*
by Léo-Paul Dana

Vol. 8 *Catalyst for Change: Chinese Business in Asia*
edited by Thomas Menkhoff, Hans-Dieter Evers, Chay Yue Wah & Hoon Chang Yau

Vol. 7 *From Adam Smith to Michael Porter: Evolution of Competitiveness Theory (Extended Edition)*
by Dong-Sung Cho & Hwy-Chang Moon

Vol. 6 *Islamic Banking and Finance in South-East Asia: Its Development and Future (Third Edition)*
by Angelo M. Venardos

Vol. 5 *Guanxi and Business (Second Edition)*
by Yadong Luo

Vol. 4 *Asian Models of Entrepreneurship — From the Indian Union and the Kingdom of Nepal to the Japanese Archipelago: Context, Policy and Practice*
by Léo-Paul Dana

The complete list of the published volumes in the series can also be found at
http://www.worldscientific.com/series/apbs

Asia-Pacific Business Series – Vol. 13

Indian SMEs and Start-Ups

Growth through Innovation and Leadership

Edited by

Léo-Paul Dana
ICD Business School, Paris, France
Dalhousie University, Canada

Omvir Gautam
Vishwakarma University, India

Ashish Gupta
Indian Institute of Foreign Trade, India

Naman Sharma
Indian Institute of Foreign Trade, India

World Scientific

NEW JERSEY · LONDON · SINGAPORE · BEIJING · SHANGHAI · HONG KONG · TAIPEI · CHENNAI · TOKYO

Published by

World Scientific Publishing Co. Pte. Ltd.

5 Toh Tuck Link, Singapore 596224

USA office: 27 Warren Street, Suite 401-402, Hackensack, NJ 07601

UK office: 57 Shelton Street, Covent Garden, London WC2H 9HE

Library of Congress Cataloging-in-Publication Data
Names: Dana, Leo Paul, editor.
Title: Indian SMEs and start-ups : growth through innovation and leadership
  / edited by Léo-Paul Dana, ICD Business School, Paris, France,
  Dalhousie University, Canada, Omvir Gautam, Vishwakarma University,
  India, Ashish Gupta, Indian Institute of Foreign Trade, India, Naman
  Sharma, Indian Institute of Foreign Trade, India.
Description: New Jersey : World Scientific, [2023] | Series: Asia-Pacific
  business series, 1793-3137 ; Vol. 13 | Includes bibliographical
  references and index.
Identifiers: LCCN 2022050636 | ISBN 9789811269547 (hardcover) |
  ISBN 9789811269554 (ebook) | ISBN 9789811269561 (ebook other)
Subjects: LCSH: Small business--India. | Small business--Growth. | New
  business enterprises--India. | Leadership--India. |
  Entrepreneurship--India.
Classification: LCC HD2346.I5 I4665 2023 | DDC
  338.6/420954--dc23/eng/20221020
LC record available at https://lccn.loc.gov/2022050636

British Library Cataloguing-in-Publication Data
A catalogue record for this book is available from the British Library.

For any available supplementary material, please visit
https://www.worldscientific.com/worldscibooks/10.1142/13239#t=suppl

Desk Editors: Aanand Jayaraman/Lai Ann

Typeset by Stallion Press
Email: enquiries@stallionpress.com

Printed in Singapore

*This book is dedicated to Anette Raaby and Bo Schöler —
Entrepreneurial leaders who understand leadership and who
lead by example, inspiring start-up teams as well as their
leaders to innovate and grow.*

About the Editors

Léo-Paul Dana is Professor at Dalhousie University and at ICD Business School. A graduate of McGill University and HEC-Montreal, he has served as Marie Curie Fellow at Princeton University and Visiting Professor at INSEAD.

Omvir Gautam is currently Assistant Professor at the Faculty of Management & Commerce, Vishwakarma University. He is also currently head of the Marketing Discipline at the Faculty. Dr Gautam has several publications in Scopus and ABDC-ranked journals and he regularly conducts research workshops at eminent institutes in India.

Ashish Gupta is Assistant Professor of Marketing at the Indian Institute of Foreign Trade. Dr Gupta is an accomplished researcher and author who has many publications in top ABDC A-ranked journals and has edited books with renowned publishers such as Springer.

Naman Sharma is currently associated with the Indian Institute of Foreign Trade. His areas of research are Entrepreneurship, Leadership and Organisational Behaviour. He has publications in ABDC-ranked journals and has edited seven books with publishers like World Scientific and IGI-Global.

Contents

About the Editors   vii

Chapter 1   SMEs and Start-Ups: The Growth Engine of India   1
             Léo-Paul Dana and Naman Sharma

Chapter 2   The SME Exchange: Issues and Challenges Faced
             by Entrepreneurs and Measures to Overcome Them   19
             Renu Bala

Chapter 3   Innovative Technologies' Adoption in Indian
             Start-Ups and SMEs   37
             Megha Sharma and V. K. Singh

Chapter 4   Export Performance and Resource Capabilities
             of Indian Manufacturing MSMEs   57
             Areej Aftab Siddiqui and Kashika Arora

Chapter 5   Leadership and Entrepreneurial Skills for SMEs:
             A Case of RP Inc.   89
             Nidhi Gupta and Ragini Tyagi

Chapter 6   Does Entrepreneurial Orientation Predict Small
             and Medium Enterprise Alliance Formation?
             Evidence from the Indian Manufacturing Sector   115
             *Rohit Prabhudesai, Ch. V. V. S. N. V. Prasad,
             Nitin Pangarkar, Abhishek Kumar Sinha
             and Akshay Bhat*

Chapter 7   COVID-19 and Learning Experiences of Women
             Entrepreneurial Leaders: An Indian Context   125
             Meghna Chhabra and Monika Agarwal

Chapter 8   Nurturing Dynamic Competencies: An Innovative
             Approach for SMEs' Sustainable Growth   151
             Swati Sharma and Jugal Kishor

Chapter 9   EdTech Start-Ups: A Mode of Transformation in
             Teaching and Learning   177
             Prateek Khanna, Reetika Sehgal, Mayank Malviya,
             Anukaran Khanna and Ashish Mohan Dubey

Chapter 10   Digital Health Innovation: Emergence of
             Digital Medical Consumer (DMC) and
             Holistic Digital Health Start-Ups (HDHSs)   203
             Girish R. Kulkarni, Daxesh M. Patel,
             Supriya Singh and Punit Saurabh

Chapter 11   A Study of Perspectives on the Growth,
             Strategy and Branding in Indian MSMEs   227
             Amol Randive, Jayashree Vispute and
             Shailendra Goswami

Chapter 12   Factors Influencing Social Media Adoption
             by MSMEs: Using the UTAUT Model   255
             Piali Haldar

Chapter 13   Free and Open-Source Software as an
             Innovation Stimulus for SMEs:
             An Indian Perspective   273
             Ruchi Jain and Ruchika Jeswal

Chapter 14   With Love for Loved Ones (WLFLO):
             A Start-Up Creating Value and Opportunities   293
             Supriya Singh, Punit Saurabh, Pradeep Kautish
             and Girish R. Kulkarni

Chapter 15   Systematic Literature Review on Retention
             in Entrepreneurial Firms: A Step Towards
             Sustainable Development   315
             Shivangi Saxena and Divya Goel

Chapter 16   Entrepreneurial Leadership and Designing
             Industry 4.0 Business Models: Towards an
             Innovative and Sustainable Future for India   333
             Slimane Ed-Dafali, Muhammad Mohiuddin,
             Md Samim Al Azad and Aidin Salamzadeh

Index   359

https://doi.org/10.1142/9789811269554_0001

Chapter 1

SMEs and Start-Ups: The Growth Engine of India

Léo-Paul Dana[*,‡] and Naman Sharma[†,§]

ICD Business School, Paris, France & Dalhousie University, Canada
†Indian Institute of Foreign Trade, Kolkata Campus, West Bengal, India
‡lp762359@dal.ca
§naman@iift.edu

Abstract

Over the past few decades, the small business and start-up ecosystem in India has undergone tremendous growth. The Indian government has implemented several policies and initiatives to support the growth of small businesses and start-ups, such as the Startup India initiative, which provides access to funding, incubation and other resources for early-stage companies. The growth of e-commerce and the increasing penetration of the Internet in India have also greatly benefited small businesses and start-ups, as they can now reach a wider market through online platforms. Overall, the small business and start-up sector has been a major contributor to the country's economic growth and job creation. However, there are a few challenges too. While the government and venture capital firms have invested heavily in Indian start-ups in recent years, competition for funding remains intense, and many start-ups struggle to make use of the funding effectively. The operating capital they need to run and scale their businesses is often not used effectively primarily due to a lack of awareness. Start-ups also face challenges in recruiting and retaining top talent, as the competition for skilled workers is fierce. This chapter provides an overview of these issues and sets the tone for the other chapters that follow.

Keywords: Start-ups, small business, start-up ecosystem, Indian start-ups, unicorns.

1. Introduction

Small businesses as a part of the MSME sector have made an immense contribution to the Indian economy as they are widening their operations through the establishment of different products through expansion of the entrepreneurship activities powered by innovation (MSME Govt. of India, 2021). The Government of India specifies the definition of small businesses as those where the investment in the plants and machinery is limited to Rs. 10 crore and the annual turnover is restricted to Rs. 50 crore. In contrast, the investments should be range bound, between Rs. 25 lakh and Rs. 5 crore for businesses catering to the manufacturing sector and between Rs. 10 lakh and Rs. 2 crore for the businesses catering to the service sector (Meghe, 2020; IBEF, 2022). Dana (2000) highlighted the importance of small business in developing countries like India. India consists of about 13 million HooReCa (Hotels, Restaurants and Catering) businesses and almost 12 million "kirana" (small retail) stores (Mediratta, 2022). The small business sector is extremely important to India as it contributes to the overall GDP of the economy by not only facilitating the upsurge of entrepreneurial avenues but also through creating jobs. According to the Centre for Monitoring Indian Economy (CMIE), there was a 7% unemployment rate till November 2021. Indian SMEs have provided employment opportunities to approximately 110 million Indians. Thus, Indian SMEs have proven to be the strongest segment of the business world that upholds the country's economic development. And, it is not immoral to calculate that Indian SMEs will expand themselves till 2025 by increasing their financial system up to $5 trillion (Mediratta, 2022).

With the increasing use of technology by people across the world, the success factor for every business is to become digital. Large organisations are blessed with the latest technological support, but SMEs lag behind the technology, especially in emerging markets. Further, digital adoption from a small vendor is a big task in a country like India. But, due to the COVID-19 pandemic, many SMEs had faced major losses due to a lack of technology. To cover up the losses, SMEs had started adopting digitisation technologies. For example, a small kirana store owner started taking orders through the mobile medium and home-delivered the orders; we also witnessed our favourite motel owner providing a digital menu just by scanning their QR code. Government bodies, financial institutions, big-tech companies and even various universities had organised paid or even free digital webinars to highlight the importance of adoption of digitisation in SMEs (Arunachalam *et al.*, 2020).

But to adopt the digitalisation and technological advances, an SME's owner needs a handsome investment which he may lack. So, the Government of India has launched a scheme for small vendors, named PM Street Vendor's Atmanirbhar Nidhi, under which loan credit is provided to such small-scale business owners like street hawkers and MUDRA (Micro Units Development and Refinance Agency) is also provided, which is a type of loan under which all the applications and legal formalities are processed smoothly (Mediratta, 2022).

Various start-ups have also emerged from SMEs. An agri-tech start-up named Khyeti attempts to connect farmers with relevant investors. Khyeti have greased the technology by initiating farmers' access to text and voice messages, voice and video calls, and social networking sites such as LinkedIn, YouTube and WhatsApp. Similarly, Krishworks is an education tech start-up that improves rural kids' learning and reading skills by teaching them the English language. This start-up has provided education to students in 10 districts of West Bengal and Tamil Nadu who were keen to learn the English language.

A SaaS start-up named Smartwinnr is promoting the adoption of digitised sales strategies by sales persons working in companies from countries like India, US, Japan and Europe by providing them adequate training and skills. The ultimate result of this personalisation method is the considerable gains in domain expertise, marketing capabilities and salesperson effectiveness (Arunachalam *et al.*, 2020). The following section delves into the growth trajectory of small businesses and start-ups till date in India, the challenges faced and the future outlook of this sector.

2. Growth Trajectory of Small Businesses in India

Different studies have already talked about the MSME sector being very lucrative and growth oriented with lot of future opportunities. While specifically referring to small businesses in India, some of the contributions to the economy of the nation are as follows: the sector constitutes a large amount of the total export of the nation and contributes to a large extent of the industrial output as well (Meghe, 2020). The sector is also one of the country's largest employment generators. Thus, being labour oriented utilises the potential of the rural and semi-urban resources, thereby leaving room for further growth through the human touch (Meghe, 2020). The following figures show the current status of small businesses in India and the growth rate till date.

Figure 1 shows the total number of registered small businesses in India year-wise from 2015–16 till 2021–22. The pattern has upward trend with a dip in the years 2017–18 and 2020–21, the latter being attributed to the impact of the COVID-19 pandemic.

It is interesting to note from Figure 2 that as a percentage of the total MSMEs in India, the trajectory of small businesses has been growing from 2016–17 till 2019–20, but declining post the pandemic, although from Figure 1, we saw that the total number of small businesses is increasing and has an uptrend post pandemic. This can be attributed to the fact that the rate of growth for the micro industries in India has surpassed the rate at which the small businesses are growing in India and this leaves us with a curious thought for further study.

Figure 3 shows the percentage of growth of small businesses in India from 2016–17 till 2021–22 and we see that post the pandemic, after the

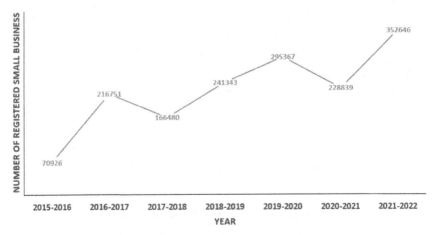

Figure 1.   Number of registered small businesses (Yearwise).

Source: Indiastat.

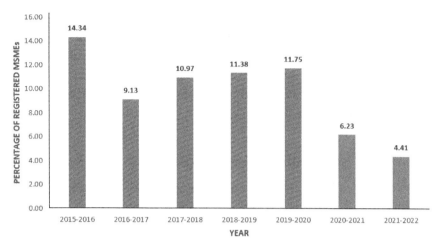

Figure 2.   Small businesses in India (Percentage of total MSME).

Source: Indiastat.

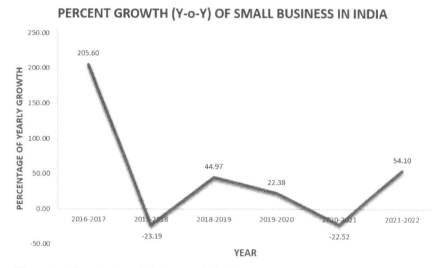

Figure 3.   Growth of small businesses in India.

Source: Indiastat.

dip, there has been a surge of 54.10% in the growth on a Y-o-Y basis from 2020–21 to 2021–22. On the contrary, the micro industries grew at 122.9% in the same period, thus contributing to the decrease of the share of small businesses in the MSME sector in India. These figures further raise curiosity with regard to the growth opportunities in the small business segment in India, which is highlighted in the next section.

3. Growth Opportunities for Small Businesses in India

Some of the studies highlight the opportunities in the telecommunications, electronics and healthcare sectors for the manufacture of cost-effective mobiles, networks and other electronics equipment, manufacture of low-cost and innovative medical devices along with providing service in this sector like data analytics solutions, software support services for customers, telemedicine services and setting up laboratories for medical diagnoses (Vasundhara, 2020). These opportunities will in turn pave the way for further employment in these businesses, while they focus on controlling the cost, expanding their operations further and influencing the local people, thereby reducing the need to import (Gandhi). However, post the COVID-19 pandemic, there has been a considerable shift towards the digital economy and thus these small businesses need to further reorient their business to sustain themselves in the future as consumers are further looking for better experiences through the usage of advanced technologies. Studies have suggested that it is very important for MSMEs to harness the power of the latest digital technologies to embark on the journey through the supply chain across the globe, thereby increasing their competitive power (Banerjee, 2021). One of the other studies has also shown that the growth for SMEs has further increased due to utilisation of the online e-commerce platform as a sales option, which further facilities cross-border sales (Vasundhara, 2020). There is untapped potential as the country moves through the fourth industrial revolution, especially in the areas of automation, robotics, digital payments, advanced connectivity and software services through customised ERP, and these small businesses can leverage the technologies to expand their businesses further and cater to the customers in these segments (Bhadada *et al.*, 2020). Also, retail, manufacturing, education, travel and tourism are among the top industrial segments wherein the opportunity lies the most in terms of revenue generation (Bhadada *et al.*, 2020). The COVID-19 pandemic has indeed been a curse to these micro and small businesses as some of them could not adapt to the rapid surge in digitisation wherein the large and medium businesses could capitalise to further grab their market share. Nevertheless, this COVID-19 pandemic can be taken as a one-off scenario, and through the learnings acquired in these transient stages, the small businesses can ride the digital wave by further investing in the upcoming technological spaces, thereby gaining the advantage of being an early mover. However, there are challenges to such moves as well, which are highlighted in the following section.

4. Challenges for Small Businesses in India

The lack of funds has always been a pain for small businesses, which operate mostly in the semi-urban or rural areas, as there is lack of access to collateral-backed securities (Meghe, 2020). Again, as the wave of the COVID-19 pandemic was ushered in, there was a significant loss to the people who took loans and set up these small businesses as there was some period of lockdown and also the people started using the e-commerce websites for buying, thereby causing these small businesses to suffer heavy losses (OkCredit, 2021). The lack of budget is also a pain point which impacts the quick access to quality raw materials and sufficient storage spaces along with the lack of marketing activities required for branding the businesses (Meghe, 2020). From the reports of Dun & Bradstreet, it is seen through a survey that access to the market, enhancing productivity, being compliant and access to finances and other resources are some of the top challenges that are faced by these small businesses (Dun & Bradstreet, 2021). While the lack of skilled labour and managerial skills remains one of the challenges throughout the operations of these small businesses, the survey shows some interesting highlights such as these businesses looking forward to a better facility of credit, help in supporting their marketing activities and utilisation of technological advancements by removing the barrier between consumers and their offerings (Meghe, 2020; Dun & Bradstreet, 2021). Although the challenges are plenty, some of which have already been highlighted in the reports, there are some other unforeseen challenges which might pop up as the country further opens up post the pandemic and another phase of transition sets in. While the small businesses will be lured towards utilisation of the digital technologies to serve their customers and tap the potential, the segments which were previously served by these businesses effectively and seamlessly, if not paid attention to, may be another challenge if there is too much focus on offering digital solutions. Thus, small businesses need to balance both their offerings by identifying the need in the market with respect to the current scenarios and then catering to the customers through appropriate channels, keeping the shortfall in budget and costs in mind. However, here comes another challenge that the survey captures: These small businesses, around 60%, have no access to marketing analytics and intelligence tools that would capture consumer sentiments to pin-point the target customers for such companies, and in the future they will be in dire need of access to such data and around 50% of them plan to use these tools (Dun & Bradstreet, 2021). Considering the points mentioned above, we discuss the road ahead for these small businesses to remain sustainable in this competitive landscape while they scale their operations.

5. Road Ahead for Small Businesses in India

On a curious note, on the future of small businesses, we start asking the following questions which may be of further interest for the readers and the community to investigate the opportunities and challenges of this sector:

- How has the COVID-19 pandemic shaped the learning curve of these small businesses in India, so that they may be able to manage these transient phases of the pandemic if any further pandemic occurs in the future?
- Are these small businesses prepared enough to harness the power of the human capital, employing upskilling, cross-skilling while utilising digitisation in their operations?

- Since small businesses are also one of the largest sources of employment for many in India, with the rapid surge in digital operations, how are they going to manage the human resources alongside harnessing the power of technology?
- Are the small businesses focusing on sustainable practices and green marketing as a means of branding their business, which may further help boost their business in India?
- Is there any practice of peer lending among the small businesses which may facilitate credit for these businesses, and if so, to what extent is it helping them?
- What is the structure of the credit facility of some of these successful small businesses and how are they leveraging empathetic relationships across the customer life cycles which may be a direction for future small businesses?

Through the above questions, some of the practices of these small businesses in India can be tracked and ascertained iteratively to note whether these are helping the businesses in the short run. In one of the reports, it was seen that around 30,000 micro-level enterprises were merged with small businesses in India as the government changed the definition of MSMEs so that their line of credit can be improved further and they get better access to financial resources (Soni, 2022). Amidst the pandemic, the government also offered several types of reliefs in the form of loans free of collateral, provisioning of debt, infusion of equities and reduction of taxes, among others (Vasundhara, 2020). As more and more small businesses adapted to the digitisation of operations, they could reduce the operational costs and by leveraging these digitisation techniques they are expected to gain more access to the behavioural patterns of consumers, enhance their competitiveness and expand their portfolio of offerings (Dun & Bradstreet, 2021). Thus, it is of utmost importance to utilise technological practices for these small businesses and at the same time understand the markets and the sentiments of the consumers in India. Thus, by doing so, such businesses will be able to face stiff competition by taking informed decisions on how to offer their services and cater to which segments of consumers, and in case some practices are not yielding much value, they can adapt to the market changes by remaining agile and competitive.

6. Start-Ups

Start-ups are getting a big share of attention with their growing importance and contribution to Indian economy (Dana & Sharma, 2021). Their rise in India has generated a good number of direct and indirect jobs driving the socioeconomic development of the country. According to India's Department for Promotion and Internal Trade (under the Ministry of Commerce and Industry), India happens to be the 3rd largest start-up eco-system in the world. The start-up ecosystem in India has witnessed a rapid evolution since the last two decades. In the beginning, they were just a handful of investors and a fewer number of entities which were called business incubators and accelerators. In India, Bangalore has constantly been topping the city charts for having sprouted the maximum number of start-ups; moreover, Genome Global Start-Up Ecosystem's project ranking report for the year 2019 identified Bangalore to be in the list of the world's 20 leading start-up cities. With time, corporates and the government have also realised the need to promote start-up organisations and the concept of entrepreneurship; hence, they are launching various opportunities for start-ups to strive and thrive in the Indian business market. As far as investment in these start-ups is concerned, Indian start-ups provide better opportunities for venture capitalists compared to the global start-up market.

On strategic front, start-ups are providing large companies the innovativeness they are looking for. Furthermore, the Government of India launched "New India" in 2016, aiming to create a window for start-ups to expand in the business market, driving sustainable economic growth. This is going to help the start-up ecosystems in India to strengthen their foundations further and create a possibility of promising outcomes. If we take a look at the recent start-ups in India, we can see that they have come a long way and have the potential to stay in the long run; some of them are as follows:

1. **Byju's:** One of India's most prominent EdTech apps, it was established in 2011 by Byju Raveendran and Divya Gokulnath. In 2017, Byju's

acquired Tutor Vista from Pearson; in 2019, it acquired Osmo, a company that makes educational games for children aged 3–8 years. Byju's has received funding from a good number of prominent investors, some of whom are Aarin Capital, Sequoia Capital India and the Chan Zuckerberg Initiative; in fact, Byju's happens to be the first in Asia to receive investment from the Chan Zuckerberg Initiative.

2. **Paytm:** An abbreviation for Pay Through Mobile, it was founded in 2010 by Vijay Shekhar Sharma. It is a Noida-based company offering payment services to consumers and merchants. Its parent company is One97 Communications Limited (OCL). Ant Group and Softbank Vision Fund are the largest shareholders with a total shareholding of 24.9% and 17.47%, respectively.

3. **OYO Rooms:** Also known as OYO Hotels & Homes, India's multinational hospitality chain was founded by Ritesh Agarwal in 2012. In 2021, OYO collaborated with Yatra, Airbnb and EaseMy Trip to form the Confederation of Hospitality, Technology and Tourism (CHATT). OYO has investments from some notable investors, such as the SoftBank Vision Fund, Sequoia Capital, Hero Enterprise and the China Lodging Group.

4. **Zomato:** Zomato is a food directory website, which was established in 2008 by Deepinder Goyal and Pankaj Chaddah, alumni of IIT and former analysts at Bain & Company. Zomato has acquired 12 start-ups globally and has received investment from a good number of investors like Info Edge and Sequoia Capital.

And the list goes on…

Now, the concept of start-ups is welcoming a new age of fast-growing unicorns. A unicorn is a privately held start-up that has a valuation of 1 billion. As of 2022, India has around 100 unicorns. Though it is not uncommon to the start-up ecosystem, building one is a challenge and requires sheer planning and dedication. The term unicorn was coined by venture capitalist and seed investor Aileen Lee. In fact, India has become the 3rd largest ecosystem to host unicorn companies. Some of the sector-wise start-ups that are now unicorns can be seen in Table 1.

Table 1. Indian unicorns.

Ecommerce	Fintech	Enterprisetech	Consumer Services	Edtech	Logistics	Health Tech	Others
Cars 24	Acko	MuSigma	Bigbasket	Byju's	Blackbuck	Curefit	Make my trip
Meesho	BharatPe	MapmyIndia	Rebel Foods	Vedantu	Delhivery	Pharmeasy	Renew Power
Flipkart	Groww	Browserstack	Swiggy	Unacademy	Rivigo	Pristyn care	No Broker
Lenskart	Zerodha	Icertis	Zomato	UpGrad	XpressBees		Ola
Snapdeal	Paytm	Zoho	Urban Company	Lead	Elasticrun		MPL

Source: Authors' compilation.

7. Start-Ups to Unicorns and the Challenges

Since the last two decades, it has already been known that India has maintained its favourable spot in the technological advancement sector through start-ups. In the previous year, 2021, the IT start-up revenue had risen up to $194 billion. In 2018, India had its first-ever unicorn success when Walmart acquired Flipkart for $16 billion. Recently, Phonepe, a subsidiary of Flipkart, was valued at $5.5 billion. Leading US and global investors like Tiger Global and Sequoia are now investing in some of the 100 such unicorns of India. In the year 2021, India became the top third country in the world in introducing unicorns (Devanur, 2022).

With the upliftment of Indian start-ups and unicorns, investors face various challenges. India on the one hand is growing its industrial setup through IT start-ups, but the number of engineering graduates is declining. In 2020, the number of engineer graduates declined to 2.2 million from 2.9 million (Chopra, 2021). This creates a great worry as qualitative engineers are decreasing, which alternatively is hiking up the salary packages. Indian IT companies like TCS, Infosys and Wipro are facing heavy resignations from engineers (Fortune India, 2022). The data show that in 2022, Infosys have faced approx. 25% attrition (BI India Bureau, 2022).

Thus, recruiting qualitative personnel, providing training to them and catching the attention of global investors and capital market are challenging tasks that Indian start-ups and unicorns may face. At present, there is an abundance of global funds floating around, but eventually, Indian start-ups may have to face the issue of fund allocation due to geo-political situations.

Indian start-ups like Paytm have not allocated funds and resources effectively. Paytm had suffered through the loss of $19 billion in the capital market within consecutive years (Bhalla, 2022). Thus, this creates more pressure on the Indian stock markets to be more alert for start-ups and unicorns flaming the funds and capital to extend their market value. To create a positive balance in the Indian market system, the upcoming start-ups must overcome such situations (Devanur, 2022).

With India's new-age start-ups reaching the top positions in the market, they must also rigorously work on having a balanced workplace for their employees, which will help the cross-pollination of knowledge. The most noticeable aspect was that only 15% of the unicorn start-ups have at least one female founder. Therefore, there are plenty of things that need to be worked upon.

To build a start-up firm is challenging for entrepreneurs, but the issues in the Indian context are different. Let us see some of the major challenges faced by Indian entrepreneurs:

1. **The Capital:** Although we previously mentioned the ease of investment in Indian start-ups compared to other countries, Indian entrepreneurs still face the issue of having enough operating capital to run the business at least in the early phase.

2. **Diversified Audience:** The product/service offered by the start-ups needs to be packaged according to the diverse population of the country where people from different religions, beliefs and occupations shall find value in the start-up's offering. Therefore, reaching out to such a large audience is difficult and next to impossible. At the same time, for a niche segment, the product or service itself has to be unique and attractive in nature.

3. **Complex Regulatory Norms:** India happens to be ranked 77th out of 190 in the World Bank's Ease of Doing Business index and 137th out of 190 in the World Bank's Starting a Business Ranking index. Therefore, the government, in spite of its "New India" concept, still has to go a long way to create a market for start-ups to flourish and sustain in the long run.

4. **Technology:** With the ever-changing technical aspects, start-ups need to keep up with these dynamics. For this, they must have a dedicated number of teams where one will keep track of the needs of consumers and another will work to provide the desired product or service.

5. **Marketing Strategy:** Today's marketing teams have a very different approach towards the consumers. They constantly subject themselves to Marketing Agility to make sense of the requirement and take up iterative experimentation before launching any product or service. This requires both human and capital resources, which can be challenging for newbie start-ups.

6. **Newbies:** As correctly stated by Albert Einstein, "The only source of knowledge is experience". Since upcoming start-ups with founders

Figure 4.   Selection of right human resources.

have the least exposure to an idea, how does one do business? With limited resources and expertise in business, and with the onset of real hardships and occasional failures in the initial phase, many start-up founders tend to lose motivation.

7. **Choosing the Right Person:** The recipe for success calls for the right people, place and time (Figure 4). Hence, choosing the right person at the right time in the business for the right position is very important and it becomes even more crucial for small businesses and start-ups as the risk is all the more higher for them. It can be challenging to identify the right pool of talent and place them at the right positions to get the best out of them.

Despite all the challenges, it is still possible for passionate entrepreneurs to build up their empires. It may be difficult in the beginning, but with patience and dedication, they can also make their mark. With the growing awareness towards entrepreneurship and business incubators, start-ups are getting stronger day by day. The biggest advantage with start-ups is the scope to invent or innovate ideas, and provide the same to their clients and consumers. Many organisations outsource their daily needs through collaborations with start-up firms. Therefore, the start-ups are not limited to common consumers; they can also serve the needs of giant corporates. Ultimately, there is a lot of evolution that is still supposed to take place in the start-up ecosystem in India, which will lead to fruitful outcomes that will aid the country's economic growth.

8. Discussion

The Indian Government has eased up doing business and collaborating with businesses of other countries to add inspiration to India's small-business and start-up ecosystem. Digital India, Skill India, Make in India, Smart cities, etc., are some of the government policies that have benefited Indian start-ups and SMEs in a broader time frame. The Startup India International Summit, held in January 2021, drew attendees from more than 25 nations. As per a news statement from the Prime Minister's Office, this was the biggest entrepreneurial convergence hosted by the Indian Government ever since the commencement of the Startup India movement. Following this, the Netherlands, Finland, Sweden and Canada implemented a slew of programmes to expand their footprint in India's innovation and start-up economy in March 2021. Through further collaborative projects via short-term technology programmes, the Government of India has instituted a network of start-up hubs to strengthen ties with other countries to find solutions in areas such as security, environmental stewardship, emission reduction, efficient affordable healthcare and renewable power, which have proven to be India's biggest weakness in recent times.

The administration rewards partnership motivates businesses and recruits shareholders from other nations to make massive investments in India's start-up and SME ecosystem through such coverage. In addition, by increasing the number of business shareholders, sensitive small businesses might be protected from fluctuations in India's international relations (Kashyap, 2021).

References

Arunachalam, S., Pingali, S., & Pedada, K. (2020). Too small to serve to too large to ignore: SMEs, the new frontier for digital vendors? https://www.forbesindia.com/article/isbinsight/too-small-to-serve-to-too-large-to-ignore-smes-the-new-frontier-for-digital-vendors/61447/1.

Banerjee, C. (2021). Integration of MSMEs into digital economy is crucial. Self-Reliant India. *Times of India*. Retrieved January 26, 2021, from https://www.mycii.in/KmResourceApplication/76885.CBsarticleinTimesofIndia27Jan.pdf.

Bhadada, P., Gupta, M., & Kejriwal, R. (2020). Tapping into SMB market opportunities. Retrieved February 14, 2020, from https://zinnov.com/the-growth-story-of-small-and-medium-business-in-india/.

Bhalla, K. (2022). Paytm says its fundamentals are 'robust', market cap now below $5 billion. https://www.businessinsider.in/stock-market/news/paytm-says-its-fundamentals-are-robust-market-cap-now-below-5-billion/articleshow/90389791.cms.

BI India Bureau (2022). The attrition at Infosys is worse than that at Wipro, Salil Parekh has increased hiring plan by 10,000. https://www.businessinsider.in/careers/news/the-attrition-at-infosys-is-worse-than-that-at-wipro-ceo-salil-parekh-has-increased-hiring-plan-by-10000/articleshow/88856648.cms.

Chopra, R. (2021). Engineering seats drop to lowest in a decade; 63 institutes to shut in 2021. https://indianexpress.com/article/education/engineering-seats-down-to-lowest-in-a-decade-63-institutes-to-shut-in-2021-7425602/.

Dana, L.-P. & Sharma, N. (2021). India. In L.-P. Dana, N. Sharma & S. R. Acharya (Eds.), *Organising Entrepreneurship and MSMEs across India* (pp. 1–30). World Scientific, Singapore. https://doi.org/10.1142/9789811212741_0001.

Dana, L.-P. (2000). Creating entrepreneurs in India. *Journal of Small Business Management*, *38*(1), 86.

Devanur, G. (2022). India's new unicorns and their current challenges. https://www.forbes.com/sites/forbesbusinesscouncil/2022/04/05/indias-new-unicorns-and-their-current-challenges/?sh=4dfadd6233a3.

Dun & Bradstreet (2021). Impact of Covid-19 on small businesses in India and the way ahead. https://www.dnb.co.in/file/reports/Whitepaper_Impact-of-COVID-19-on-Small-Businesses.pdf.

fortune india.com (2022). 2022 salary hikes to hit 6-yr high amidst the 'Great Resignation'. https://www.fortuneindia.com/enterprise/2022-salary-hikes-to-hit-6-yr-high-amidst-the-great-resignation/107153.

Gandhi, T. (2021). Growth of SME ecosystem in India & what it means for small business? Retrieved from https://digest.myhq.in/growth-of-ecosystem-of-sme-in-india/.

IBEF (2022). *MSME Industry in India*. Retrieved March 2022, from https://www.ibef.org/industry/msme.

Kashyap, K. (2021). How India is leveraging its foreign relations to benefit its startups. https://www.forbes.com/sites/krnkashyap/2021/03/28/how-india-is-leveraging-its-foreign-relations-to-benefit-its-startups/?sh=2a45a358af38.

Mediratta, A. (2022). Prioritise small businesses and MSMEs to support inclusive growth. https://www.forbesindia.com/article/new-year-special-2022/prioritise-small-businesses-and-msmes-to-support-inclusive-growth-arvind-mediratta/72783/1.

Meghe, K. (2020). Challenges and opportunities of small businesses in India after pandemic. *International Journal of Creative Research Thoughts*, 8(8), 3751–3755. https://ijcrt.org/papers/IJCRT2008447.pdf.

Ministry of Micro Small and Medium Enterprises (2021). Annual Report 2020–21. Government of India. https://msme.gov.in/sites/default/files/MSME-ANNUAL-REPORT-ENGLISH%202020-21.pdf.

OkCredit (2021). Growth of small businesses in India over the years: Some interesting stats & figures. OkCredit. Retrieved June 16, 2021, from https://okcredit.in/blog/growth-of-small-business-in-india/#:~:text=According%20to%20the%20International%20Journal,and%20medium%20enterprises%20(MSME).

Soni, S. (2022). Nearly 30,000 micro enterprises scaled up to become small businesses: Govt data. Retrieved March 27, 2022, from https://www.financialexpress.com/industry/sme/msme-eodb-nearly-30000-micro-enterprises-scaled-up-to-become-small-businesses-govt-data/2473187/.

Vasundhara, R. (2020). Micro, small, and medium enterprises in India — An explainer. India Briefing. Retrieved May 14, 2020, from https://www.india-briefing.com/news/micro-small-medium-enterprises-india-explainer-17887.html/#:~:text=As%20per%20the%20official%20estimates,medium%20enterprises%20in%20the%20country.

What's MSME. (2020). *Ministry of Micro, Small & Medium Enterprises, Government of India*. Retrieved June 6, 2020, from https://msme.gov.in/know-about-msme.

https://doi.org/10.1142/9789811269554_0002

Chapter 2

The SME Exchange: Issues and Challenges Faced by Entrepreneurs and Measures to Overcome Them

Renu Bala

Jan Nayak Chaudhary Devi Lal Vidyapeeth (JCDV),
Sirsa, Haryana, India
renu820kamboj@gmail.com

Abstract

Small and medium-sized enterprises (SMEs) are considered the backbone of the Indian economy. But for the last few years, a large numbers of issues have been generating severe hurdles for the small and medium-sized enterprises in India. As SMEs enter the new era of globalisation and face different kinds of dramatic challenges, an attempt has been made to examine those challenges and determine the measures to overcome such types of challenges. For the present study, data have been gathered from entrepreneurs of the IT sector, banking sector and pharmaceutical sector. A sample of 240 entrepreneurs, i.e., eighty from each sector, was taken. The primary data were gathered with the help of a questionnaire on a five-point Likert scale and analysed by various descriptive statistics such as frequency distribution, mean and standard deviation. ANOVA and Factor analysis have been used to test research hypotheses and validate the results of the study. The analysis shows that entrepreneurs have to face various types of issues and challenges, and such challenges can be solved by reducing the compliances of the listing procedure, using social media for advertisements, conducting business conferences and seminars periodically, providing tax incentives to the investors and minimising the risk factor.

Keywords: SMEs, challenges, issues, measures, entrepreneurs

1. Introduction

In India, Small and Medium-sized Enterprises (SMEs) are considered an essential contributor to the development and economic growth of the country (https://www.world-exchanges.org). These are also called the backbone of the Indian economy (Mukherjee, 2018) as these enterprises contribute to employment generation, social stability, industrial production, GDP growth, regional development, export earnings and economic diversification (Khatri, 2019). Small and medium-sized enterprises perform a dominant role in industrial and economic development as various types of social and economic sectors of a country depend upon SMEs (Lalhriatchhungi & Prasain, 2017). SMEs are the second largest sector after the agriculture sector in the Indian economy (Bhoganadam & Rao, 2017). SMEs provide more employment opportunities than big industries at a lower comparative cost and provide support in the industrialisation of rural as well as backward areas by reducing the regional imbalances and assuring equitable distribution of wealth and national income (Kour, 2014). SME exchanges provide a trading platform to small and medium enterprises and work under recognised stock exchanges such as the BSE and the NSE of India (https://economictimes.indiatimes.com). In Indian history, in the beginning, the first SME exchange was established by the BSE with only one company, and after that, the NSE started its SME platform named "EMERGE" (Pimpale & Rai, 2015). In India, large numbers of emerging issues create severe challenges for SMEs. SMEs have to go through various stages of growth, commonly known as life cycles (Gupta *et al.*, 2013). During the different phases of life cycles, they have to face various dramatic challenges like globalisation, financial constraints, the establishment of new enterprises, lack of human capital building, indeterminate turnover and low motivation among employees (Mathai, 2015). So, due to such issues, entrepreneurs have to face different kinds of hurdles to start up a new business, such as productivity, quality, computer-based technology, credit at a reasonable rate of interest, market-ability of products and timely availability of finance (http://www.dcmsme. gov.in). To tackle all these problems, various remedies can be adopted by SME exchanges such as diversification of the channels of financing, developing specialised private banks for SME financing, developing SME databases, developing credit risk analysis of SMEs, providing tax incentives, innovations and collaborations, and mentoring-style assistance to SMEs (Yoshino & Hesary, 2016). After launching two separate platforms for SME exchange through the BSE and NSE, the Government of India also paid attention to the growth of SMEs (Shroff & Sengupta, 2016). As per the annual report of the Government of India, during the period 2020–2021, the Indian Government spent 3125.55 crores on the MSME sector, and in the previous years, the government spent 6714.14, 6513.13 and 6222.21 crores in 2019–20, 2018–19 and 2017–18, respectively (https://msme.gov.in). However, SME exchanges have to face various kinds of problems in promoting trade among MSMEs and the investors, as there exist some shortcomings that restrict SME exchanges from getting popular among the investors (https://www.bseindia.com).

2. Review of Literature

Ackah & Vuvor (2011) presented the issues faced by SMEs in Ghana. SMEs have to tackle different kinds of problems, including high tariffs, taxes, lack of finance, infrastructure gaps and increased competition. On the other hand, several factors are responsible for the birth of such issues like the lack of management, defaulting on previous loans, collateral and small equity base. Venkatesh & Muthiah (2012) presented the importance and contribution of small- and medium-scale enterprises in India. SMEs perform a very important role in the creation of structure of the Indian economy due to their advantages in terms of employment, exports and output. Due to the importance of this sector, the Indian Government has included it in its agenda of five-year plans. But till now, SMEs have had to face many problems in terms of marketing, finance and quality, which can be solved by the collective action of policymakers and entrepreneurs. Gupta *et al.* (2013) explained the factors responsible for firms' growth. All the factors contributing to the development of a firm can be broadly divided into two parts: internal and external. Under the area of internal factors, synergy, resources and distinctive competencies of the firm are covered, and on the other side, under the umbrella of external factors, political environment, demographical environment and financial background are covered. Kour (2014) explained why SMEs are considered a boon for the development of the Indian nation. SMEs play a crucial role in India's manufacturing sector and are considered the engine of economic growth. For a developing country like India, where capital is scarce and labour is abundant, SMEs act as a significant source of employment for many people. Such a sector is the solution to various problems like unemployment, poverty and insecurity. Mathai (2015) explained the issues and challenges faced by the Micro, Small and Medium Enterprises (MSMEs) in India in the current scenario. Due to the changes in the globalised economy, various changes take place at different stages of the enterprises. Enterprises have to tackle multiple financial constraints, lack of motivation among workers, indeterminate turnover and lack of human capital. Shroff & Sengupta (2016) explained how the opportunities could be exploited for the growth of SMEs. The regulator should evaluate the volumes periodically and remove the operational difficulties faced during the listing.

Yoshino & Hesary (2016) highlighted the main challenges faced by Small and Medium-sized Enterprises at the Asian level and suggested solutions for mitigating such challenges. Lack of comprehensive databases, shortage of finance, low level of R&D expenditures and lack of technical knowledge are the primary reasons for the slow growth of SMEs. Problems of SMEs can be sorted with the adoption of various measures such as the diversification of financing channels, development of credit risk analysis, development of SME databases and providing tax incentives. Bhoganadam *et al.* (2017) explained the challenges which create hurdles for the growth of SMEs. A variety of challenges exist in the development of SMEs, which include poor quality control, lack of machinery, unorganised nature of operations, lack of demand, lack of experience, imperfect knowledge of market conditions, poor project planning, poor promotional skills, lack of distribution of marketing channels, identification of new markets, low returns, managing employees, limited capital and limited capital. Lalhriatchhungi & Prasain (2017) presented the situation of micro, small and medium enterprises in the state of Manipur. SMEs are considered very important as they perform a significant role in the development of Manipur by providing employment, exports and production facilities. Such enterprises are considered an essential segment of the economy, contributing in different forms to the nation's development. Mukherjee (2018) presented that in this present era of globalisation, the difficulties for Indian small- and medium-scale enterprises include the absence of the latest technology, lower profit margins and maintenance of product quality. For the growth of small- and medium-scale enterprises, attention should be paid to digital technology, investment in human resources, reduced infrastructural gaps, easy access to finance and lesser complicated business regulations. Khatri (2019) assessed the challenges faced by the Indian MSME sector. Many initiatives taken by government bodies for the improvement of small- and medium-scale enterprises have to tackle different kinds of hurdles. Issues related to low ICT literacy, finance, human resource, operations, marketing, complicated documentation, lack of motivation, inefficient logistics, informational gap, complex laws, infrastructural gaps, etc., create challenges for the entrepreneurs. Lema *et al.* (2020) focused on performance measurements in SMEs based on a literature review. For the study, 131 articles from the period 2006 to 2019 were covered. The main focus was on the manufacturing sector by excluding the service sector. The results indicated that most of the studies concentrated on individual companies; on the other hand, clusters, networks and supply chains have received less attention. Saunila (2020) elaborated on the innovation capabilities of SMEs on the basis of a literature review. Organisational actions which relate to the development of firms involve very meaningful basics. The innovation capabilities of SMEs depend upon several factors such as innovative production, innovative management and creation. Steinhauser *et al.* (2020) throw light on the internationalisation of SMEs in the last twenty years. During the study, the period of twenty years (1998–2017) has been divided into four sub-periods of five years. The clusters which have emerged in the four sub-periods presented the relevant results for the study.

3. Research Gaps

The above-mentioned review of the literature indicates that different studies have been conducted in this field. However, the results provided by those studies are inconclusive in nature as the focus was on finding out the issues for the slow growth of SME exchanges and the challenges faced by the SMEs; but, the present study examines the problems and challenges faced by the entrepreneurs regarding SME exchange procedures and suggests the measures to overcome such kinds of issues.

4. Research Questions

1. What are the main issues and challenges faced by the entrepreneurs during SME exchange procedures?
2. What are the required measures to solve issues and challenges faced by entrepreneurs during SME exchange procedures?

5. Research Objectives

1. To identify the main issues and challenges faced by entrepreneurs during SME exchange procedures.
2. To analyse the required measures to solve issues and challenges faced by the entrepreneurs during SME exchange procedures.

6. Sample Profile

A sample of 240 respondents, including from the IT sector, banking sector and pharmaceutical sector entrepreneurs, has been taken. Eighty entrepreneurs from each sector were selected. The judgment sampling method was adopted to select the sample. In this method, entrepreneurs of different sectors have been included so that the views of different areas can be analysed as a whole. To explore the difficulties faced by the entrepreneurs of different streams, a sample selection was made of 240 respondents.

7. Data Collection and Analysis

To conduct the present study, both primary and secondary data were collected. Secondary data have been gathered from different blogs, journals, reference books, articles, newspapers, magazines and reports. On the other hand, primary data have been collected with the help of a pre-structured questionnaire on a five-point Likert scale, i.e., Strongly Agree (SA), Agree (A), Neutral (N), Disagree (D) and Strongly Disagree (SD). The collected data have been analysed with the help of various descriptive techniques such as mean, standard deviation, ANOVA and factor analysis, and to compare the results of the present study, ANOVA was applied. To examine the reliability of the gathered data, the Cronbach Alpha coefficient (0.936) has been used, which is considered a good measure for the internal consistency.

8. Results and Discussions

The frequency distribution of views of entrepreneurs of the IT sector, banking sector and pharmaceutical sector regarding issues and challenges faced during SME exchange procedures presents that most of the entrepreneurs strongly agree/agree with the complex procedure of listing ($n = 232$, $p = 96.67$), lack of modern skills ($n = 226$, $p = 94.17$), lack of experience ($n = 212$, $p = 88.33$), lack of finance ($n = 208$, $p = 86.67$), lack of skilled management ($n = 204$, $p = 85$), lack of awareness ($n = 200$, $p = 83.33$), lack of updated technology ($n = 188$, $p = 78.33$), lack of good business relations ($n = 172$, $p = 70.83$), lack of capable and required human resources ($n = 161$, $p = 66.08$), ethical issues ($n = 144$, $p = 60$), lack of motivation infrastructure ($n = 118$, $p = 49.17$) and lack of infrastructure ($n = 107$, $p = 44.58$).

Table 1 presents the descriptive and inferential statistics of the views of entrepreneurs of the IT sector, banking sector and pharmaceutical sector regarding issues and challenges faced during the SME exchange procedure. Entrepreneurs of the IT sector focused on the complex procedure of listing ($\bar{x} = 4.91$, $\sigma = 0.763$), lack of experience ($\bar{x} = 4.78$, $\sigma = 0.784$), lack of modern skills ($\bar{x} = 4.42$, $\sigma = 0.792$), lack of finance ($\bar{x} = 4.39$, $\sigma = 0.808$), lack of skilled management ($\bar{x} = 3.83$, $\sigma = 0.823$), lack of awareness ($\bar{x} = 3.66$, $\sigma = 0.843$), lack of good business relations ($\bar{x} = 3.54$, $\sigma = 0.864$), lack of updated technology ($\bar{x} = 3.41$, $\sigma = 0.878$), lack of capable and required human resources ($\bar{x} = 3.39$, $\sigma = 0.881$), ethical issues ($\bar{x} = 3.34$, $\sigma = 0.886$), lack of infrastructure ($\bar{x} = 3.12$, $\sigma = 0.891$) and lack of motivation ($\bar{x} = 2.99$, $\sigma = 0.898$). On the other hand, entrepreneurs of the

Table 1. Sector-wise entrepreneurs' viewpoints towards issues and challenges faced during SME exchange procedure.

Statements	IT Sector			Banking Sector			Pharmaceutical Sector			ANOVA	
	N	$\bar{x}$	σ	N	$\bar{x}$	σ	N	$\bar{x}$	σ	F	Sig
Lack of finance	80	4.39	0.808	80	4.42	0.823	80	4.68	0.802	4.840	0.064
Lack of modern skills	80	4.42	0.792	80	4.61	0.804	80	4.54	0.818	2.565	0.212
Lack of capable and required human resources	80	3.39	0.881	80	3.99	0.886	80	3.88	0.890	1.835	0.436
Lack of infrastructure	80	3.12	0.891	80	3.22	0.931	80	3.62	0.901	1.644	0.000*
Lack of experience	80	4.78	0.784	80	4.71	0.789	80	4.72	0.783	2.335	0.000*
Complex procedure of listing	80	4.91	0.763	80	4.66	0.799	80	4.81	0.771	3.392	0.251
Lack of awareness	80	3.66	0.843	80	4.18	0.866	80	4.31	0.848	1.400	0.201
Lack of skilled management	80	3.83	0.823	80	4.22	0.845	80	4.32	0.844	2.036	0.324
Ethical issues	80	3.34	0.886	80	3.76	0.892	80	4.16	0.882	3.553	0.131
Lack of updated technology	80	3.41	0.878	80	4.06	0.871	80	4.26	0.856	5.962	0.232
Lack of good business relations	80	3.54	0.864	80	4.02	0.877	80	4.22	0.862	3.746	0.0121
Lack of motivation	80	2.99	0.898	80	3.48	0.906	80	3.71	0.895	4.781	0.010*

Note: N = number of respondents, * = significant at 5% level.
Source: Primary survey (author's calculation).

banking sector concentrated on lack of experience ($\bar{x} = 4.71$, $\sigma = 0.789$), complex procedure of listing ($\bar{x} = 4.66$, $\sigma = 0.799$), lack of modern skills ($\bar{x} = 4.61$, $\sigma = 0.804$), lack of finance ($\bar{x} = 4.42$, $\sigma = 0.823$), lack of skilled management ($\bar{x} = 4.22$, $\sigma = 0.845$), lack of awareness ($\bar{x} = 4.18$, $\sigma = 0.866$), lack of updated technology ($\bar{x} = 4.06$, $\sigma = 0.871$), lack of good business relations ($\bar{x} = 4.02$, $\sigma = 0.877$), lack of capable and required human resources ($\bar{x} = 3.99$, $\sigma = 0.886$), ethical issues ($\bar{x} = 3.76$, $\sigma = 0.892$), lack of motivation ($\bar{x} = 3.48$, $\sigma = 0.906$) and lack of infrastructure ($\bar{x} = 3.22$, $\sigma = 0.931$). However, entrepreneurs of the pharmaceutical sector paid more attention to the complex procedure of listing ($\bar{x} = 4.81$, $\sigma = 0.771$), lack of experience ($\bar{x} = 4.72$, $\sigma = 0.783$), lack of finance ($\bar{x} = 4.68$, $\sigma = 0.802$), lack of modern skills ($\bar{x} = 4.54$, $\sigma = 0.818$), lack of skilled management ($\bar{x} = 4.32$, $\sigma = 0.844$), lack of awareness ($\bar{x} = 4.31$, $\sigma = 0.848$), lack of updated technology ($\bar{x} = 4.26$, $\sigma = 0.856$), lack of good business relations ($\bar{x} = 4.22$, $\sigma = 0.862$), ethical issues ($\bar{x} = 4.16$, $\sigma = 0.881$), lack of capable and required human resources ($\bar{x} = 3.88$, $\sigma = 0.890$), lack of motivation ($\bar{x} = 3.71$, $\sigma = 0.895$) and lack of infrastructure ($\bar{x} = 3.62$, $\sigma = 0.901$).

Statistically, the results of ANOVA show that there is a significant difference in the views of entrepreneurs of the IT sector, banking sector and pharmaceutical sector regarding lack of infrastructure ($p = 0.000$), lack of experience ($p = 0.000$) and lack of motivation ($p = 0.010$) at the 5% level of significance; hence, the null hypothesis (H01) is rejected.

The frequency distribution of views of entrepreneurs of the IT sector, banking sector and pharmaceutical sector regarding measures to overcome the issues and challenges faced during the SME exchange procedure indicates that most entrepreneurs strongly agree/agree with reduce compliances of listing procedure ($n = 226$, $p = 94.17$), use social media for the advertisement ($n = 212$, $p = 88.33$), conduct business conferences and seminars periodically ($n = 197$, $p = 82.08$), provide tax incentives to the investors ($n = 194$, $p = 80.83$), minimise the risk factor ($n = 188$, $p = 78.33$), motivate the youth ($n = 156$, $p = 65$), create awareness ($n = 151$, $p = 62.92$) and use of print media ($n = 124$, $p = 51.67$).

Table 2 presents the descriptive and inferential statistics of the views of entrepreneurs of the IT sector, banking sector and pharmaceutical sector regarding measures to overcome the issues and challenges faced during the SME exchange procedure. Entrepreneurs of the IT sector paid

Table 2. Sector-wise entrepreneurs' viewpoints towards measures to overcome the issues and challenges faced during SME exchange procedure.

Statements	IT Sector			Banking Sector			Pharmaceutical Sector			ANOVA	
	N	$\bar{x}$	σ	N	$\bar{x}$	σ	N	$\bar{x}$	σ	F	Sig
Reduce compliances of listing procedure	80	4.66	0.756	80	4.91	0.706	80	4.62	0.756	4.840	0.204
Create awareness	80	4.16	0.841	80	4.21	0.844	80	4.26	0.811	2.565	0.212
Use social media for the advertisement	80	4.82	0.711	80	4.72	0.742	80	4.84	0.731	1.835	0.436
Use of print media	80	3.88	0.886	80	3.98	0.856	80	3.91	0.887	01.644	0.204
Motivate the youth	80	4.11	0.861	80	3.71	0.821	80	4.08	0.864	4.335	0.112
Conduct business conferences and seminars periodically	80	4.52	0.791	80	4.44	0.796	80	4.51	0.782	2.392	0.251
Provide tax incentives to the investors	80	4.36	0.802	80	4.51	0.784	80	4.55	0.774	1.400	0.421
Minimise the risk factor	80	4.31	0.818	80	4.26	0.821	80	4.11	0.851	2.036	0.000*

Note: N = number of respondents, * = significant at 5% level.
Source: Primary survey (author's calculation).

great attention to use social media for the advertisement ($\bar{x}$ = 4.82, σ = 0.711), reduce compliances of listing procedure ($\bar{x}$ = 4.66, σ = 0.756), conduct business conferences and seminars periodically ($\bar{x}$ = 4.52, σ = 0.791), provide tax incentives to the investors ($\bar{x}$ = 4.36, σ = 0.802), minimise the risk factor ($\bar{x}$ = 4.31, σ = 0.818), create awareness ($\bar{x}$ = 4.16, σ = 0.841), motivate the youth ($\bar{x}$ = 4.11, σ = 0.861) and use of print media ($\bar{x}$ = 3.88, σ = 0.886). On the other hand, entrepreneurs of the banking sector concentrated on reduce compliances of listing procedure ($\bar{x}$ = 4.91, σ = 0.706), use social media for the advertisement ($\bar{x}$ = 4.72, σ = 0.742), provide tax incentives to the investors ($\bar{x}$ = 4.51, σ = 0.784), conduct business conferences and seminars periodically ($\bar{x}$ = 4.44, σ = 0.796), minimise the risk factor ($\bar{x}$ = 4.26, σ = 0.821), create awareness ($\bar{x}$ = 4.21, σ = 0.844), use of print media ($\bar{x}$ = 3.98, σ = 0.856) and motivate the youth ($\bar{x}$ = 3.71, σ = 0.821). However, entrepreneurs of the pharmaceutical sector paid more attention to use social media for the advertisement ($\bar{x}$ = 4.84, σ = 0.731), reduce compliances of listing procedure ($\bar{x}$ = 4.62, σ = 0.756), provide tax incentives to the investors ($\bar{x}$ = 4.55, σ = 0.774), conduct business conferences and seminars periodically ($\bar{x}$ = 4.51, σ = 0.782), create awareness ($\bar{x}$ = 4.26, σ = 0.811), minimise the risk factor ($\bar{x}$ = 4.11, σ = 0.851), motivate the youth ($\bar{x}$ = 4.08, σ = 0.864) and use of print media ($\bar{x}$ = 3.91, σ = 0.887).

Statistically, the results of ANOVA show that there is a significant difference in the views of entrepreneurs of the IT sector, banking sector and pharmaceutical sector regarding minimising the risk factor (p = 0.000) at the 5% level of significance; hence, the null hypothesis (H02) is rejected.

9. Factor Analysis

To identify the issues and challenges faced by the entrepreneurs in the SME exchange procedure, factor analysis has been applied, which has been considered to be a statistical measure to reduce the initial variables as well as combine them to produce a broad range of factors on the basis of common variables (Inkova, 2014). Table 3 indicates that the value of Cronbach's Alpha coefficient is 0.842, which represents the reliability as well as consistency of the data used for analysis purposes

Table 3.   Coefficients of sampling adequacy.

Coefficients		Value
Kaiser–Meyer–Olkin (KMO)		0.842
Bartlett's test of sphericity	Chi-square	3554.862
	d.f.	76
	Sig.	0.000*

Note: N = number of respondents, * = significant at 5% level.
Source: Compiled from primary data (SPSS output).

Table 4.   Anti-image matrix (measure of sampling adequacy).

Anti-image	1	2	3	4	5	6	7	8	9	10	11	12
1	**.927**[a]	−.161	.052	.074	.013	−.034	−.088	.052	.008	−.217	.076	−.279
2	−.061	**.912**[a]	−.026	.098	−.173	.037	.059	.042	−.001	.142	−.025	−.117
3	.152	−.036	**.864**[a]	−.080	.025	−.831	.025	.002	.015	−.232	.082	.083
4	.174	.095	−.080	**.826**[a]	−.466	.084	−.119	.023	.078	−.012	−.067	−.295
5	.113	−.153	.025	−.466	**.843**[a]	−.030	−.711	−.135	−.183	.031	−.092	.237
6	−.134	.036	−.831	.084	−.030	**.873**[a]	−.010	−.011	−.014	.214	−.514	−.077
7	−.188	.057	.025	−.119	−.711	−.010	**.891**[a]	.016	−.002	−.060	.020	−.104
8	.042	.045	.002	.023	−.135	−.011	.016	**.893**[a]	−.073	.065	−.125	−.125
9	.018	−.041	.015	.078	−.183	−.014	−.002	−.073	**.961**[a]	−.024	−.025	−.005
10	−.117	.141	−.232	−.032	.030	.216	−.010	.062	−.034	**.829**[a]	−.432	−.267
11	.036	−.035	.082	−.067	−.092	−.514	.020	−.125	−.025	−.442	**.817**[a]	.125
12	−.179	−.127	.083	−.295	.237	−.077	−.104	−.125	−.005	−.297	.125	**.820**[a]

[a]Denotes the variables building anti image matrix.
Source: Compiled from primary data (SPSS output).

(Nunnaly, 1978). For the factor analysis, two tests have been applied, namely, Kaiser–Meyer–Olkin (KMO) and Bartlett's Test of Sphericity. Kaiser–Meyer–Olkin (KMO) examines the suitability of factor analysis and is a good measure of sampling adequacy. The calculated value of KMO is 0.842, which presents the appropriateness of the factor analysis.

For the analysis of the anti-image matrix as shown in Table 4, diagonals containing the value of more than 0.6 are retained. Measures of

Sampling Adequacy (MSA) are presented through the diagonal elements of the anti-image correlation matrix, and are facilitated to achieve more stable results of factor analysis and to drop out the collections of variables which seem to be non-factorable.

Table 5 presents those factors which were drawn through the principal component method, and reduces a large number of variables by preserving much information of the initial variables. The twelve variables were divided into three factors. The initial Eigenvalues represent the total dispersion attributed to that factor. The variance share of the first factor is 5.223 (43.529%) of the total variance, the second factor is 1.222 (10.181%) of the total variance and similarly the third factor is 1.011 (08.426%) of the total variance. The first three factors combined account for 62.137% of the total variance.

Table 6 indicates the communalities that amount to dispersion of variables shared by three factors. The values of communalities vary from

Table 5. Total variance explained.

| Component | Initial Eigenvalues | | | Extraction Sums of Squared Loadings | | |
	Total	% of Variance	Cumulative %	Total	% of Variance	Cumulative %
1	5.223	43.529	43.529	5.223	43.529	43.529
2	1.222	10.181	53.710	1.222	10.181	53.710
3	1.011	8.426	62.137	1.011	8.426	62.137
4	.875	7.288	69.425			
5	.765	6.372	75.797			
6	.587	4.890	80.687			
7	.492	4.103	84.790			
8	.450	3.749	88.538			
9	.384	3.200	91.738			
10	.366	3.050	94.788			
11	.351	2.925	97.713			
12	.274	2.287	100.000			

Note: Extraction method: principal component analysis.

Table 6.   Extraction of the variables.

S. No.	Statements	Initial	Extraction
1	Lack of finance	1.000	0.864
2	Lack of modern skills	1.000	0.833
3	Lack of capable and required human resources	1.000	0.856
4	Lack of infrastructure	1.000	0.852
5	Lack of experience	1.000	0.845
6	Complex procedure of listing	1.000	0.677
7	Lack of awareness	1.000	0.751
8	Lack of skilled management	1.000	0.834
9	Ethical issues	1.000	0.878
10	Lack of updated technology	1.000	0.822
11	Lack of good business relations	1.000	0.741
12	Lack of motivation	1.000	0.733

Source: Compiled from primary data (SPSS output).

0.677 to 0.878 and all the values were more than 0.5 as required. Hence, all the variables were retained, which shows adequate explanation of the drawn factors.

Table 7 exhibits the factor labelling known as rotated component matrix. This matrix presents the association between twelve variables forming three factors.

• The first factor named "Factors related to Personal Issues" consists of six variables such as lack of modern skills (0.950 loading) followed by lack of motivation (0.943 loading), lack of experience (0.936 loading), lack of good business relations (0.932 loading), lack of awareness (0.911 loading) and ethical issues (0.907 loading).
• The second factor named "Factors related to Financial Issues" consists of three variables such as lack of finance (0.862 loading), lack of capable and required human resources (0.844 loading), and lack of infrastructure (0.826 loading).
• The third factor labelled "Factors related to Technical Issues" consists of three variables such as lack of updated technology (0.758 loading),

Table 7.   Factors labelling and loading.

Factor(s)	Factors Labelling	Statements	Factor Loading I	II	III
Factor-I	Factors related to personal issues	Lack of modern skills	**0.950**		
		Lack of motivation	0.943		
		Lack of experience	0.936		
		Lack of good business relations	0.932		
		Lack of awareness	0.911		
		Ethical issues	0.907		
Factor-II	Factors related to financial issues	Lack of finance		**0.862**	
		Lack of capable and required human resources		0.844	
		Lack of infrastructure		0.826	
Factor-III	Factors related to technical issues	Lack of updated technology			**0.758**
		Complex procedure of listing			0.724
		Lack of skilled management			0.712
Cronbach's Alpha coefficient of the Factors					
0.863		0.824		0.982	

Source: Compiled from primary data (SPSS output).

complex procedure of listing (0.724 loading) and lack of skilled management (0.712 loading).

The obtained Cronbach's alpha coefficient values of all the three factors are 0.863, 0.824 and 0.982, respectively.

10. Conclusion and Recommendations

The present study concluded that during the SME exchange procedure, entrepreneurs of the IT sector faced challenges such as complex procedure of listing, lack of experience and lack of modern skills. In contrast, entrepreneurs of the banking sector faced issues such as lack of experience, complex procedure of listing and lack of modern skills. However, entrepreneurs of the pharmaceutical sector find difficulties in procedure of listing, lack of experience and lack of finance. Various measures can be adopted to solve such kinds of issues, such as reducing compliance of listing procedures, using social media for the advertisements, conducting business conferences and seminars periodically, providing tax incentives to the investors and minimising the risk factor. The Indian Government should try to support SMEs by providing required and necessary services from time to time to improve and grow the nation. SMEs play a significant role in the Indian economy, so there is a need to take collective measures for betterment.

11. Implications of Study

The present study describes the issues and challenges faced by entrepreneurs regarding SME exchange procedures and measures to improve such problems. In a nutshell, it will provide valuable suggestions to the management of SME exchanges to enhance the image of the exchange as per the entrepreneurs' requirements. The study results can also be used as a reference by researchers to conduct research in the respective fields.

12. Limitations and Further Scope of the Study

The study is restricted to less number of the sectors as it can be further expand to the another sectors and secondly a sample of 240 respondents is also small, which cannot be used to generalise the outcomes of the study. So for the generalisation of results, number of respondents can be increased. The study of a particular sector can be conducted to analyse that sector in detail or researchers can analyse area-wise sectors as per their interest.

References

Ackah, J. & Vuvor, S. (2011). The challenges faced by small & medium enterprises (SMEs) in obtaining credit in Ghana. Master's thesis, BTH School of Management, pp. 1–56.

Bhoganadam, S. D. & Rao, N. S. (2017). A study on issues and challenges faced by SMEs: A literature review. *Research Journal of SRNMC*, *1*(2), 48–57.

Gupta, P. D., Guha, S., & Krishnaswami, S. (2013). Firm growth and its determinants. *Journal of Innovation and Entrepreneurship*, 2(15), 1–14.

Khatri, P. (2019). A study of the challenges of the Indian MSME sector. *IOSR Journal of Business and Management (IOSR-JBM)*, 21(2), 5–13.

Kour, M. (2014). Entrepreneurship in SMEs: A boon for development of India. Paper presented at *Entrepreneurship Development in India: Challenges and Opportunities*, pp. 207–214.

Lalhriatchhungi, M. & Prasain, G. P. (2017). Growth of micro, small and medium enterprises in Manipur. *International Journal of Business and Management Invention*, 3(12), 22–26.

Lema, X. R., Saiz, J. A., Rodríguez, R., & Verdecho, M. J. (2020). Performance measurement in SMEs: Systematic literature review and research directions. *Total Quality Management & Business Excellence*, 32(15), 1–8.

Mathai, G. P. (2015). Challenges and issues in micro, small and medium enterprises (MSMEs) in India: A current scenario of economic growth. *Global Journal for Research Analysis*, 4(7), 162–163.

Mukherjee, S. (2018). Challenges to Indian micro small scale and medium enterprises in the era of globalization. *Journal of Global Entrepreneurship Research*, 1(28), 1–19.

Shroff, S. & Sengupta, S. (2016). SME exchange: Transformation opportunities of SMEs. *IOSR Journal of Business and Management (IOSR-JBM)*, 2(2), 103–107.

Steinhauser, V. P. S., Paula, F. D., & Soares, D. M. (2020). Internationalization of SMEs: A systematic review of 20 years of research. *Journal of International Entrepreneurship*, 19(1), 46–53.

Venkatesh, S. & Muthiah, K. (2012). SMEs in India: Importance and contribution. *Asian Journal of Management Research*, 11(2), 792–796.

Yoshino, N. & Hesary, F. T. (2016). Major challenges facing small and medium-sized enterprises in Asia and solutions for mitigating them. 1(3), ADBI Working Paper Series 564, pp. 1–20.

Websites

https://www.world-exchanges.org.
https://economictimes.indiatimes.com.
http://www.dcmsme.gov.in.
https://msme.gov.in.
https://www.bseindia.com.

© 2023 World Scientific Publishing Company
https://doi.org/10.1142/9789811269554_0003

Chapter 3

Innovative Technologies' Adoption in Indian Start-Ups and SMEs

Megha Sharma[*,‡] and V. K. Singh[†,§]

*School of Management, Graphic Era Hill University, Dehradun, India
†Faculty of Management Studies, Gurukula Kangri
(Deemed to Be University), Haridwar, India
‡meghaas663@gmail.com
§drvksingh1969@gmail.com

Abstract

The world is changing, and so are businesses, customers and technological advancement. With new innovations of technological advances, various new businesses have established to make themselves the market leaders just like large organisations, which are known as start-ups. Similarly, several small- and medium-sized businesses (SMEs) have also adopted the latest and innovative technologies in their businesses, to make themselves competitive and attract a large customer base. Artificial intelligence, deep learning, robotics, machine learning, Internet of Things (IoT) and blockchain technologies are the latest technologies, which are being adopted by start-ups and shall be adopted by SMEs. This chapter aims to explore and provide insights about the importance of the latest innovative technologies and their usage by the start-ups and SMEs by reviewing the literature. Indian society has adopted digitalisation and so as the start-ups and SMEs which have flourished the Indian markets and engaged the customers and it builds the brand strong and credible.

Keywords: Innovation, digitalisation, technologies, brands, customers, artificial intelligence, machine learning

1. Introduction

At the end of 2020, many successful companies focused on improving their investment policies by welcoming a new decade. Most of the companies prioritised implementation and embracing the latest and progressing technologies. To flourish in the core competitive market, start-ups and small- and medium-sized businesses (SMEs) should aim to adapt and upgrade the latest technologies by discarding old and outdated technologies. This helps preserve work efficiency, build up a strong position in the market and helps in maintaining a strong relationship with the existing customers and invite new customers. By adopting and upgrading the latest technologies, start-ups and SMEs can lead a strong position in the competitive market by meeting all the customers' needs and demands with sterling practices. Therefore, adopting the latest technologies by replacing the old ones is called the digital revolution (*Forbes*, 2021).

The digital revolution, and innovation, improves the business environment externally as well as internally. Digitalisation enhances the communication terms of SMEs and start-up owners to communicate with existing and potential customers. Besides this, it also advances employees' efficiency. As for the latest technologies, employees use them at their best and can increase production efficiency by cutting extra costs and recruiting the most deserving candidate.

In the previous year, 2021, Indian start-ups had upraised their funding by $42 billion, including Meesho, Sharechat, Upgrad, Mamaearth, MPL, Grofers and Cred. India is the third largest economy to have experienced a growth through start-ups. In the year 2021, Indian start-ups experienced tremendous growth through public offerings.

Paytm has raised the highest offering for a total valuation of $2.46 billion (Rs. 18,300 crore as per Indian currency). Following it, Zomato has reached the maximum capitalisation in the Indian market of the amount $14.8 billion. Similarly, Nykaa also has a capitalisation of $13.5 billion (*The Economic Times*, 2022).

On Twitter, an Indian start-up entrepreneur joked that the definition of a "Unicorn" in the venture capital market should now be $1 billion in investment raised. India produced 42 unicorns, a threefold increase from 11 new unicorns in 2020 and nine in 2015. With an $18 billion value,

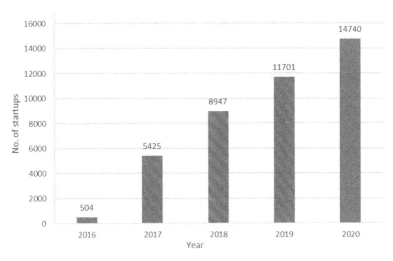

Source: *Statista* (2022).

Byju's became a unicorn this year. After China required all online education enterprises to register as non-profits, Indian EdTech entrepreneurs gained investor trust (Vanamali, 2021).

The unicorn club in India is in the midst of a talent war, as companies are increasing their staff by 10–100% in order to drive market growth and invest in product development. Among surveyed unicorns, they admitted that they want to recruit between 2000 and 2500 people in the year 2021 and 2022. According to the executives, hiring will be driven by the need to expand capabilities in artificial intelligence (AI), technology and product development, and foreign market growth (Sarkar & Basu, 2021).

Innovation is supposed to drive the economic development of the country at two levels. First is the organisational level, which aims to increase the profit value of the business, and second is the social level, which aims to increase the overall GDP of the country. Conventionally, innovation used to lay emphasis on inventing advanced technologies and expertise by investing majorly in the research and development (R&D) sector. However, this method did not last well because it was generating the expected results. For example, Canada is the highest investment-generating country in the education and R&D sector but has not yet produced the estimated output, country's GDP and technological system.

Therefore, in the Global Innovation Index 2020, 131 markets across 80 pointers were measured on the basis of innovation enactment and Canada ranked 17th in it which is subsequently acknowledged for its innovative infrastructure (Cukier *et al.*, 2021).

Broadly acknowledging, innovation and advancement are beyond the formation of modern technologies and increase of R&D. Innovation is all about presenting and implementing fresh and first-hand ideas which advance and generate development, achieve the desired results and invent a product or service for the advantage of the business, society and stakeholders. Therefore, innovative technological development is not successful until it is adopted by companies and industries, whether it is the latest application, software or digital innovation, or an injection. It will not be measured as innovation until it is accepted by the organisations and society.

Innovation adoption can be clarified more particularly. The significant part to succeed a business is to implement the latest technologies and modern commercial models. Innovation was defined by the economist Joseph Schumpeter as business that needs to be arranged by producing new and latest products as per the need of society, adopting latest approaches of production, implementing new techniques to supply, and exploring the new markets and latest techniques to conduct a business (Cukier *et al.*, 2021).

Businesses that empower themselves with the latest digital transformation technologies may profit by various methods, including simplifying systems and processes, lowering expenses and increasing staff efficiency. Whereas every organisation is now at a distinct point in its digital competency, here are five technologies that enterprises, particularly SMEs, and start-ups should adopt to ensure long-term success:

• Considering the use of mobile cloud computing opportunities
In today's era, almost every business considers using mobile cloud computing. It includes e-mail storage and software processors such as Microsoft 365 and Google workstations. For adopting digitalisation in the industry, SMEs and start-ups should increase the use of the mobile cloud for internal business operations. Clouding provides several possible cost reductions, improves record protection, increases customisation

and increases freedom of movement. These features contribute to the competitive edge of start-ups and SMEs to take them to a leading position in the market and attract more customers. Mobile cloud computing enables businesses to access business information only through the latest smartphones and tablets. It safeguards the employees' constant link safety and keeps employees informed about all the latest activities of the business.

- Investing in AI

Technology behemoths like Facebook, Google and Microsoft pour massive amounts of money into AI every year. Certain firms can leverage AI's strategic benefits with minimum investment. SMEs and start-ups, for example, can benefit from ongoing operations which are instantly integrated into the bookkeeping system thanks to AI-powered accounting software. Computational technologies analyse information and find trends, allowing computers to anticipate and perform regular tasks like changing wages or sending cash receipts. Furthermore, AI-powered business software liberates accounting employees from ordinary activities, allowing them to pay greater attention to significantly greater activities.

- Upgrading to software-defined vast area network

To make the business's work smooth, installing a good network is essential. SMEs and start-ups need to upgrade their networks by installing and updating software-defined vast area networks (SD-WAN). SD-WAN conglomerates access advanced technology and a scalable management solution to meet your specific business requirements. It can improve networking transparency, streamline and centralise management, and provide high reliability and effective network efficiency. Another advantage is that industry apps may be prioritised for optimum efficiency.

- Make use of the IoT capabilities

The IoT enables businesses to tackle challenges in creative ways. A nationwide transportation firm can now effectively monitor the position of its cars (and transported items) due to IoT instead of phoning its drivers to verify geolocation and projected delivery times. Similarly, IoT-enabled remote access enables the transportation firm to distribute its cars along more effective paths by accessing essential information supplied by linked transportation companies and data itself from automobiles.

However, ship control is just one example. In practically every corporate field, IoT technology is creating game-changing potential. By providing firms with the ability to gather additional information to make better-educated decisions, it may deliver valuable insights to develop efficiency and give the business a strategic advantage it did not previously possess. Thus, start-ups and SMEs must adopt and consume IoTs.

- Concentrate on data analytics

An emphasis on data analytics can help to enhance profitability. A B2B firm, e.g., may use data analytics to examine clients and determine the regularity of the bills payments from the clients and to the clients. Furthermore, it is easy to maintain and are well-positioned for the sustained growth. Once these elevated clients have been discovered, a firm may focus on nurturing those connections and analysing critical features about some of these companies to identify and seek equal opportunities.

Thus, in the current era, the transformation a business adopts as per the latest trends and technologies is known as Industry 4.0. Industry 4.0 is the fourth revolution in the business world. Industry 4.0 has revolutionised since the automation of production through steam and water processes, i.e., first revolution of business. The second revolt includes increased production through the use of electricity. In contrast, the third industrial revolution succeeded by adopting computers and mechanisation with machine and data learning (Marr, 2018).

Therefore, with the increased adoption rate of technology and digitalisation through companies, start-ups and SMEs, this chapter aims to throw light on the importance of technology and digital adoption by Indian start-ups and SMEs to maintain a strong competitive position in the domestic and globalised market.

2. Materials and Methods

This study is based on a literature review of research papers from the year 1990–2021. The studies have been extracted through major databases such as Scopus and Web of Science. We also referred to the individual publisher databases such as Emerald, Springer and Elsevier. Further, the online articles were also analysed to gather the facts related to the subject. This chapter analyses the unknown facts of innovative theories and their impact on Indian start-ups and SMEs.

3. Analysis of Literature

3.1 *Blockchain adoption*

Blockchain has been successfully used in private and public enterprises (Pilkington, 2016; Nowiński & Kozma, 2017; Antoniadis *et al.*, 2019; Jain *et al.*, 2021). Blockchain was initially introduced through the cryptocurrency Bitcoin in 2008 (Antoniadis *et al.*, 2019). It has been analysed that the businesses that lack the latest technologies fall behind the competition. The way to obtain and retain big data applications has increased at an extraordinary speed. The technological ability to integrate and analyse these heterogeneous amounts of data is now starting to catch up (De Vivo, 2018). Thus, this inspires SMEs and start-ups to adopt blockchain technology.

Blockchain technology helps businesses examine their customers' data instantly, maintaining privacy and security. Blockchain is used in every aspect of a company, including finance, production, marketing and even analysing the customers' needs and purchase behaviour. Combining blockchain technologies and development has reduced the costs and difficulty, rendering it much more acceptable for SMEs and start-ups. Thus, to make blockchain technology successful in a business, owners need to cater to their company's big data.

Therefore, big data can also improve the utility and efficiency of SMEs and start-ups. Given in the following are some of the benefits that SMEs and start-ups will achieve from bid data:

- **Enhanced clarity:** Big data provide opportunities to a business by analysing the data quickly. They implement operational policies according to consumers' needs and their buying behaviour.
- **Improvement in product/service line:** Understanding the customers' needs may assist the SMEs and start-ups to produce specific products

and services that fulfil the customers' desires and outlooks. Big data facilitate post-launch product and service enhancement, ensuring superiority across the product and service time.

- **Core competency:** SMEs and start-ups are able to compete in the competitive market environment according to the relative time period. This allows the organisation to analyse the actual situation in their sector in the competitive market. Core competency enables SME and start-up owners to examine themselves against their competitors. This feature helps owners identify how better and more significant their competitors are.

Big data provide potential benefits to a business. For SME and start-up owners, the knowledge is required to produce advanced business analytics. Fortunately, with the advent of technology, this gap has been recognised and closed.

3.2 *Forms of Advanced Innovation*

For decades, the market has invented the latest technologies such as robotics, AI, cloud computing, machine learning are the innovations which cannot be separated from the companies sustained either in developed or developing countries. With growing innovative technologies, businesses have started producing products and services with advanced features, upgraded skills and promotion as per the customers' needs.

These innovative technologies play a key role in the succession story of start-ups and SMEs once they adopt it. However, adoption of such technologies makes a business strong and successful as without its implementation there is no actual development (Cukier *et al.*, 2021).

According to a report by McKinsey & Company (2019), small businesses adopt digital technology more as compared to large companies, such as IoT and AI. With lower digital costs, it becomes reasonable for SMEs and start-ups to adopt such technologies. Small businesses have adopted the digital payment system at a rate of 94%, whereas large companies have accepted digital payments at 79%.

With the growing adoption rate of innovative technologies and digitalisation by SMEs and start-ups, there is a grown demand for these innovations to be tuned to their customers and suppliers, as it helps to shape the customers' purchase behaviour and increase the revenue system of the business.

Businesses are launching the latest goods and services or upgrading the former one by adopting innovative technologies. For example, Spotify, the music app, during the year 2020 and 2021, faced a downfall in revenues when advertisers decreased their budgets. So, to overcome this situation, this start-up launched the option of uploading podcasts, which increased the customers' entertainment and gave a positive output. Start-ups and SMEs have adopted the AI technology for their marketing strategy. AI enable the companies to access the data of their potential customers which they for on web browsers, and then creates the pop-up ads at every digital marketing platform which the customers use. This effects to persuade the buying behavior of the customers. Moreover, start-ups and SMEs have led chat bots to make direct contact with customers, answering their queries and asking for the honest feedback through AI.

SMEs and start-ups have adopted various business models to boost their sales and customers' interaction. For example, Sugar, the cosmetic brand, started its business by launching personal mobile applications and also by selling its products through the e-commerce platform, Nykaa. Restaurants and bakeries started taking orders by launching their social media accounts and websites. Therefore, by shifting the business totally to the digital mode by branding themselves strongly and adopting the latest business model, businesses have made a smart decision and profitable business.

Process optimisation is aided by innovation and digital technology. Companies are attempting to incorporate technology into their daily operations in order to accelerate growth and enhance quality. Across sectors, there is a growing need for industrial automation systems that provide a connected and digitised factory experience. Embracing next-generation change, gaining efficiency and resilience, sustainability, and people-centricity are the four fundamental elements driving the transition towards universal automation. Universal automation is significant because it tackles current system constraints while unleashing limitless creativity. Machine-driven procedures provide major economic advantages while also improving employee satisfaction. Digital transformation has the potential to tackle a wide range of challenges in a more flexible and imaginative way. Companies that are fast to adjust to the new standard will have a competitive edge (Verma, 2022).

4. Challenges Faced by Start-ups and SMEs

There have been some tremendous technologies introduced since the previous decade. Android and iOs industries are one of the example which use technology to upgrade and amend their features. Famed technology giants Snapshot, Uber, Instagram, Facebook and Make my trip are products of the latest technology.

It has also been witnessed that mobile cloud computing is becoming an essential access and digital resource for companies without using computer systems or laptops. At the same time, AI has also marked its presence with upgrading technology. Some of the technologies like mobile clouding and apps can be quickly adopted by small and big companies. But AI is the only technology that only large companies can adopt.

Due to cyberattacks like phishing and inadequate cyber security, many small Indian businesses have lost a lot of their money, customer trust and financial information as surveyed by Cisco through a double-blinded survey of 3700 small businesses (*The Economic Times*, 2021).

Undoubtedly, AI is long-lasting technology in the digital era. Many brands and companies are investing massive capital in adopting AI. Unfortunately, start-ups and SMEs face challenges in the adoption of AI technology. Start-ups and SMEs are business set-ups with fewer resources, small capital and fewer employees. But, like every business, start-ups and SMEs also expect to grow more in less time in the competitive market. Hence, for these reasons, SMEs and start-ups deal with a gap in the adoption of AI in their businesses. There are few drawbacks of artificial intelligence which are faced by start-up and SMEs owners, as follows (Agarwal, 2021).

4.1 *Data determined*

As AI relies on data, a business can achieve better outcomes through AI in the presence of more data. With the changing world of digitalisation, it is easy for people to access the internet and businesses. Thus, with the internet increment, companies are gathering a considerable quantity of data and contrary to big companies, SMEs and start-ups lack in collecting vast data. Having less data creates a big problem for start-ups and SMEs in adopting AI, as AI will not provide expected outcomes.

Recently, Facebook used a billion photographs from Instagram users who have public profiles, i.e., do not have private accounts, to build a machine learning system. Facebook notified the account holders of Instagram in their general data protection regulations that they have utilised the data from their account to promote Facebook's technology and development and technological advancements. Despite the users' feelings regarding security, start-ups and SMEs lack the data of existing customers and traffic required to collect a large quantity of data and train AI in this manner.

For the classification model, most SMEs and start-ups depend upon public databases like ImageNet. ImageNet is an imagery collection database arranged as part of speech structure with numerous photos representing each cluster of the network. After nine consecutive years of research by professors from the top-most universities worldwide, only 14 million images were collected in the carrier.

Collecting data is not the only issue that start-ups and SMEs face; there is one more issue they face, i.e., quality of information. Those companies that adopt AI need to be characterised, classified and accurate. Although SMEs and start-ups face the issue of collecting fresh, accurate and original data because of lack of resources, start-ups are new to the market world.

4.2 *Shortage of AI ability*

With the ongoing technology graph, various companies have also adopted and used AI. But, AI needs a specialist who must comprehend analytics and sequential equations. Also, the specialists need to develop representations and identify the problem, attribute and structure. As a result, the number of people with AI experience is restricted, resulting in a technological skills gap. This gap is distressed even further when it comes to start-ups. Big companies now recruit qualified AI scientists and give them premium wages, which leads to increased prices and a limited supply of AI professionals.

Indeed, large tech firms recruit AI academics, resulting in a significant decline in AI talent at the higher education level. Offering a good salary is unrealistic for start-ups and SMEs, and it is far more probable that an AI specialist would want to work for a major firm with the means to do so.

4.3 *Calculation price*

Another growing problem that SMEs and start-ups are facing is the AI expense. AI includes learning methods like machine learning, which require substantial effort and time. Creating a "strong quality" network requires a minimum of training rounds for feature subset adjustment and modification. Thus, a model must be trained several times, which incurs significant expenses in computing capacity and production time.

Simply training an established model will increase the cost through a monthly salary being paid to the engineer. Other than price calculation, start-ups and SMEs must also manage their infrastructures. Large firms have IT specialists and the resources needed to handle the expenses involved with AI; therefore, this is not a significant barrier.

5. Tax Haul by Start-ups and SMEs

Direct and indirect tax, named GST (goods and services tax) collection, increased in FY22 (Sharma, 2021). The Indian taxing system have raised the establishment of start-ups in the country, and have helped to expand the old-businessess of the country. However, the increased collection of taxes uplifts the economy of the country. Similarly, India had experienced great benefits while collecting taxes. Ernst & Young Private Limited (EY) is India's largest firm in India, which analyses the tax collection calculations. It stated that corporate income tax had grown in revenue by 21% during FY22 in April–October. Besides the downfall of India's GDP due to the pandemic and lockdowns, tax collection has still seen an upswing (Sharma, 2021).

As per EY's analysis, there are three significant reasons why the country has observed two graphs of collection of taxes and GDP in unbalanced as follows:

1. With the increased adoption of digitalisation by companies, start-ups and SMEs have increased the country's revenue graph and have formalised the country's economy.
2. During the COVID-19 pandemic, large companies improved the productivity of their business, which led to cutting extra costs. Hence, they adopted the cost-optimised technique to increase production, sales and revenue. This taught the start-ups and SMEs a big lesson. Therefore, this technique was also adopted by start-ups and SMEs and increased their productivity and revenue.
3. During the COVID-19 pandemic, there has been observed the impressive growth in the designated sectors named, IT departments in the companies, pharmaceutical sector, FMCG, etc.

6. Results and Discussion

6.1 *Importance of digitalisation adoption*

SMEs and start-ups were invented to support the economic growth of a country. Adopting the latest technologies is very important for these businesses to stabilise their position in the market. But, due to few resources being available, lesser capital, etc., adopting the latest technologies has become a challenge for start-ups and SMEs. In such a situation, digitalisation adoption by start-ups and SMEs is the right decision to make the businesses strong and unique in the marketplace.

Digitalisation is one of the most robust tools for start-ups and SMEs to compete in a strong market. As per the research finding of CRISIL (2020), the sales of start-ups and small businesses have been boosted by 53% in the past two years by relying on social media marketing, mobile marketing and another online market. Besides SMEs and start-ups, micro-enterprises are also dependent on digital mode to boost their sales and observed an increment of digital sale by 47% in 2020.

In one of the studies by Soni (2021), digitalisation adoption among SMEs is expected to grow by 25% CAGR, rounding off to $85 billion by the year 2024. In India, out of all SME owners, only 34% adopt the digitalisation mode for customer engagement, endorsing brands and interacting with employees and suppliers. However, only 7% of SMEs had adopted digitalisation all over.

Thus, digitalisation helps to influence the customers' mindset and helps businesses grow. Start-ups and SMEs owners shall adopt and use the multiple digital platforms that are available in the market to overcome the technological barrier and face the competition in the market. Given in the following are the key steps to embrace digitalisation by SMEs and start-ups (Kan, 2020).

6.1.1 *Identifying the need of digitalisation*

The digitalisation need is assessed by identifying the real problem going on in a business. Every business needs to adopt new technology to resolve such issues, for example, purchasing the latest machinery for efficient production, turning the marketing strategy around by going digital as it reduces the unnecessary cost incurred as compared to traditional marketing techniques and interacting with the customers to increase the engagement power of the business. Therefore, those sectors and departments of the companies which does not produce the efficient output shall be improved and revived by adopting the latest information technology.

6.1.2 *Selecting the correct tool of digitalisation*

By doing the proper research, a business can identify the best digital tool necessary. The correct digital device is a technology that successfully identifies the problem and solves it by setting the organisational goals. Selecting the right digital tool may be a time-consuming process, but is the best and most potent way to make the business firm.

They should also interact and consult with business owners which functions in less budget and yet are successful in the market, to acknowledge the gaps that SMES and start-ups might face.

6.1.3 *Providing training to employees*

Proper technology training should be provided to the employees to make digital learning easier. After all, the company's employees make the latest technologies work successfully. So, by educating them on the objectives and advantages of such technologies, it perhaps shows the productive output. Though it is the most challenging step, it provides faster and better results.

6.1.4 *Result measurement*

Digital transformation may not succeed in the way it was planned due to numerous reasons. Thus, to measure the actual performance against the planned one, it is necessary to find the loopholes in the plan.

Therefore, digital transformation is a valuable part of the business externally and internally. External parties such as customers, suppliers and stakeholders get assistance through digital transformation. On the other hand, for the business employees, digital transformation makes work easier by utilising less of their time to achieve more goals. Digital adoption makes SMEs and start-ups as competitive in the market as large corporations.

7. Building Brand Credibility of SMEs and Start-ups

Start-ups such as Tesla, Facebook, Airbnb and Uber have ruled the market by framing themselves to be the most competitive leaders by adopting the latest technologies and digital adoption, which helped make their brand strong in the market. Over a decade ago, brand-building was just for large companies and was not for SMEs or start-ups. But due to evolving technological advancement, and with the latest information and communication technology, branding is a significant component for promoting and diversifying the business of SMEs and start-ups (Ruzzier *et al.*, 2013; Rus, 2018). Branding is necessary to ensure a business's survival and sustainability.

Credibility is the authenticity of a business in a definite time (Erdem & Swait, 2004). Credibility consists of two main dimensions, i.e., trustworthiness and expertise (Ohanian, 1990). Therefore, brand credibility is termed as the products' and services' authenticity delivered by the brand owners by comparing it in the real terms and by the information conveyed by the brands. Thus, any information conveyed to the customers regarding the brand should be trustworthy or authentic in nature (Erdem & Swait, 2004; Kim *et al.*, 2020).

Building a strong brand is the most crucial part of the business. Therefore, making the brand credible for start-ups is a big task. Customer engagement is the most effective technique to make the brand credible. When customers relate with the brands through marketing communications, they create a mutual belief and spread awareness in society. The mutual belief between customers and brands increases the customers' positive attitude towards the products/services of the brand. Therefore, the customers' positive attitude increases the intention to purchase the product/service (Kim *et al.*, 2020). Thus, start-ups and SMEs can be significantly affected by brand credibility which enhances the sales of the company.

8. Blockchain Facilitates Exposures to Big Data Solution

Despite all the benefits of exploiting big data, according to the IBM Big Data & Analytics Hub, just 23% of firms have a big data strategy. Creating a big data strategy might be difficult for SMEs and start-ups.

However, welcoming blockchain technology is a novel alternative for SMEs and start-ups as it reduces the cost and complexity of building a big data strategy. Small company owners may now boost their competitiveness by utilising big data analytics.

AI and machine learning blockchain technologies enable access to reliable information and commercial understandings. For example, Endor Protocol Ecosystem is a blockchain infrastructure that utilises AI and blockchain technologies to boost big data analytics for enterprises. A business may use behavioural science tools and equipment to investigate by asking prospective questions and receiving exact forecasts. How can companies receive forecasts regarding the questions they ask? Customers will choose whether or not to communicate their thoughts with Endor. When customers opt in, they are compensated in EDRs, which may be converted into cash or cryptocurrency.

MedRec is yet another fantastic example of blockchain technology being used in conjunction with big data in the medical profession. Patients and health professionals may use MedRec to grant others entry into the EHR communities, authorise updates and communicate information among each other (De Vivo, 2018).

9. Conclusion

Upon reviewing the literature, researchers have noted that technological implementation is the most significant tool for making start-ups and SMEs stronger and successful in the Indian market. Start-ups and SMEs should make their brands stronger and credible to engage customers, which ultimately makes the brand a great success. With the growing usage of AI, blockchain technology and machine learning, start-ups and SMEs aim to attract and satisfy the customers, and thereby improve their business.

With the use of AI and IoT, start-ups and SMEs maintain their quality of products/services, and analyse the customers' behaviour. Khatabook, the Fintech start-up, has created a successful market within three years of its launching, and has registered more than 10 million customers (Dey, 2021). Similarly, a social commerce platform named Meesho has made its brand the competitor of Flipkart and Amazon by gaining the customer trust. With the help of AI, machine learning and IoT, Meesho made a heavy investment to reach out to its target customers by making the right type of advertisement.

Similarly, there are several Indian start-ups that are completely based on AI, ML and IoT. Some of them are Mad Street Den, Haptik, Manthan, Flutura, Dailyhunt, ShipRocket and INDWealth. Such start-ups lead in blockchain technology, different AI technologies, etc., to identify the data gap with regard to the customers' needs, create the technologies and innovations to curb such gaps, and launch the products/services with the help of the latest technologies. These latest technologies have modified the customers' purchase behaviour and expectations from the market. Thus, this has created a tough and competitive market for start-ups and SMEs and has also provided them the opportunity to compete with large-scale organisations.

Bibliography

Agarwal, G. (2021). Three key factors making AI adoption hard for startups. Forbes. https://www.forbes.com/sites/forbestechcouncil/2021/04/23/three-key-factors-making-ai-adoption-hard-for-startups/?sh=9929ccf796e8.

Antoniadis, I., Kontsas, S., & Spinthiropoulos, K. (2019). Blockchain applications in marketing. *The Proceedings of 7th ICCMI.*

CRISIL (2020). Smaller enterprises in big digital shift to shore up sales in pandemic times. https://www.crisil.com/en/home/newsroom/press-releases/2020/12/smaller-enterprises-in-big-digital-shift-to-shore-up-sales-in-pandemic-times.html.

Cukier, W., McCallum, K. E., Egbunonu, P., & Bates, K. (2021). The mother of invention: Skills for innovation in the post-pandemic world. In *Public Policy Forum, Diversity Institute, Future Skills Centre.* https://www.ryerson.ca/diversity/reports/MotherOfInvention_EN.pdf.

De Vivo, M. (2018). How small-business owners can use Blockchain and Big Data for bigger profits. Forbes. https://www.forbes.com/sites/theyec/2018/07/12/how-small-business-owners-can-use-blockchain-and-big-data-for-bigger-profits/?sh=23e1b8c01ccb.

Dey, A. (2021). How start-ups use AI to spur business growth, companies are increasingly leveraging technology to build varied products and services for users across segments. Fortune India. https://www.fortuneindia.com/enterprise/how-start-ups-use-ai-to-spur-business-growth/106083.

Erdem, T. & Swait, J. (2004). Brand credibility, brand consideration, and choice. *Journal of Consumer Research, 31*(1), 191–198.

Forbes (2021). The top 5 digital transformation trends in 2021 for small and mid-size businesses. *Forbes.* https://www.forbes.com/sites/tmobile/2021/01/11/the-top-5-digital-transformation-trends-in-2021-for-small-and-mid-size-businesses/?sh=6faf995554bb.

Jain, G., Sharma, N., & Shrivastava, A. (2021). Enhancing training effectiveness for organizations through blockchain-enabled training effectiveness measurement (BETEM). *Journal of Organizational Change Management, 34*(2), 439–461.

Kaka, N., Madgavkar, A., Kshirsagar, A., Gupta, R., Manyika, J., Bahl, K., & Gupta, S. (2019). Digital India: Technology to transform a connected nation. Mckinsey Global Institute.

Kan, P. (2020). How small businesses can embrace digital transformation. *Forbes.* https://www.forbes.com/sites/forbesbusinesscouncil/2020/06/03/how-small-businesses-can-embrace-digital-transformation/?sh=5ad0715a4363.

Kim, J., Melton, R., Min, J. E., & Kim, B. Y. (2020). Who says what? Exploring the impacts of content type and blog type on brand credibility, brand similarity and eWOM intention. *Journal of Fashion Marketing and Management, 24*(4), 1361–2026.

Konecnik Ruzzier, M. & Ruzzier, M. (2013). A modern approach to brand conceptualisation. *Transformations in Business and Economics*, *12*(3), 30.

Konstantinidis, I., Siaminos, G., Timplalexis, C., Zervas, P., Peristeras, V., & Decker, S. (2018). Blockchain for business applications: A systematic literature review. In *International Conference on Business Information Systems* (pp. 384–399). Cham: Springer.

Limburn, J. (2021). Data Fabric and the search for the single source of truth. *Forbes*. https://www.ibm.com/blogs/journey-to-ai/2021/11/data-fabric-and-the-search-for-the-single-source-of-truth/.

Marr, B. (2018). *What is industry 4.0? Here's a super easy explanation for anyone. Forbes*. https://www.forbes.com/sites/bernardmarr/2018/09/02/what-is-industry-4-0-heres-a-super-easy-explanation-for-anyone/?sh=6c744b799788.

Nowiński, W. & Kozma, M. (2017). How can blockchain technology disrupt the existing business models? *Entrepreneurial Business and Economics Review*, *5*(3), 173–188.

Ohanian, R. (1990). Construction and validation of a scale to measure celebrity endorsers' perceived expertise, trustworthiness, and attractiveness. *Journal of Advertising*, *19*(3), 39–52.

Pilkington, M. (2016). Blockchain technology: Principles and applications. In F. Xavier Olleros & Majlinda Zhegu (Eds.), *Research Handbook on Digital Transformations* (pp. 225–253). USA: Edward Elgar Publishing.

Rus, M., Konecnik Ruzzier, M., & Ruzzier, M. (2018). Startup branding: Empirical evidence among Slovenian startups. *Managing Global Transitions*, *16*(1), 79–94.

Ruzzier, M. K., Ruzzier, M., & Hisrich, R. D. (2013). *Marketing for Entrepreneurs and SMEs: A Global Perspective*. USA: Edward Elgar Publishing.

Sarkar, B. & Basu, S. (2021). *The Economic Times*. https://economictimes.indiatimes.com/tech/startups/startup-jobs-2020s-unicorns-look-to-ramp-up-hiring-in-2021/articleshow/80116567.cms?from=mdr.

Sharma, S. N. (2021). The big tax haul. *The Economic Times*.

Soni, S. (2021). National Technology Day: How pandemic served as force multiplier for tech adoption among MSMEs. *Financial Express*. https://www.financialexpress.com/industry/sme/national-technology-day-how-pandemic-served-as-force-multiplier-for-tech-adoption-among-msmes/2250018/.

Statista (2022). Startup India: Number of recognized businesses 2020 | Statista. *Statista*. https://www.statista.com/statistics/1155602/india-start-up-recognized-businesses/.

The Economic Times (2021). When cyber attacks wreaked havoc on SMBs in India. *The Economic Times*. https://economictimes.indiatimes.com/tech/tech-bytes/when-cyber-attacks-wreaked-havoc-on-smbs-in-india/articleshow/86572972.cms.

The Economic Times (2022). Indian startups raised $42 billion in 2021. *The Economic Times*. https://economictimes.indiatimes.com/tech/funding/indian-startups-raised-42-billion-in-2021-report/articleshow/88875670.cms.

Vanamali, K. V. (2021). What explains India's unicorn boom in 2021? *Business Standard*. https://www.business-standard.com/podcast/current-affairs/what-explains-india-s-unicorn-boom-in-2021-121122200092_1.html.

Verma, P. A. (2022). Business sustainability: How sustainability can help businesses stay relevant in future. *The Economic Times*. https://economictimes.indiatimes.com/news/company/corporate-trends/how-sustainability-can-help-businesses-stay-relevant-in-future/articleshow/89013137.cms?utm_source=contentofinterest&utm_medium=text&utm_campaign=cppst.

© 2023 World Scientific Publishing Company
https://doi.org/10.1142/9789811269554_0004

Chapter 4

Export Performance and Resource Capabilities of Indian Manufacturing MSMEs

Areej Aftab Siddiqui[*,‡] and Kashika Arora[†,§]

Dubai Business School, University of Dubai, UAE
†*Ministry of Commerce, Government of India, New Delhi, India*
‡*areej@iift.edu*
§*10kashika@gmail.com*

Abstract

Micro, Small and Medium Enterprises (MSMEs) are regarded as the backbone of India's current and future commercial growth. These institutions are equipped to nurture and assist the growth of a new generation of entrepreneurs with the potential to build globally competitive firms in India. However, for these businesses, finding the correct balance in resource use is crucial. This is why, in order to capture their impact on MSMEs' export performance, a set of 14 relevant elements from the resource-based view (RBV) model were discovered and ranked using modified total interpretive structural modelling. This method, together with the MICMAC technique, creates a hierarchical link between the elements. The nature of the interaction between the factors is shown through reliance and driving power. Strategic direction, upper echelon orientation, financial capacity and the external environment all have a significant impact on MSMEs' export performance.

Keywords: MSMEs, manufacturing sector, trade performance, m-TISM, MICMAC

1. Introduction

With increasing market globalisation and strong competition, many
growth-oriented domestic firms are looking for opportunities in foreign
marketplaces to complement their local market size and get scale economies (Cavusgil & Zou, 1994). Due to low business risks and significant
flexibility possibilities, exporting has been the preferred means of joining
the global arena (Leonidou *et al.*, 2007). In international business and
strategy, it has also become a well-studied topic (Xu *et al.*, 2008).
Although there is a lot of literature in the field of exporting that managers,
researchers and policymakers would be interested in, a few areas remain
untouched (Kakkos *et al.*, 2007) involving its subtopics that have gained
a lot of attention from a theoretical aspect (Morgan *et al.*, 2004; Douglas
& Craig, 2006; Styles *et al.*, 2008). Theoretical research has been performed in three important areas: the framework for industrial organisation
performance (Cavusgil & Zou, 1994), behavioural and relational elements
(Styles *et al.*, 2008), and the firm's resource-based view (RBV) (Morgan
et al., 2004).

The RBV contributes to export performance in a variety of ways due
to its theoretical approach. This is one of the most significant theoretical
frameworks in the area of entrepreneurship and international business
(Barney, 2001; Powell, 2001; Newbert, 2007; Barney *et al.*, 2001; Alvarez
& Busenitz, 2001). RBV promotes the importance of firm resources and
capabilities in achieving performance goals, particularly export success,
by taking into consideration the global business environment and institutional difficulties (Zou *et al.*, 2003). Export performance has mostly been
built on the RBV theoretical approach in the world of international business (Lages *et al.*, 2009). External business environmental aspects that
may affect export success have been discovered to stimulate the performance of a firm's resources and capabilities (Katsikeas *et al.*, 2000;
Spyropoulou *et al.*, 2011). RBV backs up concerns that exporting enterprises' resources and competences are unfairly divided, even when it
comes to market diversification and fresh market research (Armstrong &
Shimizu, 2007; Crook *et al.*, 2008). However, in recent years, there has
been a dearth of thorough study, notably on the strategic impact of
resources and talents on export performance, despite the fact that just a

few recent research studies have focused on competitive advantage and export performance (Tan & Sousa, 2015).

Studies on export performance have primarily been conducted for established countries (Zou & Stan, 1998), with very few for developing and emerging countries (Aulakh *et al.*, 2000; Zou *et al.*, 1997). Global export commerce accounts for over 30% of the world's gross domestic product, with emerging countries accounting for roughly 41% of global exports (World Bank, 2019). This has demonstrated the need of exporting for economies to do international business (Peng & York, 2001). Unlike enterprises in industrialised economies, which rely on FDI and other modes of international expansion, emerging economy firms, including MSMEs, mostly expand internationally through exporting (Vernon-Wortzel *et al.*, 1988; Leonidou *et al.*, 2002). As a result, study into the elements that determine the performance of emerging economy exports is critical. In the case of India, which is one of the world's fastest-growing emerging economies (ITC 2019 ranks it third in terms of purchasing power parity), the country ranked 19th in total world exports in 2019, with $304.1 billion in exports (CIA World Factbook, 2020). There was a considerable increase in competitiveness and consumer awareness after India's borders were opened to global and domestic private firms in 1991. In such a dynamic environment, domestic MSMEs began to confront increasing competition from large-scale firms. Despite this, these companies surmounted obstacles like economies of scale, a lack of resources, environmental unpredictability and market fragility (Gronum *et al.*, 2012).

These companies have now established themselves as growth engines for India's economic progress and prosperity (Eggers *et al.*, 2013). They are an important part of most industrial businesses and are essential for job creation and provision in most nations (Lee *et al.*, 2016). MSMEs have long been considered India's economic backbone, capable of withstanding global economic shocks and accounting for 33.4% of manufacturing output and 45% of total exports (CII, 2020). As a result, despite ranking low in the global competitiveness index, MSMEs have thrived in order to compete and maintain long-term competitiveness, particularly in growing countries like India (WEF, 2020).

The literature has primarily concentrated on the direct and indirect effects of available resources on the export performance of large-scale firms from developed countries, despite all of these contributions from MSMEs (Avci *et al.*, 2011). This is because MSMEs in emerging economies operate in a distinct business environment (Batra *et al.*, 2015). Large manufacturing firms, on the one hand, gain competitive advantage through cost efficiencies achieved through formalised structures and systems (Porter, 1990; Benner & Tushman, 2003; Bessant & Tidd, 2007), whereas MSMEs gain competitive advantage through their employees' creative potential to develop differentiated products for niche markets (Porter, 1990; Benner & Tushman, 2003; Bessant & Tidd, 2007; Damanpour, 1992).

The current study seeks to contribute to the existing export performance literature by examining the sets of abilities associated to resources. In international business studies, capabilities have been shown to be crucial in creating value, retaining competitive advantage and achieving profitability (Knight & Cavusgil 2004; Yalcinkaya *et al.*, 2007; Fang & Zou, 2009). Company resources and capabilities, according to RBV, are closely intertwined (Grant, 1991). As a result, the fundamental objective of this study is to determine the key and driving aspects of RBV as a platform for integrating and explaining current MSME export success. As a result, given the dynamic nature of global commerce and emerging economies' rising reliance on exporting to get access to global markets, doing research in emerging economies while taking various external environment characteristics into account in theoretical development is critical.

Modified total interpretive structural modelling (m-TISM), which is seen to be a potential qualitative method for establishing the structure of any social or technical system with related identifiable features, is used to build the hierarchical inter-relationships among the qualities (Lim *et al.*, 2017). While the ISM methodology creates noteworthy cross-component correlations (Hsu *et al.*, 2013; Venkatesh *et al.*, 2015), it lacks strong link interpretations and clear qualitative analysis. ISM is further modified to TISM in order to get around this. An interpretive matrix is used by TISM to represent causal links and expert opinions for extended systematic analysis (Shibin *et al.*, 2015). The present chapter employs the m-TISM technique, which is based on TISM and detects both dependants and drivers for various parameters, to measure export success from an RBV aspect. As a result, the following are the research questions to be addressed:

- What are the interconnections between the variables?
- What are the driving forces and dependencies for manufacturing MSMEs to improve their export performance through RBV?
- What are the consequences?

Furthermore, through a systematic knowledge base in a highly difficult context, this study contributes to the literature of resource and capability utilisation for long-term competitiveness. The rest of this chapter is laid out as follows. The backdrop and conceptual foundation are presented in the second section. The methodology is described in the third section. The fourth section contains the results and discussion. The study's consequences are addressed in section five, which includes pertinent theoretical, managerial, policy and future research. Finally, section six discusses the study's conclusion and limitations.

2. Broader Background and Theoretical Foundation

2.1 *Long-term export performance*

Over time, export research has progressed by looking into questions like why companies export, what factors influence exporting and whether export performance improves or declines over time (Bilkey & Tesar, 1977; Johanson & Vahlne, 1977). Export behaviour has changed over time, much like internationalisation approaches (Bilkey & Tesar, 1977). The export performance models emphasised learning by experience (Penrose, 1959); however, this approach was questioned, and revisions were proposed to meet real-life settings rather than just geographical distance and foreign activities (Sullivan & Bauerschmidt, 1990; Turnbull, 1987). Operating in a market defined by geographic distance, where enterprises must struggle with new competitive rules in a foreign cultural, economic or political environment, is what exporting means. Exporting improves a company's learning process (Crespi *et al.*, 2008), in part by establishing tools to record, preserve and apply information through operations in foreign markets.

The second stage of empirical study examines the export performance of small and medium-sized firms. Scholars have discovered a correlation between the scale of a company, its technological skills and its management's desire to succeed in worldwide markets (Pla-Barber & Alegre, 2007; Wilkinson & Brouthers, 2006). More advanced indicators of export success, such as resources and product-related properties, as well as company characteristics, performance and strategy, were examined for ease of decision-making and policy formation (Cavusgil & Naor, 1987; Cooper & Kleinschmidt, 1985). The relationship between export strategy and export performance was also emphasised (Baird *et al.*, 1994; Cavusgil & Naor, 1987).

Prior research has been limited by a lack of a good theoretical framework and the prevalence of empirical approaches (Gemunden, 1991). Other limitations include the presence of studies that focus on the decision to export rather than the export strategy and firm performance (Cavusgil & Zou, 1994), the explanation of export behaviour and performance, and the lack of explanatory variables, all of which stem from methodological constraints. A majority of studies have assessed the relationship between export performance and its dependent factors rather than a thorough theoretical structure (Morgan *et al.*, 2004). Thus, there is an urgent need to focus on developing explanatory factors utilising methods in order to gain a better theoretical knowledge of export performance connections.

2.2 *RBV and export results*

Internal capabilities are thought to play a role in a company's capacity to quickly internationalise and thrive in new markets (Autio *et al.*, 2000; Zahra *et al.*, 2000). Internal capabilities, based on evolutionary economics (Nelson & Winter, 1982), have explicitly detailed the innovative processes by which certain businesses might generate new knowledge, leading to the development of organisational skills such as critical competencies and embedded routines. As a result, firms will be able to better coordinate their activities and maximise their assets (Teece *et al.*, 1997). This captures the diversity of businesses, many of which are in the same industry, and so underscores the RBV structure's core principles (Barney, 1991). Internal corporate resources such as physical, human and organisational capital can help a company achieve a competitive advantage, but resource heterogeneity and immobility can suffocate that advantage (Barney, 1991).

Several studies have looked at export performance and internal company characteristics using the RBV approach. In export markets, firms from various countries and cultures are more diverse than in domestic markets (Zou *et al.*, 2003). Improved export performance has been linked to a company's competitive advantage resulting from specialised skills (Aaby & Slater, 1989; Wolff & Pett, 2000). According to the RBV approach, exporting companies' marketing and financial capabilities have a positive and significant relationship (Zou *et al.*, 2003). Resources and capabilities, as well as positional advantages, have been discovered to have an impact on export performance (Morgan *et al.*, 2004). Previous research has concentrated on export marketing and product adaptation rather than establishing a direct link between the RBV paradigm and export performance (Lages *et al.*, 2008). Product adaptation and export performance, as evaluated by export propensity and intensity, have produced contradictory results (Cavusgil & Kirpalani, 1993).

2.3 *Conceptual foundation*

Based on the findings of the brief literature review, the conceptual framework recognises and considers the causal relationship between antecedent resources and capabilities, capability drivers and competitive export performance. The resource-based perspective theory, which states that accumulating resources leads to long-term advantage, also translates to enhanced export performance (Ipek, 2018). The capability-building components to engage in exports by MSMEs must be given special attention.

We treat strategy and performance as two separate entities when building the export strategy and performance model. Because most export models are interested in maximising country-level exports, export intensity is used as a performance metric (Gemunden, 1991). As a result, it becomes a macro-level measure. Although export profitability can be used at the firm level, the actual value of exports is obtained through a primary survey, which also answers questions about products and market reachability, capturing export diversity in line with the market expansion strategy

(Cooper & Kleinschmidt, 1985; Ayal & Zif, 1979) using the number of markets served. As a result, export performance is reliant on export concentration and diversification.

Figure 1 depicts the conceptual framework, which is based on the RBV. This model reflects the impact of RBV characteristics found in the literature on the 14 key capability driving factors that influence firm export performance. The focus of this research is on exporting firms; it has been established in the literature that a firm's internal resources include managerial, physical, technological and entrepreneurial resources (Penrose, 1959). Relational resources such as network and relationship quality, on the other hand, are considered external to the firm.

Competence drivers or techniques, such as firm-specific qualities, are highly associated with export performance (Dhanaraj & Beamish, 2003; Sousa & Novello, 2014). Company size, followed by firm age, has emphasised the accumulation of resources and skills with time and age, which has influenced firm exports (Singla & George, 2013). Small enterprises

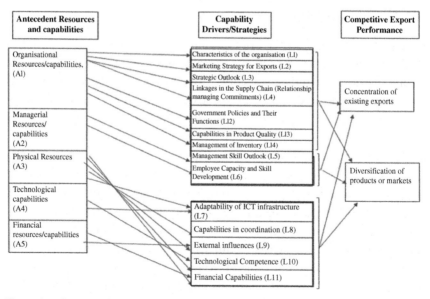

Figure 1.   Conceptual foundation.

Source: Authors' compilation/inference based on existing literature.

with minimal resources, on the other hand, may find exporting and internationalisation difficult. The export marketing strategy and performance relationship are driven by managerial characteristics and the external environment (Katsikeas *et al.*, 2006).

The literature lists various types of strategic orientation typologies. The synergistic effect of market orientation and other strategic orientation features improves the firm's competitive advantage and growth rather than adopting them independently (Hult & Ketchen, 2001). This makes it possible to develop, integrate and maintain internal and external capabilities (Teece *et al.*, 1997). As a result of the competitive advantage and higher firm performance, export performance has improved. Building long-term orientation in commercial interactions is an important aspect of organisational competencies. Relationship-building skills are crucial in the exporting environment since they focus on forming and maintaining long-term relationships with supply chain partners, external stakeholders and customers.

The notion of organisational capacities includes quality capabilities, which are a required antecedent to outstanding business performance both at the firm and at the international level (Leonidou *et al.*, 2013). Due to rapid imitation by competitors, MSMEs must focus on both product strategies and product quality, which is more difficult to achieve (Zhang *et al.*, 2003). As a result, product innovation is becoming increasingly important in attaining export performance (Porter, 1980). Inventory management, which focuses on obtaining the correct quality and amount of material from the right source at the right time to reduce waste and boost production and efficiency, is also covered in organisational competencies (Vokurka *et al.*, 2007).

Following that, the literature has extensively examined managerial resources in the context of exporting, including international outlook, management attitude, qualities, commitment and other managerial resources (Ipek, 2018). Small-business CEOs are usually the key decision-makers, with control over the composition of their company's senior management team. CEOs of smaller organisations may have more needs for overseas operations information processing (Tihanyi & Thomas, 2005). The management skill orientation of the exporting organisation needs, above all, the managers' global view. Managers, according to the upper echelon's premise, must have characteristics that allow them to assimilate information quickly in order to deal with worldwide complexity (Herrmann & Datta, 2002). This includes a variety of top executive traits such as global experience, educational level, age and tenure. As a result, the company's internationalisation strategy will be harmed.

In line with the endogenous growth hypothesis, for firm-level export performance, technological competitiveness is especially important, which is dependent on the level of creative activity (Grossman & Helpman, 1995). Buckley & Casson (1976) claim that technology is a crucial factor in determining product mobility and quality across national borders. The firm's RBV also emphasises the importance of technology capabilities, which can give businesses a long-term competitive advantage, especially in international markets (Alvarez, 2004; Anand & Kogut, 1997). These qualities enable a company's tangible and intangible assets to be converted into new innovative items and technology, hence increasing its competitiveness (Buckley & Casson, 1976). This is why many businesses invest in R&D in order to develop products for worldwide markets (Kuemmerle, 1999).

In this study, the function of the external environment is also considered in terms of financial risk, with a focus on payment and currency concerns. One of the most significant impediments to internationalisation for MSMEs, according to Braaksma & Hessels (2007), is the external environment. MSMEs are discouraged from expanding internationally due to the danger of non-payment by international clients and frequent currency changes in international markets. Lack of immediate interaction with clients overseas, as well as many clients' needs for additional credit, increases the likelihood of slower payments (Leonidou, 2004), affecting export performance. Following that, the research approach is proposed in the next part.

3. Research Methodology

3.1 *Considering Modified TISM*

As a result of the data collected for numerous aspects, the necessity to determine contextual inter-relationships develops automatically, as there is not a single factor that underpins the export performance of Indian MSMEs, but rather a slew of them. As a result, the research methodology requires the use of interpretive structural modelling (ISM). This requires contextual and interpretive techniques for addressing difficult problems using structural linking of interconnections among attributes into multi-level structural equation modelling (Watson, 1978). The idea is to break down a complicated system into a number of sub-systems from which a multi-level structure model can be built using specialists' practical expertise and knowledge (Mathiyazhagan *et al.*, 2013). This model recognises the influence while explaining the system's features. It also links many elements together to pinpoint an issue or problem premised on their interrelationship and driving force. Because of the way ISM understands nodes, the link interpretations are comparable to the node meanings. It is also challenging to deal with qualitative criteria. ISM has been fine-tuned and renamed TISM as a result. We used the m-TISM technique, which is a TISM extension, for this research. This is a more advanced version of the ISM that is used to convert a system's fuzzy and poorly articulated mental model into an unambiguous and well-defined representation (Sushil, 2017).

3.1.1 *Steps in the proposed m-TISM*

1. Creation of a matrix of structural self-interaction (SSIM)
The context of "leads to" is taken into account. The interactions and connections among the variables are identified using four symbols (*i* and *j*), namely:

V: The parameter *i* leads to the parameter *j*, but not the other way around.
A: Parameter *j* points to *i*, but not the other way around.
X: Both *i* and *j* link to one another.
O: Both *i* and *j* are unrelated parameters.

The SSIM is created based on contextual relationships, as shown in Table 1.

2. Creating a matrix of reachability
The reliance and driving strength of each criterion may be seen by replacing 1 and 0 for V, A, X and O, and incorporating transitivity. The 1 and 0 substitution criteria are as follows:

Table 1. Structural self-interaction matrix.

Notation	Drivers of Capability	1	2	3	4	5	6	7	8	9	10	11	12	13	14
L1	Characteristics of the Organisation	X	X	V	V	V	V	V	V	O	V	V	A	V	V
L2	Marketing Strategy for Exports		X	A	V	A	V	O	A	A	V	A	A	A	A
L3	Strategic Outlook			X	V	X	V	V	V	V	V	A	X	V	V
L4	Linkages in the Supply Chain (Relationship Managing Commitments)				X	A	O	O	V	A	A	X	X	V	X
L5	Management Skill Outlook					X	V	V	V	X	V	V	V	V	V
L6	Employee Capacity and Skill Development						X	V	V	X	X	A	A	V	V
L7	Adaptability of ICT Infrastructure							X	V	O	X	A	A	V	V
L8	Capabilities in Coordination								X	O	A	A	A	O	X
L9	External Influences									X	O	X	A	O	V
L10	Technological Competence										X	A	X	V	V
L11	Financial Capabilities											X	A	V	V
L12	Government Policies and Their Functions												X	V	V
L13	Capabilities in Product Quality													X	V
L14	Management of Inventory														X

If the (i, j) item in the SSIM is V, the reachability matrix entries (i, j) and (j, i) become 1 and 0, appropriately.

If the (i, j) entry in the SSIM is A, the reachability matrix entries (i, j) and (j, i) become 0 and 1, appropriately.

If the (i, j) entry in the SSIM is X, the reachability matrix entries (i, j) and (j, i) become 1 and 1, appropriately.

If the (i, j) entry in the SSIM is O, then (i, j) entry and (j, i) entry in the reachability matrix becomes 0 and 0, appropriately.

Table 2 shows the reachability matrix for the capability drivers using the stated rules. This table also shows the driving and dependent power of each variable. A variable's driving power is the total number of variables (including itself) that it can assist in achieving. Dependence power, on the other hand, refers to the total number of factors (including itself) that can help you achieve your goal. These terms are also used to categorise variables into four groups: autonomous, dependent, linkage and driver variables (independent).

3. Dividing the reachability matrix levels

When the intersection of the reachability set and the antecedent set equals the reachability set, that component is considered at the top of the hierarchy. To determine the level of all other components, we keep eliminating the element that turns out to be at the top of the hierarchy. The digraph and the final model are built using these layers.

At level 1, Table 3 shows the competence factors of MSMEs' export performance. As a result, it occupies the highest position in the ISM hierarchy. This procedure is done until all of the factors' levels are known as shown in Tables 3–6. The levels mentioned contribute to the development of the TISM's final model. Table 7 shows the growth-accelerating factors in their hierarchical order.

4. Depiction of a digraph

The digraph is used to construct the link between the elements, which is based on the levels determined after numerous rounds. The components are organised by level, and the relationships are represented by a reachability matrix.

Table 2. Reachability matrix.

Notation	Drivers of Capability	1	2	3	4	5	6	7	8	9	10	11	12	13	14	Driving Power
L1	Characteristics of the Organisation	1	1	1	1	1	1	1	1	1	1	1	1	1	1	14
L2	Marketing Strategy for Exports	1	1	1	1	1	1	1	1	1	1	1	1	1	1	14
L3	Strategic Outlook	1	1	1	1	1	1	1	1	1	1	1	1	1	1	14
L4	Linkages in the Supply Chain (Relationship Managing Commitments)	1	1	1	1	1	1	1	1	1	1	1	1	1	1	14
L5	Management Skill Outlook	1	1	1	1	1	1	1	1	1	1	1	1	1	1	14
L6	Employee Capacity and Skill Development	1	1	0	1	1	1	1	1	1	1	1	1	1	1	13
L7	Adaptability of ICT infrastructure	1	1	0	1	0	1	1	1	0	1	0	1	1	1	10
L8	Capabilities in Coordination	1	1	0	1	0	1	0	1	0	1	0	0	1	1	8
L9	External Influences	1	1	1	1	1	1	1	1	1	1	1	1	1	1	14
L10	Technological Competence	1	1	1	1	0	1	1	1	1	1	1	1	1	1	13
L11	Financial Capabilities	1	1	1	1	1	1	1	1	1	1	1	1	1	1	14
L12	Government Policies and Their Functions	1	1	1	1	1	1	1	1	1	1	1	1	1	1	14
L13	Capabilities in Product Quality	1	1	0	1	0	1	0	1	0	1	0	0	1	1	8
L14	Management of Inventory	1	1	1	1	0	1	0	1	0	1	1	1	1	1	11
Dependence Power		14	14	10	14	9	14	11	14	10	14	11	12	14	14	175

Table 3. Iteration-1.

Variables	Reachability Set	Antecedent Set	Intersection Set	Level
L1	1,2,3,4,5,6,7,8,9,10,11,12,13,14	1,2,3,4,5,6,7,8,9,10,11,12,13,14	1,2,3,4,5,6,7,8,9,10,11,12,13,14	1
L2	1,2,3,4,5,6,7,8,9,10,11,12,13,14	1,2,3,4,5,6,7,8,9,10,11,12,13,14	1,2,3,4,5,6,7,8,9,10,11,12,13,14	1
L3	1,2,3,4,5,6,7,8,9,10,11,12,13,14	1,2,3,4,5,9,10,11,12,14	1,2,3,4,5,9,10,11,12,14	
L4	1,2,3,4,5,6,7,8,9,10,11,12,13,14	1,2,3,4,5,6,7,8,9,10,11,12,13,14	1,2,3,4,5,6,7,8,9,10,11,12,13,14	1
L5	1,2,3,4,5,6,7,8,9,10,11,12,13,14	1,2,3,4,5,6,9,11,12	1,2,3,4,5,6,9,11,12	
L6	1,2,4,5,6,7,8,9,10,11,12,13,14	1,2,3,4,5,6,7,8,9,10,11,12,13,14	1,2,4,5,6,7,8,9,10,11,12,13,14	
L7	1,2,4,6,7,8,10,12,13,14	1,2,3,4,5,6,7,9,10,11,12	1,2,4,6,7,10,12	
L8	1,2,4,6,8,10,13,14	1,2,3,4,5,6,7,8,9,10,11,12,13,14	1,2,4,6,8,10,13,14	
L9	1,2,3,4,6,7,8,9,10,11,12,13,14	1,2,3,4,5,6,9,10,11,12	1,2,3,4,5,6,9,10,11,12	
L10	1,2,3,4,6,7,8,9,10,11,12,13,14	1,2,3,4,5,6,7,8,9,10,11,12,13,14	1,2,3,4,6,7,8,9,10,11,12,13,14	
L11	1,2,3,4,5,6,7,8,9,10,11,12,13,14	1,2,3,4,5,6,9,10,11,12,14	1,2,3,4,5,6,9,10,11,12,14	
L12	1,2,3,4,5,6,7,8,9,10,11,12,13,14	1,2,3,4,5,6,7,9,10,11,12,13,14	1,2,3,4,5,6,7,9,10,11,12,14	
L13	1,2,4,6,8,10,13,14	1,2,3,4,5,6,7,8,9,10,11,12,13,14	1,2,4,6,8,10,13,14	
L14	1,2,3,4,6,8,10,11,12,13,14	1,2,3,4,5,6,7,8,9,10,11,12,13,14	1,2,3,4,6,8,10,11,12,13,14	

Table 4. Iteration-2.

Variables	Reachability Set	Antecedent Set	Intersection Set	Level
L3	3,5,6,7,8,9,10,11,12,13,14	3,5,9,10,11,12,14	3,5,9,10,11,12,14	
L5	3,5,6,7,8,9,10,11,12,13,14	3,5,6,9,11,12,	3,5,6,9,11,12	
L6	5,6,7,8,9,10,11,12,13,14	3,5,6,7,8,9,10,11,12,13,14	5,6,7,8,9,10,11,12,13,14	2
L7	6,7,8,10,12,13,14	3,5,6,7,9,10,11,12	6,7,10,12	
L8	6,8,10,13,14	3,5,6,7,8,9,10,11,12,13,14	6,8,10,13,14	2
L9	3,5,6,7,8,9,10,11,12,13,14	3,5,6,9,10,11,12	3,5,6,9,10,11,12	
L10	3,6,7,8,9,10,11,12,13,14	3,5,6,7,8,9,10,11,12,13,14	3,6,7,8,9,10,11,12,13,14	2
L11	3,5,6,7,8,9,10,11,12,13,14	3,5,6,9,10,11,12,14	3,5,6,9,10,11,12,14	
L12	3,5,6,7,8,9,10,11,12,13,14	3,5,6,7,9,10,11,12,14	3,5,6,7,9,10,11,12,14	
L13	6,8,10,13,14	3,5,6,7,8,9,10,11,12,13,14	6,8,10,13,14	2
L14	3,6,8,10,11,12,13,14	3,5,6,7,8,9,10,11,12,13,14	3,6,8,10,11,12,13,14	2

Table 5. Iteration-3.

Variables	Reachability Set	Antecedent Set	Intersection Set	Level
L3	3,5,7,9,11,12	3,5,9,11,12	3,5,9,11,12	
L5	3,5,7,9,11,12	3,5,9,11,12	3,5,9,11,12	
L7	7,12	3,5,7,9,11,12	7,12	3
L9	3,5,7,9,11,12	3,5,9,11,12	3,5,9,11,12	
L11	3,5,7,9,11,12	3,5,9,11,12	3,5,9,11,12	
L12	3,5,7,9,11,12	3,5,7,9,11,12	3,5,7,9,11,12	3

Table 6. Iteration-4.

Variables	Reachability Set	Antecedent Set	Intersection Set	Level
L3	3,5,9,11	3,5,9,11	3,5,9,11	4
L5	3,5,9,11	3,5,9,11	3,5,9,11	4
L9	3,5,9,11	3,5,9,11	3,5,9,11	4
L11	3,5,9,11	3,5,9,11	3,5,9,11	4

Table 7. The final reachability matrix is partitioned into multiple layers.

Notation	Capability Drivers	Level in TISM
L1	Characteristics of the Organisation	I
L2	Marketing Strategy for Exports	I
L3	Strategic Outlook	IV
L4	Linkages in the Supply Chain (Relationship Managing Commitments)	I
L5	Management Skill Outlook	IV
L6	Employee Capacity and Skill Development	II
L7	Adaptability of ICT Infrastructure	III
L8	Capabilities in Coordination	II
L9	External Influences	IV
L10	Technological Competence	II
L11	Financial Capabilities	IV
L12	Government Policies and Their Functions	III
L13	Capabilities in Product Quality	II
L14	Management of Inventory	II

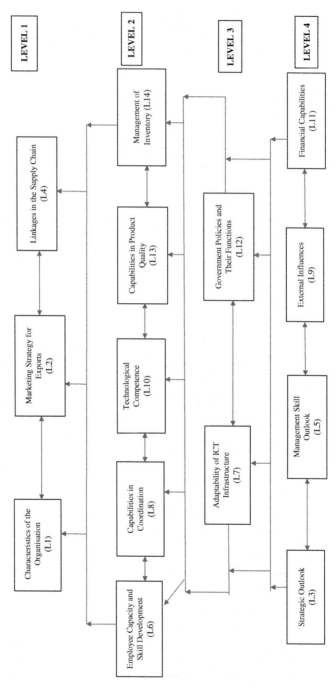

Figure 2.   TISM model of factors influencing Indian MSMEs' export success (digraph illustration).

5. A total structural interpretive model

The TISM is made up of pair-wise interpretive logic comparisons, a transitivity reachability matrix and a binary interaction matrix. In TISM, each relationship in the digraph is assigned a meaning. The TISM model used for this study is shown in Figure 2.

3.2 The m-TISM (modified-TISM) process

The TISM ran into severe issues when the number of paired comparisons expanded in lockstep with the number of components. Another concern was the transitivity of the reachability matrix (Yadav & Sushil, 2014; Singh & Sushil, 2013; Meena & Dhir, 2020). The m-TISM concept addressed both of these issues (Sushil, 2017). A transitive inspection is conducted in this approach, simultaneously with paired comparison, resulting in a fully transitive reachability matrix in a single step and dramatically lowering the number of repeats. Figure 2 depicts the different levels captured by various elements.

3.3 A factor relationship analysis

The reachability matrix with transitivity can be used to complete the MICMAC analysis. This research assists in classifying and categorising components based on their reliance and driving force. Therefore, in a two-dimensional chart, the 14 elements can be graphically classified into four categories depending on their dependence and driving intensity. In the upper-left frame of Figure 3, "independent" components are depicted. There is a lot of driving power here, but not much dependence power. Because they are dependent on the bulk of the system's other elements, they are critical to understanding the system's behaviour. The "linkage" factors of the chart are in the upper-right frame. Those are all characterised by a great deal of power as well as a great deal of reliance. The "linkage" factors channel the activity or effect of the influent elements. As a result, these variables may magnify or obstruct the influence of the influent elements, depending on their relevance. Because of their nature, these aspects become strategic. This quadrant, as can be seen, contains all of the variables that influence Indian MSMEs' exports. The "dependent"

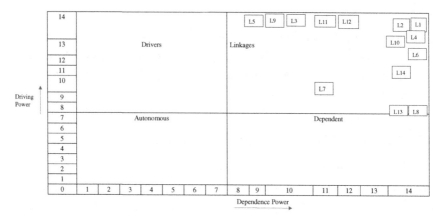

Figure 3.   The MICMAC evaluation.

components of the chart are in the lower-right frame. These factors have a high level of dependency and little influence. The action of these factors is greatly influenced by the independent and connecting variables' effects. Finally, "autonomous" factors are found in the lower-left frame of the graph. These variables have a small amount of sway and dependency.

4. Discussion and Conclusion

Our findings, which support an earlier study, confirm the impact of the 14 key variables, revealed through the literature review on RBV modelling adoption on MSMEs' export success. The modelling also demonstrates how each of these criteria influences the employment of RBV techniques to improve Indian MSMEs' export performance and how they are ranked. The components covered in the analysis have emerged as linkage elements, establishing a strong basis for MSMEs to internationalise competitively and become robust in their approach by developing a deep strategic connection among themselves.

The factors at level 4 are the major driving components for export, starting with the digraph illustrating the capability drivers of MSMEs' competitive approach to export performance. These factors include things like "strategic outlook", "management skill outlook", "external influences" and "financial capacities". Organisational, managerial and physical resources are split into three groups. The combination of these traits, as well as other elements, is now putting a strain on top management's socio-cognitive abilities in providing the firm with a valued, unique, inimitable and non-substitutable resource and potential competitive advantage (Barney *et al.*, 2001). Managing a hostile external environment and providing timely financial solutions are both top managerial skills that are rarely found in resource-constrained firms, and they interact. Level 4 factors, such as "Adaptability of ICT infrastructure" and "Government policies & regulations", have an impact on level 3 issues. Businesses can dominate and sustain market dominance by utilising ICT. The complexities of information gathering and processing have increased as a result of globalisation, resulting in a dynamic environment. As a result, ICT operations have become required to improve technological abilities, provide accuracy, minimise uncertainty about future global demand and aid in resource management to support the business (Luthra *et al.*, 2015; Gitupulos *et al.*, 2017). Furthermore, because emerging market corporations have less experience handling international projects, skilled CEOs with stronger lobbying skills and political clout can get through bureaucratic roadblocks. As a result, government policies can have a big impact on how internationalisation works, and they need to be applied correctly to organisational capacities. As a result, this component is highly reliant on RBV methods and has a substantial impact on them.

The Indian Government has liberalised FDI policy to attract investments, incorporating sophisticated and cutting-edge technologies in order to boost overall productivity and competitiveness. Many industries/activities allow 100% FDI through an automated process. India will also be able to benefit due to its capabilities in small-scale goods and services exports if e-commerce becomes more widely accepted. As a result of the digitalisation process, MSMEs should be able to find affordable and skilled employees. The government's introduction of the production-linked incentive (PLI) plan may boost emerging industries such as electronics, electrical and mechanical equipment, textiles and garments.

At level 2, the greatest number of components can be found. These are important concerns for MSMEs, as expanding into new geographic markets can provide major opportunities for growth and value creation. "Employee capacity & skills building", "coordination capabilities", "technology capabilities", "product quality" and "inventory planning management" are all highly reliant factors. Each company's variables are unique, and they interact with one another. The firm's success hinges on the growth of employees' skills and competences, as well as the transmission of knowledge through training and programmes. MSMEs are motivated to improve their performance because of their commitment to coordinating efforts. Furthermore, the capability of MSMEs to innovate is essential to the economy's long-term competitiveness (Madrid-Guijarro *et al.*, 2009).

For exports, the procedure of adhering to product quality requirements is critical. However, despite its low driving strength, this factor remains a potent strategic weapon in international competitiveness and commerce. Waste is reduced and productivity is increased when quality is improved. As a result, inventory management is aided. Firms can expand their market share and charge greater prices for their products as their quality and productivity improve, resulting in higher profitability. Furthermore, as competition has become more intense, constant planning and quality improvement have become a requirement for all types of businesses to survive (Temtime, 2003). Finally, the variables at level 1 are the most dependent on other factors due to their placement in the linking quadrant, but they also have a strong driving power. MSMEs have a difficult time maintaining their competitiveness since they are more sensitive to a number of challenges. This is why a company's outward orientation, inter-organisational networks that increase international exposure and managers' ability to adapt to different cultures, economic environments, and consumer tastes and preferences in international markets are valued as "characteristics of the organisation", "marketing strategies for exports" and "supply chain links".

The findings show that by combining their relevance and interdependence, the TISM model, which is based on RBV modelling, provides significant insights into the growth-inducing factors of MSMEs' export performance. As indicated by the relevance of each aspect selected systematically from the review, our findings support and enhance the literature review. The m-TISM model's effective presence of direct and transitive links, which results in the development of linkage factors, enables the factors' enhancement. Our findings indicate the importance of the factors, their interrelationship and their impact on one another. The necessary resources and competencies for products and global expansion (Barney *et al.*, 2001) are considered using RBV's applicable theoretical framework. This viewpoint has gained widespread acceptance as a key theoretical paradigm in the export literature (Morgan *et al.*, 2004; Freeman & Styles, 2014; Kaleka, 2012). Due to the scarcity of resources and their optimal utilisation, the potential sources of comparative advantage can be observed.

5. Consequences

5.1 *Theoretical consequences*

This study examines aspects relating to various resources and capacities, with a focus on their relationship to export performance. The outcomes contribute in a variety of ways as a result of the application of RBV procedures. To begin, restricted resources with the potential to generate a superior market offering are considered the basic source of comparative advantage. When combined with Hunt's (2011) heterogeneous demand theory, such a concept can also provide concrete solutions. Second, understanding how elements interact is required for comprehending the evolutionary and complex structures, resolving path dependencies, internal growth processes and the roles of social institutions in achieving productivity. Third, in addition to internal issues, external forces can have an impact on a company's ability to navigate global crises. The current global pandemic serves as an illustration. MSMEs have discovered new ways to export by establishing new routes, reducing transportation costs, collaborating with the shipping sector and buyers, and even buyers who recognise the depth of the problem are renegotiating product rates. Such campaigns also advocate for government policies that provide prompt financial assistance.

5.2 *Implications for managers*

The TISM model shows that managers' orientation towards the drivers of export is a significant deciding factor in their desire to engage in internationalisation efforts, based on a review of the relevant literature and brainstorming sessions with experts in the field. MSMEs in rising economies and developing countries face a variety of challenges when it comes to competing successfully in the global marketplace. Qualitative evaluations show that organisations can notice, focus on and manage complications connected with internationalisation, which aligns with the assumptions of RBV modelling. A firm's export orientation is also influenced by management and corporate factors. Because establishing and managing a worldwide firm is a difficult endeavour (Ghoshal & Bartlett, 1990), MSMEs' success is heavily reliant on their management's commitment to international activities, favourable domestic market circumstances and established international networks. Top executives face a wide range of challenges, particularly in smaller businesses when resources and talents are restricted. As a result, creating systematic relationships with the external world by the top echelon is beneficial. Firms with subsidiaries can also use prior learnings to expand their base, capabilities and competitiveness. MSMEs are threatened by challenges such as defining the target exchange rate, foreign buyer insolvency, export credit delays and other political, economic and social hazards. Thus, top management must have a full understanding of export promotion factors in order to hire people, offer ICT infrastructure, take advantage of government incentives and, most significantly, improve product quality and anticipate export expansion activities.

6. Summary and Limitations

The study begins by evaluating the existing literature and identifying 14 major characteristics that influence export performance when RBV practices are taken into account. The research uncovered a variety of resources and competences connected to export success in the literature, some of which were more relevant than others. The role of various firm-specific characteristics, strategic orientation, export marketing expansion strategy, maintaining product quality, inventory management and supply chain capabilities has become more closely linked to export-related activities, with a greater emphasis on the role of various organisational characteristics, strategic outlook, export marketing expansion strategy, maintaining product quality, inventory management and supply chain capabilities. The importance of R&D resources involving innovation and technology orientation in generating increased export performance has also been underlined by technological resources in the form of ICT infrastructure readiness and skills. Managerial resources, such as top management commitment and employee skill and competency development, are also essential.

The TISM was supposed to be useful for building hierarchical relationships and analysing links and nodes effectively. MICMAC analysis was used to graphically present the discovered determinants in four quadrants (independent, linked, dependent and autonomous antecedents) depending on reliance and driving power. Strategic resources are a key antecedent for export performance. The connecting quadrant encompasses all of the elements, emphasising the importance of relationships as a foundation for MSMEs' growth. According to the research, the top two barriers to internationalisation experienced by MSMEs are management competency and a lack of knowledge. As a result of this research, management should focus on a diversity of resources and competencies, as well as knowledge computing capabilities, in order to fulfil international standards.

In addition, India's foreign trade policy should concentrate on new ways for small businesses to grow their global footprint. By making substantial changes to incentives and definitions, as well as building a talent platform, India can enable fundamental changes in global commerce and emerge as a winning leader. This will help the country's economy both now and in the future. MSMEs are likely to play a significant part in India's rise to one of the world's top economies during the next decade, thanks to a favourable political and economic environment. The country's national goals of financial inclusion and job creation in both towns and cities require the expansion of this segment. It can also encourage and assist the growth of a new generation of entrepreneurs in India who have the potential to build globally competitive firms. MSMEs will be the backbone for current and future high-growth firms, with a significant impact, thanks to the implementation of the "Make in India" initiative. Future research could focus on applying structural equation modelling to statistically validate the model. It is also suggested that a comparative TISM for inter-linkages for service industry innovation implementation be established.

Bibliography

Aaby, N. E. & Slater, S. F. (1989). Management influences on export performance: A review of the empirical literature 1978–1988. *International Marketing Review*.

Alvarez, S. A. & Busenitz, L. W. (2001). The entrepreneurship of resource-based theory. *Journal of Management*, 27(6), 755–775.

Anderson, E. & Weitz, B. (1992). The use of pledges to build and sustain commitment in distribution channels. *Journal of Marketing Research*, 29(1), 18–34.

Armstrong, C. E. & Shimizu, K. (2007). A review of approaches to empirical research on the resource-based view of the firm. *Journal of Management*, 33(6), 959–986.

Attri, R., Grover, S., Dev, N., & Kumar, D. (2013). An ISM approach for modelling the enablers in the implementation of Total Productive Maintenance (TPM). *International Journal of System Assurance Engineering and Management*, 4(4), 313–326.

Aulakh, P. S., Kotabe, M., & Teegen, H. (2000). Export strategies and performance of firms from emerging economies: Evidence from Brazil, Chile, and Mexico. *Academy of Management Journal*, 43(3), 342–361.

Avci, U., Madanoglu, M., & Okumus, F. (2011). Strategic orientation and performance of tourism firms: Evidence from a developing country. *Tourism Management*, 32(1), 147–157.

Ayal, I. & Zif, J. (1979). Market expansion strategies in multinational marketing. *Journal of Marketing*, 43(2), 84–94.

Baker, W. E. & Sinkula, J. M. (1999). The synergistic effect of market orientation and learning orientation on organizational performance. *Journal of the Academy of Marketing Science*, 27(4), 411–427.

Barney, J. B. (2001). Resource-based theories of competitive advantage: A tenyear retrospective on the resource-based view. *Journal of Management*, 27(6), 643–650.

Barney, J., Wright, M., & Ketchen Jr, D. J. (2001). The resource-based view of the firm: Ten years after 1991. *Journal of Management*, 27(6), 625–641.

Batra, S., Sharma, S., Dixit, M. R., & Vohra, N. (2015). Strategic orientations and innovation in resource-constrained SMEs of an emerging economy. *The Journal of Entrepreneurship*, 24(1), 17–36.

Beleska-Spasova, E., Glaister, K. W., & Stride, C. (2012). Resource determinants of strategy and performance: The case of British exporters. *Journal of World Business*, 47(4), 635–647.

Benner, M. J. & Tushman, M. L. (2003). Exploitation, exploration, and process management: The productivity dilemma revisited. *Academy of Management Review, 28*(2), 238–256.

Bessant, J. & Tidd, J. (2007). *Innovation and Entrepreneurship.* John Wiley & Sons.

Bilkey, W. J. & Tesar, G. (1977). The export behavior of smaller-sized Wisconsin manufacturing firms. *Journal of International Business Studies, 8*(1), 93–98.

Braaksma, R. M. & Hessels, S. J. A. (2007). SMEs and international business: The orientation of SMEs in markets and sectors abroad. EIM, Zoetermeer, commissioned by the EVD, The Hague.

Broad Conceptualization of Global Marketing Strategy and Buckley, P. J. & Casson, M. C. (1998). Analyzing foreign market entry strategies: Extending the internalization approach. *Journal of International Business Studies, 29*(3), 539–561.

Cadogan, J. W., Diamantopoulos, A., & Siguaw, J. A. (2002). Export market-oriented activities: Their antecedents and performance consequences. *Journal of International Business Studies, 33*(3), 615–626.

Cavusgil, S. T. (1976). Organizational determinants of firms' export behaviour: An empirical analysis. PhD Thesis, University of Wisconsin, Madison.

Cavusgil, S. T. & Kirpalani, V. M. (1993). Introducing products into export markets: Success factors. *Journal of Business Research, 27*(1), 1–15.

Cavusgil, S. T. & Naor, J. (1987). Firm and management characteristics as discriminators of export marketing activity. *Journal of Business Research, 15*(3), 221–235.

Cavusgil, S. T. & Zou, S. (1994). Marketing strategy-performance relationship: An investigation of the empirical link in export market ventures. *Journal of Marketing, 58*(1), 1–21.

Cooper, R. G. & Kleinschmidt, E. J. (1985). The impact of export strategy on export sales performance. *Journal of International Business Studies, 16*(1), 37–55.

Crespi, G., Criscuolo, C., & Haskel, J. (2008). Productivity, exporting, and the learning-by-exporting hypothesis: Direct evidence from UK firms. *Canadian Journal of Economics/Revue canadienne d'économique, 41*(2), 619–638.

Crook, T. R., Ketchen Jr, D. J., Combs, J. G., & Todd, S. Y. (2008). Strategic resources and performance: A meta-analysis. *Strategic Management Journal, 29*(11), 1141–1154.

Damanpour, F. (1992). Organizational size and innovation. *Organization Studies, 13*(3), 375–402.

Dhanaraj, C. & Beamish, P. W. (2003). A resource-based approach to the study of export performance. *Journal of Small Business Management, 41*(3), 242–261.

Dierickx, I. & Cool, K. (1989). Asset stock accumulation and sustainability of competitive advantage. *Management Science, 35*(12), 1504–1511.

Dubey, R., Gunasekaran, A., Sushil, & Singh, T. (2015). Building theory of sustainable manufacturing using total interpretive structural modelling. *International Journal of Systems Science: Operations & Logistics, 2*(4), 231–247.

Eggers, F., Kraus, S., Hughes, M., Laraway, S., & Snycerski, S. (2013). Implications of customer and entrepreneurial orientations for SME growth. *Management Decision, 51*(3), 524–546.

Eisenhardt, K. M. & Martin, J. A. (2000). Dynamic capabilities: What are they? *Strategic Management Journal, 21*(10–11), 1105–1121.

Fang, E. E. & Zou, S. (2009). Antecedents and consequences of marketing dynamic capabilities in international joint ventures. *Journal of International Business Studies, 40*(5), 742–761.

Gemunden, H. G. (1991). Success factors of export marketing: A meta-analytic critique of the empirical studies. *New Perspectives on International Marketing*, 33–62.

Ghoshal, S. & Bartlett, C. A. (1990). The multinational corporation as an interorganizational network. *Academy of Management Review, 15*(4), 603–626.

Grant, R. M. (1991). The resource-based theory of competitive advantage: Implications for strategy formulation. *California Management Review, 33*(3), 114–135.

Griffith, D. A., Cavusgil, S. T., & Xu, S. (2008). Emerging themes in international business research. *Journal of International Business Studies, 39*(7), 1220–1235.

Gronum, S., Verreynne, M. L., & Kastelle, T. (2012). The role of networks in small and medium-sized enterprise innovation and firm performance. *Journal of Small Business Management, 50*(2), 257–282.

Grossman, G. M. & Helpman, E. (1995). Technology and trade. *Handbook of International Economics, 3*, 1279–1337.

Herrmann, P. & Datta, D. K. (2002). CEO successor characteristics and the choice of foreign market entry mode: An empirical study. *Journal of International Business Studies, 33*(3), 551–569.

Herrmann, P. & Datta, D. K. (2005). Relationships between top management team characteristics and international diversification: An empirical investigation. *British Journal of Management, 16*(1), 69–78.

Hsu, W. T., Chen, H. L., & Cheng, C. Y. (2013). Internationalization and firm performance of SMEs: The moderating effects of CEO attributes. *Journal of World Business*, *48*(1), 1–12.

Hult, G. T. M. & Ketchen Jr, D. J. (2001). Does market orientation matter? A test of the relationship between positional advantage and performance. *Strategic Management Journal*, *22*(9), 899–906.

Hunt, S. D. (2011). On the intersection of marketing history and marketing theory. *Marketing Theory*, *11*(4), 483–489.

Ibeh, K. I. & Wheeler, C. N. (2005). A resource-centred interpretation of export performance. *The International Entrepreneurship and Management Journal*, *1*(4), 539–556.

Jayalakshmi, B. & Pramod, V. R. (2015). Total interpretive structural modeling (TISM) of the enablers of a flexible control system for industry. *Global Journal of Flexible Systems Management*, *16*(1), 63–85.

Johanson, J. & Vahlne, J. E. (1977). The internationalization process of the firm — A model of knowledge development and increasing foreign market commitments. *Journal of International Business Studies*, *8*(1), 23–32.

Kaleka, A. (2002). Resources and capabilities driving competitive advantage in export markets: Guidelines for industrial exporters. *Industrial Marketing Management*, *31*(3), 273–283.

Katsikeas, C. S., Leonidou, L. C., & Morgan, N. A. (2000). Firm-level export performance assessment: Review, evaluation, and development. *Journal of the Academy of Marketing Science*, *28*(4), 493–511.

Kazlauskaitė, R., Autio, E., Gelbūda, M., & Šarapovas, T. (2015). The resource-based view and SME internationalisation: An emerging economy perspective. *Resource*, *3*(2), 53–64.

King, A. W. & Zeithaml, C. P. (2001). Competencies and firm performance: Examining the causal ambiguity paradox. *Strategic Management Journal*, *22*(1), 75–99.

Kirpalani, V. H. & Macintosh, N. B. (1980). International marketing effectiveness of technology-oriented small firms. *Journal of International Business Studies*, *11*(3), 81–90.

Kuemmerle, W. (1999). The drivers of foreign direct investment into research and development: An empirical investigation. *Journal of International Business Studies*, *30*(1), 1–24.

Lages, L. F. & Montgomery, D. B. (2004). Export performance as an antecedent of export commitment and marketing strategy adaptation: Evidence from small and medium-sized exporters. *European Journal of Marketing*, 38(9/10), 1186–1214.

Lee, V. H., Foo, A. T. L., Leong, L. Y., & Ooi, K. B. (2016). Can competitive advantage be achieved through knowledge management? A case study on SMEs. *Expert Systems with Applications, 65,* 136–151.

Leonidou, L. C. (1995). Empirical research on export barriers: Review, assessment, and synthesis. *Journal of International Marketing, 3*(1), 29–43.

Leonidou, L. C., Katsikeas, C. S., & Samiee, S. (2002). Marketing strategy determinants of export performance: A meta-analysis. *Journal of Business Research, 55*(1), 51–67.

Leonidou, L. C., Katsikeas, C. S., Palihawadana, D., & Spyropoulou, S. (2007). An analytical review of the factors stimulating smaller firms to export: Implications for policy-makers. *International Marketing Review, 24*(6), 735–770.

Lim, M. K., Tseng, M. L., Tan, K. H., & Bui, T. D. (2017). Knowledge management in sustainable supply chain management: Improving performance through an interpretive structural modelling approach. *Journal of Cleaner Production, 162,* 806–816.

Madrid-Guijarro, A., Garcia, D., & Van Auken, H. (2009). Barriers to innovation among Spanish manufacturing SMEs. *Journal of Small Business Management, 47*(4), 465–488.

Mangla, S., Madaan, J., Sarma, P. R. S., & Gupta, M. P. (2014). Multi-objective decision modelling using interpretive structural modelling for green supply chains. *International Journal of Logistics Systems and Management, 17*(2), 125–142.

Mathiyazhagan, K., Govindan, K., NoorulHaq, A., & Geng, Y. (2013). An ISM approach for the barrier analysis in implementing green supply chain management. *Journal of Cleaner Production, 47,* 283–297.

Meena, A. & Dhir, S. (2020). An analysis of growth-accelerating factors for the Indian automotive industry using modified TISM. *International Journal of Productivity and Performance Management.*

McDougall, P. P., Shane, S., & Oviatt, B. M. (1994). Explaining the formation of international new ventures: The limits of theories from international business research. *Journal of Business Venturing, 9*(6), 469–487.

Murray, J. Y., Gao, G. Y., & Kotabe, M. (2011). Market orientation and performance of export ventures: The process through marketing capabilities and competitive advantages. *Journal of the Academy of Marketing Science, 39*(2), 252–269.

Nelson, R. R. & Winter, S. G. (1982). The Schumpeterian tradeoff revisited. *The American Economic Review, 72*(1), 114–132.

Newbert, S. L. (2007). Empirical research on the resource-based view of the firm: An assessment and suggestions for future research. *Strategic Management Journal, 28*(2), 121–146.

Peng, M. W. & York, A. S. (2001). Behind intermediary performance in export trade: Transactions, agents, and resources. *Journal of International Business Studies, 32*(2), 327–346.

Penrose, E. T. (1959). *The Theory of the Growth of the Firm*. New York: John Wiley.

Pla-Barber, J. & Alegre, J. (2007). Analysing the link between export intensity, innovation and firm size in a science-based industry. *International Business Review, 16*(3), 275–293.

Porter, M. E. (1990). *The Competitive Advantage of Nations*. New York: The Free Press.

Powell, T. C. (2001). Competitive advantage: Logical and philosophical considerations. *Strategic Management Journal, 22*(9), 875–888.

Shibin, K. T., Gunasekaran, A., Papadopoulos, T., Dubey, R., Singh, M., & Wamba, S. F. (2016). Enablers and barriers of flexible green supply chain management: A total interpretive structural modeling approach. *Global Journal of Flexible Systems Management, 17*(2), 171–188.

Singla, C. & George, R. (2013). Internationalization and performance: A contextual analysis of Indian firms. *Journal of Business Research, 66*(12), 2500–2506.

Sousa, C. M. & Novello, S. (2014). The influence of distributor support and price adaptation on the export performance of small and medium-sized enterprises. *International Small Business Journal, 32*(4), 359–385.

Sullivan, D. & Bauerschmidt, A. (1990). Incremental internationalization: A test of Johanson and Vahlne's thesis. *Management International Review*, 19–30.

Sushil, A. (2017). Modified ISM/TISM process with simultaneous transitivity checks for reduced direct pair comparisons. *Global Journal of Flexible Systems Management, 18*(4), 331–351.

Tan, Q. & Sousa, C. M. (2015). Leveraging marketing capabilities into competitive advantage and export performance. *International Marketing Review, 32*(1), 78–102.

Teece, D. J., Pisani, G., & Shuen, A. (1997). Dynamic capabilities and strategic management. *Strategic Management Journal, 18*(7), 509–533.

Temtime, Z. T. (2003). The moderating impacts of business planning and firm size on total quality management practices. *The TQM Magazine, 15*(1), 52–60.

Tihanyi, L. & Thomas, W. B. (2005). Information-processing demands and the multinational enterprise: A comparison of foreign and domestic earnings estimates. *Journal of Business Research, 58*(3), 285–292.

Turnbull, P. W. (1987). Interaction and international marketing: An investment process. *International Marketing Review, 4*(4), 7–19.

Venkatesh, V. G., Rathi, S., & Patwa, S. (2015). Analysis on supply chain risks in Indian apparel retail chains and proposal of risk prioritization model using Interpretive structural modelling. *Journal of Retailing and Consumer Services, 26*, 153–167.

Vernon-Wortzel, H., Wortzel, L. H., & Deng, S. (1988). Do neophyte exporters understand importers? *Columbia Journal of World Business, 23*(4), 49–56.

Vokurka, R. J., Lummus, R. R., & Krumwiede, D. (2007). Improving manufacturing flexibility: The enduring value of JIT and TQM. *SAM Advanced Management Journal, 72*(1), 14.

Watson, R. H. (1978). Interpretive structural modeling — A useful tool for technology assessment? *Technological Forecasting and Social Change, 11*(2), 165–185.

Wernerfelt, B. (1984). A resource-based view of the firm. *Strategic Management Journal, 5*(2), 171–180.

Wilkinson, T. & Brouthers, L. E. (2006). Trade promotion and SME export performance. *International Business Review, 15*(3), 233–252.

Wolff, J. A. & Pett, T. L. (2000). Internationalization of small firms: An examination of export competitive patterns, firm size, and export performance. *Journal of Small Business Management, 38*(2), 34.

Yadav, N. (2014). Total interpretive structural modelling (TISM) of strategic performance management for Indian telecom service providers. *International Journal of Productivity and Performance Management, 63*(4), 421–445.

Yalcinkaya, G., Calantone, R. J., & Griffith, D. A. (2007). An examination of exploration and exploitation capabilities: Implications for product innovation and market performance. *Journal of International Marketing, 15*(4), 63–93.

Zahra, S. A., Hayton, J. C., & Salvato, C. (2004). Entrepreneurship in family vs. non-family firms: A resource-based analysis of the effect of organizational culture. *Entrepreneurship Theory and Practice, 28*(4), 363–381.

Zou, S. & Stan, S. (1998). The determinants of export performance: A review of the empirical literature between 1987 and 1997. *International Marketing Review, 15*(5), 333–356.

Zou, S. & Cavusgil, S. T. (2002). The GMS: A broad conceptualization of global marketing strategy and its effect on firm performance. *Journal of Marketing, 66*(4), 40–56.

© 2023 World Scientific Publishing Company
https://doi.org/10.1142/9789811269554_0005

Chapter 5

Leadership and Entrepreneurial Skills for SMEs: A Case of RP Inc.

Nidhi Gupta and Ragini Tyagi

ASB, Amity University, Noida, India
ngupta2@amity.edu
raginikb@gmail.com

Abstract

Currently, SMEs are facing challenges across the globe, and to overcome these, there is a need for entrepreneurial competencies. Various past research studies had already proven that entrepreneurship leads to economic growth and development. Education institutions are also focusing on building entrepreneurial ecosystems and providing skill sets through workshops and training programmes so that students are industry ready. But the question in front of educational institutions is one of which skills are required for creating, managing and growing SMEs. The present case describes the entrepreneurial competencies of Mr. Pankaj Tyagi, founder of RP Inc., in creating and leading an entrepreneurial venture. The study also discusses and analyses the VRIO model of the company to know the business performance and how the entrepreneur utilises his resources optimally by applying his entrepreneurial and leadership skills. An exploratory study was done to know the types of skill required for the growth and management of SMEs, for which an unstructured interview with an entrepreneur was conducted to get in-depth knowledge about the entrepreneurial competencies, which was supported by past literature review. The key findings were that there is a strong need to focus on entrepreneurial and leadership skills for managing and growing SMEs. The study seeks to report the value and usefulness of these skills to persons pursuing entrepreneurial activities. This research forms the theoretical basis for future qualitative research.

Keywords: Entrepreneurship, entrepreneurial competencies, entrepreneurial skills, leadership, VRIO, business performance, growth

1. Introduction

In the Indian economy, micro, small and medium enterprises (MSMEs) have emerged as a remarkably progressive sector, which play a vital role in presenting major employment opportunities at a comparatively lower capital price than large industries. The MSMEs have been continuously contributing to the growth of entrepreneurial endeavours through business innovations. They help in the industrialisation of rural and backward areas, thus reducing regional disparities, persuading a more equitable distribution of national income and wealth. The MSMEs are in harmony to improve the large industries as auxiliary units, and this sector provides equity for the socioeconomic development of the country. The MSMEs are widening their domain across various sectors by producing a diverse range of products and services to meet domestic as well as global market needs. This sector occupies a key place in terms of output, exports and employment created in the country. It produces about 45% of manufacturing output and 40% of the total exports. Furthermore, about 110.99 million persons are engaged in MSME units in over 63.39 million units throughout the country. It plays a very important role in industrialising rural areas and thereby reducing regional imbalances (Agrawal *et al.*, 2019).

SMEs are a driving force in the economic growth of the country by providing job opportunities, regional growth, national income and raising the standard of living of the people in the country (Jinadal & Bhardwaj, 2016). But SMEs face many challenges in the disruptive world and to strengthen these SMEs there is a need to develop entrepreneurial and leadership skills. These entrepreneurial skills enable one to face environmental changes and intense competition in the marketplace (Lee *et al.*, 2018). SMEs' supporting role in the advancement of prosperity among communities is highly appreciated, but to ensure the consistency of SMEs towards economic prosperity of the country, the focus should be on increasing entrepreneurs at the micro, small and medium levels (Martin *et al.*, 2013).

However, the SME sector faces many challenges, like lack of financial and non-financial resources, inefficient management practices and lack of latest technical know-how, which are some of the main causes of failure of small enterprises (Bowen *et al.*, 2009). While SMEs face many constraints, lack of access to financial resources is one of the major challenges (Waari & Mwangi, 2015). SMEs face many challenges in India that are related to the lack of credit facilities from banks and other financial institutions, infrastructural problems, non-availability of raw materials, absence of training for employees, deficiency of organisational and technical skills, and intense competitions from large-scale enterprises. Gamage *et al.* (2020) review global challenges faced by SMEs, mainly the global market competition, global financial and economic crises, information communication technology, the emergence of multinational corporations, transnational corporations, consumer changes and their preferences, trade dumping, international terrorism and religious conflicts (Gamage *et al.*, 2020). These major challenges are creating a hindrance in competing with other companies globally and ultimately affecting business growth, sales and profit.

More than 85% of innovative small and medium firms see unavailability of skilled workers as a barrier to innovation, making it one of the foremost challenges in SME innovation. SMEs are generally unable to recruit a highly skilled workforce due to financial constraints and lack of adequate infrastructure. This includes internal management. The lack of the right internal management can adversely impact both the firm's innovation capability and its overall performance due to lack of direction, rising inefficiencies and the absence of market focus, among others. More than 38% of innovative small and medium firms perceive internal management as a barrier to innovation (Agrawal *et al.*, 2019).

2. Importance of Entrepreneurship Skills and Leadership in SMEs' Business Performance

2.1 *Entrepreneurship skills*

Entrepreneurship is the ability and willingness to begin, put together and maintain a business undertaking, alongside any of its vulnerabilities to generate profits. The entrepreneurial vision is characterised by revelation and hazard taking and is a basic piece of a country's ability to prevail in a consistently changing and competitive global market. It is an inventive errand of imagining and embellishing a business by making something where nothing existed previously. Thus, entrepreneurs must acquire skills which enable them to manage and assist their business. It is an entrepreneur who identifies opportunities, starts a business, manages resources and always seeks excellence because of his/her entrepreneurial skills and competencies (Gürol and Atsan, 2006).

Entrepreneurial skills incorporate different ranges of abilities like initiative, leadership, using time productively, business management, creativity and critical thinking (Prabhu, 2020). One can apply these abilities in their small businesses and grow the venture to the next level.

The following are a list of skills and abilities which are favourable when possessed by SMEs:

1. **Communication skills:** Each business visionary should have the verbal proficiency to discuss adequately with customers, clients, business owners and other stakeholders through face-to-face meetings or any other medium. Communication skills build confidence to influence people within and outside the organisation. The entrepreneur must be a good listener to understand others' perspectives and to handle situations in a creative manner (Akhter *et al.*, 2020).

2. **Risk-taking ability:** Entrepreneurs are always ready to excel in their life, take challenges and are ready to face uncertainties to bring innovations to the economy. They realise that risk is a chance to learn and grow a business to a higher level. Even the management hires those candidates who are ready to take risks and bring innovative solutions for business growth (Stuetzer *et al.*, 2013).

3. **Networking skills:** Networking Skills include assembling and overseeing relationships with different experts to develop and advance a business. Networking abilities can open doors to new opportunities for the business. It permits businesspeople to meet like-minded people, learn, develop and stay up to date with industry patterns (Dohse & Walter, 2012). It is perhaps one of the best abilities of business visionaries as it creates a robust organisation by helping them to learn and access proficient business skill and get criticism on their new pursuit or thought by industry experts.

4. **Critical thinking skills:** Critical reasoning is an entrepreneur's expertise that equitably examines the data and makes a fruitful inference. It assists business visionaries with evaluating circumstances and thinking of a coherent arrangement. SMEs need these critical thinking skills to improvise their products and services, to tackles issues and construct procedures for business development (Pool & Sewell, 2007).

5. **Problem-solving abilities:** Businesses regularly face several issues and challenges in their day-to-day operations. A majority of challenges relate to employees' behaviour, business rivals, debt management and resource management. To overcome these challenges, problem-solving skills need to be developed to come up with viable solutions (Pool & Sewell, 2007).

6. **Creativity:** Innovation follows creativity. For any business to grow and be sustainable, the employees need to be curious to learn new things in a disruptive environment. Learning ability gives rise to creative thought in managing business activities to face the competition globally. Businessmen with imaginative reasoning abilities are never reluctant to take alternate routes that others might disregard in light of fear of failure (Chen, 2015). It is perhaps the most pursued entrepreneurial ability since it permits one to see designs and fosters creative approaches to settle business issues (Chang & Rieple, 2013).

7. **Time management and organisational abilities:** Time management leads to discipline in life and entrepreneurs understand the importance of time. Effective time management leads to prioritising activities and helps in completion of tasks without any delays. Therefore, business organisations, to improve the efficiency of the employees and to monitor their activities, have complete time schedules which help them to plan their tasks accordingly. To manage work properly, it is important to plan tasks and assign activities accordingly, which leads to accountability and self-responsibility among the employees (Pintoa *et al.*, 2020).

8. **Technical skills:** Specialised abilities are hard abilities that are acquired by utilising advanced apparatuses and programming. Entrepreneurs should learn and apply technical skills in managing and growing a business. The digital skills enables entrepreneurs to create web presence, understand customer behaviour with the help of artificial intelligence and able to create its competitive advantage. Hence,

technical skills are important for business success (Smith *et al.*, 2007; Johnson *et al.*, 2015).

9. **Adaptability:** As the business environment is dynamic, it is important to adapt to new strategies, techniques, means and methods to face the competition. The entrepreneurs need to adapt to changes to bring about creativity and innovation and to gain competitive advantage.

10. **Competitive aggressiveness:** Aggressive competitiveness refers to a company's tendency to challenge directly and intensively its competitors when entering into a market or to enhance its position by outperforming its rivals (Junior, 2015). The entrepreneurs need to have competitive aggressiveness which leads to innovations in the businesses with an objective to offer something different from one's competitors.

2.2 *Leadership*

The role of leadership among SMEs cannot be ignored as it greatly impacts the SMEs' performance and subsequently their growth and continuity (Özer & Tınaztepe, 2014). Therefore, leadership has been the key interest of entrepreneurial and management studies for two decades and has gradually become a topic of increasing concern. Leadership plays a vital role in day-to-day functioning of SMEs and influences business performance So as to prosper, the SMEs require consultants with knowledge, skills and education for their operations (Atamian & VanZante, 2010).

To start a business and to run it smoothly, along with entrepreneurial skills, there is a need of a leader in SMEs who can keep motivating people towards a common goal, build trust and confidence of the employees, appreciate them for their performance and foster values among them (Souitaris *et al.*, 2007). Effective leadership skills enable owners and managers to build an intrapreneurial culture and create a competitive advantage at the marketplace.

Leadership ability enables SMEs to expand their venture to new heights (Mukherjee, 2018). The following leadership skills need to be inculcated among small entrepreneurs to grow and sustain their business during crises (Sousa, 2018):

1. **Motivation to other:** Business is uncertain as it influenced by an external environment, so to build the confidence of employees and to

keep them motivated through economic and non-economic rewards, an effective leader is required. A motivated person will have greater job satisfaction, heightened performance and a willingness to succeed, while the unmotivated employees lack interest in their job, take no initiative to come up with new ideas, spend little or no effort to complete work within the time framework and have no desire for quality outcomes (Asah *et al.*, 2015). They try to evade their duties and responsibilities. Thus, motivating staff or a team is a great way to drive performance results and improve workplace morale. With continued motivation, organisations will be able to foster constant productivity and ensure the output of high-quality work in the long term. Thus, it is a leader who keeps inspiring one's subordinates and sparks the creativity and innovation which lead to business growth.

2. **Initiative for innovation:** To lead any venture, it is important to take initiative for the goals to be achieved. The leader is the one who initiates and communicates company goals, plans and policies to achieve the desired outcomes. The ability to take initiative during a crisis is very important to take a step ahead to push your boundaries with your innovative strategies. The leader with these abilities will be able to lead and guide his team.

3. **Building confidence and trust among team members:** Effective leaders always guide their employees, give clarity on their roles and responsibilities, and in this way employees develop their confidence and are able to complete their task efficiently and effectively. The good leaders win the trust of their team by boosting their morale and get full cooperation from their employees at a time when the business is facing a challenge.

4. **Recognition and appreciation of subordinates:** Recognising the team strengths and allocating tasks accordingly will help create a positive workplace environment and ensure that employees work passionately and with commitment. To maintain their consistency and regularity towards their work, it is important for leaders to appreciate their efforts in front of others to boost their morale. Thus, good leaders spend time and observe their employees or team members to get more insights about their strength so as to recognise and reward them accordingly.

5. **Empower subordinates:** When an employee is empowered, they are able to take responsibilities and be influential in a particular situation.

Empowerment is powerful. Therefore, leaders empower employees by delegating authority. The freedom to make decisions and take owner-ship of the good, and the not so good, outcomes can only come from someone who is motivated. An employee who desires to have their voice heard, who wants to contribute in a pivotal role and who seeks results will thrive with empowerment.

6. **Foster values:** Leadership imparts a common set of values to all employees, improving their cohesion and readiness to work in the changing environment. A leader or manager has similar principles and often boosts employees to follow their instruction, increasing the chance of success with every goal. The value-based leadership pro-vides meaning and purpose to employees, stakeholders, successors and the company as a whole. This type of leadership inspires both strong association and innovation through shared values within its community. It expands business opportunities in the same way by attracting new customers, suppliers and investors with similar values and beliefs.

Leadership and entrepreneurial skills help enhance and strengthen business performance. They help businesses in increasing productivity, efficiency and profitability. By studying the influence of these skills, this chapter seeks to establish an understanding towards the importance of leadership and entrepreneurial skills in business growth. This will be done by examining and interviewing Mr. Pankaj Tyagi, founder, partner and business director of M/s RP Inc. The role of entrepreneurial skills with respect to business success and efficiency in dealing with work and profit-ability will be defined by observing the entrepreneur's attitude towards business problems, opportunities and threats (Cooney, 2012).

3. About the Enterprise

RP Inc. is an ISO 9001:2008 CERTIFIED, IRS- and CE-certified, profes-sionally operated firm employed in manufacturing white water rafts/inflatable boats and other inflatable products made of Hypalon and PVC fabric. This decade-old group of firms has been working with the civilian and defence sectors.

The company is the only manufacturer who carries the esteemed CE certification for its rafts in the India. Since it uses the finest raw materials and workmanship in the market, its inflatable product range is unparalleled. The headquarters serves as the administrative complex, production warehouse and wholesale channel in Tehri Garhwal. The import facilitation office is in New Delhi.

Its brand of rafts "JP Rafts" is celebrated all over India as being one of the finest in the country. The JP brand of paraphernalia has a market share in the following regions:

- Northeast
- Ladakh
- J&K
- Maharashtra
- Karnataka
- Himachal
- Uttarakhand
- Miscellaneous world markets

Source: http://jprafts.com.

RP Inc. enjoys excellent trade relations with national and international businesses around the world. It, along with its other group of enterprises, is engaged in the following diverse activities:

- *Adventure equipment of leading brands for civilian and military usage.*
- *Aero sports equipment for civilian and military usage.*
- *Water sports equipment for private and military usage.*

It has been selling and dealing in varied outdoor and water sports products/equipment for more than a decade and consequently it decided to move into manufacturing to help serve its clients better.

The firm's philosophy is to the high-quality top-of-the-market materials (which are all imported). For example, the fabric it uses is sourced from the Number 1 company in the world, Pennel and Flippo (France), and the glue used to bind the fabric is sourced from the Original Equipment Manufacturer (OEM) of the fabric manufacturer (Pennel and Flippo), custom-made to fit the specifications of the fabric. This ensures no quality issues in the products' production and hence facilitates Total Quality Management (TQM).

Its range of products is inclusive of the following:

- Inflatable Boats up to 5 m
- Inflatable White Water Rafts Up to 18ft
- Boats
- Inflatable Kayaks
- Inflatable Catarafts
- Life Buoys (Inflatable)
- Inflatable Fenders
- Life Jackets
- Rescue Throw Bags

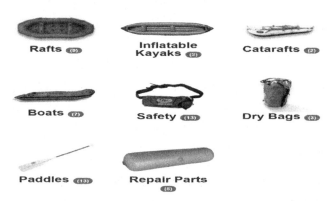

Source: http://jprafts.com.

3.1 *About the entrepreneur*

Mr. Pankaj Tyagi is the founder, partner and business director of RP Inc., a firm based in Uttarakhand, involved in the manufacturing of inflatable rafts and other products. He did his schooling from Welham Boys' School (Dehradun) and completed his graduation from Hindu College (Delhi University) in 1991. Prior to establishing his own company, he worked in several organisations, start-ups and NGOs, where he was engaged in a wide variety of work. He had exposure in marketing, finance, IT and other sectors of business. He proved to be quite an all-rounder as far as entrepreneurial skills are concerned due to his vast interests and work experiences. He founded the company in 2009 along with his associates. He had always been adventurous, outgoing and communicative since childhood, and this aided and inspired him greatly to start this venture as it fit well with his personality and was in line with his skill set. Mr. Tyagi was the first to identify the need for the production of white water rafts and other inflatables in India as there was great scope for rafting and other water sport activities throughout the country. Over the years, RP Inc. has been successfully manufacturing and distributing its quality products all over India and lately even internationally (Japan, China, etc.).

Due to Mr. Tyagi's diligent, meticulous and high-quality work since the inception of the enterprise, the firm has been bestowed with the prestigious CE certification for its products. It is currently the only firm in the country that possesses this certification in that field of work. Slowly and surely, with hard work and dedication, the firm managed to secure over 90% of the market share in the industry.

A 90-minute unstructured face-to-face interview was conducted with Mr. Pankaj Tyagi on 19 July 2021. During the course of the interview, his entrepreneurial journey was discussed along with his start-up story. The entire list of questions along with answers can be referred to in the annexure. Further research and information about Mr. Tyagi and his company RP Inc. was obtained via online sources and incorporated into the study and findings.

Source: Sent via email by Mr. Tyagi on request.

- Name of founder: Mr. Pankaj Tyagi
- Nationality: Indian
- Age: 53
- Title: Founder, Partner and Business director of RP Inc.

4. VRIO Analysis of RP Inc.

VRIO Analysis is a logical strategy used for the assessment of an organisation's resources and in this manner its competitive edge (Barney, 1991).

VRIO is an abbreviation of the initials of the names of the assessment measurements:

- Value
- Rareness
- Imitability
- Organisation

This technique was invented by Jay B. Barney as a method of assessing the resources of a firm, that is, its micro-environment, which consists of the following:

- Financial assets
- Human resources
- Material supplies
- Non-tangible assets

Once a firm knows its resources, it can better understand its competitive edge or its weaknesses. The VRIO analysis considers every type of resource by taking into account the following questions (known as evaluation dimensions) both for one's own firm and its competitors.

The following are the dimensions of VRIO:

- **Value** — How costly is the resource and what is the ease of obtainment?
- **Rareness** — How rare/limited is the asset?
- **Imitability** — How tricky it is to imitate the asset?
- **Organisation** — Can the resource be capitalised on by the organisation?

The diagram further explains how the analysis is conducted.

VRIO Model

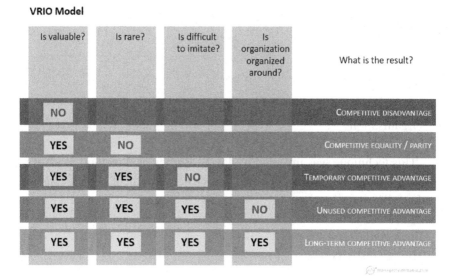

Source: https://managementmania.com/en/vrio-analysis.

After running this analysis on the firm RP Inc., the following points were noted:

1. RP Inc. is very competent at capitalising on its resources which fall into the "permanent competitive advantage" category (like superior quality at competitive prices, top-quality sources of raw material, rarity of white water rafts, inimitable production standards and uniqueness of products). RP Inc. has a very stable and successful method of operation as it is playing to its strengths and side by side working on its weaknesses.
2. It possesses the added advantage of being the first mover in the Indian market (by being the first to venture into inflatable products' production (2009)).
3. It is yet to expand its business onto E-business platforms so that remains in the "unused competitive advantage" category, as it is planning to do so in the coming time period.

5. Strategies for Sustainability and Growth Adopted by Entrepreneur

All this would not have been possible without the entrepreneur's initiative and critical thinking skills which motivated him to recognise the need for his product in the market at a time when no one else was engaged in a similar activity and hence rose to success by delivering quality equipment and products to the concerned market segments.

Further, RP Inc. has a system of prudent spending and timely investment of funds and is very prompt in meeting its payment obligations towards vendors, creditors and other parties. In doing so, its effective financial management skills can be seen.

Mr. Tyagi and his partners are also very competent in communication which has helped them secure deals and maintain a large client base both in India and abroad. It is an essential skill in their line of business as convincing the clients about the necessity and reliability of their product is imperative if they wish to have a loyal and supportive customer base (Akhter *et al.*, 2020).

In conclusion, it can be observed that RP Inc. possesses the entrepreneurial skills that are required to be successful and to ensure growth of the enterprise in the market (Chatterjee & Das, 2016). Thereby, it simultaneously proves the necessity and validity of possessing entrepreneurial skills in order to attain business success (Cooney, 2012).

6. Findings

1. Entrepreneurial skills play an essential role in business development (Do Paco *et al.*, 2011), growth and success (Iakovleva, 2002). Initiative, risk-taking, communication and more skills were visibly seen in Mr. Tyagi and had a clear effect on business performance (Cooney, 2012).

2. Having an entrepreneurial orientation is very important to have a cutting edge in one's respective industry and field. Without this, one cannot easily become the market leader. RP Inc. holds regular brainstorming sessions with its partners and employees to chalk out plans for expansion, growth and to explore new avenues. The company is very dynamic and does its best to capitalise on all opportunities it

comes across. Possessing this kind of entrepreneurial orientation helps the firm to continuously grow and be profitable (Chaston & Sadler-Smith, 2012).

3. Innovation, risk-taking capacity, adaptability, proactiveness and competitive aggressiveness are some of the few essential skills required for lucrative functioning of an organisation (Chatterjee & Das, 2016). For example, after conducting market research among clients and prospective buyers, it was found that PVC fabric rafts were preferred for short-term raft requirements as they are slightly cheaper than Hypalon fabric rafts. Consequently, RP Inc. adapted by starting a line of PVC rafts and marketed them to the appropriate clients. Also, to match up to his competitors, Mr. Tyagi pioneered the idea of providing dry bags and attaching rope-holding D-rings to the raft, which increased the safety and dexterity standards of his rafts as compared to his competitors.

4. Digital literacy and being up to date with technological trends are a must in today's age of business. This aspect will be implemented by the firm as soon as possible. There is an ongoing digital literacy training programme being executed at the company where administrative executives are being taught the required technical skills to go forward with their digital expansion plan (selling rafts purely through digital platforms).

5. Understanding the kind of market one is in and the type of customer base that is being dealt with is extremely critical before the marketing/financing strategy is decided by the entrepreneur. He/she must be well informed about the environment in which he/she is operating. By being and operating in this industry for over a decade, Mr. Tyagi has gained a vast amount of knowledge about the market that he is operating in. By regularly scanning and studying his environment for opportunities, he keeps his firm updated, flexible and adaptable to changes and potential growth prospects.

6. Prudent saving and intelligent investing of financial resources have also been advised so as to ensure timely availability of funds as and when required by the entrepreneur to employ in any projects and to facilitate consistent growth. During the period of COVID-19, RP Inc. was financially secure as throughout the life of the organisation, it followed financial policies which encouraged prudent spending and

extensive saving. It was able to meet its liabilities and all other miscellaneous payment obligations. It did initially have to do a salary cut for its employees due to a lack of business during the COVID-19 pandemic, but it promptly came back to the original salary levels. During the hard times, the company was always very supportive of its staff and sponsored the factory workers' meals for at least 3–4 months till things became more normalised and business was back to booming.

7. Conclusion

The study concludes that entrepreneurial skills, knowledgeable market orientation and networking among entrepreneurs have a constructive and visibly identifiable positive outcome on entrepreneurial competency. Along with this, entrepreneurial competency, entrepreneurial skills and networking have a visible impact on a firm's performance. In addition to entrepreneurial skills, there should be a need for effective leadership skills required to manage and grow a business (Mamabolo *et al.*, 2017). The leadership skills which are essential in SMEs are empowering employees, listening to others' views, negotiation skills, initiative for innovation, etc. Without these skills, it is nearly impossible for entrepreneurs to survive in today's competitive environment. They help the entrepreneur navigate through challenging times by helping them adapt and grow in a manner favourable to the firm's growth. As in the case taken up and analysed in this chapter, Mr. Pankaj Tyagi showed by example that being attentive, alert and enterprising, one can become the market leader in one's respective fields. The importance of having an entrepreneurial orientation was also stressed upon as without it the firm will not be able to capitalise on the opportunities which it comes across nor will it achieve maximum potentially attainable profitability in its future.

Recommendations

The study found that leadership and entrepreneurial skills have had a positive effect on the growth of RP Inc. Therefore, the study recommends that SME leaders enhance their entrepreneurial and leadership skills in attempt to improve business performance (Sousa *et al.*, 2014). The skills can be enhanced by seeking more education on entrepreneurship, leadership, attending workshops, seminars and reading widely (Undiyaundeye & Otu, 2015). SMEs should also arrange training programmes for their employees to empower them. This will ensure that the SMEs' entrepreneurial and leadership culture will enhance business performance.

The study therefore recommends that SME leaders be more charismatic, foster values in employees and empower them by delegating authority and making them accountable for their decisions. This will ensure employees' commitment towards their work and improve business productivity. This study also recommends that SMEs should build intrapreneurial culture by giving due recognition to the ideas presented by the team or employees of the organisation as this will lead to innovations in their strategies for growth.

References

Agarwal, W., Agrawal, U., Mk, A., & Khan, S. (2019). A study on challenges faced by SMEs in India. *International Journal of Engineering Research and Management, 6*(9), 33–37.

Akhter, N., Khan, S. I., & Akter, N. (2020). A total communication package for the business executives: Importance of attitude, culture, leadership and other factors. *International Business Research, 13*(11), 1–1.

Asah, F., Fatoki, O. O., & Rungani, E. (2015). The impact of motivations, personal values and management skills on the performance of SMEs in South Africa. *African Journal of Economic and Management Studies, 6*(3), 308–322.

Atamian, R. & VanZante, N. R. (2010). Continuing education: A vital ingredient of the success plan for small business. *Journal of Business & Economics Research (JBER), 8*(3), 37–42.

Bowen, M., Morara, M., & Mureithi, M. (2009). Management of business challenges among small and micro enterprises in Nairobi-Kenya. *KCA Journal of Business Management, 2*(1), 16–31.

Chang, J. & Rieple, A. (2013). Assessing students' entrepreneurial skills development in live projects. *Journal of Small Business and Enterprise Development, 20*(1), 225–241.

Chaston, I. & Sadler-Smith, E. (2012). Entrepreneurial cognition, entrepreneurial orientation and firm capability in the creative industries. *British Journal of Management, 23*(3), 415–432.

Chatterjee, N. & Das, N. (2016). A study on the impact of key entrepreneurial skills on business success of Indian micro-entrepreneurs: A case of Jharkhand region. *Global Business Review, 17*(1), 226–237.

Chen, S. C., Hsiao, H. C., Chang, J. C., Chou, C. M., Chen, C. P., & Shen, C. H. (2015). Can the entrepreneurship course improve the entrepreneurial intentions of students? *International Entrepreneurship and Management Journal, 11*(3), 557–569.

Cooney, T. M. (2012, November). Entrepreneurship skills for growth-orientated businesses. In *Report for the Workshop on 'Skills Development for SMEs and Entrepreneurship*, (Vol. 28).

Dohse, D. & Walter, S. G. (2012). Knowledge context and entrepreneurial intentions among students. *Small Business Economics, 39*(4), 877–895.

Gürol, Y. & Atsan, N. (2006). Entrepreneurial characteristics amongst university students: Some insights for entrepreneurship education and training in Turkey. *Education + Training, 48*(1), 25–38.

Hsieh, C., Parker, S. C., & van Praag, C. M. (2017). Risk, balanced skills and entrepreneurship. *Small Business Economics, 48*(2), 287–302.

Iakovleva, T. (2002). Theorizing on entrepreneurial performance. In *In 1ère Conférence Européenne d'été, Valence, France* (pp. 1–42).

Jindal, M. K. & Bhardwaj, A. (2016). Entrepreneurship development in India: A new paradigm. In *Proceedings of the World Congress on Engineering* Vol. 2, (pp. 724–726).

Johnson, S., Mukhuty, S., Fletcher, B., Snowden, N., & Williams, T. (2015). Entrepreneurship skills: Literature and policy review. London: Department of Business, Innovation & Skills.

Junior, A. B. O. (2015). The aggressive competitiveness influence on the retailer company performance. *Future Studies Research Journal: Trends and Strategies, 7*(1), 183.

Lee, Y., Kreiser, P. M., Wrede, A. H., & Kogelen, S. (2018). University-based education and the formation of entrepreneurial capabilities. *Entrepreneurship Education and Pedagogy, 1*(4), 304–329.

Mamabolo, M. A., Kerrin, M., & Kele, T. (2017). Entrepreneurship management skills requirements in an emerging economy: A South African outlook. *Southern African Journal of Entrepreneurship and Small Business Management, 9*(1), a111. https://doi.org/10.4102/sajesbm.v9i1.111.

Martin, L. M., Warren-Smith, I., Schofield, C., & Millman, C. (2013). Exploring SME advice and training needs for entrepreneurial rural firms. *The International Journal of Entrepreneurship and Innovation, 14*(2), 95–102.

Mukherjee, S. (2018). Challenges to Indian micro small scale and medium enterprises in the era of globalization. Retrieved from https://journal-jger. springeropen.com/articles/10.1186/s4 0497-018-0115-5.

Naradda Gamage, S. K., Ekanayake, E. M. S., Abeyrathne, G. A. K. N. J., Prasanna, R. P. I. R., Jayasundara, J. M. S. B., & Rajapakshe, P. S. K. (2020). A review of global challenges and survival strategies of small and medium enterprises (Smes). *Economies*, *8*(4), 79.

Özer, F. & Tınaztepe, C. (2014). Effect of strategic leadership styles on firm performance: A study in a Turkish SME. *Procedia-Social and Behavioral Sciences*, *150*, 778–784.

Pintoa, S., Pintob, P., Darwishc, S. Z., & Thonse, I. (2020). Entrepreneurial skills and intention of graduate students for business start-ups: A survey from India. *International Journal of Innovation, Creativity and Change*, *14*(3), 951–970.

Pool, L. D. & Sewell, P. (2007). The key to employability: Developing a practical model of graduate employability. *Education + Training*, *49*(4), 277–289.

Prabhu, J. J. (2020). A study and analysis of entrepreneurial skills and entrepreneurship education: Recommendation for arts and science college students. *IJSART*, *6*(3), 849–855.

Smith, W. L., Schallenkamp, K., & Eichholz, D. E. (2007). Entrepreneurial skills assessment: An exploratory study. *International Journal of Management and Enterprise Development*, *4*(2), 179–201.

Souitaris, V., Zerbinati, S., & Al-Laham, A. (2007). Do entrepreneurship programmes raise entrepreneurial intention of science and engineering students? The effect of learning, inspiration and resources. *Journal of Business Venturing*, *22*(4), 566–591.

Sousa, M. J. (2018). Entrepreneurship skills development in higher education courses for teams leaders. *Administrative Sciences*, *8*(2), 18.

Sousa, M. J., Almeida, M. D. R., Mastorakis, N. E., Pardalos, P. M., & Katehakis, M. N. (2014). Entrepreneurial skills development. Recent Advances in Applied Economics, 135–139.

Stuetzer, M., Obschonka, M., Davidsson, P., & Schmitt-Rodermund, E. (2013). Where do entrepreneurial skills come from? *Applied Economics Letters*, *20*(12), 1183–1186.

Undiyaundeye, F. & Otu, E. A. (2015). Entrepreneurship skills acquisition and the benefits amongst the undergraduate students in Nigeria. *European Journal of Social Science Education and Research*, *2*(3), 9–14.

Waari, D. N. & Mwangi, W. M. (2015). Factors influencing access to finance by micro, small and medium enterprises in Meru County, Kenya. *International Journal of Economics, Commerce and Management*, 3(4), 1–15.

Annexure

Interview

1. Tell us about your company?

We present ourselves as a competently managed firm employed in the manufacturing of white water rafts/inflatable boats and other inflatable products made using PVC and Hypalon fabric, dealing with the private and defence segments in India.

We enjoy excellent trade relations in conjunction with national and international businesses around the world. We along with our other group of enterprises are engaged in the following diverse activities:

Adventure equipment of leading brands for civilian and military usage.
Aero sports equipment for civilian and military usage.
Water sports equipment surf for private and military usage.

We have been selling and dealing in varied outdoor and water sports products/equipment for more than a decade and consequently we decided to move into manufacturing to help serve our clients better.

Our firm's philosophy is to employ the high-quality top-of-the-market materials (which are all imported). For example, the fabric we use is sourced from the Number 1 company in the world, Pennel and Flippo (France), and the glue used to bind the fabric is sourced from the Original Equipment Manufacturer (OEM) of the fabric manufacturer (Pennel and Flippo), custom-made to fit the specifications of the fabric. This ensures no quality issues in our products' production and hence facilitates Total Quality Management (TQM).

Our range of products is Inclusive of the following:

- Inflatable Boats up to 5m
- Inflatable White Water Rafts up to 18ft

- Boats
- Inflatable Kayaks
- Inflatable Catarafts
- Life Buoys (Inflatable)
- Inflatable Fenders
- Life Jackets
- Rescue Throw Bags

We are striving to produce top-quality Inflatables in the Indian marketing scenario. Slowly and surely, we are getting there, one step at a time.

Our List of Clients is as follows:

1. Mercury Himalayan Exploration
2. PAC
3. Army
4. Air Force
5. Tata Adventure Foundation
6. ITBP
7. SDRF
8. Exports to Japan
9. Forest Department

2. What inspired you to start the enterprise?

RP Inc. with our "JP" Brand of Rafts was created out of a necessity for the white water rafting industry in Uttarakhand.

We conquered the deficiencies of design and compatibility issues of the other international brands in the distinctive Indian market where extreme temperature and operating conditions are found.

Our endeavour became an instantaneous success, as for the first time in India we were able to produce a raft which was perfect for Indian conditions and at the same level as some of the world's most competitive and leading manufacturers.

3. What is the age and size of your business?

We started operations in 2012 and we are a medium-scale enterprise.

4. Which all segments of the market do you cater to?
We cater to commercial operators in India, to the Indian Armed Forces and export to a few countries as well. We will be looking to expand these segments as and when opportunities permit.

5. What is your USP?
We offer high-quality products at affordable prices with exceptional after-sales services. We were one of the few firms to begin with in this industry so we have the advantage of being the "first mover" and hence have a lot of experience in terms of manufacturing and selling rafts.

6. Do you believe that entrepreneurial orientation increases your firm's performance and productivity?
Yes, it most certainly does. Without having such an orientation, one cannot grow in business. An entrepreneur must always seek to capture and capitalise as many opportunities as they can so as to be successful while at the same time, creating value for customers. One should engage in innovative, risk-taking, and proactive behaviours for optimum output.

7. What kind of entrepreneurial skills would you say attribute towards the success of the firm?
Low-cost high-quality product sourcing and understanding and import substitution without lower standards are key.

8. How have you been coping up during COVID-19 times?
It has been tough as our business is tourist dependent, and since there is no travel, no adventure sports and no business from b2b, but we have managed to secure sufficient orders as we are the market leaders.

9. How did your entrepreneurial skills help you in challenging times?
We are improvising and keeping our cost to the minimum and lean to tide over these unprecedented times. Having a go-getter attitude and the ability to take risky out-of-the-box decisions is what helps a lot in difficult times. One must be willing to step out of their comfort zone and make the best of what is offered in the environment in which they are placed. The more

innovative a person is, the more he or she can extract from a given set of resources.

10. What would you say is the most essential thing needed to survive in the Indian market with respect to your line of work?

Competitive pricing while still being able to offer good quality and catering to the ever-changing demands of the customer on a timely and appropriate basis are essential. Along with this, to be successful, understanding customer psychology and using appropriate marketing strategies to promote your product efficiently are very important. While this sounds very cliché, to actually be able to execute this effectively is quite a task in a country like India which is home to such a diverse range of people, each having varied tastes, preferences and outlooks.

11. How has the application of entrepreneurial skills changed with time, from the inception of your firm till date?

We have to be more digitally and technologically updated. The importance of technical skills has grown significantly over time, and we have been adapting to it as and when possible. We are working on expanding our online customer base as E-commerce is quite prevalent today and we do not want to leave out any expansion opportunities. To be able to fully reach out to all potential clients having a prominent digital presence is imperative.

12. What is your advice for the upcoming generations of entrepreneurs?

Never compromise on the quality of products, constantly upgrade your skill set to adapt with your environment, stay lean and save for a rainy day. Do not spend more than you earn. Save and invest 70% of what you earn to ensure prosperity and fruitful usage of funds.

13. What is your plan in the coming future with regard to expansion and growth of your firm?

We will explore more international markets as we already have 90% of the Indian market share in our industry.

14. How imperative are these skills on a scale of 1 to 10?

- Risk-Taking — 7
- Proactiveness — 9
- Innovativeness — 10
- Competitive Aggressiveness — 8

Chapter 6

Does Entrepreneurial Orientation Predict Small and Medium Enterprise Alliance Formation? Evidence from the Indian Manufacturing Sector

Rohit Prabhudesai[*,¶], Ch. V. V. S. N. V. Prasad[†,‖],
Nitin Pangarkar[‡,**], Abhishek Kumar Sinha[§,††]
and Akshay Bhat[*,‡‡]

[*]Goa Institute of Management, Poriem Sattari, Goa, India
[†]Department of Economics, Birla Institute of Technology and Science (BITS)
Pilani, Goa Campus, Goa, India
[‡]NUS Business School, Singapore
[§]NMIMS Mumbai, Mumbai, India
[¶]rohit@gim.ac.in
[‖]prasad@goa.bits-pilani.ac.in
[**]bizpn@nus.edu.sg
[††]abhishekkumar.sinha@nmins.edu
[‡‡]akshay@gim.ac.in

Abstract

While entrepreneurial SMEs are known to explore their strategic options for acquiring the resources necessary for achieving competitiveness, relatively little research exists on how their entrepreneurial orientation affects the formation of strategic alliances. Using a unidimensional perspective of entrepreneurial orientation conceptualised by Covin and Slevin (1989), this study aims to determine how it affects the alliance formation tendencies of SMEs. Utilising a sample of 127 SMEs from the manufacturing sector in Goa, the study finds that entrepreneurial orientation positively affects alliance formation tendencies. Furthermore, size of the SME was also found to affect its alliance formation tendencies.

Keywords: Small and medium enterprise, SME, manufacturing SME, SME alliance formation, entrepreneurial orientation

1. Introduction

Small and Medium Enterprises (SMEs) often compensate for the lack of resources at their disposal by exhibiting higher levels of entrepreneurial orientation (EO). Using their entrepreneurial approach, SMEs tend to proactively explore their strategic options for acquiring resources, which can yield them a competitive advantage in the marketplace (Brouthers *et al.*, 2015; Dana, 2021; Sawyer, 2009; Prabhudesai & Prasad, 2018; Troise *et al.*, 2021). Viewed from Williamson's (1985) perspective, a firm can undertake either a market or hierarchical decision for acquiring resources. Since both approaches become difficult for an SME to undertake due to the associated high transaction costs, opting for a hybrid structure such as strategic alliances remains the only viable option. However, very little is known about the impact of the EO of an SME on its alliance formation patterns. Studies that have analysed this relationship have either focused on the moderating influence of EO (Brouthers *et al.*, 2015; Dickson & Weaver, 1997) or its impact on future alliance formation intentions (Marino *et al.*, 2008). While Franco and Haase (2013) studied the impact of EO on SME alliance formation, they studied the impact of each EO dimension separately. Thus, holistic insight into the impact of EO on SME alliance formation patterns is missing in the extant literature. This study seeks to bridge this theoretical gap by determining how the EO of an SME influences its alliance formation patterns.

2. Theory and Hypothesis

EO is a construct which represents the state of organisational policies, processes and practices that result in entrepreneurial actions and decisions

(Lumpkin & Dess, 2015). Miller (2011) emphasises that the conceptualisation of EO answers what is basically meant by an entrepreneurial firm, in practical and behavioural terms. Thus, the construct of EO of a firm has been traditionally defined based upon three dimensions — innovativeness, proactiveness and risk-taking (Covin & Slevin, 1989; Miller, 1983; Zahra & Neubaum, 1998). While innovativeness refers to the ability of a firm to engage in activities which can give rise to new products, processes or services, proactiveness determines how quickly the firm seizes an opportunity in the marketplace ahead of its competitors, with risk-taking encompassing the extent to which firm managers undertake risky commitments involving large payoffs (Kreiser & Davis, 2010). While Covin & Slevin (1989) argue that all three dimensions represent a composite factor, EO, Lumpkin & Dess (1996) state that the dimensions essentially capture heterogeneous phenomena and must be considered separately. Covin & Lumpkin (2011) state that both approaches are distinct and researchers must view them as such, rather than considering them as substitutes to each other.

Holistically, higher EO leads to exploration of opportunities for a firm, thereby resulting in greater alliance formation tendencies (Brouthers *et al.*, 2015; Dana, 1999; Nakos *et al.*, 2018; Prasad & Prabhudesai, 2018). While alliances represent a double-edged sword for SMEs, entailing the risks of partner opportunism alongside the benefit of resource acquisition, those with higher EO tend to focus on benefits rather than risks associated with alliances, thereby exhibiting higher propensity for alliance formation (Marino *et al.*, 2008; Prasad & Prabhudesai, 2018). Thus, it can be posited that

Hypothesis 1: The higher the entrepreneurial orientation of an SME, the greater its alliance formation tendency.

3. Methods and Results

3.1 *Variables and their measurement*

The independent variable for the purpose of the study was entrepreneurial orientation and was measured on a scale of 1–5, based on Covin & Slevin's (1989) work. Thus, a total of eight items measuring the three

Table 1.   Details of the firms.

Firm Size	Number of Firms (Percentage)
0–50 employees	93 (73%)
50–100 employees	16 (13%)
>100 employees	18 (14%)

Firm Age	Number of Firms (Percentage)
<10 years	14 (11%)
10–20 years	63 (50%)
>20 years	50 (39%)

Firm Industry	Number of Firms (Percentage)
Chemical	7 (6%)
Electrical and electronic equipment	15 (11%)
Food	13 (10%)
Industrial and computer equipment	9 (7%)
Paper	10 (8%)
Primary metals	27 (21%)
Rubber	7 (6%)
Stone, clay and concrete	9 (7%)
Other	30 (24%)

dimensions of EO — innovativeness, proactiveness and risk-taking — were included to measure the construct of EO. Alliance formation by SMEs was the dependent variable, measured as to whether the SME was currently engaged in a strategic alliance or not. The definition of alliances was based on the conceptualisation by Das & Teng (2000), wherein four alliances types are identified — unilateral contractual arrangements, bilateral contractual arrangements, minority equity purchases and joint ventures. Years since the establishment of the firm, calculated as the age of the firm, and the number of full-time employees working in the firm, analysed as firm size, were both used as control variables. Details of the firms are provided in Table 1.

3.2 Sample and data collection

Given the differences which exist in the definitions of SMEs across countries, it was considered expedient to limit the study to Indian SMEs (Gilmore *et al.*, 2013). Furthermore, SMEs in India are defined differently for manufacturing and service sectors (MSME, 2021). Thus, to obtain reliable insights, only manufacturing sector SMEs were considered for the study purpose.

Given the comparatively higher reliability of the personal survey method against other methods (Sax *et al.*, 2003), it was chosen as the means of data collection. However, this limited the number of firms that could be approached for the purpose of the study. After pilot testing the survey with a sample of eight academicians and practitioners, the convenience sampling approach was used and all the manufacturing SMEs in the state of Goa were selected for this study. A total sample of 770 firms was obtained. Key respondents — CEOs, MDs and proprietors — involved in the strategic decision-making in each SME were approached to seek their responses to the survey on behalf of their firm (Coviello & Jones, 2004). 127 firms ultimately completed the survey, yielding a response rate of 16%.

4. Results

4.1 Validity and reliability analysis

Given that the scale for EO measures three dimensions, exploratory factor analysis was conducted to determine the factor structure. All eight items loaded onto one factor — entrepreneurial orientation — with the factor explaining 76% of the variance in the variables, with each factor loading above 0.70 (Joliffe & Morgan, 1992). Similarly, the internal reliability analysis conducted using Cronbach's Alpha yielded a score of 0.95, indicating the high reliability level of the scale (Gliem & Gliem, 2003).

4.2 Model fit and hypothesis testing

Given that the independent variable was continuous and the dependent variable was categorical in nature, logistic regression analysis was used to

R. *Prabhudesai et al.*

Table 2.   Results of logistic regression.

	Model 1	Model 2
Firm Size	0.020*** (0.006)	0.016** (0.006)
Firm Age	0.013 (0.023)	0.015 (0.026)
Food Industry	−0.988 (0.753)	−0.341 (0.823)
Paper Industry	−1.547* (0.872)	−1.269 (0.931)
Chemical Industry	−1.411 (0.972)	−1.535 (1.203)
Rubber Industry	−0.982 (0.905)	−0.953 (1.014)
Stone and Clay Industry	−1.679* (0.942)	−1.579 (1.061)
Primary Metals Industry	−1.136* (0.602)	−1.224* (0.720)
Computer and Industrial Equipment Industry	−0.892 (0.845)	−0.900 (0.966)
Electrical and Electronics Industry	−1.072 (0.744)	−1.794** (0.899)
EO		1.206*** (0.264)
Constant	−0.376 (0.588)	−3.930 (1.028)
Nagelkerke R-square	0.302	0.501
Correct Classification Percentage	66%	78%

Notes: $*p < 0.10$, $**p < 0.05$, $***p < 0.001$; standard error in parentheses.

analyse the relationship. While model 1 tests only the control variables of firm age and firm size to determine their impact on SME alliance formation, the independent variable of EO is introduced in model 2.

Hypothesis 1 was validated as it was found that EO of an SME positively affects alliance formation ($p < 0.05$). The exponential coefficient was observed to be 7.98, indicating that every unit increase in EO of an SME increases the odds of alliance formation by a factor of 7.98. Firm size was also found to affect alliance formation patterns, with every unit increase resulting in a corresponding increase in the odds of alliance formation by a factor of 1.021. Table 2 shows the results of logistic regression analysis.

5. Discussion and Conclusion

The aim of the study was to determine how EO of an SME influences its alliance formation patterns. Firstly, while Franco & Haase (2013) tested the multidimensional approach of EO and found that each dimension has a differential impact on alliance formation of SMEs, the results of this study indicate that EO functions as a unidimensional construct and has a strong positive influence on the SME alliance formation tendency. Thus, support is obtained for the findings of Covin & Lumpkin (2011) who find that the unidimensional and multidimensional approaches essentially measure different phenomena.

Among the control variables, size of an SME was also found to affect its alliance formation tendencies. The finding resonates with those of Shan *et al.* (1994), and Colombo *et al.* (2006), who find that the greater the size of an SME, the greater the tendency for alliance formation.

From a practical perspective, the study determines the importance of EO holistically in the formation of alliances by SMEs. SMEs which have key decision-makers with higher EO — those who exhibit a higher propensity towards innovativeness, proactiveness and risk-taking — are more likely to form alliances and thereby become competitive in the marketplace. Theoretically, the study finds a positive relationship between EO and SME alliance formation, thereby providing important insights into a topic which has hitherto been ignored in the extant literature.

Despite the key findings, the study carries certain limitations. While the study finds a strong relationship between EO and SME alliance formation, certain variables such as environmental uncertainty faced by an SME also affect its strategic choices; thus, it would be worthwhile to determine their impact on the EO–alliance formation relationship (Marino *et al.*, 2008; Prasad & Prabhudesai, 2018). Furthermore, the relatively small sample size of the study necessitates the need for replicating the model in other geographical contexts for generalising study results.

References

Brouthers, K. D., Nakos, G., & Dimitratos, P. (2015). SME entrepreneurial orientation, international performance, and the moderating role of strategic alliances. *Entrepreneurship Theory and Practice*, *39*(5), 1161–1187.

Colombo, M. G., Grilli, L., & Piva, E. (2006). In search of complementary assets: The determinants of alliance formation of high-tech start-ups. *Research Policy*, *35*(8), 1166–1199.

Coviello, N. E. & Jones, M. V. (2004). Methodological issues in international entrepreneurship research. *Journal of Business Venturing*, *19*(4), 485–508.

Covin, J. G. & Lumpkin, G. T. (2011). Entrepreneurial orientation theory and research: Reflections on a needed construct. *Entrepreneurship Theory and Practice*, *35*(5), 855–872.

Covin, J. G. & Slevin, D. P. (1989). Strategic management of small firms in hostile and benign environments. *Strategic Management Journal*, *10*(1), 75–87.

Dana, L.-P. (Ed.) (2021). *World Encyclopedia of Entrepreneurship*. Edward Elgar Publishing. Cheltenham, United Kingdom.

Das, T. K. & Teng, B. S. (2000). A resource-based theory of strategic alliances. *Journal of Management*, *26*(1), 31–61.

Dickson, P. H. & Weaver, K. M. (1997). Environmental determinants and individual-level moderators of alliance use. *Academy of Management Journal*, *40*(2), 404–425.

Eisenhardt, K. M. & Schoonhoven, C. B. (1996). Resource-based view of strategic alliance formation: Strategic and social effects in entrepreneurial firms. *Organization Science*, *7*(2), 136–150.

Franco, M. & Haase, H. (2013). Firm resources and entrepreneurial orientation as determinants for collaborative entrepreneurship. *Management Decision*, *51*(3), 680–696.

Gilmore, A., McAuley, A., Gallagher, D., Massiera, P., & Gamble, J. (2013). Researching SME/entrepreneurial research: A study of Journal of Research in Marketing and Entrepreneurship (JRME) 2000–2011. *Journal of Research in Marketing and Entrepreneurship*, *15*(2), 87–100.

Gliem, J. A. & Gliem, R. R. (2003). Calculating, interpreting, and reporting Cronbach's alpha reliability coefficient for Likert-type scales. *Midwest Research-to-Practice Conference in Adult, Continuing, and Community Education*, Columbus, pp. 82–88.

Joliffe, I. T. & Morgan, B. J. T. (1992). Principal component analysis and exploratory factor analysis. *Statistical Methods in Medical Research*, *1*(1), 69–95.

Kreiser, P. M. & Davis, J. (2010). Entrepreneurial orientation and firm performance: The unique impact of innovativeness, proactiveness, and risk-taking. *Journal of Small Business and Entrepreneurship*, *23*(1), 39–51.

Lumpkin, G. T. & Dess, G. G. (1996). Clarifying the entrepreneurial orientation construct and linking it to performance. *Academy of Management Review*, *21*(1), 135–172.

Lumpkin, G. T. & Dess, G. G. (2015). Entrepreneurial orientation. *Wiley Encyclopedia of Management*, *3*, 1–4.

Marino, L. D., Lohrke, F. T., Hill, J. S., Weaver, K. M., & Tambunan, T. (2008). Environmental shocks and SME alliance formation intentions in an emerging economy: Evidence from the Asian financial crisis in Indonesia. *Entrepreneurship Theory and Practice, 32*(1), 157–183.

Miller, D. (1983). The correlates of entrepreneurship in three types of firms. *Management Science, 29*(7), 770–791.

Miller, D. (2011). Miller (1983) revisited: A reflection on EO research and some suggestions for the future. *Entrepreneurship Theory and Practice, 35*(5), 873–894.

MSMEs, M. O. (2021). *What are Micro, Small and Medium Enterprises.* Retrieved from http://www.dcmsme.gov.in/ssiindia/defination_msme.htm.

Nakos, G., Dimitratos, P., & Elbanna, S. (2019). The mediating role of alliances in the international market orientation-performance relationship of SMEs. *International Business Review, 28*(3), 603–612.

Prabhudesai, R. & Prasad, C. V. (2018). Understanding the international strategic alliances of SMEs: A case-study approach. *International Journal of Entrepreneurship and Small Business 35*(1), 102–125.

Prasad, C. V. & Prabhudesai, R. (2018). What drives SME explorative-exploitative alliance formation: An integrated perspective. *International Journal of Business Innovation and Research, 15*(1), 79–98.

Sax, L. J., Gilmartin, S. K., & Bryant, A. N. (2003). Assessing response rates and nonresponse bias in web and paper surveys. *Research in Higher Education, 44*(4), 409–432.

Sawyer, J. (2009). Product differentiation and the choice of alliance partners. *Global Business and Economics Review, 11*(3–4), 281–287.

Shan, W., Walker, G., & Kogut, B. (1994). Interfirm cooperation and startup innovation in the biotechnology industry. *Strategic Management Journal, 15*(5), 387–394.

Troise, C., Dana, L.-P., Tani, M., & Lee, K. Y. (2021). Social media and entrepreneurship: Exploring the impact of social media use of start-ups on their entrepreneurial orientation and opportunities. *Journal of Small Business and Enterprise Development, 29*(1), 47–73.

Wales, W. J. (2016). Entrepreneurial orientation: A review and synthesis of promising research directions. *International Small Business Journal, 34*(1), 3–15.

Williamson, O. E. (1985). *The Economic Institutions of Capitalism.* Simon and Schuster. New York, United States of America.

Zahra, S. A. & Neubaum, D. O. (1998). Environmental adversity and the entrepreneurial activities of new ventures. *Journal of Developmental Entrepreneurship, 3*(2), 123–140.

© 2023 World Scientific Publishing Company
https://doi.org/10.1142/9789811269554_0007

Chapter 7

COVID-19 and Learning Experiences of Women Entrepreneurial Leaders: An Indian Context

Meghna Chhabra[*,‡] and Monika Agarwal[†,§]

*Faculty of Management Studies, Manav Rachna International Institute of Research and Studies, Faridabad, Haryana, India
†Jagan Institute of Management Studies, Rohini, Delhi, India
‡meghnachhabra1@gmail.com
§monikaagg85@gmail.com

Abstract

This chapter aims to explore the factors that motivate or demotivate women entrepreneurs to continue their businesses amid COVID-19 in the context of the Indian environment and the leadership style approached by women entrepreneurs amid COVID-19. The study has employed qualitative research methods (thematic analysis) for the data collection and data analysis. The authors conducted in-depth semi-structured interviews with the participants to collect the required data for the study. The study highlighted various motivating and demotivating factors for women entrepreneurs in small businesses to continue their business in India during the pandemic period. The factors that motivated women entrepreneurs amid COVID-19 to continue their business are support from family and society for enhanced homely responsibilities, favourable nature of business in which women are operating, considering adversity as an opportunity and self-assessment of their skills because of the unprecedented situation of

COVID-19. But the lack of family support, the unfavourable nature of business and having a high risk of infection from COVID-19 demotivated them from continuing their business. The study will help the government and other policy-makers devise strategies and policy frameworks to enhance the motivation level of women entrepreneurs to continue their business. The study will also help gain deeper insights into the problems associated with women's entrepreneurship.

Keywords: India, developing country, women entrepreneur, entrepreneurial leader, small businesses, COVID-19

1. Introduction

Every setback is an opportunity.

Women are confidently taking on leadership roles in all sectors of the economy. Leadership is growing in different career clusters, especially entrepreneurial roles (Dana, 1990, 1997; Jang, 2013). The increasing presence of women leaders as entrepreneurs has led to the change in the demographic characteristics of the business and economic growth of the country. Women entrepreneurship has gained a lot of importance with its materialistic contribution to economic development (Noguera *et al.*, 2013). Women entrepreneurial leaders have significantly contributed to employment creation and economic growth (Chhabra *et al.*, 2020). In the last few years, the Government of India has given much importance to the development of women entrepreneurial leaders (Kangal, 2019). However, women-operated self-owned firms stand at approximately 8.5 million out of 58.5 million established firms in India (Government of India, 2016). Women self-owned firms in India are less than 20% of the total existing firms (Chawla *et al.*, 2020). As per Chawla *et al.* (2020), the potential of the 432 million employable women's group is still not utilised. Therefore, the enhanced focus on the growth of women entrepreneurs can generate approximately 170 million jobs by 2030 (Chawla *et al.*, 2020). But in India, there are numerous hindrances and challenges which hamper the flourishing of women entrepreneurs and their contribution to the economic growth of the country (Chhabra & Karmarkar, 2016).

The Mastercard Index report on Women Entrepreneurs (2018) states that India is a lower-middle-income developing country that provides an unfavourable environment for nourishing women's entrepreneurship. The report further says that deep-rooted cultural biases and lack of financial support for women entrepreneurs negatively affect their business growth and continuation. Furthermore, the pandemic has made women entrepreneurs more vulnerable (Manolova, 2020). Moreover, the COVID-19 pandemic has impeded all businesses, but it has badly affected the women entrepreneurs predominantly (Chmura, 2020). It has been found that a majority of women entrepreneurs exist in tourism, beauty, wholesale, retail, health, education and social services (Elam *et al.*, 2019; Salla, 2020; Women Budget Group, 2020), and hence, COVID-19 has affected these sectors most (Chaudhary *et al.*, 2020; Chmura, 2020; Orser, 2020). The damaging effect of the COVID-19 pandemic on women-owned small businesses has worsened the socioeconomic inequalities (ET Rise, 2020). Other than COVID-19, there are many factors responsible for the vulnerable position of women entrepreneurs during COVID-19. Factors such as organisational inequalities of women-owned firms expose women entrepreneurs to more susceptible economic impacts (Chmura, 2020; WE Forum, 2020). Women entrepreneurs rely more on informal borrowing and have fewer financial resources, facing more financial crunch (Orser, 2020).

Further, during COVID-19, women's homely responsibilities were enhanced because of the non-availability of domestic helpers, the shutting down of schools and child care services, posing an immense challenge for women entrepreneurs to run their businesses smoothly (Chmura, 2020; Salla, 2020). Amid this crisis, gender inequalities have become more visible in highly male-dominated developing countries (Priola & Pecis, 2020) and have generated more obstacles in women entrepreneurs' paths (Jaim, 2020b). Various restrictions because of COVID-19 and poor support availability to women in developing countries have affected women's entrepreneurial activity engagement (Mathew *et al.*, 2020; Peto *et al.*, 2020). The entire critical situation of women entrepreneurs in existing problems and the COVID-19 crisis posit some appealing research questions. How do women in the unfavourable environment of India deal with their business with the issues enhanced due to the COVID-19 situation, and what was the effect of the crisis on their business?

For this reason, it is an excellent opportunity to discover the factors that affect women entrepreneurial leaders in continuing their firms in the unfavourable environment posed due to the ongoing pandemic situation (Jaim, 2020b). Past literature shows that very few studies explain the intricacies for women entrepreneurs to go beyond the established societal obligations and problems (Ahl, 2004; Holmes, 2007) for starting entrepreneurial activities. Also, few studies have explored the issues faced by women entrepreneurs for the continuation of business amid the pandemic in developing countries (Popović-Pantić, 2020; Jaim, 2020a). Therefore, looking into the women entrepreneur's experiences in developing countries during COVID-19 can be insightful.

This research aims to discover the effect of COVID-19 on women entrepreneurs' business in India, where there exists a high level of unfavourable culture for women entrepreneurs (Mastercard Index report, 2020), and uncovers their initiatives as business leaders to combat the adversities faced during the time of the pandemic. This study profiled women who own and manage small to medium-sized businesses. The chapter's framework is as follows. It starts with an extensive literature review exploration, followed by research methodology and results. The study is further classified into discussion sections, conclusion and implications, and limitations.

2. Review of Literature

Women's entrepreneurship has recently had good scope for contributing to socioeconomic development and has received remarkable attention worldwide (Popovic-Pantic *et al.*, 2020). Many studies on women's entrepreneurship have been conducted in developed countries, but these studies have ignored the concept of women's entrepreneurial leaders in developing countries (Jaim & Islam, 2018). Many authors viewed that women's homely responsibilities have unconstructive impacts on their business (Ahl, 2006; Mehtap *et al.*, 2017). Moreover, innate and unusual hurdles (Popovic-Pantic *et al.*, 2020) make entrepreneurship a gender-biased sphere in developing countries (Ahl, 2006). The restrictions on women's communication in many developing countries impede the creation of an exemplary communication network for their business (Roomi, 2009; Rutashobya *et al.*, 2009). Thus, these social and economic barriers negatively affected women entrepreneurs (Popovic-Pantic *et al.*, 2020).

COVID-19 has inflicted various restrictions such as lockdowns, social distancing and curb on travelling, (Danish & Smith, 2012; Jaim, 2020a), which have impeded the smooth operation of self-owned business, specifically women entrepreneurs. Women are already facing inherent and deliberately generated problems in developing countries (Amine & Staub, 2009; Jaim, 2020b). Little information exists about women entrepreneurs' business practices, survival and growth strategies (Ahmad, 2011). The outbreak of this pandemic created the need to study women entrepreneurs' issues with COVID-19 to continue their ventures. Therefore, the present study explores the problems of women entrepreneurs in connection with COVID-19 in India.

Many support initiatives from the government, formation of self-help groups (SHGs), support from NGOs, enhanced women's education, etc., have increased the participation of women in entrepreneurial activities; regardless of all this, women's representation in entrepreneurial activities remains slow in comparison to men in India (Mathew & Panchanatham, 2011; Lenka & Agarwal, 2017). As per the GEM report (2018–2019), the female share in entrepreneurial activity is only 38%. Above it, the pandemic has badly impacted 73% of women-owned businesses and put 20% of women's ventures on the verge of closure (Chawla *et al.*, 2020). Countrywide lockdowns due to COVID-19 resulted in the closure of economic operations of the businesses, which hit the budding entrepreneurs hard (Gregurec *et al.*, 2021; Sahoo & Ashwani, 2020). It has affected all self-owned firms' financial positions and operational activities. Majority of the women-owned businesses have been adversely impacted by the pandemic (Fabrizio *et al.*, 2020). Thus, this study examines women entrepreneurs' experiences in the COVID-19 pandemic of carrying on or shutting down their ventures in the developing country of India and their traits as entrepreneurial leaders.

3. Research Methodology

The authors used the thematic text analysis to explore women entrepreneurs' experience amid COVID-19 (Braun & Clarke, 2006; Dana & Dana, 2005; Dana & Dumez, 2015). Positivist prefer scientific quantitative methods. Constructivist or interpretative ideal models are favoured in qualitative research methodologies (Dana & Dumez, 2015). There is a growing understanding that qualitative research may be used to discover and present innovative findings in the entrepreneurial arena (Gartner & Birley, 2002; Javadian *et al.*, 2020). The qualitative method may be a more effective way to learn about the participants' perceptions of the underlying issue. It offers "valuable insights into how people construct meaning in various social settings" (Neuman, 2006).

As a result, the study was conducted using a qualitative research design, namely, the narrative inquiry methodology (Bruner, 1991; Kohler Riessman, 2002). Narrative inquiry is a research method that focuses on "detailed histories or life experiences of a single event or a series of events for a small number of individuals" (Elliott, 2005). "A narrative study aims to describe the understanding and meaning of the experiences from the participant's perspective. The combination of content and reflection of the researcher is called a narrative inquiry. Data analysis may be carried out by reorganising the stories into chronological order, identifying key aspects, and may include interpretation and thematic analysis" (Groenland & Dana, 2020). The approach used, narrative inquiry, is appropriate for the study because our primary goal was to conduct exploratory research. Narrative inquiry is most appropriate when the goal is to understand why and how to investigate a phenomenon in its natural setting (Elliott, 2005).

3.1 *Sample for the study*

The data collection for the study was based on extensive interviews with Indian women entrepreneurs. The respondents were chosen using purposeful rather than random sampling to ensure a "knowledge-rich" sample on issues pertinent to the study's goal (Hamilton & Catterall, 2006). The main requirement was that all women were self-employed and started their own modest companies in India. Because the purpose of the study is to look at the impact of gender on women's entrepreneurial challenges, no other firm members should be included in the running of the business. Another criterion for evaluating the pandemic period's experiences was that all women had at least five years of experience running their businesses during normal periods (non-pandemic times). It made it easier for individuals to recognise and reflect on their unique experiences during the pandemic. Women entrepreneurs were interviewed in semi-structured face-to-face interviews to obtain primary data on the continuation of their business activity throughout the continuing epidemic.

The research aims were explained to the participants, and their agreement was obtained. The participants were assured of their anonymity, and no identities were revealed at the presentation of the findings. The interview method was chosen because it allows the authors to gain deep insights and in-depth knowledge about the topics under investigation (Groenland & Dana, 2020). Depending on the respondents' responses, the semi-structured questionnaire provided flexibility in question sequence and tempo. The tool was first tested for reliability and validity with the help of five entrepreneurship experts, who recommended minor changes. The revisions were incorporated, and five academicians were consulted to ensure concept and face validity. The instrument was completed after all of the appropriate validations. The structured questions were related to the demographic profile of the participants.

In contrast, the semi-structured questions addressed the primary components under consideration for this study (i.e., the role of family, human capital, social capital and government support services) (Groenland and Dana, 2020). The authors, starting with questions related to demographic details, asked two prompting questions to the participants: "How did COVID-19 affect your business?" "What made you continue or discontinue your business?" All the interviews were carried out at the participants' workplaces. The mean time duration of the interviews was 40 minutes, though the overall timings fluctuated between 30 and 60 minutes.

The authors stopped collecting data when they reached theoretical saturation, which means there were no more themes that could be generated with further data (Glaser & Strauss, 1967). Heuristics were used to organise and understand the data instead of following predetermined instructions. Thematic groups of related codes were created to aid in the identification of essential concepts (Strauss & Corbin, 1998). The authors used open coding, and any discrepancies were resolved after extensive discussion and mutual agreement. It was then followed by axial coding, which cultivated second-order codes and themes by identifying relationships between sub-categories on a conceptual level (Strauss & Corbin, 1998). Participants in the study were also given the opportunity to provide input on the authors' interpretations.

The outcome is a script that divides the story into two critical themes as elucidated by the authors. According to Smith & Firth (2011), if the sample size is more than eight, reference extracts from three to four respondents will be enough for each identified topic. Because of the word length constraints, each respondent's perspective could not be detailed. On the other hand, the total responses have been condensed and organised into topics. QDA Miner version 4, a sophisticated qualitative data analysis software for coding textual data, extracting and revising data, and annotating the coded data, was used to conduct the research (La Pan, 2013).

3.2 *Sample characteristics*

An analysis of the sampled respondents shows that the mean age of the respondents is 42 years (41–50 years old), and the mean age of the business is nine years. 81.25% of the respondents are married and 62.5% have acquired postgraduate degrees, thus depicting a higher education level. The level of education is a significant variable in understanding the motivations and the difficulties of women entrepreneurs (Huarng *et al.*, 2012). From among the business type, 56.25% of the respondents are from the service sector, running businesses like a salon, naturopathy centre, beauty training centre, event management, tailoring shop, EdTech company and pre-school chain; 18.75% are in the manufacturing sector (handicraft products, farming, dairy farming and artificial jewellery); and 25% are in the retail/wholesale business sector (boutique, stationery shop and clothing). Table 1 gives a snapshot of the respondents' demographic profile. The name has been specified either for the respondent or the name of her enterprise.

4. Results

This section reports findings from the analysis of the 14 interviews using IPA. The results have been grouped under two "themes". One of the themes talks about the impact of COVID-19 on women's business, and

Table 1. Overview of respondents.

S. No.	Name of the Respondent	Business Product/Service	Age	Education	Business Experience	Members (Living with Women)
1.	Amita Bhatia	Stationary	49	Postgraduate	17 years	One child (29 years old)
2.	Chanchal	Kirana shop	52	Uneducated	25 years	Husband, two children (18 and 13 years old)
3.	Preethi Rawat	Naturopath, acupressure and other medical services	45	Postgraduate	14 years	Husband, two children (14 and 2 years old)
4.	Sumita Narang	Boutique	46	Postgraduate	6 years	Husband, two children (18 and 7 years old)
5	Asha	Tea stall and snacks	52	Uneducated	15 years	Daughter (30 years old), no servant
6	Farha	Boutique	28	Graduation	7 years	Parents, grandmother, grandfather and other family members
7.	Aaleen	Makeup	47	Graduation	6 years	Husband, two children (20 and 15 years old) and mother-in-law
8.	Bobby Chopra	Parlour	33	Until secondary school (till 12th class)	16 years	Husband, mother-in-law, father-in-law and other family members
9.	Rupreet Kaur	NGO and dresses for females	35	Postgraduate	7 Years	Husband and one child (2.5 years old)
10.	Prachi	Lead-free jewellery	36	Postgraduate	6 years	Husband and one child (10 years old)
11	Madhu Sharma	Dairy farming, milk, butter, cheese, pulses and other	55	Postgraduate	6 years	Husband, two children (26 and 28 years old) and mother-in-law
12.	Preeti Kalp	Health advisor, makeup tutor and NGO	28	Postgraduate	7 years	Husband and one child (2.5 years old)
13.	Savita	Hosiery shop	34	Graduate	6 years	Husband, mother-in-law, father-in-law and other family members. Two children (12 and 5 years old)

other speaks about the factors that motivated the women entrepreneurs to continue their business. The respondents revealed that their businesses suffered huge setbacks during the current pandemic, had lower profits and had high operating costs; therefore, it was challenging to run their business. However, various factors such as family support for their financial and household needs, self-assessment of their skills and the favourable nature of the business they operate in motivated them to continue their business. On the other hand, recognising an opportunity from the COVID-19 pandemic encouraged them to start a new venture. The findings reveal the traits and capabilities of the women entrepreneurs as leaders where they effectively safeguarded their enterprises and managed to survive through the pandemic.

4.1 *Theme 1: Impact of COVID-19*

The various impacts of COVID-19 on women's self-owned firms were reduced business and enhanced losses.

4.1.1 *Reduced business/sales*

The outbreak of COVID-19 in India imposed an enforceable lockdown throughout the country. Many women entrepreneurs stated that their business sales were reduced due to the unprecedented pandemic situation and lockdown. Some of the women entrepreneurs even closed their businesses temporarily. They held a view that due to the closure of schools, offices, markets, transportation and social distancing, their business suffered a lot:

> *As the schools and offices are not open, it is resulting in our business suffering a lot. COVID-19 resulted in a lockdown and shifted education to the online mode. Thus, fewer people buy stationary from us, reducing sales. (Participant 1: Amita Bhatia)*

> *COVID-19 has resulted in lots of problems. After lockdown, offices and markets are closed, the work in our tea hop has reduced. Currently, it is only sustenance for us, and we cannot even provide for the kids' education. I had to pull them out of school, and I am earning just enough to provide for the family to eat two meals a day. Earlier, there was good*

work in this area, and the footfall in our tea shop was never-ending. (Participant 5: Asha)

I am into "Event Management", and now, due to COVID-19, there is no business for us. The going had been good for us in the past few years and resulted in good profits and savings. But currently, we are surviving on past savings only. Let's see when the situation improves and when we can start back. (Participant 9: Rupreet Kaur)

4.1.2 Enhanced operating cost

The emergence of the pandemic has resulted in inconsiderable disruptions in businesses. The majority of the women participants stated that they suffered losses because of the pandemic. As per the participants, they could not generate revenue and were bearing a financial crunch. They retrenched the employees to reduce their costs, but it was still challenging to manage the business.

Just see the neighbouring big salon; my business was operating well before COVID-19, making good profits and continuously expanding. But after the COVID-19 pandemic, there was no business, rent became a burden and losses mounted. Thus, I had to shift to this smaller outlet. I had to cut down on my number of employees substantially. Online salon services like Urban Clap pose a significant threat as the customer has more trust in these more prominent hygiene and safety brands. They offer attractive packages and discounts that I cannot even dream of providing because of the high operating cost. Earlier, even I used to give discounts as my numbers (customers) increased. Now, I do not have enough money to hire good-quality staff, requiring higher salaries. The situation is now becoming dire for me, and this salon is my only hope to help me survive after my husband's untimely death. (Participant 4: Sumita Narang)

Another participant in the salon business had a similar view that during COVID-19, she could not control her business's operating cost, and there was no revenue generation. She reduced the staff to control the cost, but the impact of COVID-19 has led to uncontrollable circumstances. However, she also confessed that she could not make ends meet currently and was living on the profits that she had earned in the course of operation of the "golden years" of her business.

> *Before COVID-19, I was able to control the cost, but currently, I cannot control it. Previously, we used to have eight workers, but now we only have 4; because of COVID-19, we cut down to that. Before, it was workable (profit generation), but it is out of our hands right now. But I am very confident that we will strike back once the situation improves. (Participant 8: Bobby Chopra)*

Thus, the participants expressed disparaging views about the business losses, and their ability to tolerate the losses depended on their previous financial position and earnings.

4.2 Theme 2: Factors that motivated women entrepreneurs to continue their business

Most of the women said that various factors such as family support, taking adversity as an opportunity, self-recognition of skills and the favourable nature of business motivated them to continue their business

4.2.1 Support from family and society

One of the participants was a physiotherapist who ran her clinic in a hospital run by a trust. The participant's comments indicated that during COVID-19, family support enabled her to continue operating her clinic. At the same time, the increased responsibilities of the participant towards her work impacted her child.

> *I don't think it might be possible to handle a small child without my husband's constant support. He used to help with all the child's responsibilities, from feeding her to making her dress. (Participant 3: Preeti Rawat)*

She also added that her family had suffered massive stress because of COVID-19.

Being a doctor, I had to go out every day in the lockdown to perform the COVID-19 duty. And then there was a constant scare and fear of catching the virus and bringing it home. My daughter is only one and a half years old. But now, I feel proud that I served my duties well during the tough time. But it was a very stressful time for the entire family, and I wouldn't have been able to manage it without the support of my husband. (Participant 3: Preeti Rawat)

Another participant (Babita), who owned a dairy farm, stated that financial support from her family motivated her to continue the business during COVID-19.

When there was a lockdown, my business suffered; we had to send essentials (food items) through "Express Delivery", and thus, costs were mounting up with reduced sales. The financial dip was insurmountable. At that time, my grown-up children supported me and funded my business out of their savings. That kept me going. (Participant 11: Madhu Sharma)

Another participant who has been running a ladies boutique stated that due to the lockdown, she had to close her business temporarily. But afterwards, the shop owner's support in running her boutique enabled her to come back into business.

When the lockdown was imposed, I had to shut down the boutique. The shop's landlord, where I run the boutique, waived the rent for three months. That was immense support for me and helped me return to the business as the financial burden was reduced. I had already dipped into my savings to start my business and wouldn't have been able to take the financial crunch if the landlord hadn't supported me. I am back on my own two feet because of his empathetic support. It is a great help. (Participant 6: Farha)

However, two participants reported the lack of support from society. As per a participant's view, the pandemic hit them so hard that there were new challenges every day, and it was challenging for them to conduct their business smoothly. Moreover, non-cooperation from society made it challenging for them to continue their business.

I run a Kirana store in a rented shop. The shop owner has not been cooperating at all. He asked us to leave the house whenever we requested leniency in the rent, but we managed to survive. Still, the condition is not good. Other shopkeepers in the area do not like us because we open our shop for more than the prescribed hours. But we do not want to disappoint our customers, and that is why we remain open for longer hours to serve our customers. (Participant 2: Chanchal)

Thus, the support from family and society motivated the women entrepreneurs to continue their businesses.

4.2.2 *Adversity as an opportunity based on self-assessment of skills*

The pandemic turned out to be an "Opportunity in Adversity" for this participant. Her family owned a place that was leased to run a salon. The salon owner could not bear the losses due to the temporary shutdown because of the imposed lockdown. The participant considered COVID-19 an opportunity and recognised her skills to start a new business. She took over the saloon business from her lessee. Because of COVID-19, her leaseholder sold the business to the participant. Thus, she found herself competent to run the business and took it as an opportunity to start her venture.

We negotiated with the salon owner, and he handed us the entire setup of the salon and the staff. My husband supported my decision to run the salon, and now after being a housewife for twenty years, I have got this opportunity amid COVID-19 to run the business. Although my in-laws were sceptical, my grown-up children also supported me. The business is slow, but we manage with a low-cost model with minimal staff. I also love the experience and wonder why I did not start working earlier. (Participant 7: Aaleen)

As per Aaleen, she also found new opportunities for business in the pandemic situation. COVID- 19 resulted in the closure of a participant's current business, an event management company, so she recognised another chance to survive and start a new venture. She temporarily closed her existing business and started the business of sanitisers, masks and blue-ray guns.

There was no scope for starting our existing business as we have an event management company. So, we started dealing in sanitisers, masks and blue-ray guns required due to the emergence of COVID-19. My partners and I have a business mind and sufficient entrepreneurial experience. It is essential to keep the shop running, and we know that this is a temporary plan. But still, we have invested and are currently managing to earn small profits. (Participant 9: Rupreet Kaur)

She further added that the above business helped them earn a profit and gain satisfaction for fulfilling their social responsibility. They used to distribute the leftover extra pieces for free to the people who could not afford to purchase them.

We were satisfied with the business because the extra pieces left, we distributed them freely in areas where people could not buy them. With that, we achieved dual objectives. We earned the profit and did the social work too. (Participant 9: Rupreet Kaur)

Thus, these women leaders revealed their commitment and motivation towards serving the social cause in the adverse time of the pandemic.

Another participant and her business partner, a woman, had been running a pre-school for the last seven years. However, their business suffered a lot due to the pandemic, and they had to close the pre-school. They decided to diversify and explore a new business and are now running a small retail shop selling hosiery and ready-made clothes. She also stated that they would restart the pre-school if the shop does not work out once the situation improves. The above facts show that self-motivation helped women consider adversity as an opportunity to create and continue their business ventures.

The pre-school was on rent, and we were not open due to regulations imposed due to COVID-19. The rent had become an enormous burden, and the landlord wanted to rent out the place to another person. So, we emptied the site and started this small shop with our savings. We do not hope to make it big in the current situation but hope to survive the business. We are inspired by Prime Minister Modi Ji's "Atma Nirbhar Abhiyan" and will continue to seek self-employment. The plan is also to go back to the pre-school business if this business model does not work out. (Participant 13: Savita)

Another participant owned a jewellery business. She considered COVID-19 an opportunity to learn many things and enhance her skills. During the lockdown, she learned new skills required for her business. Henceforth, she cut down some of the staff and began to do more work by herself. Hence, it helped her control her cost and operate the business smoothly.

When lockdown started, I had to reduce my staff, mainly engaged in business social media activities. And I became involved in this creative social media process of the organisation. But this was a different ball game. But I took it up wholeheartedly and did a miniature course on digital and social media marketing. I even learned photography to do the jewellery piece photoshoots on our website and social media portals. I am a very intuitive person and had started cutting down on my operating expenses even before the lockdown was announced. So, we are managing well with the smaller team and will go back to our original team size when things start improving. (Participant 10: Prachi)

Thus, these participants could turn adversity into an opportunity based on their self-belief, learned about their capabilities, developed their abilities as innovative leaders and managed their businesses to survive and thrive in the adverse market. Their self-efficacy prompted them to learn new skills, upgrade themselves and sometimes diversify their business. In all the cases, these women decided to help themselves and became their own saviours instead of looking for support outside of their family or society.

4.3 *Nature of business and risk of COVID-19 infection*

The participants whose products were of the nature of "essential items" reported that their sales did not suffer. Thus, COVID-19 did not affect their business sales, and they continued their business. Therefore, one can discern that woman who operated their ventures in essential products could continue their business.

When the pandemic started, migrant labourers were having problems, and many other industries were suffering, but this dairy sector wasn't suffering. At least we were inside a safe place on the farm, and things kept moving, and in essentials, our supply was there, machinery was working, I had in-house workers, and we were safe. (Participant 11: Madhu Sharma)

A participant had started an NGO (Non-Government Organisation) providing makeup classes to disabled students. However, the occurrence of the pandemic affected her venture. She had to temporarily discontinue the venture, given the high risk of infection to children who attended the classes. Her comments explicated that taking COVID-19 as a threat to getting infected made the women entrepreneurs discontinue their venture.

I started an NGO because I know that everyone cannot afford these makeup classes, and many disabled students aspire to learn, and there are not many provisions available to teach them about self-grooming. The makeup products are costly, services are expensive and most people cannot afford them. Thus came the idea to start an NGO, but things became slow with the onset of the pandemic. Eventually, we had to close down the centre as there was a high risk of COVID-19 infection in our business. However, that has not deterred me, and I plan to start back as soon as the situation improves. (Participant 12: Preeti Kalp)

Thus, the continuation/discontinuation of the business also depends upon the nature of the business, with women running businesses of essentials reporting continuation of business activity during the pandemic. Additionally, women entrepreneurs quickly shifted their business models to those with greater relevance to the COVID-19 situation projecting their effective leadership traits.

5. Discussion

The role of Indian women as entrepreneurs is a vital active factor in society and the economy in this era of globalisation. Women entrepreneurs confront societal pressures and, despite these conflicts, work hard to thrive and run their businesses, particularly in the present epidemic crisis. The findings of this study enhance and deepen our understanding of the key factors that affected the continuation/discontinuation of women-run enterprises in these tough times. A good understanding of these factors will enable policymakers to direct their efforts towards improving the overall business performance of women entrepreneurs.

The minimal literature on the impact of the coronavirus on women entrepreneurs to date emphasises financial losses of ventures (Chmura, 2020) or mainly revolves around problems caused by well-known issues, such as the sector or structure of women's firms (Chmura, 2020) or a lack of financial and human capital (Chmura, 2020; Orser, 2020). Furthermore, while the limited literature on women's entrepreneurship outside of Western developed countries (Danish & Smith, 2012; Jaim, 2020a; Lerner & Almor, 2002) focuses on gendered experiences during the normal period, this article has the potential to add to the general knowledge about women business owners in a developing country experiencing a pandemic. The research could help researchers better understand the elements that influence whether or not women stay in the workforce.

Furthermore, while the menfolk of the family are given due consideration in the literature (Amine & Staub, 2009; Roomi *et al.*, 2018) for their positive or negative influences on the entrepreneurial activities of women in developing countries, this study broadens the perspective on the roles of family members during the COVID-19 pandemic. While the assisting roles of husbands have been recognised in the literature (Barragan *et al.*, 2018, Jaim, 2020a), this paper adds to the information by demonstrating how a husband's assistance might help a woman continue her business throughout the pandemic's critical stage. As a result, this essay helps to better understand the responsibilities of male family members and society in women's businesses during times of crises.

The women entrepreneurs in our study are primarily from small businesses in the service sector. This finding aligns with Alexandre & Kharabsheh's (2019) results. The research provides valuable insights into women's experiences during COVID-19 while confronting challenges to their small businesses from the pandemic. Regarding the continuation of the firms during the pandemic period, the study results reveal that most of the respondents bring to light how support from family and society helped them overcome problems related to finance and enhanced homely responsibilities due to COVID-19. Thus, these findings are in line with Welsh *et al.* (2014) and Stevenson & St-Onge (2005) that family support and societal support are two significant antecedent factors leading to the growth of women entrepreneurs.

Jaim (2020a) discerns that family and society play an essential role in developing women entrepreneurs. This study infers family and society's role during COVID-19 for a woman to continue her business. Many of the women said that support from family and community at the time of COVID-19 helped them continue their business smoothly.

Some of the women entrepreneurs gave insights into how they recognised the adversity of COVID-19 as an opportunity and started new ventures, levelling up their skills during the lockdown to smoothen their business operations. They also started innovative ventures based on the self-assessment of their capabilities as entrepreneurial leaders. These findings are in line with the results of Javadian *et al.* (2012) that the possession of personal internal factors such as high levels of self-efficacy and risk-taking positively impacted the success of women entrepreneurs. The result of the study also corroborates with the work of Manolova *et al.* (2007) that any changes in economic situations lead to changes in women's entrepreneurial intentions. Nevertheless, this research significantly contributes to understanding the issues that emerge due to the pandemic. The research deciphers the factors that motivates the women entrepreneurs to continue their business during the pandemic. Without the women entrepreneurs' vision, leadership, tenacity and drive, their businesses would be nowhere, thus signifying the role they played as business leaders in pivoting, downsizing, streamlining and adjusting their business operations well in time and thus minimising the bolts they would have felt had they not taken the initiatives as entrepreneurial leaders.

6. Conclusion and Implications

This study yields valuable insights by establishing that support from the family and society, favourable nature of business, taking adversity as an opportunity and therefore recognising their skills are enabling factors for women to continue their businesses against the adverse situation of the pandemic. The study potentially contributes to understanding critical factors, such as the risk of getting infected with COVID-19 and non-availability of family and social support for enhanced homely responsibilities and financial needs because of the COVID-19 crisis, generated difficulties for women entrepreneurs to continue their business; hence, they have to close down their small businesses because of the COVID-19 crisis in a developing country. The study explores the experience of women entrepreneurs amid unfavourable environments because of the spread of COVID-19 in a developing country. It discloses various problems women faced in continuing their business in India during the pandemic period.

This article reveals that during COVID-19, many sensitive issues led women entrepreneurs to discontinue their businesses or bear additional financial burdens to continue their ventures. And if women get support from the family and society, are made to recognise their potential as business leaders and are trained with new skills, it can help them continue their business during the time of crisis. Because few studies have looked into the impact of COVID-19 on women entrepreneurship in developing countries (Jaim, 2020b; Welter *et al.*, 2020), this research paper will be invaluable in assisting various stakeholders, such as the government, NGOs and others, in developing effective policies to support women entrepreneurs in times of crises and training them to deal with such situations. This study reveals the kind of support and training women entrepreneurs need to recognise their potential for establishing a start-up and surviving the crisis. The study will enable the practitioners to formulate policies to provide training and support to women entrepreneurs. Academicians and researchers can extend the research further to identify the issues women entrepreneurs face in other developing countries and different parts of India and explore the intrinsic factors of developing countries that worsen the situation for women entrepreneurs in a time of crisis.

7. Limitations of the Study

The current study describes the women entrepreneurs' experiences amid COVID-19 in India. These experiences are exclusively based on the interviews of some of the women entrepreneurs, and therefore results from the survey cannot be generalised to the whole group of women entrepreneurs. Academicians and researchers can extend the studies to a more significant number of women entrepreneurs and can empirically validate the results. Further research can also be extended to other parts of India and other developing countries to generalise results. The results may be influenced by the biasness of the authors while conducting manual analysis of the data in order to classify the themes. However, the authors have tried to eliminate unintentional bias while analysing the study's findings.

Acknowledgement

This study and research were funded by the Indian Council of Social Science (ICSSR) through a research grant (No. IMPRESS/P1083/489/18-19/ICSSR).

References

Ahl, H. (2004). *The Scientific Reproduction of Gender Inequality: A Discourse Analysis of Research Texts on Women's Entrepreneurship*. Stockholm, Sweden: Liber.

Ahl, H. (2006). Why research on women entrepreneurs needs new directions. *Entrepreneurship, Theory and Practice, 30*(5), 595–621.

Ahmad, S. Z. (2011). Evidence of the characteristics of women entrepreneurs in the Kingdom of Saudi Arabia: An empirical investigation. *International Journal of Gender and Entrepreneurship, 3*(2), 123–143.

Alexandre, L. & Kharabsheh, R. (2019). The evolution of female entrepreneurship in the Gulf Cooperation Council, the case of Bahrain. *International Journal of Gender and Entrepreneurship, 11*(4), 390–407.

Amine, L. S. & Staub, K. M. (2009). Women entrepreneurs in sub-Saharan Africa: An institutional theory analysis from a social marketing point of view. *Entrepreneurship & Regional Development, 21*(2), 183–211.

Barragan, S., Erogul, M. S., & Essers, C. (2018). 'Strategic (dis) obedience': Female entrepreneurs reflecting on and acting upon patriarchal practices. *Gender, Work & Organisation, 25*(5), 575–592.

Braun, V. & Clarke, V. (2006). Using thematic analysis in psychology. *Qualitative Research in Psychology, 3*(2), 77–101.

Bruner, J. (1991). The narrative construction of reality. *Critical inquiry, 18*(1), 1–21.

Chaudhary, M., Sodani, P. R., & Das, S. (2020). Effect of COVID-19 on Economy in India: Some Reflections for Policy and Programme, *Journal of Health Management, 22*(2), 169–180.

Chawla, M., Sahni, P., & Sadhwani, K. (2020). Can COVID-19 Be the Turning Point for Women Entrepreneurs in India? Retrieved from https://www. bain.com/insights/can-COVID-19-be-the-turning-point-for-women-entrepreneurs-in-india/#.

Chhabra, M. & Karmarkar, Y. (2016). Gender gap in entrepreneurship-a study of small and micro enterprises. *ZENITH International Journal of Multidisciplinary Research, 6*(8), 82–99.

Chhabra, S., Raghunathan, R., & Rao, N. M. (2020). The antecedents of entrepreneurial intention among women entrepreneurs in India. *Asia Pacific Journal of Innovation and Entrepreneurship, 14*(1), 76–92.

Chmura, M. (2020). Pandemic impacts entrepreneuring women at work and home. Babson College. Retrieved from https://entrepreneurship.babson.edu/ pandemic-impacts-entrepreneuring-women-at-work-and-home/

Dana, L.-P. (1990). Saint Martin/Sint Maarten: A case study of the effects of culture on economic development. *Journal of Small Business Management, 28*(4), 91.

Dana, L.-P. (1997). The origins of self-employment in ethno-cultural communities: distinguishing between orthodox entrepreneurship and reactionary enterprise. *Canadian Journal of Administrative Sciences, 14*(1), 52–68.

Dana, L.-P. & Dana, T. E. (2005). Expanding the scope of methodologies used in entrepreneurship research. *International Journal of Entrepreneurship and Small Business, 2*(1), 79–88.

Dana, L.-P. & Dumez, H. (2015). Qualitative research revisited: Epistemology of a comprehensive approach. *International Journal of Entrepreneurship and Small Business, 26*(2), 154–170.

Danish, A. Y. & Smith, H. L. (2012). Female entrepreneurship in Saudi Arabia: Opportunities and challenges. *International Journal of Gender and Entrepreneurship, 4*(3), 216–235.

Elam A. B., Brush C. G., & Greene P. G. (2019). Global Entrepreneurship Monitor 2018/2019: Women's Entrepreneurship Report. Global Entrepreneurship Research Association; Babson College; Smith College; Korean Entrepreneurship Foundation. Retrieved from https://www.babson. edu/media/babson/assets/blank-center/GEM-2018-2019-Women%27s-Report.pdf.

Elliott, J. (2005). *Using narrative in social research: Qualitative and quantitative approaches*. Sage.

ET Rise (2020). COVID-19 impact on women-led micro businesses widens socio-economic gap: Survey, Retrieved from https://economictimes. indiatimes.com/small-biz/entrepreneurship/COVID-19-impact-on-women-led-micro-biz-widens-socio-economic-gap-survey/articleshow/79473035. cms.

Gartner, W. B. & Birley, S. (2002). Introduction to the special issue on qualitative methods in entrepreneurship research. *Journal of business venturing, 17*(5), 387–395.

Glaser B. G. & Strauss A. L. (1967). The discovery of grounded theory: strategies for qualitative research. *New York, Adline de Gruyter, 17*(4), 364.

Government of India (2011). Census of India, Office of the Registrar General and Census Commissioner, Ministry of Home Affairs, retrieved from https://censusindia.gov.in/census_data_2001/india_at_glance/workpart.aspx (accessed April 18, 2020).

Gregurec, I., Tomičić Furjan, M., & Tomičić-Pupek, K. (2021). The impact of COVID-19 on sustainable business models in SMEs. *Sustainability, 13*(3), 1098.

Groenland, E. & Dana, L.-P. (2020). *Qualitative methodologies and data collection methods: Toward increased rigour in management research*. World Scientific.

Hamilton, K. & Catterall, M. (2006). Consuming love in poor families: Children's influence on consumption decisions. *Journal of Marketing Management, 22*(9–10), 1031–1052.

Holmes, M. (2007). *What Is Gender? Sociological Approaches*. London, UK: Sage

Huarng, K. H., Mas-Tur, A., & Yu, T. H. K. (2012). Factors affecting the success of women entrepreneurs. *International Entrepreneurship and Management Journal, 8*(4), 487–497.

Jaim, J. (2020a). Bank loans access for women business-owners in Bangladesh: Obstacles and dependence on husbands. *Journal of Small Business Management, 59*(1), S16–S41.

Jaim, J. (2020b). Exist or exit? Women business-owners in Bangladesh during COVID-19. *Gender, Work and Organization, 28*(1), 209–226.

Jaim, J. & Islam, M. N. (2018). Context specificities in entrepreneurship research. *Journal of Entrepreneurship, Business and Economics, 6*(1), 59–77.

Jang, Y. (2013). Modeling student entrepreneurship: A longitudinal study. *Journal of Entrepreneurship Education, 16*, 93–114.

Javadian, G. & Singh, R. P. (2012). Examining successful Iranian women entrepreneurs: An exploratory study. *Gender in Management, 27*(3), 148–164.

Javadian, G., Dobratz, C., Gupta, A., Gupta, V. K., & Martin, J. A. (2020). Qualitative research in entrepreneurship studies: A state-of-science. *The Journal of Entrepreneurship, 29*(2), 223–258.

Kangal, S. (2019). *Development of Women Entrepreneurs in India.* Retrieved from https://medium.com/@eduarticle/development-of-women-entrepreneurs-in-india-.

Kohler Riessman, C. (2002). Accidental cases: Extending the concept of positioning in narrative studies. *Narrative Inquiry, 12*(1), 37–42.

La Pan, C. (2013). Review of QDA Miner. *Social Science Computer Review, 31*(6), 774–778.

Lenka, U. & Agarwal, S. (2017). Role of women entrepreneurs and NGOs in promoting entrepreneurship: Case studies from Uttarakhand, India. *Journal of Asia Business Studies, 11*(4), 451–465.

Lerner, M. & Almor, T. (2002). Relationships among strategic capabilities and the performance of women-owned small ventures. *Journal of Small Business Management, 40*(2), 109–125.

Manolova, T. S., Brush, C. G., Edelman, L. F., & Elam, A. (2020). Pivoting to stay the course: How women entrepreneurs take advantage of opportunities created by the COVID-19 pandemic. *International Small Business Journal, 38*(6), 481–491.

Manolova, T. S., Carter, N. M., Manev, I. M., & Gyoshev, B. S. (2007). The differential effect of men and women entrepreneurs' human capital and networking on growth expectancies in Bulgaria. *Entrepreneurship Theory and Practice, 31*(3), 407–426.

Mastercard Index of Women Entrepreneurs (MIWE) (2018). Mastercard Index of Women Entrepreneurs (MIWE) Report. Retrieved from https://newsroom.mastercard.com/eu/files/2018/03/MIWE-2018-Report.compressed.pdf.

Mathew, N., Deborah, I., Karonga, T., & Rumbidzai, C. (2020). The impact of COVID-19 lockdown in a developing country: Narratives of self-employed women in Ndola, Zambia. *Health Care for Women International, 41*(11–12), 1370–1383.

Mathew, R. V. & Panchanatham, N. (2011). An exploratory study on the work-life balance of women entrepreneurs in South India. *Asian Academy of Management Journal, 16*(2), 77–105.

Mehtap, S., Pellegrini, M. M., Caputo, A., & Welsh, D. H. (2017). Entrepreneurial intentions of young women in the Arab world: Socio-cultural and educational barriers. *International Journal of Entrepreneurial Behavior & Research, 23*(6), 880–902.

Neuman, M. (2006). Infiltrating infrastructures: On the nature of networked infrastructure. *Journal of Urban Technology, 13*(1), 3–31.

Noguera, M., Alvarez, C., & Urbano, D. (2013). Sociocultural factors and female entrepreneurship. *International Entrepreneurship and Management Journal*, *9*(2), 183–197.

Orser, B. (2020). Women enterprise policy and COVID-19: Towards a gender-sensitive response. Retrieved from https://sites.telfer.uottawa.ca/were/files/2020/06/OECD-Webinar-Women-Entrepreneurship-Policy-and-COVID-19_Summary-Report.pdf.

Peto, J., Alwan, N. A., Godfrey, K. M., Burgess, R. A., Hunter, D. J., Riboli, E., Romer, P., Buchan, I., Colbourn, T., Costelloe, C., & Smith, G. D. (2020). Universal weekly testing as the UK COVID-19 lockdown exit strategy. *The Lancet*, *395*(10234), 1420–1421.

Popović-Pantić, S., Vasilić, N., & Semenčenko, D. (2020). Women entrepreneurship in the time of COVID-19 pandemic. *Journal of Women's Entrepreneurship and Education*, *3–4*, 23–40.

Priola, V. & Pecis, L. (2020). Missing voices: The absence of women from Italy's COVID-19 pandemic response. *Gender in Management*, *35*(7/8), 619–627.

Roomi, M. A. (2009). Impact of social capital development and use in the growth process of women-owned firms. *Journal of Enterprising Culture*, *17*(04), 473–495.

Sahoo, P. & Kumar, A. (2020). COVID-19 and Indian economy: Impact on growth, manufacturing, trade and MSME sector. *Global Business Review*, *21*(5), 1159–1183.

Salla, S. (2020). How will COVID-19 affect women entrepreneurs? Retrieved from https://idronline.org/how-will-COVID-19-affect-women-entrepreneurs/.

Smith, J. & Firth, J. (2011). Qualitative data analysis: The framework approach. *Nurse Researcher*, *18*(2), 52–62.

Stevenson, L. & St-Onge, A. (2005). Support for growth-oriented, women entrepreneurs in Kenya. International labour organisation. Retrieved from https://www.empowerwomen.org/en/resources/documents/2014/4/support-for-growth-oriented-women-entrepreneurs-in-kenya?lang=en.

Strauss, A. L. & Corbin, J. M. (1998). *Basics of Qualitative Research: Techniques and Procedures for Developing Grounded Theory* (2nd ed). Sage Publications.

WE Forum (2020). *Our recovery from the coronavirus crisis must have gender empowerment at its heart*. Retrieved from https://www.weforum.org/agenda/2020/05/industries-gender-women-coronavirus-COVID19-economic.

Welsh, D. H., Kim, G., Memili, E., & Kaciak, E. (2014). The influence of family moral support and personal problems on firm performance: The case of

Korean female entrepreneurs. *Journal of Developmental Entrepreneurship*, *19*(03), 1450018.

Welter, F., Wolter, H. J., & Holz, M. (2020). *Exit from the Shutdown–How the "Mittelstand" Businesses can Optimally Survive the Coronavirus Pandemic Crisis*. Bonn: IfM-Background Paper.

Women Budget Group (2020). Crises collide: Women and COVID-19. Retrieved from https://wbg.org.uk/wp-content/uploads/2020/04/FINAL.pdf.

Chapter 8

Nurturing Dynamic Competencies: An Innovative Approach for SMEs' Sustainable Growth

Swati Sharma[*,‡] and Jugal Kishor[†,§]

*Assistant Professor, School of Business & Commerce,
Manipal University Jaipur, Rajasthan, India
†Assistant Professor, Central University of Rajasthan, Ajmer, India
‡swati.coer18@gmail.com
§jugal77@gmail.com

Abstract

In this chapter, the authors have envisaged the various dynamic competencies that are instrumental and probable rationales for SMEs' sustainable growth. Innovative entrepreneurship is portrayed as an integration of opportunity optimisation and advantage optimisation. This in turn offers unique start-up concepts. The authors have built upon the resource perspective of the enterprise. This chapter specifically conceptualised the elaboration of the dynamic competencies instrumental in the innovation and growth perspectives of the enterprise. On the basis of an extensive literature review in a relevant field, four dynamic competencies, viz., innovative resource recognition, resource acquisition, networking capabilities and path aligning, have been dissected as part of an innovative approach that is critical for SMEs' sustainable growth. From an SME standpoint, these dynamic competencies are observed to be constructive innovative strategies. A thematic analysis approach was employed to provide insights into the probable dynamic competencies of the SMEs.

Keywords: SMEs, resource, recognition, learning, competencies, networking, innovation, sustainable growth

1. Introduction

In recent times, the market has become more intensive and turbulent; therefore, established enterprises must have a desire to do something better or more efficient than has been done ever before. Enterprises are required to develop their entrepreneurial competencies and turn towards development and innovation-oriented concepts. In this chapter, the authors have stressed on establishing and organising optimised conduct. From an enterprise standpoint, this chapter outlines the dynamic capabilities of enterprises to develop new resources and transform their existing resources into valuable and innovative inputs (Venkataraman *et al.*, 1992; Burgelman, 1984; Dess *et al.*, 1999). It has been observed that enterprises confront a fundamental challenge to explore new business opportunities business opportunities and compromise their existing business prospects (Hitt *et al.*, 2003; Hitt & Ireland, 2000). In modest terms, the entrepreneurial organisational mechanism may confront entrepreneurial short-term objectives. On account of strategic implementation, SME confront obstacles that arises due to the dearth of adequate resources (Stinchcombe, 1965). Developing resources concerning innovation and growth perspective strategies may be a call for unique capabilities within a firm.

In this chapter, the authors propound the dynamic competencies for SMEs that may contribute to the sustainable establishment of new entrepreneurial platforms. Dynamic competencies are important for building an enterprise by assimilating and revitalising both existing and potential resources (Teece *et al.*, 1997; Eisenhardt & Martin, 2000; Zahra *et al.*, 2006; Zahra & George, 2002). It is evident from the literature that dynamic competencies offer a special edge to firms for their entrepreneurial growth. Nevertheless, there is potential scope for exploring dynamic competencies for the development of innovative strategies within small- and medium-scale firms.

On the contrary, SMEs may require different competitive strategies than big firms (Zahra *et al.*, 2006). In recent times, the modern organisational mechanism must include dynamic processes to protect the sustainable resources and offer a functional setting. The real entrepreneurial system must include transforming existing resources into innovative business opportunities (McGrath & MacMillan, 2000; Hitt & Ireland, 2000).

Zahra *et al.* (2006) contended that there is a huge scope for exploring organisational competencies. The foregoing discussion suggests that, today, SMEs need dynamic competencies, emphasising innovation at all management levels. The firm's resource perspective emphasises the contribution of dynamic competencies in developing and reconfiguring new resources (Peteraf, 1993; Barney, 1991; Amit & Shoemaker, 1993). The literature available on resource portfolio addressed that it is not only the resource availability that becomes the dynamic competency but also the organising capability of the firm to arrange the resources into a dynamic configuration (Grant, 1991).

Optimised configuration of the available resources results in innovative business strategies (Brush *et al.*, 2001). Current article stressed further about the dynamic competencies that may be built upon better entrepreneurial strategies. From the dynamic competencies perspective, the configuration of resource recognition, acquisition capabilities, network competencies and strategic aligning competencies contributes to the innovative platform of SMEs. Dynamic competencies are instrumental in figuring and reengineering the action approach development for SMEs. The dynamic competency studies emphasised tools, viz., resource acquisition, resource transformation and reconfiguration, to induct innovative entrepreneurial strategies (Teece *et al.*, 1997; Grant, 1996; Eisenhardt & Martin, 2000).

One of the important goals of a developing economy involves the design and building of SMEs, which is a challenging task that includes different stakeholders (Muhammad *et al.*, 2010). SMEs have not only put efforts to enhance innovation but also acted as a fundamental mode for growing managers to contribute to the emerging economy through new invention and learning (Katua, 2014). The resource-based view and dynamic competencies act as an essential element while identifying a suitable strategy for SMEs. Dynamic, as the name depicts, refers to an organisation's ability to frequently observe and update operational competencies to align with the changing competitive scenario and competencies describe the significance of handling and sustaining those operating competencies. Thus, dynamic competencies are defined as the ability of Small and Medium Enterprises (SMEs) to incorporate, grow and update micro and macro competencies to cope with the current scenario. It was developed to eliminate the problems of the resource-based view of an organisation (Teece *et al.*, 1997). The resource-based view is defined as a firm's competency to gain distinct resources and expertise (Wernerfelt, 1984). Further, resources and competencies that are vital and irreplaceable become a probable centre for competitive advantage. According to the resource-based view, there is an extensive range of resources, i.e., human capital and fixed capital (Barney, 1991), and these resources are combined together to develop a competency (Grant, 1991).

Integrating competencies, a fundamental principle of dynamic competencies, enables SMEs to access sustainable growth and build value (Mikalef & Pateli, 2017). Further (Teece, 2012), to face the current dynamic environment, SMEs are required to manage their resources and functions through solidarity of interdependencies. It was also acknowledged again in Teece *et al.* (1997) that dynamic competencies are enforced in different ways of collaborating. Further, dynamic competencies not only assist managers to develop their strategy but also help them to safeguard their competitive gain (Wade & Hulland, 2004). Enough research is conducted on analysing the effect of dynamic competencies on a firm's sustainable growth but very few studies focus on the role of dynamic competencies in building value for SMEs. Value is termed as a parameter to analyse the performance from the viewpoint of different participants of the market (Amit & Zott, 2001). Due to high competition and internalisation, SMEs are bound to create value to increase competitive advantage (Karaev *et al.*, 2007). Therefore, SMEs are expected to recognise dynamic competencies as a fundamental factor in building value in the organisation. Further, it will enable SMEs to avail opportunities and denounce limitations by utilising the firm's competencies (Teece, 2018). Dynamic competencies act as an integral part of SMEs which enable to perform strategic decision-making (Hatum *et al.*, 2010; Pisano, 2017). In addition, it is evident from research that dynamic competency involves two important elements, i.e., learning and information, and therefore it is termed as unprecedented and a significant competency of SMEs (Jantunen *et al.*, 2012). Therefore, by implementing dynamic competencies in an efficient manner, SMEs are able to generate high value (Ringov, 2017). In addition, it is argued that if SMEs provide support in building competitive approaches, dynamic competencies assist them in building significant value (Rashidirad *et al.*, 2015) and undoubtedly it is evident that affirmative acknowledgement of competitive approaches helps in building value (Kim *et al.*, 2004). In fact, SMEs build policies to enhance value for different participants of the organisation. Hence, it is proved that organisational competencies of aligning strategy are vital to structure a firm's competitive advantage.

In a world full of competition, survival has become challenging for all existing organisations and innovation is the only way to survive. The idea of innovation depicts the development of advanced technology and approaches to achieve the desired objective (Tornatzky *et al.*, 1990). With reference to SMEs, fulfilling customer needs and desires more effectively and efficiently by introducing new products and services leads to innovation (O'Regan & Ghobadian, 2006). Innovative strategies refer to approaches to elucidate the limitations and developing new products and services (Damanpour, 1992). The primary element of innovative strategies is to set a goal for achieving sustainable growth. Henceforth, innovation can be described as updating organisational policies that lead to deepen the growth (Curristine, 2006). Further, it was explored that acknowledging innovation in organisation leads to divergent growth in SMEs (Freeman, 2004).

Strategic path-aligning competencies are a result of capability rather than chance, as they enable organisations to generate financial returns (Powell, 1992). It has also been observed that the success of strategic aligning competency depends mainly on a set of organisational competencies (Gupta *et al.*, 1997). On the basis of extensive literature, it can be stated that if strategic alignment is maintained for a stipulated duration, it is regarded as organisational dynamic competencies which enable firms to construct their competitive advantage.

Firm's thought of making and updating alignment behaviour to support strategic path alignment for a specified duration also depicts its policies and procedures which is regarded as dynamic competencies (Luftman, 2000). Similarly, strategic path alignment is an output of organisations' sincere strategic planning structure and procedure (Grover & Segars, 2005). Hence, the initial foundation of this research is to identify how dynamic competencies facilitate the strategic path aligning competencies in SMEs.

2. Literature Review

2.1 Resource recognition

Splitting, combining and adding resources to the SMEs are some of the important functions of entrepreneurship (Eisenhardt & Brown, 1999). Out of all important strategic functions of entrepreneurship, the ability to realign an enterprise is considered to be a significant strategic feature. Any SME consists of a simple organisational structure where day-to-day operational functions are centralised to the manager. Hence, this enables the manager to have an exceptional overview regarding the probable and prevailing resources. Now, it is argued that entrepreneurial firms must map the existent and emergent resource base and competencies for sustainable growth perspectives. Entrepreneurship today requires a value chain and competitive strategy to enhance the enterprise's functioning (Argyres & McGahan, 2002). Dynamic competencies also build up platforms to create a new venture. The enterprises must dissect the potential advantages of resource integration and its productivity within the enterprise. Brainstorm technique may foster the link between existing resource combinations and potential resources (Venkataraman et al., 1992).

An enterprise's continued adaptation lies with the ongoing connection of several ventures with different resources. It has been envisaged that the association between potential resources and ventures contributes to lead to innovation management activities. Furthermore, this strategic configuration process provides new ways to explore and reconfigure resources (Dougherty, 1995). A simple organisational structure helps the entrepreneur in flexible decision-making. For instance, lesser reporting in the decision-making hierarchy results in fast decision-making, and lesser organisational frontiers offer better opportunities to allocate resources to the organisation's operational areas (Miller & Toulouse, 1986; D'Amboise & Muldowney, 1988). It also builds a mutual ground for linking resources with environmental fortification (Borch, 1994). The SMEs may not give direct competition to the big giants. Therefore, SMEs may synch up and draw upon the capabilities of vendors and develop futuristic relationships with stakeholders.

2.2 *Resource acquisition competency*

A major challenge for SMEs is to seek access to existing and potential resources to offer opportunities to gain necessary skills and help determine how resource acquisition capabilities can improve entrepreneurial competencies. Resource acquisition aims to provide SMEs with insight into the design and development of innovative solutions for SME transformation. Resource acquisition capability enables SMEs to build expertise in domains such as resource optimisation and resource allocation. This dynamic competency aims to enable managers in different fields to drive organisational growth and reduce costs using innovative technologies.

Many studies have revealed that using this dynamic competency will transform the theory into real market practice. Dynamic competencies extend the acquisition of new resources through equity capital accumulation. Conversely, while dealing with big giants, there have been situations that revealed high risk associated with investing in unsuitable resources. To cure this challenge, SMEs must develop business relations with their stakeholders through customisation relationship techniques; this type of acquisition is reportedly expected to benefit SMEs in urban as well as rural areas by primarily focusing on underserved segments.

Dynamic competencies aim to strengthen SMEs' social as well as societal roles. The resource-based organisational structure has emerged with human relations and witnessed a slew of measures to improve the organisational mechanism (Hall, 1993). This innovative and dynamic approach has ensured that SMEs offer quality solutions to society. The resource bundle not only focuses on reciprocity but also on exchange relationships (Borch, 1992). Subsequently, it also aims to establish harmony in organisational ties such as norming and storming. Resource acquisition capabilities avoid looming economic crises. In one of the studies, the author described the contribution of intangible resources, viz., network, reputation and culture, to SMEs' growth (Hall, 1993).

Contextual operations in the business environment also play an integral part in SMEs' sustainable growth (Johannisson *et al.*, 1994). Small business development sees a plan laid out for all aspects of networking, functional areas, social and emotional ingredients to build up start-ups (Johannisson *et al.*, 1994; Larsson, 1991). Resource-based entrepreneurs deal with the challenges of evaluating a candidate's potential. The resource-based view of the entrepreneur seeks development in the early stages and provides an effective information processing system. The unrealistic mobility of resources restricts enterprises from maintaining a sustainable competitive advantage. The mobility of resources may be avoided by linking organisational resources with external resources and establishing a higher level of operational platforms (Black & Boal, 1994).

2.3 *Innovative learning competency*

Competitive advantage is largely influenced by competencies which play an integral role in gaining knowledge. Learning is a process of acquiring new skills and opportunities to achieve organisational goals (Lane & Lubatkin, 1998).

Enhancing skills in all areas of an organisation contributes to strategy formulation and the ability to acquire knowledge more frequently than another contender in the market, which is the only competitive advantage of a firm (López *et al.*, 2005). This indirectly affects the growth of the firm through the practice of innovation and is regarded as a significant contribution to firm profitability (Antonello & Godoy, 2011). Learning enables a firm to identify updated operation facilities and opportunities and also support repetitive and investigating work to be performed effectively and efficiently (Teece *et al.*, 1997). It acts as a constant source of providing resources in an organisation, and for an effective plan of action, there is a requirement for primary operational competencies (Zollo & Winter, 2002). A firm updates its expertise and learning through continuous effort which leads to acquiring new techniques and expertise. In the current scenario, it becomes vital to practice updated knowledge and technology (Cohen & Levinthal, 1990; Levinthal & March, 1993), but there is a gap between expectations of SMEs to make themselves more viable and their initiatives towards implementing it, which is affected by different factors, including training and learning competencies (Tilley, 1999). A network generates a platform for SME owners to communicate and exchange their thoughts and solve limitations that arises in day-to-day activities. This builds trust in the environments, which leads to increased welfare and decreased insecurity for SMEs (Tell, 2001). Integrating competencies supports SMEs in harmonising individual learning with the organisation's functional competencies (Pavlou & El Sawy, 2011). In the current scenario, this form of dynamic competency is sensitive for SMEs as they need to integrate their internet system (Kim *et al.*, 2004).

Managers play a crucial role in forecasting and planning. A small-sized firm's prospects and knowledge and skill acquiring procedure are required to be synchronised with the policy of the firm. Fundamental knowledge includes provoking thoughts and beliefs initiated by the professional appointees. It enables one to introduce innovative ideas, critical thinking of current learning aspects, rules and regulations. Further, by contributing to learning networks, SMEs achieve technological competencies which are restricted by a lack of internal resources (Dosi, 1988). The success of learning network competencies relies on the spirit and capacity of the contributors to support each other. Dynamic competencies dominate the frequency of alteration or change in the normal competencies of an organisation (Collis, 1994).

Innovative knowledge procedure requires updates depending on expert routines for delivering, coding and growth of capabilities, together with efficient investigation. Combined learning (Zollo & Winter, 2002) requires individuals to involve themselves in constructive debates, share their thoughts and encounter the ideas of other individuals (Argyris & Schon, 1978; Duncan & Weiss, 1979). Small-sized firms use blended learning that enables them to use different online resources to attain growth. SMEs face challenges in innovation due to a dearth of competencies and resources (Cassells & Lewis, 2011). As is evident, SMEs do not function in barrenness and are enable to conquer their limitations together with different meetings; hence, network competencies and support stakeholders are essential components (Bos-Brouwers, 2010).

Fundamental updates take place due to some external and internal forces, which include support from external agencies and internal long-term objectives and investigations of a firm. This leads to the inclusion of different networks of information exchange and a matrix of different functional teams that enhance the source of learning. The knowledge process involves different schedules such as exchanging expertise and knowledge among groups and exploring communication with external agencies, which enhance the demands.

2.4 *Strategic resource aligning competency*

Alignment has a wider scope which is developed by a notion that firms must allocate their resources in an efficient manner to gain a competitive advantage (Andrews, 1971; Chandler, 1962; Venkatraman & Camillus, 1984). In other words, alignment can be described as a balance of one element with another element with respect to objectives, goals, demands and functions (Nadler & Tushman, 1980). In the last few decades, different types of alignments have been introduced which focused on a firm's policies and strategy, competitive advantage and business possessions or resources. Small-sized firms always involve themselves in existing strategies due to which they often face disagreement and criticism. Usually, small-sized firms are incorporated by an older person of the family who laid down strategies and policies for the firm. This elder person is termed as founder president of a firm. So, it becomes difficult to alter the strategies due to the family traditions and ownership structure. As these firms worked in family relationships, they do not follow any formal structure that includes a board of directors or specific designation that operates in more organised and formal ways. As each SME has a different organisational structure (Ghobadian & Gallear, 1996), there are different factors that work as aligning competencies for SMEs (Ramsay, 2008). Efficient strategy implementation involves aligning competencies too. Small-scale operations of SMEs should not be the reason for ignorance of strategic decision-making as it leads to success in the future (Lim & Teoh, 2021). Time constraint is one of the biggest features of SMEs and it leads to the perception of the manager that SMEs do not require any update in the functioning and if required the manager can manage it without support from macro-environmental factors (Zaridis & Mousiolis, 2014). On the contrary, some entrepreneurs evaluate the performance of SMEs in terms of monetary gain and organisation success (Gyimah, 2014). Hence, entrepreneurs play a major role in building strategies for SMEs (Lefebvre & Lefebvre, 1993).

Dynamic competencies involve a process of policy formulation wherein decision-makers seek various prospects and organisation functions, and on the basis of these functions investments are made. In this process, various alternatives are analysed to prepare and plan a strategy for the firm (Eisenhardt, 1989; Fredrickson, 1984; Judge & Miller, 1991).

In the process of decision-making, the firm's vision is created to seek its overall path in the coming years. The dynamic competency framework advocates that SMEs' ability to conquer alignment is an unending competency that becomes a foundation for competitive advantage (Hambrick & Fredrickson, 2001; Helfat & Peteraf, 2003). Therefore, the strategic decision-making process is used by organisations to create a structure to alter and analyse the strategic functions of the firm. This process enables the organisation to find ways to alter strategic movement and action plans to find solutions. Innovative strategies and activities are introduced to support SMEs in updating their organisation vision and enhancing different promotion techniques to increase sales.

According to the concept of path dependencies, it is believed that future plans will be influenced by the nature of past actions. Various prospects available for strategy formulation are considered as paths for an organisation (Teece *et al.*, 1977) and the organisation not only requires a strategy but also requires an effective strategy; there are various strategic tools available, i.e., industry and technology analysis, completive advantage and value chain analysis, which will make the strategy more effective and sound (Hambrick & Fredrickson, 2001). The biggest obstacle in implementing change in the organisation is the imbalance of strategies and art of organisational change (Woodman, 1993). Strategic decision-making involves a process that focuses on creating symmetry in persistence and change, which leads to creating stability in an organisation (Pettigrew, 1998). Hence, succeeding and maintaining a strategic path aligning competencies is often annoying and challenging (Grant, 2003; Sabherwal *et al.*, 2001), but strategic alignment has always topped the position when it comes to managers (Chan & Reich, 2007).

Research Question — *Do dynamic competencies enhance SMEs' sustainable growth?*

3. Procedure

To explore the objectives of this chapter, a qualitative phenomenon was employed to conduct an in-depth analysis of the dynamic competencies of SMEs. The qualitative approach was employed here because the purpose of this chapter was to "explore instead of forecast" (Leavy, 1994) and to comprehend the variable instead of quantify it (Gordon & Langmaid, 1988). Thus, the qualitative approach is deemed to be a suitable phenomenon to understand dynamic competencies of SMEs (Gilmore *et al.*, 2001).

Managers of SMEs were directly contacted to participate in a one-to-one structured interview. The contacted managers were directly involved in the decision-making of the variables of interest of this chapter. In-depth interviews were conducted which were deemed to be an optimal way to elicit information from SMEs' managers regarding dynamic competencies, viz., resource recognition, resource acquisition capabilities, learning network capabilities and strategic aligning ability. This technique also offers convenience as per the interviewee's consent to customise the content and sequence of information (Carson *et al.*, 2001).

Furthermore, the in-depth questioning procedure enabled the interaction to be more interpersonal and focused on deriving a rationale of their dynamic competency execution and benefits. Every interaction with the respondent was provided appropriate time to discuss the course of action aligning to dynamic competencies. Each interaction was allocated around 20–30 min to complete the interview procedure. For analysis purposes, every respondent consented to the interaction sessions being recorded and transcribed to facilitate in-depth analysis. To obtain the relevant information regarding the dynamic competencies, SMEs which had existed in the market for five years were included for the depth analysis.

4. Findings

The findings of the chapter are linked with the key themes of dynamic competencies executed in SMEs. The findings are based on the critical thematic analysis of the literature and envisaged from the study carried out. SMEs execute many dynamic competencies specifically related to resource recognition, resource acquisition, network capabilities and strategic aligning competencies as discussed in this chapter. The foregoing discussion and findings suggest that SMEs include stumbling blocks to dynamic competencies. For instance, a majority of SMEs reported that incorporating dynamic competencies in operations enabled them to invest an exorbitant amount of resources and time on meta business opportunities.

Of the 30 SMEs, 24 believed that skilled and trained human resources had a constructive influence on designing and executing dynamic competencies. For instance, optimised resource recognition for SMEs is positively associated with SME sustainability. From the resource recognition standpoint, the chapter has addressed the sustainable implementation of the resources (Darnall & Edwards, 2006; Zhu *et al.*, 2008). The literature review and the data recovered from the SMEs conveyed that small-scale enterprises accomplish a competitive edge through optimised resource recognition. SMEs' managers believed that to grasp this competitive advantage, the resource recognition process must be accompanied by valuable and inimitable inputs.

SMEs' managers remarked that internal as well as external environments enabled them to have access to potential resources. This chapter conveyed that resource acquisition has its advantages for the SMEs; hence, it is likely that SMEs operating in smaller business fields acquired more projects with a needed budget and gained access to solve problems. In a nutshell, this dynamic competency enables SMEs to tap into the local market and do something better or more efficient than has been done before. Resource acquisition may be executed by budget, material, time and space. Several managers in SMEs have further acknowledged that the dearth of needed organisational resources brought dependency and vulnerability. Environmental eventualities have developed through a sense of self-efficacy and enterprise mechanism. Resource acquisition has been employed as a key variable in entrepreneurial activities (Huang & Knight, 2017). As of now, it has been argued that resource acquisition has proved to be a crucial ingredient for SMEs to enhance their productivity. Therefore, many social researchers have given their attention to set out the critical contribution of resource acquisition to SMEs.

Network competency is recommended as an important variable to enhance SMEs' innovative strategies. The lack of network ability has been acknowledged in the literature; from a dynamic capability perspective, this chapter tried to explore the existing and futuristic scope of this competency. This chapter has corroborated the contribution of network competency to enable SMEs to discover and explore opportunities through exceptional networking insights. Furthermore, it has envisaged that network competency brings sterilised, formatted and organised platforms that are meaningful, useful and the best possible solutions to a situation. This concept stalls many obstacles, viz., work halts, waste of resources and time infringement at SMEs. It further enhances the probability to lead to the immediate evolvement of existing tasks. Network competency conceptualised the organisational need for both internal and external inputs to eradicate uncertainties. This finding has a resemblance with the study conducted by Potnis (2015). For instance, network competency nurtures an enterprise's transformation and opportunity development. From the SMEs' standpoint, it is a concept that emerged to spur enterprise innovative strategies, which turn the resources into a positive outcome. Moreover, network competency serves as a regularity system that reduces ambiguity, increases efficiency and maintains procedures. Therefore, a lack of adequate networking resources may negatively affect the sustainability and performance of SMEs.

5. Discussion

This chapter dealt with the challenges being confronted by SMEs in the execution and formulation of innovative strategies. The central input of this chapter is to outline the relationship between dynamic competencies and innovative strategies. For instance, on the topic of proactive innovative strategies, internal flexibility, external reconfiguration and integration competencies, all were considered to be important. The integration and reconfiguration competencies for SME productivity led to flexible changes in responsibilities. SMEs being a small scale level firm consisting of few employees, direct towards innovative mechanism. Citing the effective implementation of existing strategies, employees can be inspired and supportive with regard to probable innovative tactics.

It is now recommended that SMEs have to be vigilant about the rationales of current success, and the existing success should not be a restraint for exploring potential entrepreneurial scope. Resource acquisition competency enables SMEs to explore potential resources through matrixes, perceptual mapping and cluster analysis. It has been observed that compatible and innovation-oriented human resources in SMEs may establish a contingency system to optimise resources. In contrast, when SMEs are facing a dearth of resources, it is external networking competency that sets up a way to explore opportunity reconfiguration and innovation discovery. It assists SMEs to establish flexibility to develop futuristic strategies and contain potential resources through networking competency.

This chapter nourishes the literature through variegated insights of resource acquisition advantages for SMEs in the form of employees' connection as a knowledge resource. Nevertheless, these dynamic competencies may not be easy to integrate but surely offer higher productivity into the current SMEs scenario. Subsequently, this chapter postulates a constructive relationship between dynamic competency and innovative strategies; this positive association turns up to make effective and realistic use of available resources. Innovative strategic tactics and reconfiguration of the external resources enable SMEs to establish clear communication with suppliers, partners and customers. Establishing contact through email/ internet, and frequent and regular hunt for collaborators to develop dynamic competency were suggestions of this chapter. Continuous collaboration with the R&D department and implementation of framed strategies lead SMEs to achieve growth patterns. These outcomes suggest that any dynamic competency in isolation is not sufficient to offer desired growth; hence, an integrative dynamic competency approach must be followed by the managers in the SMEs to contain the continuous utilisation of resources.

Due to the dearth of resources and competencies, SMEs encounter difficulties in maintaining sustainable growth. Hence, positive and growth periods quickly convert into negative and declining phases for SMEs. Therefore, SMEs are required to survive in this type of unstable circumstances (Detarsio *et al.*, 2013). Over the years, researchers have focused on developing that competitive advantage that is dependent on competencies that support them to build customer value (Javalgi *et al.*, 2006)

Rising and learning in unstable circumstances in order to gain competitive advantage is a crucial role of SMEs, but practically it is tough for SMEs to find out solutions to such limitations. This is supported by Macpherson & Holt (2007) in their research on skills, ability and growth, which depicted a lack of an efficient process of knowledge acquiring and its connotation with SME expansion. Firms are required to upgrade policies and procedures to enable learning. These policies and procedures involve internal aspects, external aspects, social aspects and all the organisation policies that create a feasible environment for learning (Mbengue & Sané, 2013). These policies are an integral part of firms' learning competency which can be identified as the group of management policies that fastens the way to knowledge and enhances the firm's capacity to build and update its learning (Alegre & Chiva, 2008). Different studies are being explored to review the association between SMEs' expansion and gaining knowledge, and hence the focus of this paper has been on developing the "knowledge to expand" concept which highlighted knowledge as a way of enhancing dynamic competencies (Zollo & Winter, 2002).

Dynamic competencies facilitate SMEs in developing innovative strategies that lead to gaining a competitive advantage. As the alignment of strategy is important for an organisation, it is also necessary to allocate resources efficiently to implement strategies. A dynamic competency framework also helps an organisation to understand and identify suitable competencies to mark its presence in the market. In the current scenario, innovation is believed to be a vital source for financial wellbeing as it builds competitive advantage (Cooper *et al.*, 2001). SMEs do not work as an individual firm or in a limited scope; rather, they operate beyond their limitation to explore resources and information that are limited in their own firm (Teece, 1986). As changes in SMEs' attitude is required to maintain innovative practices, it is essential to explore the different factors supporting and limiting its implementation (Heiskanen *et al.*, 2005). It is evident from the literature that SMEs' learning is associated with innovation (Dodgson, 1993) and has an affirmative impact on innovative practices (Alegre & Chiva, 2013). Therefore, any technological advancement in SMEs encompasses the firm's knowledge (Antonello & Godoy, 2011). Studies have witnessed that innovation has a significant impact on the SMEs' performance, although there are many other factors that also impact the performance, which include the number of years of organisation, cultural background and an array of innovation (Rosenbusch *et al.*, 2011). SMEs can avail the benefits of innovation in analysing the needs and wants of customers, approaches of competitive firms and technological advancement (Calantone *et al.*, 2002). Therefore, innovation acts as a catalyst in increasing market capitalisation and competency (Gunday *et al.*, 2011; Frasquet *et al.*, 2013). Dynamic competency is a part of the state decision-making process of globalisation through which companies can build competitive advantage. A significant relationship between the frequency of globalisation and the growth of foreign firms was found by Pehrsson *et al.* (2015) on the basis of dynamic competencies. With regard to globalisation, it is essential that firms acquire knowledge and information of the foreign market before making an entry into it. It becomes more important in a situation where distance is significant in terms of both physical and psychological (Frasquet *et al.*, 2013). Further, dynamic competencies play a significant role in the organisational environment where workforce and cultural diversity are great (Zollo & Winter, 2002).

Regarding dynamic competency theory, it is evident that competencies approaches of SMEs entrepreneurs in fulfilling the market sentiments impacts the strategic alignment. Although there are some similar characteristics, the process of dynamic competencies differs from organisation to organisation. Further, as the firm's size increases, it becomes more difficult for the SME to evolve dynamic competencies. Therefore, SMEs are required to identify the potential resources that enhances their unique characteristics to gain profits and achieve success in the long run (Barney, 1991). Dynamic competencies are useful tools for the organisation even if they are built unknowingly; they impact the organisation in a positive way. The government has also built policies and strategies to support SMEs to make their way and avoid barriers in availing government sector contracts (Patil, 2017). Research should focus on analysing the impact of change in structure and type of dynamic competencies. On the basis of the current research, it is suggested that if strategic path aligning competencies are maintained in the long run, it leads to organisation dynamic competencies on which competitive benefits are based.

Moreover, the available resources must be integrated and aligned with the strategy and efficiently implemented through other resources.

Regular scanning for collaborators and strategic mapping of resources are considered to be crucial activities for the proactive innovation reconfiguration. The continuous growth perspective of SMEs requires skilled employees and a wider competency setup. However, it is attention-grabbing that strategic aligning competency is positively associated with development-oriented innovative strategies. Growth-oriented firms gain the best possible benefits from dynamic competency like strategic aligning capabilities. This may be understood as a way of expressing the strategic aligning capabilities of the enterprises, where business activities and opportunities are framed and evaluated through a panel of the advisory board. This chapter suggests that SMEs should consider the most probable dynamic competency to collaborate and furnish essential resources to grow enterprises.

6. Limitations and Suggestions for Future Research

This chapter limits its recommendations for general inferences in many ways. This study has incorporated SMEs from Bangalore and it must be validated in other regions. Citing this concern, further studies must be carefully designed to incorporate these inferences for small-scale enterprises. This study is based on SMEs with less than 45 employees, which restricts its inferences for medium-scale enterprises.

This chapter also recommends some of the directions for further studies. The authors can dissect strategic level and take out the best of dynamic competency. There can be another way to interconnect these distinct dynamic competencies. Another way to explore dynamic competencies could be establishing a cause-and-effect relationship with the SMEs' productivity. Subsequently, the authors expect that dynamic competencies may incur additional costs in the short run and may give returns in the long run. Therefore, further research is required to conduct longitudinal research exploring the dynamic competency development process, cost incurred and returns in the long run. This chapter has emphasised entrepreneurial competencies and day-to-day activities at the organisational level. Further study is required to connect these dynamic competencies to the individual level, paying special attention to the role of the entrepreneur.

References

Alegre, J., Lapiedra, R., & Chiva, R. (2006). A measurement scale for product innovation performance. *European Journal of Innovation Management, 9*(4), 333–346.

Amit, R. & Shoemaker, P. J. (1993). Strategic assets and organizational rent. *Strategic Management Journal, 14*(1), 3–46.

Amit, R. & Zott, C. (2001). Value creation in e-business. *Strategic Management Journal, 22*(6), 493–520.

Andrews, K. R. (1971). *The Concept of Corporate Strategy*. Homewood, IL: Irwin.

Argyres, N. & McGahan, A. M. (2002). An interview with Michael Porter. *Academy of Management Executive, 16*(2), 43–52.

Argyris, C. & Schon, D. (1978). *Organizational Learning*. Reading, MA: Addison-Wesley.

Barney, J. B. (1991). Firm resources and sustained competitive advantage. *Journal of Management, 17*(1), 99–120.

Black, J. A. & Boal, K. B. (1994). Strategic resources: Traits, configuration and paths to sustainable competitive advantage. *Strategic Management Journal, 15*(1), 131–148.

Borch, O. J. (1992). Small firms and the governance of environmental exchange. *Scandinavian Journal of Management, 8*, 321–334.

Borch, O. J. (1994). The process of relational contracting. Developing trust-based strategic alliances among small business enterprises. In J. D. Shrivastava & A. Huff (Eds.), *Advances in Strategic Management*. Greenwich, CT: JAI Press Inc.

Bos-Brouwers, H. E. J. (2010). Corporate sustainability and innovation in SMEs: Evidence of themes and activities in practice. *Business Strategy and the Environment, 19*, 417–435.

Brush, C. G., Greene, P. G., & Hart, M. M. (2001). From initial idea to unique advantage: The entrepreneurial challenge of constructing a resource base. *Academy of Management Executive, 15*(1), 64–78.

Burgelman, R. A. (1984). Designs for corporate entrepreneurship in established firms. *California Management Review, 26*(1), 23–34.

Calantone, R., Cavusgil, S., & Zhao, Y. (2002). Learning orientation, firm innovation capability, and firm performance. *Industrial Marketing Management, 31*, 515–524.

Carson, D., Gilmore, A., Perry, C., & Gronhaug, K. (2001). *Qualitative Marketing Research*. London: Sage.

Cassells, S. & Lewis, K. (2011). SMEs and environmental responsibility: Do actions reflect attitudes? *Corporate Social Responsibility and Environmental Management, 18*(3), 186–199.

Chan, Y. E. & Reich, B. H. (2007). IT alignment: What have we learned? *Journal of Information Technology, 22*(4), 297–315.

Cohen, W. M. & Levinthal, D. A. (1990). Absorptive capacity: A new perspective on learning and innovation. *Administrative Science Quarterly, 35*, 128–152.

Collis, D. J. (1994). Research note: How valuable are organizational capabilities? *Strategic Management Journal, 15* (Winter Special Issue), 143–152.

Cooper, R. G. (2001). *Winning at New Products: Accelerating the Process from Idea to Launch* (4th ed.). Cambridge, MA: Perseus.

Curristine, T. (2006). Performance information in the budget process: Results of the OECD 2005 questionnaire. *OECD Journal on Budgeting, 5*(2), 87–131.

D'Amboise, G. & Muldowney, M. (1988). Management theory of small business: Attempts and requirements. *Academy of Management Journal, 13*(2), 226–240.

Damanpour, F. (1996). Organizational complexity and innovation: Developing and testing multiple contingency models. *Management Science, 42*(5), 693–716.

Darnall, N. & Edwards, D. (2006). Predicting the cost of environmental management system adoption: The role of capabilities, resources and ownership structure. *Strategy Management Journal, 27*(1), 301–320.

Dess, G. G., Lumpkin, G. T., & McGee, J. E. (1999). Linking corporate entrepreneurship to strategy, structure, and process: Suggested research directions. *Entrepreneurship Theory and Practice, 23*(3), 85–102.

Detarsio, R., North, K., & Ormaetxea, M. (2016). Surviving and competing in times of crisis: Cases of strategies by Argentine SMEs. *Competitive Strategies for Small and Medium Enterprises*, 139–151.

Dodgson, M. (1993). Organizational learning: A review of some literatures. *Organization Studies, 14*(3), 375–394.

Dosi, G. (1988). Sources, procedures, and microeconomic effects of innovation. *Journal of Economic Literature, 26*, 1120–1171.

Dougherty, D. (1995). Managing your core incompetencies for corporate venturing. *Entrepreneurship Theory and Practice, 19*(3), 113–135.

Eisenhardt, K. M. & Brown, S. L. (1999). Patching: Restitching business portfolios in dynamic markets. *Harvard Business Review, 78*(1), 91–101.

Eisenhardt, K. M. & Martin, J. K. (2000). Dynamic capabilities: What are they? *Strategic Management Journal, 21*, 1105–1121.

Frasquet, M., Dawson, J., & Mollá, A. (2013). Post-entry inter-nationalisation activity of retailers. An assessment of dynamics capabilities. *Management Decision, 51*(7), 1510–1527.

Freeman, C. (2004). Technological infrastructure and international competitiveness. *Industrial and Corporate Change, 13*(3), 541–569.

Ghobadian, A. & Gallear, D. N. (1996). Total quality management in SMEs. *Pergamon Omega. International Journal of Management and Science, 24*(1), 83–106.

Gilmore, A., Carson, D., & Grant, K. (2001). SME marketing in practice. *Marketing Intelligence & Planning, 19*(1), 6–11.

Gordon, W. & Langmaid, R. (1988). *Qualitative Market Research: A Practitioner's and Buyer's Guide*. Aldershot: Gower.

Grant, G. G. (2003). Strategic alignment and enterprise systems implementation: The case of Metalco. *Journal of Information Technology, 18*(3), 159–175.

Grant, R. M. (1991). The resource-based theory of competitive advantage: Implications for strategy formulation. *California Management Review, 33*(3), 114–135.

Grant, R. M. (1996). Toward a knowledge-based theory of the firm. *Strategic Management Journal, 17* (Special Issue), 109–122.

Grover, V. & Segars, A. H. (2005). An empirical evaluation of stages of strategic information systems planning: Patterns of process design and effectiveness. *Information & Management, 42*(5), 761–779.

Gunday, G., Ulusoy, G., Kilic, K., & Alpkan, L. (2011). Effects of innovation types on firm performance. *International Journal of Production Economics, 133*(2), 662–676.

Gupta, Y. P., Karimi, J., & Somers, T. M. (1997). Alignment of a firm's competitive strategy and information technology management sophistication: The missing link. *IEEE Transactions on Engineering Management, 44*(4), 399–413.

Gyimah, K. N., Owiredu, A., & Antwi, F. (2020). Effects of entrepreneurial trait on the success. *International Journal of Scientific & Technology Research, 9*(3), 7177–7186.

Hall, R. (1993). A framework linking intangible resources and capabilities to sustainable competitive advantage. *Strategic Management Journal, 14*, 607–618.

Hambrick, D. C. & Fredrickson, J. W. (2001). Are you sure you have a strategy? *Academy of Management Executive, 15*(4), 48–59.

Hatum, A., Pettigrew, A., & Michelini, J. (2010). Building organizational capabilities to adapt under turmoil. *Journal of Change Management, 10*(3), 257–274.

Heiskanen, E., Kasanen, P., & Timonen, P. (2005). Consumer participation in sustainable technology development. *International Journal of Consumer Studies, 29*(2), 98–107.

Hitt, M. A. & Ireland, R. D. (2000). The intersection of entrepreneurship and strategic management research. In D. L. Sexton & H. Landström (Eds.), *Handbook of Entrepreneurship* (Vols. 46–63). Oxford, UK: Blackwell Publishers.

Hitt, M. A., Ireland, R. D., & Sirmon, D. G. (2003). A model of strategic entrepreneurship: The construct and its dimensions. *Journal of Management, 29*(6), 963–989.

Huang, L. & Knight, A. P. (2017). Resources and relationships in entrepreneurship: An exchange theory of the development and effects of the entrepreneur-investor relationship. *Academy of Management Review, 42*(1), 80–102.

Jantunen, A., Ellonen, H. K., & Johansson, A. (2012). Beyond appearances — Do dynamic capabilities of innovative firms actually differ? *European Management Journal, 30*(2), 141–155.

Javalgi, R. G., Martin, L. C., & Young, R. B. (2006). Marketing research, market orientation and customer relationship management, a framework and implications for service providers. *Journal of Service Marketing, 20*(1), 12–24.

Johannisson, B., Alexanderson, O., Nowicki, K., & Senneseth, K. (1994). Beyond anarchy and organization — Entrepreneurs in contextual network. *Entrepreneurship and Regional Development, 6,* 329–356.

Judge, W. Q. & Miller, A. (1991). Antecedents and outcomes of decision speed in different environments. *Academy of Management Journal, 34*(2), 449–464.

Karaev, A., Koh, S. C. L., & Szamosi, L. T. (2007). The cluster approach and SME competitiveness: A review. *Journal of Manufacturing Technology Management, 18*(7), 818–835.

Katua, N. T. (2014). The role of SMEs in employment creation and economic growth in selected countries. *International Journal of Education and Research, 2*(12), 461–472.

Kim, E., Nam, D., & Stimpert, J. L. (2004). Testing the applicability of Porter's generic strategies in the digital age: A study of Korean cyber malls. *Journal of Business Strategies, 21*(1), 19–45.

Lane, P. J. & Lubatkin, M. (1998). Relative absorptive capacity and interorganizational learning. *Strategic Management Journal, 19*(5), 461–477.

Larsson, A. (1991). Partner networks: Leveraging external ties to improve entrepreneurial performance. *Journal of Business Venturing, 6*, 173–188.

Leavy, B. (1994). The craft of case-based qualitative research. *Irish Business and Administrative Research, 15*(1), 105–118.

Lefebvre, L. A. & Lefebvre, E. (1993). Competitive positioning and innovative efforts in SMEs. *Small Business Economics, 5*, 297–305.

Lim, C. H. & Teoh, K. B. (2021). Factors influencing the SME business success in Malaysia. *Annals of Human Resource Management Research, 1*(1), 41–54.

López, S. P., Peón, J. M. M., & Ordás, C. J. V. (2005). Organizational learning as a determining factor in business performance. *The Learning Organization, 12*(3), 227–245.

Luftman, J. (2000). Assessing business-IT alignment maturity. *Communications of the AIS, 4*(14), 1–50.

Macpherson, A. & Holt, R. (2007). Knowledge, learning and small firm growth: A systematic review of the evidence. *Research Policy, 36*(2), 172–192.

McGrath, R. G. & MacMillan, I. C. (2000). *The Entrepreneurial Mindset: Strategies for Continuously Creating Opportunity in an Age of Uncertainty.* Boston, MA: Harvard Business School Press.

Mikalef, P. & Pateli, A. (2017). Information technology-enabled dynamic capabilities and their indirect effect on competitive performance: Findings from PLS-SEM and fsQCA. *Journal of Business Research, 70*, 1–16.

Miller, D. & Toulouse, J. M. (1986). Strategy, structure, CEO personality and performance in small firms. *American Journal of Small Business, 10*(3), 47–62.

Muhammad, M. Z., Char, A. K., Yasoa, M. B., & Hassan, Z. (2010). Small and medium enterprises (SMEs) competing in the global business environment: A case of Malaysia. *International Business Research, 3*(1), 66–75.

Pavlou, P. A. & El Sawy, O. A. (2011). Understanding the elusive black box of dynamic capabilities. *Decision Sciences, 42*(1), 239–273.

Pehrsson, T., Ghannad, N., Pehrsson, A., Abt, T., Chen, S., Erath, F., & Hammarstig, T. (2015). Dynamic capabilities and performance in foreign markets: Developments within inter-national new ventures. *Journal of International Entrepreneurship, 13*(1), 28–48.

Peteraf, M. A. (1993). The cornerstones of competitive advantage: A resource-based view. *Strategic Management Journal, 14*, 179–191.

Potnis, D. D. (2015). Beyond access to information: Understanding the use of information by poor female mobile users in rural India. *The Information Society, 31*(1), 83–93.

Powell, T. C. (1992). Organizational alignment as competitive advantage. *Strategic Management Journal, 13*(2), 119–134.

Ramsay, J. (2008). Purchasing theory and practice: An agenda for change. *European Business Review, 20*(6), 567–569.

Rashidirad, M. (2014). The impact of strategic alignment between competitive strategy and dynamic capability on e-business value: An empirical analysis of the UK telecommunications firms, Kent Business School. Canterbury: University of Kent. Unpublished PhD thesis.

Ringov, D. (2017). Dynamic capabilities and firm performance. *Long Range Planning, 50*(5), 653–664.

Rosenbusch, N., Brinckmann, J., & Bausch, A. (2011). Is innovation always beneficial? A meta-analysis of the relationship between innovation and performance in SMEs. *Journal of Business Venturing, 26*(4), 441–457.

Sabherwal, R., Hirschheim, R., & Goles, T. (2001). The dynamics of alignment: Insights from a punctual equilibrium model. *Organization Science: A Journal of the Institute of Management Sciences, 12*(2), 179–197.

Stinchcombe, A. L. (1965). Social structures and organizations. In J. G. March (Ed.), *Handbook of Organizations* (pp. 142–193). Chicago: Rand McNally.

Teece (1986). Profiting from technological innovation: Implications for integration, collaboration, licensing and public policy. *Research Policy, 15*(6), 285–305.

Teece, D. J. (2012). Dynamic capabilities: Routines versus entrepreneurial Action. *Journal of Management Studies, 49*(8), 1395–1401.

Teece, D. J. (2018). Business models and dynamic capabilities. *Long Range Planning, 51*(1), 40–49.

Teece, D. J., Pisano, G., & Shuen, A. (1997). Dynamic capabilities and strategic management. *Strategic Management Journal, 18*(7), 509–533.

Tilley, F. (1999). The gap between the environmental attitudes and the environmental behaviour of small firms. *Business Strategy and the Environment, 8*(4), 238–248.

Tornatzky, L. G., Fleischer, M., & Chakrabarti, A. K. (1990). *Processes of Technological Innovation.* New York: Lexington Books.

Venkataraman, S., MacMillan, I. C., & McGrath, R. G. (1992). Progress in research on corporate venturing. In D. L. Sexton and J. D. Kasarda (Eds.), *The State of the Art of Entrepreneurship.* Boston: PWS-Kent.

Wade, M. & Hulland, J. (2004). Review: The resource-based view and information systems research: Review, extension, and suggestions for future research. *MIS Quarterly, 28*(1), 107–142.

Wernerfelt, B. (1984). A resource-based view of the firm. *Strategic Management Journal, 5*(2), 171–180.

Woodman, R. W. (1993). Observations on the field of organizational change and development from the lunatic fringe. *Organization Development Journal, 11*(2), 71–75.

Zahra, S. A. & George, G. (2002). The net-enabled business innovation cycle and the evolution of dynamic capabilities. *Information Systems Research, 13*(2), 147–150.

Zahra, S. A., Sapienza, H. J., & Davidsson, P. (2006). Entrepreneurship and dynamic capabilities: A review, model and research agenda. *Journal of Management Studies, 43*(4), 917–955.

Zaridis, A. D. & Mousiolis, D. T. (2014). Entrepreneurship and SME's organizational structure-elements of a successful business. *Procedia-Social and Behavioral Sciences, 148*, 463–467.

Zhu, Q., Sarkis, J., Lai, K. H., & Geng, Y. (2008). The role of organizational size in the adoption of green supply chain management practices in China. *Corporate Social Responsibility and Environmental Management, 15*(1), 322–337.

Zollo, M. & Winter, S. G. (2002). Deliberate learning and the evolution of dynamic capabilities. *Organization Science, 13*(3), 339–351.

https://doi.org/10.1142/9789811269554_0009

Chapter 9

EdTech Start-Ups: A Mode of Transformation in Teaching and Learning

Prateek Khanna[*,¶], Reetika Sehgal[†,‖], Mayank Malviya[*,**], Anukaran Khanna[‡,††] and Ashish Mohan Dubey[§,‡‡]

*Department of Business Administration,
Shambhunath Institute of Engineering and Technology,
Prayagraj, Uttar Pradesh, India
†Department of Management, United College of Engineering &
Management D-II, UPSIDC Industrial Area, Prayagraj, Uttar Pradesh, India
‡Department of Electrical and Electronics Engineering, Birla Institute of
Technology and Science, Pilani, Rajasthan, India
§Department of Management, Birla Institute of Technology,
Mesra, Ranchi (Patna Campus), Patna, Bihar, India
¶fdp16prateekk@alumni.iimidr.ac.in
‖reetikasehgal@united.edu.in
**mayank.joinwith@gmail.com
††anukaran84@gmail.com
‡‡amdubey@bitmesra.ac.in

Abstract

The emergence of COVID-19 has led to an inclination towards the adoption of online teaching learning processes. The education sector witnessed massive changes for both students and educators. In the year 2020, there was a gigantic change in the teaching and learning methodology due to the occurrence of the COVID-19 pandemic and implementation of NEP (New Education Policy) by the Central Government of India. We at present live in the generation of learners, with millennials being the first generation to come to campus with laptops in hand and generation X using desktops in computer labs. Learners force educators to live with advanced artificial intelligence. EdTech start-ups became prevalent and transformed the COVID-19 pandemic into an opportunity. The EdTech approach intends to customise the learning process on the basis of learners' skills, interests and strengths. The prerequisite for EdTech is the use of technology and its integration with the education process. EdTech needs to bridge this gap through curriculum innovation. Educators must be aware of the potential barriers of technology. The delivery of instruction is influenced by advance technologies which provide adequate knowledge and skills to the learners as per their convenience. The aim of the current chapter is to find out the critical success factors of the EdTech start-ups. After examining the extensive available literature, the authors found the six factors which changed the education sector and led to a rise in the demand of EdTech start-ups. The findings of this chapter can be useful for companies, students and even for educators to design policies related to the online teaching process.

Keywords: EdTech, learning, start-ups, technology

1. Introduction

Educational technology is a combination of two terms, education and technology. Educational technology (EdTech) is becoming one of the foremost investment sectors in recent times. EdTech has become the favourite destination for investors and venture capital (VCs). The emergence of COVID-19 changed the preferences and there has been a significant jump in the adoption of online education during the pandemic (Dhawan & Dhawan, 2020) and in the post-pandemic world (Teras *et al.*, 2020). In countries like India, the EdTech space leapt forward and turned the COVID-19 pandemic into an opportunity (Tauson & Stannard, 2018). EdTech refers to how the people use their inventions and discovery to satisfy their educational needs and desires (Bailetti, 2012). It also refers to the application of physical sciences and engineering technology to provide mechanical instruments or hardware which can be used for instructional purposes (Duval-Couetil *et al.*, 2020). Examples are motion picture technology, computer-based teaching and other comprehensive aspects. EdTech implies planning, implementing and evaluating a system in education according to scientific principles to achieve the educational objectives at the maximum level (Alhomod & Shafi, 2013). Technology can make education more effective because with its use, instructions given to the learners can have more of a scientific basis (Al-Fraihat *et al.*, 2019). It also makes instructions more powerful as with the use of available resources the technology provides immediate and equal access to information (Rujira *et al.*, 2020). Technology has transformed the manner of learning (Beckman *et al.*, 2012a) in the classrooms for teachers keen to emulate new learning techniques with the help of technology (Aderinoye, 2008). EdTech businesses are positively changing the education industry. EdTech start-ups have come a long way, especially during the pandemic, by bringing teaching and learning to an entirely digitised form (Arguel *et al.*, 2017). The emergence of advanced learning tools such as mobile apps makes education easier and innovative (Ardito *et al.*, 2015). Smart classes, live online tuitions, doubt clarification sessions, exam preparation support or competitive exams classes are all part of the digital learning revolution that is engulfing the entire country (Selim, 2007). In the post-COVID world, there has been a significant change noticed in terms of the way the teachers teach as compared to the past (Dishon, 2021). Now, teachers want to incorporate advanced teaching and learning tools which help them to transform physical classes into digital classes (Fayolle *et al.*, 2020). EdTech spaces solve and simplify the learning with the help of sharing videos, assignments, quiz and reports (Hennessy *et al.*, 2010). The pandemic has transformed the way of learning for students compared to pre pandemic. The transformation of teaching and learning equips teachers with advanced digitalised tools.

Advancement of digitalisation and the emergence of artificial intelligence have made the job of instructors easy with the use of multiple tools (Ejermo & Xiao, 2014). Universities, schools, coaching institutes and other conventional institutions faced gargantuan challenges during the COVID-19 pandemic (Allen & O'Shea, 2014). This led to the increase in scope of EdTech start-ups. EdTech start-ups utilise emerging technologies such as artificial intelligence, robotics, virtual reality and augmented reality. To ensure business and learning continuity, learning classes have to swiftly upload all of the work on the internet, making access to education easy (Balven *et al.*, 2018). The largest companies in this space are unicorns like Byju's, Udemy, Eruditus and UpGrad. EdTech improves the traditional education system by improving pedagogy and the learning process. EdTech is not limited only to education but has brought along massive job opportunities in large corporate learning organisations in the last two years. During the COVID-19 pandemic, students, teachers and even parents faced a number of challenges. EdTech is the only option to solve such issues faced by all these three sides in a time of crisis. To build EdTech start-ups from the ground up requires significant research and knowledge of the education industry. EdTech companies are setting new equations by empowering the Indian education system with awe-inspiring learning products and solutions. The purpose of EdTech is to improve teaching and learning through technology. The COVID-19 pandemic changed the preferences of teachers to move from physical schools to the world of virtual schools and this was only possible because of EdTech.

2. Theoretical Contribution

2.1 *Existing theories*

EdTech learning experiences can be understood by identifying the learning theory. Learning theories are the ideas that attempt to describe how humans learn. One of the important aspects to witness success in the learning process is the change in behaviour. In other words, any sort of learning results in a change in behaviour. To make the teaching learning process successful, it is important to concentrate on the behaviour aspects (Gunnars, 2021) of individuals. Therefore, the main focus will be on behaviour theory. Behaviourism is a theory of learning that is based on the idea that all behaviours are acquired through conditioning. There is something called operant conditioning where behaviour is learned through a stimulus which leads to a response and then the stimulus that follows that response (Agarkar, 2019). BF Skinner, a behaviourist, implemented operant conditioning into academic learning which is called programmed instruction. This type of instruction involves the use of a mechanical device, a teaching machine, that provides stimuli to students and additionally reinforces based on their responses. Behaviours and behaviourism-based tech are very popular in EdTech because they help the students to increase their performance and examples are apps and other online platforms that break down learning (To & Wong, 2013) into smaller sections with each section requiring students to respond to stimuli and then getting immediate feedback.

3. Background: Evolution of Education

In India, the Fourth Industrial Revolution reshaped the pattern of teaching and learning at a time of crisis with the use of technology. A comprehensive EdTech policy architecture is needed in India which should focus on providing access to learning, especially to disadvantaged groups, enabling processes of teaching, learning and evaluation, facilitating teacher training and continuous professional development, and improving governance systems (Garrison, 2011). Man and his quest for knowledge can be traced back from the period of 30,000 B.C. In those days, to express his thoughts and communicate ideas, early man used the method of cave painting. The cave paintings of that time have red and black pigments, which on further investigation were revealed to come from ochre and charcoal, respectively. The first evidence of formal education in history was in the form of the Pythagoras academy founded by one of the great philosopher, Pythagoras, in 510 B.C. in ancient Greece where students were taught philosophy, science and mathematics in open classrooms. It was the invention of paper around 105 A.D. during the Han Dynasty in China that revolutionised the world as it was cheaper and more convenient than its counterparts bamboo, silk and wood. With the advent of paper technology and subsequent developments, around 328 A.D., manuscript transcription helped a lot in the growth of education because students could develop their writing (Garrison, 2011) and thus have very comprehensible letters which could be easily understood by others.

The invention of the printing press by Johannes Gutenberg in 1450 changed the world forever as books finally became available on a mass scale for the first time in human history. The cost efficiency led to the opening of more libraries, which accelerated the literacy rate; new ideas could now spread very quickly which further advanced the Renaissance and helped to support the science revolution. With all these developments happening, basic education was still limited to a certain class of people only and it was still considered a luxury (Garcia-Huidobro *et al.*, 2017). In the period of 1600–1800, formal education or, in other words, public education came into existence, which helped many attain formal education in the typical classroom with a chalk and blackboard setup. This method of teaching with chalk and board proved to be very helpful for students as well as teachers to exchange their views and knowledge easily.

With technological developments in every sphere, education technology (Garrison, 2011) also improved in the period of the 1920s, which is referred to as multimedia or audio-visual age. The strip projector along with the microphone was introduced in class to deliver content. After World War II, when world stabilised, a rapid surge in technological advancement was observed and the same was incorporated into the education as well. During the 1960s, to arouse more interest among students, VCR, VHS and audio tapes were introduced in the classroom. By 1990, VCR and VHS were outdated, and this is when the computer first hit the classroom and the computer age began, which very soon became an integral part of our life. In the beginning of the 21st century, the entire landscape changed and this was felt in the classroom as well; this period of the early 2000s is termed as the digital age. The progress of technology is observed through the interaction between people irrespective of their geographical presence, as the teacher and student both have access to greater communication through the internet (Chaston & Scott, 2012). In the present decade, augmented reality, virtual reality, artificial intelligence and other technological advancements got placed in the classroom, which make subjects more interesting and easy to understand (Habler *et al.*, 2018). The complete journey of man in the quest for knowledge is shown in Figure 1.

According to Figure 2, which represents the various domains of educational technology, the primary purpose of education is to enrich a child's mind and make him future ready by numerous teaching practices and schemes. As discussed earlier, imparting education radically changed over time, with technological advancement shifting the entire paradigm of

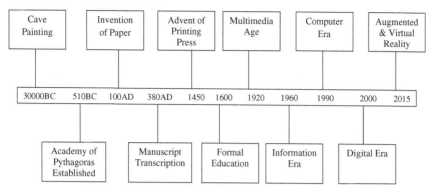

Figure 1.   Evolution of technology in education.

Source: Authors' own contribution.

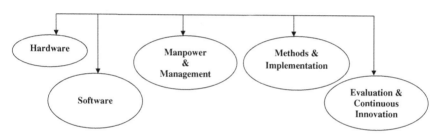

Figure 2.   Domains of educational technology.

Source: Authors' own contribution.

education to make learning more impactful (Wright *et al.*, 2004). Education technology is basically an integration of scientific techniques (Wright *et al.*, 2007) with hardware and software to enhance teaching and learning processes and achieve educational goals as shown in Figure 2. The five major domains or components of education technology are as follows:

1. **Hardware:** In education technology, all the physical components, which include mechanical equipment, materials and electronic equipment such as projectors, computers, laptops, television and motion pictures which help in improving the learning process, come under the umbrella of hardware.

2. **Software:** Software denotes the scientific and systematic application of various fields to improve the teaching learning process. It utilises aspect of psychology for designing the course material, teaching learning strategies, etc. Software turns out to be productive only when aided by hardware technology.

3. **Manpower and management:** For successful implementation of any technology, manpower and proper management are key aspects. To manage educational technology, one requires diversified professional manpower with enormous expertise in different domains and fields to help improve the teaching learning process.

4. **Methods and implementation:** In education technology, knowledge is imparted with the help of different devices, tools and techniques through various ways, such as evidence-based learning, micro-teaching, personalised delivery of instructions and programmed learning, which help facilitate the application of cognition, memory and senses and therefore lead to improved teaching practices resulting in better learning outcomes.

5. **Evaluation and continuous innovation:** To evaluate the entire process, continuous feedback in a closed loop is a must for its stability. Teaching and learning outcomes can be meaningful only if there is continuous evaluation and scope for exploration in adoption of innovative technology. There must be a periodic assessment of outcomes, and accordingly methodology must change depending upon the desired result.

Figure 3 presents a holistic education model which is an all-inclusive approach that addresses (Schreiner, 2009; Martin, 2015) the three basic aspects, namely, base knowledge, meta knowledge and anthropomorphic knowledge of learning, where educators strive to deal with emotional, social, ethical and academic demands of students in an integrated learning structure. Other than academic excellence, educators must focus on developing critical thinking skills among students to solve real-world problems.

Education has multiple attributes. The first is instructive, like history, geography and other subjects of humanities which can be dealt with by computer. The second is the examination of scientific subjects, which is

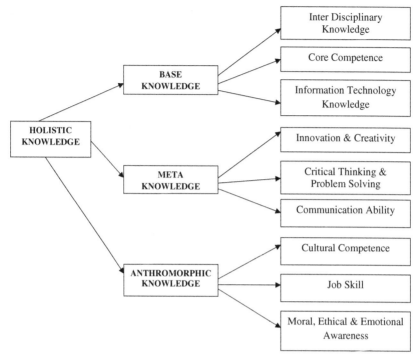

Figure 3.   Knowledge model.
Source: Authors' own contribution.

enormously significant because it is half of reality. They can also be dealt with by computer, but as they are more complex and human intervention is unavoidable. The third is the art of living; every student must be taught to transform his resentment, anger and animosity into love. An important aspect of the art of living is a sense of humour: One who forgets the expression of laughter has forgotten much of life. The foundation of the art of living is a reverence for life. The fourth is art and creativity: painting, music, craftsmanship, pottery — anything that is creative, because unless individuals learn how to create, they never become a part of existence, which is constantly creative. To make people educated in the true sense, they must be educated as a whole.

Figure 4 shows EdTech Business Models. The pandemic crisis has accelerated the prevalence of EdTech business models (Beehner, 2018; Hamari *et al*., 2020; Teras *et al*., 2020).

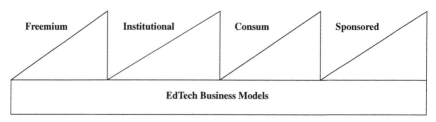

Figure 4.   EdTech business models.
Source: Authors' own contribution.

3.1 *Freemium model*

This model for start-ups is very appealing as it permits speedy trust of a brand and builds a position as an influential leader. The freemium pricing model is employed by many EdTech companies. This model facilitates the customers to use the product without any payment, just free of cost, with an opportunity to upgrade to a paid version at a later stage. For example, Coursera initiated offering free-of-cost courses on several topics along with the opportunity to obtain a certificate. With this initiative, the company became a prominent and motivating force for other EdTech companies. Coursera is an outstanding pattern of an EdTech start-up. Approximately 30 million new consumers were added in the year 2020 alone (*Business Today*, 2021). The company operates on the freemium model (Hamari *et al.*, 2020) where various paid courses are offered in parallel to free products. The availability of these free courses is an attraction for the consumers. The company also enjoys the monetary benefits with this approach.

This method leads to rapid acceleration of the momentum and ensures the availability of the product in a straight line to the consumer without any interference from intermediaries. Udemy is a renowned EdTech company that has reallocated itself to a marketplace model. Udemy offers online courses to individuals and businesses through its online platform. Currently, the total worth of its online courses is approximately $3 billion. Udemy splits course fees with instructors and collect it's 50 percent of the course revenue.

3.2 *Institutional model*

The institutional model or top-down model is a conventional technique of trading with schools through district managers and executives (Beehner, 2018). The proposed penetration rate and the size of the market decide the market volume which is required and then the target is set accordingly. Consequently, after determining the required market volume, a strategy for accomplishing the prospective revenue is developed. The area head or a district executive takes control of the purchases by a single purchasing method for the requirement of each school under its command. One of the advantages with this model is that it has the ability to allow districts to undertake contracts of huge amounts.

3.3 *Consumer model*

The consumer perspective is an innovative online education business model which allows a trial deal before its actual use. Schools can try the product free of cost before charging families to use at home. This approach is more suitable for business as it provides stuff that can be used by children independently. In this manner, schools efficiently act as a leader for the adoption of more consumers (Teras *et al.*, 2020). In this approach, it is significant to develop a "product loop" among schools and homes, where teachers can use the product in the classroom for students followed by advice given to parents to use it at home for children. This approach is advantageous to schools as they prefer free-of-cost and high-quality items which in turn will result in increased adoption by users. At the same time, parents are expected to follow the suggestions of instructors for using the technology at home. The same is apparent in products available for toddler and kindergarten children offered by EdTech.

3.4 *Sponsored model*

It is a fascinating and unique strategy where school and parents both do not pay any amount. In spite of the conventional payment method, the company takes the responsibility of sponsorship by paying for the development of the product. It acts as Corporate Social Responsibility (CSR) for the company (Beehner, 2018). The advantage is that when an extraordinary product is offered to schools free of cost, its consumption will be high, which is a favourable move for the sponsor. Further, the sponsors also have the opportunity to enhance the goodwill of the company by making customers aware about the brand.

3.5 EdTech turns into decacorn and unicorns

The education sector in India is a marketplace having a wide range of complications and opportunities. The pandemic has disturbed the traditional way of education, giving birth to the start-ups of EdTech, and the transition from offline to online. According to the report of KPMG, approximately 3,500 EdTech start-ups are there in India today (KPMG & Google, 2017). Further, it is expected that in next 10 years the EdTech industry will run a business of $30 billion (*The Economic Times*, 2021). It has been observed in recent reports that since the lockdown, there was a tremendous increase in the business of Byju's where 33 million users were added to touch the 75 million mark. (*Business Standard*, 2021). Unacademy's count of users rose more than triple amount, making it around 40 million users by January 2021. In the initial months of FY 2020–21, there was a 100 percent increase in the number of users of an online course platform of UpGrad.

In India, till 2019, Education technology or EdTech was one of the smallest sectors in terms of funding but with the occurrence of the pandemic and increase in the teaching learning process in rural areas, EdTech got a new path and direction, giving a new set of wings to education which earlier remained untouched.

In the year 2021, there were five major start-ups in India that turned into decacorn and unicorn (*Business Standard*, 2021b). A unicorn start-up is valued at more than $1 billion and a decacorn is valued at more than $10 billion (*Business Standard*, 2020). One of the main reasons for the increase in the EdTech unicorn series in India is the huge interest of the shareholders in this sector. Since 2020, there has been a continuous improvement in the EdTech start-up amount. It was raised to $2.2 billion in 2020 and $1.9 billion between 3 January and 3 August, 2021. The first

Indian EdTech company to become a unicorn was Byju's in 2018. Byju's has the highest value among Indian start-ups across the globe. The company's current value is $16.5 billion and it is the first decacorn status company. In September 2020, Unacademy became the second largest Indian EdTech unicorn after two years of struggle and a pandemic. Two more giants, Ashwin Damera-led Eruditus and Ronnie Screwvala-led UpGrad, were found in 2021 in India (*Business Standard*, 2021a). Vedantu became the latest unicorn in the EdTech space in September 2021 after raising $100 million from Singapore-based ABC World Asia (*Business Insider India*, 2021). Table 1 represents the EdTech company status and valuations.

It is a known fact that the COVID-19 pandemic and subsequent lockdowns dealt a severe blow to the Indian education sector. The Indian education sector has broadened due to the COVID-19 pandemic and periodic lockdowns. In metropolitan cities, schools adopted emerging technology on an urgent basis using the updated technology for the teaching learning process and quality education. But unfortunately, at the same time, the students in small cities and rural areas were deprived of these education aids during lockdowns. The COVID-19 pandemic brought changes in the teaching learning process across the range for students. The classrooms in the current scenario have moved far ahead from conventional desktops, which are now being replaced with technology-infused LEDs, tablets, interactive online courses, etc., for the teaching learning process.

On the basis of a vast literature review, six critical success factors for EdTech start-ups have been identified as shown in Table 2.

Table 1.   EdTech company status and valuation.

Decacorn and Unicorns Status	Year	Company Valuation
Byju's	2018	$16.5 billion
Unacademy	2020	$3.4 billion
Eruditus	2021	$3.2 billion
UpGrad		$1.2 billion
Vedantu		$1 billion

Source: *Business Insider* (2021).

Table 2. Factors identified from literature review.

S. No.	Factors	Source
1	Availability of Wider Resources	Al-Fraihat *et al.* (2019); Butler *et al.* (2020); Daoud *et al.* (2020); Kordel *et al.* (2021); Mosey *et al.* (2016)
2	Accessibility	Arguel *et al.* (2017); Daoud *et al.* (2020); Habler *et al.* (2015); Mertala (2020); Schindler *et al.* (2012)
3	Customised and Blended Learning	Bailetti (2012); Dishon (2020); Sancho-Gil *et al.* (2019)
4	Technology As a Tutor	Mertala (2020); Mosey & Wright (2007); Ross & Lowther (2010)
5	Real-Time Support	Dishon (2021); Kordel & Wolniak (2021); Laufer *et al.* (2021); Mertala (2020); Secundo *et al.* (2021); Williamson *et al.* (2020)
6	NEP Implementation	Aithal & Aithal (2020); MHRD Government of India (2020)

Source: Authors' own findings.

4. Research Method

A detailed analysis of the available published surveys and recent studies related to EdTech was undertaken. In-depth discussions and personal interview sessions were organised with different experts such as tech-savvy educators, students, parents and EdTech executives. The current chapter examined the major changes which came out in the teaching and learning process for educators and students. After analysing the various surveys, reports and studies related to education technology, six critical

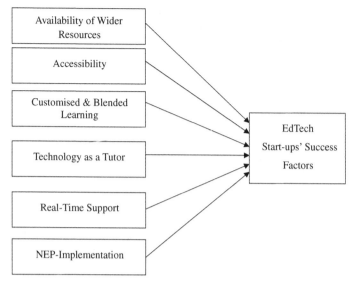

Figure 5.   Research framework of EdTech start-ups' success factors.
Source: Authors' own contribution.

success factors were identified for EdTech in India. These factors are availability of wider resources, accessibility, customised and blended learning, technology as a tutor, real-time support and NEP implementation. Figure 5 shows the research framework of EdTech start-ups' success factors proposed for the current study.

The detailed descriptions of the identified factors are given below:

(1) **Availability of wider resources:** In the modern world, the internet is used as a multi-purpose weapon for organisations and industries. On the one hand, it supports immediate access and usage of infinite data, while on the other hand data frequently fluctuates in quality and profundity, making people all over the world spend excessive time looking for precious and useful content (Daoud *et al.*, 2020). The EdTech platform must hold the potential to gather content in totality from contributors across the world. This can assist a company in securing itself as a brand that can be trusted and establish a position as an industry kingpin. In the absence of best-quality materials, it is impossible to achieve the target of the teaching

learning process. The target for the EdTech platform is to make a foundation of creating quality and wider content for learners who can access the learning materials and enhance their skills (Butler *et al.*, 2020). The capacity to organise and share computerised learning content is a significant part of the vigorous framework for adopting needs and providing guarantee for both consistent quality and a wide range of choices.

(2) **Accessibility:** Accessibility is defined as the layout of applications, gadgets, materials and conditions that help and empower access to the content and exercises for all the learners. In order to empower learners with adequate learning and overcome inabilities, learners must be taught to utilise the content and take part in exercises, for example, English language students, learners from rustic networks or from financially weaker sections. Technology and innovation can be encouraged through embedded assistance (Corrales-Estrada, 2019). For instance, text-to-disclosure, sound and advanced text configurations of informative materials, programmes that separate guidance, versatile testing and assistive technology are essential to establish a successful learning atmosphere. Learners and educators cannot move on the opportunity to associate and connect around the world or influence best-quality learning materials without steady and dependable access to the internet (Mertala, 2020). Technology and innovation have altered most areas of the economy. It has changed the way the knowledge is imparted to learners and how one can access data. The conventional "Chalk and Talk" method in classroom teaching has been substituted by separate guidance, personalised and customised training, and sincere commitment to the technology-based teaching learning process. Educators are aided with technology and innovative learning methodology for imparting the knowledge and skills among learners (Azevedo & Cromley, 2004).

(3) **Customised and blended learning:** Customised learning refers to training in which the pace of learning and the instructional approach are optimised for the needs of the learner (Bhuasiri *et al.*, 2012). On the basis of the learners' need, instructional content, instructional approach and learning objectives may vary. In addition to this, learning activities

become more meaningful and relevant for learners when it is backed by interest and initiation (King & Boyatt, 2015). Online and in-person learning form a blended learning environment. Blended learning manages the pace of learning, place, path and time for learners. The blended learning approach facilitates face-to-face interaction with a teacher in a large group, small group and also with learning from peer groups. Blended learning facilitates individual focused study and adaptable learning (Dishon, 2020). Traditionally, the teaching learning process and its resources were limited only to the boundaries of the school (Kozma, 2003). Technology-led learning facilitates the utilisation of resources in a better manner and develops an expertise in the learner to learn anywhere in the world.

(4) **Technology as a tutor:** Augmented connectivity enhances the significance of teaching and learning by adopting digital modes. The focus should be on developing competencies to use technology in better ways that are respectful, meaningful, protected and productive (Ross & Lowther, 2009), for example, aiding students in developing the skills and etiquettes required for online teaching, knowing how their personal details may be collected and used online and how vast access to a worldwide society can assist in improving the globe around them (Greve & Salaff, 2003). The fundamental knowledge of tools and technology and the capacity to make the right decisions for their usage in our daily life will make an individual an expert of these skills. The term digital citizenship refers to the responsible, ethical, secured and informed use of technology (Beckman *et al.*, 2012b). This concept includes a variety of skills and literacies that can consist of privacy and security, internet safety, communication skills, online reputation management, information literacy, cyber bullying and creative credit and copyright. The careful and thoughtful application of technology has the possibility to increase, strengthen and enlarge the impact of influential principles of learning. The procedure of learning is not directly visible; therefore, understanding the learning process involves producing models and conclusions that develop with time.

(5) **Real-time support:** EdTech spaces provide real-time effective feedback and automated responses for assignments. Real-time updates help educators identify the problems faced by the other side and resolve them within a time frame compared to the traditional mode of assessments (Azevedo *et al.*, 2004). Effective and efficient feedback in adequate time enhances the performance of the students and allows educators to give the solution to the individual. The availability of advanced teaching learning tools helps one identify the strengths and weaknesses of the individual. EdTech spaces give multiple options to educators to solve the generated queries given by the learners (Boh *et al.*, 2016). Queries can be resolved through an open discussion forum, chat box, email, with the help of videos, etc. Real-time feedback has some benefits like being transparent, actionable and completion within a time frame. Today, with the aid of advanced technology, educators and learners connect together to achieve desire results. Connectivity is the essence of EdTech, which shares experiences between educators and learners. Real-time technology assesses the performance of learners and allows educators to demonstrate resources at the same time. In the world of print-based resources, it is difficult for educators to showcase the resources. Real-time solution is a win–win situation for educators and learners.

(6) **National Education Policy (NEP) implementation:** One of the most important success factors for the EdTech start-ups is their preparedness and readiness to implement the new education policy in 2020 (Aithal & Aithal, 2020). As it is evident from the policy, it focuses on heuristic development that will change the learning environment as well as learning process. On the one hand, it brings a lot of prospects for EdTech players and, on other hand, it brings challenges as well. Post NEP implementation, only those EdTech companies will survive in the markets that are able to adapt themselves as per the new regime. EdTech spaces that connect with artificial intelligence will gain momentum, and the development of the AI interface will promote productive learning. The AI-driven deep learning algorithm reduces the burden of content developers and instructors and also easily fills the gap in the learning cycle by providing customised content as per the need (IBEF, 2021). Other than enabling artificial intelligence techniques, EdTech companies must develop learning

management systems, ERP software, online labs, etc. To make their presence felt in the market as NEP will open the door for many players in the education ecosystem, NEP will promote digitisation in physical classrooms as well (*India Today*, 2020). Hence, it opens the horizon for creating innovative products and content (*Higher Education Digest*, 2021). Companies can indulge in designing immersive technology for classroom learning. The primary focus of the NEP is on skill development of EdTech players, particularly the ones who are into language-based learning, cognitive and analytical skill development, game-based learning, and VR- and AR-assisted skilling, which will be able to substantially exploit the situation. EdTech players with a proficiency in blockchain technology can help build vibrant learning ecosystems that are learner-centric, equitable, modular, interoperable and resilient, and have got the ability to introduce a surge of innovation around learner data. The new education policy will shift the entire paradigm in adaptation of technology in education (*The Hindu*, 2020) and provide an ocean of opportunities to EdTech companies.

5. Conclusion

The outbreak of COVID-19 led to the shutting down of education institutions, propelling an urgent need for technological solutions and upgrading technological infrastructure to ensure continuity in education. This brought about an unprecedented opportunity for the educational technology "EdTech" sector in India. The traditional face-to-face interaction between a teacher and students suffered a setback; there was a paradigm shift to the unconventional mode of online learning. With the announcement of the National Education Policy (NEP) by the Ministry of Human Resource and Development in the FY 2020–2021, it offered a policy impetus to the EdTech sector. The NEP recognises the role of technology in making education more effective. This change put a spotlight on the EdTech industry. With this emergence, there has been a meteoric growth in new start-ups in the EdTech sector in India. The current chapter is an attempt to present before the readers the historical evolution of the education system and how technology has played a major role in development of the EdTech industry. In countries like India, young entrepreneurs and start-ups have taken this as an opportunity to bring revolutionary change by blending technology in education and are earning good returns and simultaneously opening new employment opportunities in the country. This chapter also makes an attempt to identify six critical success factors through a widespread literature review that can be used for such start-ups that are seeking opportunities in setting up EdTech businesses.

Acknowledgements

The authors would like to thank all the respondents who spared their precious time to provide data essential for the current study. The authors also express their appreciation for the experts of the pilot study for sharing their pearls of wisdom that improved the work significantly.

The authors are also immensely grateful to the editors for their critical and valuable comments to improve the manuscript. They would also like to express their sincere appreciation to the anonymous referees for their valuable comments which enhanced the quality of the paper.

Declaration of Conflicting Interests

The authors declared no potential conflicts of interest with respect to the research, authorship and/or publication of this article.

Funding

The authors received no financial support for the research, authorship and/or publication of this article.

References

Aderinoye, R. (2008). Literacy and communication technologies: Distance education strategies for literacy delivery. *International Review of Education*, *54*(5–6), 605–626.
Agarkar, S. C. (2019). Influence of learning theories on science education. *Resonance*, *24*, 847–859.

Aithal, P. S. & Aithal, S. (2020). Analysis of the Indian National Education Policy 2020 towards achieving its objectives. *Munich Personal RePEc Archive (MPRA)*, 5(2), 19–41, 102549.

Al-Fraihat, D., Joy, M., & Sinclair, J. (2019). Evaluating e-learning systems success: An empirical study. *Computers in Human Behavior, 102*, 67–86.

Alhomod, S. & Shafi, M. M. (2013). Success factors of e-learning projects: A technical perspective. *Turkish Online Journal of Educational Technology-TOJET, 12*(2), 247–253.

Allen, T. J. & O'Shea, R. P. (2014). *Building Technology Transfer within Research Universities*. Cambridge, UK: Cambridge University Press.

Ardito, L., Messeni Petruzelli, A., & Albino, V. (2015). Technological inventions to new products: A systematic review and research agenda of the main enabling factors. *European Management Review, 12*(3), 113–147.

Arguel, A., Lockyer, L., Lipp, O. V., Lodge, J. M., & Kennedy, G. (2017). Inside out: Detecting learners confusion to improve interactive digital learning environments. *Journal of Educational Computing Research, 55*(4), 526–551.

Azevedo, R. & Cromley, J. G. (2004). Does training of self-regulated learning facilitate students' learning with hypermedia? *Journal of Educational Psychology, 96*, 523–535.

Azevedo, R., Cuthrie, J. T., & Seibert, D. (2004). The role of self-regulated learning in fostering students' conceptual understanding of complex systems with hypermedia. *Journal of Educational Computing Research, 28*(1), 15–30.

Bailetti, T. (2012). Technology entrepreneurship: Overview, definition, and distinctive aspects. *Technology Innovation Management Review, 2*(2), 5–12.

Balven, R., Fenters, V., Siegel, D. S., & Waldman, D. (2018). Academic entrepreneurship: The roles of identity, motivation, championing, education, work-life balance, and organizational justice. *Academy of Management Perspectives, 32*(1), 21–42.

Beckman, C. M., Eisenhardt, K., Kotha, S., Meyer, A., & Rajagopalan, N. (2012a). The role of the entrepreneur in technology entrepreneurship. *Strategic Entrepreneurship Journal, 6*(3), 203–206.

Beckman, C. M., Eisenhardt, K., Kotha, S., Meyer, A., & Rajagopalan, N. (2012b). Technology entrepreneurship. *Strategic Entrepreneurship Journal, 6*(2), 89–93.

Beehner, C. G. (2018). Expanding sustainable business education beyond business schools. In S. Dhiman & J. Marques (Eds.), *Handbook of Engaged Sustainability*. Cham: Springer.

Bhuasiri, W., Xaymoungkhoun, O., Zo, H., Rho, J. J., & Ciganek, A. P. (2012). Critical success factors for e-learning in developing countries: A comparative analysis between ICT experts and faculty. *Computers & Education, 58*(2), 843–855.

Boh, W. F., De-Haan, U., & Strom, R. (2016). University technology transfer through entrepreneurship: Faculty and students in spinoffs. *The Journal of Technology Transfer, 41*(4), 661–669.

Business Insider India (2021, August 14). From Byju's to Eruditus — India now has four edtech unicorns, thanks to a $4 billion fund flowing in since 2020. Retrieved December 27, 2021 from https://www.businessinsider.in/business/ startups/news/india-now-has-four-edtech-unicorns-byju-unacademy-eruditis-upgrad/articleshow/85300757.cms.

Business Standard (2020, June 27). Covid-19 pandemic helped Byju's become a decacorn, cross $10.5 bn valuation. https://www.business-standard.com/ article/companies/covid-19-pandemic-helped-byju-s-become-a-decacorn-cross-10-5-bn-valuation-120062701068_1.html.

Business Standard (2021, April 26). With Temasek's $120 mn, Ronnie Screwvala's UpGrad set for $1 bn valuation. https://www.business-standard.com/article/ companies/will-get-there-soon-ronnie-screwvala-s-upgrad-heads-for-1-bn-valuation-121042600140_1.html.

Business Standard (2021, December 22). What explains India's unicorn boom in 2021? https://www.business-standard.com/podcast/current-affairs/what-explains-india-s-unicorn-boom-in-2021-121122200092_1.html.

Business Today (2021, November 9). India becomes Coursera's second-largest market with 13.6 million users. https://www.businesstoday.in/latest/story/ india-becomes-courseras-second-largest-market-with-136-million-users-311723-2021-11-09.

Butler, J. S., Garg, R., & Stephens, B. (2020). Social networks, funding, and regional advantages in technology entrepreneurship: An empirical analysis. *Information System Research, 31*(1), 198–216.

Chaston, I. & Scott, G. J. (2012). Entrepreneurship and open innovation in an emerging economy. *Management Decision, 50*(7), 1161–1177.

Corrales-Estrada, M. (2019). *Innovation and Entrepreneurship: A New Mindset for Emerging Markets* (pp. 267–278). Emerald Publishing Limited. doi: 10.1108/9781789737011.

Daoud, R., Starkey, L., Eppel, E., Vo, T. D., & Sylvester, A. (2020). The educational value of internet use in the home for school children: A systematic review of literature. *Journal of Research on Technology in Education, 53*(4), 353–374.

Dhawan, S. & Dhawan, S. (2020). Online learning: A panacea in the time of COVID-19 crisis. *Journal of Educational Technology Systems*, *49*(1), 5–22.

Dishon, G. (2020). The new natural? Authenticity and the naturalization of educational technologies. *Learning, Media and Technology*, *46*(2), 156–173.

Dishon, G. (2021). What kind of revolution? Thinking and rethinking educational technologies in the time of COVID-19. *Journal of the Learning Sciences*, *31*(3), 458–476.

Duval-Couetil, N., Ladisch, M., & Yi, S. (2020). Addressing academic researcher priorities through science and technology entrepreneurship education. *The Journal of Technology Transfer*, *46*, 288–318.

Ejermo, O. & Xiao, J. (2014). Entrepreneurship and survival over the business cycle: How do new technology-based firms differ? *Small Business Economics*, *43*(2), 411–426.

Fayolle, A., Lamine, W., Mian, S., & Phan, P. (2020). Effective models of science, technology and engineering entrepreneurship education: Current and future research. *The Journal of Technology Transfer*, *46*(2), 277–287.

Garcia-Huidobro, J. C., Nannemann, A., Bacon, C. K., & Thompson, K. (2017). Evolution in educational change: A literature review of the historical core. *Journal of Educational Change*, *18*(3), 263–293.

Garrison, D. R. (2011). *E-Learning in the 21st Century: A Framework for Research and Practice*. Routledge. doi: 10.4324/9780203838761.

Greve, A. & Salaff, J. W. (2003). Social networks and entrepreneurship. *Entrepreneurship Theory and Practice*, *28*(1), 1–20.

Gunnars, F. (2021). A large-scale systematic review relating behaviorism to research of digital technology in primary education. *Computers and Education Open*, *2*(100058), 1–10.

Habler, B., Broadbent, E., Cunningham, A., Chimombo, J., Jamil, B. R., Kauthria, R., Lake, L., Rose, P., Sarfraz, S., & Szekely, M. (2018). Synergies between the principles for digital development and four case studies. In *Research for Equitable Access and Learning (REAL) Centre*, Faculty of Education, University of Cambridge. https://zenodo.org/record/1219919#. XfJKv3X7Qeo.

Habler, B., Major, L., & Hennessy, S. (2015). Tablet use in schools: A critical review of the evidence for learning outcomes. *Journal of Computer Assisted Learning*, *32*(2), 139–156.

Hamari, J., Hanner, N., & Koivisto, J. (2020). "Why pay premium in freemium services?" A study on perceived value, continued use and purchase intentions in free-to-play games. *International Journal of Information Management*, *51*(102040), 1–15.

Hennessy, S., Harrison, D., & Wamakote, L. (2010). Teacher factors influencing classroom use of ICT in sub-Saharan Africa. *Itupale Online Journal of African Studies*, *2*, 39–54.

Higher Education Digest (2021, March 24). NEP 2020 and online education — A paradigm shift. https://www.highereducationdigest.com/nep-2020-and-online-education-a-paradigm-shift.

India Brand Equity Foundation (2021). New educational schemes — One year completion of NEP, the road ahead. https://www.ibef.org/blogs/new-educational-schemes-one-year-completion-of-nep-the-road-ahead.

India Today (2020, August 22). Will NEP give a much needed boost to online education in India? https://www.indiatoday.in/education-today/featurephilia/story/will-nep-give-a-muchneeded-boost-to-online-education-in-india-1713926-2020-08-22.

Joshi, A., Meza, J., Costa, S., Puricelli Perin, D. M., Trout, K., & Rayamajih, A. (2013). The role of information and communication technology in community outreach, academic and research collaboration, and education and support services (IT-CARES). *Perspectives in Health Information Management*, *10*(Fall), 1–15.

King, E. & Boyatt, R. (2015). Exploring factors that influence adoption of e-learning within higher education. *British Journal of Educational Technology*, *46*(6), 1272–1280.

Kordel, P. & Wolniak, R. (2021). Technology entrepreneurship and the performance of enterprises in the conditions of COVID-19 pandemic: The fuzzy set analysis of waste to energy enterprises in Poland. *Energies*, *14*, 3891.

Kozma, R. B. (2003). Technology and classroom practices: An international study. *Journal of Research on Technology in Education*, *36*(1), 1–14.

KPMG & Google (2017). Online education in India: 2021. https://assets.kpmg/content/dam/kpmg/in/pdf/2017/05/Online-Education-in-India-2021.pdf.

Laufer, M., Leiser, A., Deacon, B., Perrin de Brichambaut, P., Fecher, B., Kobsda, C., & Hesse, F. (2021). Digital higher education: A divider or bridge builder? Leadership perspectives on edtech in a COVID-19 reality. *International Journal of Educational Technology in Higher Education*, *18*(1), 51.

Martin, R. (2015). Holistic education and teacher professional learning in the twenty-first century. In S. Tang & L. Logonnathan (Eds.), *Taylor's 7th Teaching and Learning Conference 2014 Proceedings*. Singapore: Springer.

Mertala, P. (2020). Paradoxes of participation in the digitalization of education: A narrative account. *Learning, Media and Technology, 45*(2), 179–192.

MHRD Government of India (2020). New education policy 2020. https://www.education.gov.in/sites/upload_files/mhrd/files/NEP_Final_English_0.pdf.

Mosey, S., Guerrero, M., & Greenman, A. (2016). Technology entrepreneurship research opportunities: Insights from across Europe. *The Journal of Technology Transfer, 42*, 1–9.

Mosey, S. & Wright, M. (2007). From human capital to social capital: A longitudinal study of technology based academic entrepreneurs. *Entrepreneurship Theory and Practice, 31*(6), 909–935.

Ross, S. M. & Lowther, D. L. (2009). Effectively using technology in education. *Better Evidence-Based Education, 2*(1), 20–21.

Ross, S. M., Morrison, G. R., & Lowther, D. L. (2010). Educational technology research past and present: Balancing rigor and relevance to impact school learning. *Contemporary Educational Technology, 1*(1), 17–35.

Rujira, T., Nilsook, P., & Wannapiroon, P. (2020). Synthesis of vocational education college transformation process toward high-performance digital organization. *International Journal of Information and Education Technology, 10*(11), 832–837.

Sancho-Gil, J. M., Rivera-Vargas, P., & Miño-Puigcercós, R. (2019). Moving beyond the predictable failure of Ed-Tech initiatives. *Learning, Media and Technology, 45*(1), 61–75.

Schindler, L. A., Burkholder, G. J., Morad, O. A., & Marsh, C. (2017). Computer-based technology and student engagement: A critical review of the literature. *International Journal of Educational Technology in Higher Education, 14*(25), 1–28.

Schreiner, P. (2009). Holistic education and teacher training. In M. de Souza, L. J. Francis, J. O'Higgins-Norman, & D. Scott (Eds.), *International Handbook of Education for Spirituality, Care and Wellbeing. International Handbooks of Religion and Education, 3.* Dordrecht: Springer.

Secundo, G., Mele, G., Vecchio, P. D., Elia, G., Margherita, A., & Ndou, V. (2021). Threat or opportunity? A case study of digital-enabled redesign of entrepreneurship education in the COVID-19 emergency. *Technological Forecasting and Social Change, 166*, 120565.

Selim, H. M. (2007). E-learning critical success factors: An exploratory investigation of student perceptions. *International Journal of Technology Marketing, 2*(2), 157–182.

Tauson, M. & Stannard, L. (2018). Using EdTech for learning in emergencies and displaced settings: A rigorous review and narrative synthesis. https://resourcecentre.savethechildren.net/pdf/edtech-learning.pdf.

Teras, M., Suoranta, J., Teras, H., & Curcher, M. (2020). Post-COVID-19 education and education technology 'solutionism': A seller's market. *Postdigital Science and Education, 2*, 863–878.

The Economic Times (2021, April 28). Indian Ed-Tech industry's market size to reach $30 billion in 10 years: Report. https://economictimes.indiatimes.com/tech/technology/indian-edtech-industrys-market-size-to-reach-30-billion-in-10-years-report/articleshow/82295097.cms.

The Hindu (2020, September 3). COVID-19, NEP fuel fund raising by education technology firms. https://www.thehindu.com/business/Industry/covid-19-nep-fuel-fund-raising-by-education-technology-firms/article32517271.ece.

Teo, T. & Wong, S. L. (2013). Modeling key drivers of e-learning satisfaction among student teachers. *Journal of Educational Computing Research, 48*(1), 71–95.

Williamson, B., Eynon, R., & Potter, J. (2020). Pandemic politics, pedagogies and practices: Digital technologies and distance education during the coronavirus emergency. *Learning, Media and Technology, 45*(2), 107–114.

Wright, M., Birley, S., & Mosey, S. (2004). Entrepreneurship and university technology transfer. *The Journal of Technology Transfer, 29*(3–4), 235–246.

Wright, M., Hmieleski, K. M., Siegel, D. S., & Ensley, M. D. (2007). The role of human capital in technological entrepreneurship. *Entrepreneurship Theory and Practice, 31*(6), 791–806.

Chapter 10

Digital Health Innovation: Emergence of Digital Medical Consumer (DMC) and Holistic Digital Health Start-Ups (Hdhss)

Girish R. Kulkarni[*,‡]**, Daxesh M. Patel**[†,§]**,**
Supriya Singh[*,¶] **and Punit Saurabh**[*,‖]

[*]*Institute of Management, Nirma University, Ahmedabad, Gujarat, India*
[†]*Intas Pharmaceuticals Pvt Ltd, Ahmedabad, Gujarat, India*
[‡]*girish.kulkarni@nirmauni.ac.in*
[§]*daxeshm_patel@intaspharma.com*
[¶]*supriya.singh@nirmauni.ac.in*
[‖]*punit@nirmauni.ac.in*

Abstract

One of the major change drivers which emerged in the 21st century is the birth of the internet. Internet-led digitalisation has impacted almost all the sectors across the board positively and in some cases negatively. The healthcare sector is no exception to the transformation. We are witnessing dramatic changes in the healthcare sector across all its verticals due to increasing digital health innovations. The Government of India is aggressively pushing for digital health reforms in India. The inception of key healthcare digitalisation initiatives, like national digital health mission, legalisation of telemedicine, E-pharmacies and the Health ID project, indicates the government's strong resolve towards taking forward the digitalisation transformation at a rapid pace.

All these digital health innovations led to new strata of medical consumers like Digital Medical Consumers. In this chapter, a conceptual framework of three types of medical consumers based on their buying behaviour has been postulated. In addition, digital health innovations are playing a major role in the evolution of the holistic digital health ecosystem in India. We anticipate the evolution of Holistic Digital Health Start-ups (HDHSs) because of the government's push towards digitalisation in health and its subsequent willingness to create digital health infrastructure and the rising penetration of health informatics. Hence, this paper has proposed a conceptual framework for Holistic Digital Health Start-ups (HDHSs).

Keywords: Digitalisation, telemedicine, E-pharmacies, health informatics, digital medical consumer, holistic digital health start-ups, digital health ecosystem, health, start-ups, digital, innovation, medical, COVID

1. Introduction

India has witnessed a significant digital transformation in the 21st century due to the increased penetration of the internet, mobile telephony, and rise of the tech-savvy generation as well as the emergence of India as an Information Technology (IT) superpower. It is known that the increased connectivity and digital technologies will have a significant impact on business model innovations (Svadberg *et al.*, 2019). The recent COVID-19 crisis induced a surge in e-commerce and online shopping (Halan, 2020), which is proof of this fact. In addition, key initiatives such as Aadhaar and Digilocker increased thrust on digital payments and black swan events such as COVID-19 pandemic have further accelerated the agenda. The government is aggressively driving digitalisation across all the sectors with special emphasis on the health sector. In August 2020, the Indian Government announced the ambitious Health ID project, thereby giving a boost to digitalisation in health (ANI, 2020). This announcement opened a world of possibilities for delivering the health services through digitalisation. The National Digital Health Mission has envisaged a detailed digital health ecosystem which is connected through a common network (Ministry of Health and Family Welfare, 2019).

Traditionally, the scope of digitalisation in the healthcare sector was considered limited due to its clinical, regulatory and physical nature. However, telemedicine and E-pharmacies are leading the digital disruption of the healthcare sector. The tech-savvy younger generation who have little time to travel to see doctors or visit a pharmacy prefers healthcare services and medicines delivered right at their doorstep. The current generation is increasingly using technology-based platforms (Meier, 2013). These technology-based platforms in healthcare, such as telemedicine and E-pharmacies, are helping medical consumers manage their healthcare needs effectively and proactively (Srivastava & Raina, 2020). Hence, in their study, Herting & Lennart (2020) considered digital health innovations like telemedicine and E-pharmacies as disruptive business models of the healthcare industry. Telemedicine and E-pharmacies which offer significant benefits in terms of cost saving and convenience are influencing a change in the consumer buying behaviour (Desai, 2016; Abanmy, 2017; Sarker *et al.*, 2019). Rapid developments in the field of health are likely to serve as a precursor to exciting digital health innovations. These digital health innovations coupled with changing behaviours of consumers will offer exciting opportunities for start-ups to explore.

In pursuance with the objective of gap identification, it is to be noted that the current research in the field of digital health is largely dedicated to three aspects. First and primary area of research is developing digital technologies for disease management and interventions. The second area of research is limited to telemedicine. The third and evolving area is building large and complex digital health ecosystems which are parallel to the existing physical public health systems. However, there is limited research available about the impact of digital health innovations on the behaviour of medical consumers. COVID-19 has created serious challenges for effective delivery of primary health services such as doctor consultations, purchase of medicines and laboratory testing. It is pertinent that digital health will be seen as an alternative to solve this challenge. However, there is limited research available which discusses the role of digital health innovations and health informatics in the evolution of start-ups that offer primary digital health services consisting of telemedicine, E-pharmacies and e-laboratories under one umbrella. The current literature is largely silent about the exciting value propositions which are on offer for start-ups in the digital health area.

Hence, the authors of this paper have tried to study the changing behaviours of medical consumers in the light of digitalisation in healthcare. In the process, the authors have postulated and proposed the conceptual framework for different types of medical consumers. Further, the chapter deliberates on the future of digital health innovation and presents the conceptual framework for Holistic Digital Health Start-ups (HDHSs).

The chapter is organised into four sections. The first section reviews the Indian healthcare sector, health informatics and the impact of COVID-19. The second section elaborates on the research methodology employed for developing conceptual frameworks. The third section proposes the conceptual framework of different types of medical consumers, whereas the fourth and final sections discuss the digital health ecosystem and postulate the conceptual framework for HDHSs, respectively.

2. Indian Healthcare and Pharmaceutical Industry: Challenges and Opportunities

The Indian healthcare and pharmaceutical industry is one of the largest healthcare industries across the globe. The Indian healthcare sector is poised to become a USD 372 billion industry by 2022 with a CAGR of 16.8%. The healthcare industry was projected to reach USD 280 billion for the year 2020, not a mean achievement considering the COVID-19 situation (IBEF, 2020a). In addition, the Indian domestic pharmaceutical industry is worth USD 20.03 billion, growing at 9.8% for FY 2019 (IBEF, 2020b). The Indian healthcare sector boasts of a huge health infrastructure consisting of 1.9 lakh government health centres (Ministry of Health and Family Welfare (Statistics Division), 2019) and 43,000 private hospitals (Statista Research Department, 2020). In India, 2 million doctors cater to the health needs of 1.35 billion people, which includes 1.2 million doctors from the allopathic system and 0.8 million doctors from alternate medicine (Jadhav, 2020). However, in India, the amount spent on public health for the financial year 2020 was merely 1.6% of GDP (IBEF, 2020b). As a result, out-of-pocket (OOP) expenditure by the patients accounts for 69% of total health expenditure (Kastor & Mohanty, 2018), while the remaining 31% includes public health expenditure by the government and health insurance. It is estimated that out-of-pocket expenditure on medication is around 80% (Prachi, 2018). In a nutshell, India lacks "affordable, available and accessible" medical services and medicines (Saurabh *et al.*, 2012) for its citizens. The above-discussed factors play a significant role in determining the consumer behaviour of a patient. The underdeveloped public health system is also responsible for the development and over-reliance on unorganised private healthcare including the retail pharmacy ecosystem.

India has 0.85 million pharmacies out of which brick-and-mortar pharmacies comprise 99%, whereas organised pharmacies constitute merely 1% in terms of the count. The Indian retail pharmacy market is about USD 18 billion, growing at 10–12% annually (Apollo Hospitals Enterprise Limited, 2020). The market is projected to reach USD 31 billion (INR 2230 billion) by 2024 with a CAGR of 10%. The Indian retail pharmacy sector is one of the most fragmented sectors, largely made up of unorganised retail stores. In terms of the revenue, unorganised retail stores hold a 93% market share, whereas the remaining 7% is with organised retail and online pharmacies (Business Wire, 2020). Additionally, the Indian retail pharmacy market is a highly regulated market both in terms of sale of drugs and pricing of drugs. The Food and Drug administration in the country is responsible for governing the retail pharmacy ecosystem in India. The Drugs and Cosmetics Act, 1940, regulates the sales of drugs, whereas the Pharmacy Act, 1948, regulates the conduct of pharmacists registered under state pharmacy councils (Legaldocs, 2018). The profit margins for pharmacy retailers in India on medicines are fixed and they range between 16% and 20% (NPPA, 2018). The pricing and regulatory environment plays an important role in creating the existing retail pharmacy ecosystem in India.

2.1 *Health informatics*

Health informatics in simple terms refers to the management of information in healthcare with the help of information technology, computer applications and telecommunications. The focal point of health informatics is patient care (Imhoff, 2001). Health informatics is all about providing tools that optimise the process of patient care across the healthcare ecosystem (Imhoff, 2001). With increasing digitalisation, the widespread availability of information technology and its growing role in healthcare systems (Aziz, 2017), health informatics is likely to play an important role in the delivery of healthcare services (Oak, 2007). Further, health informatics can significantly reduce the cost of healthcare services and improve quality (Luna, 2014). Two important reasons that argue in favour of the evolution of health informatics in India are as follows:

(i) India's significant digital transformation due to increased penetration of the internet, mobile telephony and rise of a tech-savvy generation (Subathra & Selvanathan, 2019).
(ii) Emergence of India as an Information Technology superpower.

2.2 COVID-19, the outpatient consultation crisis and the need for health informatics

The current COVID-19 pandemic is the single biggest health, socioeconomic, financial, cultural and technological disrupter of the century (Scott, 2020). India is one of the worst-hit countries by the pandemic (Worldometer, 2021). The pandemic exposed the limitations of the physical health infrastructure in dealing with such health emergencies (Chetterje, 2020). Hence, when the country was hit with COVID-19, it triggered an outpatient consultation crisis. Multiple factors, such as lockdown, inability to seek outpatient consultation due to the contagious nature of the disease, quarantine of COVID-positive patients and inability to seek logistics for travel, led to this. With COVID-positive patient numbers reaching as high as 400,000 cases per day (Worldometer, 2021), outpatient consultations became a challenge for both COVID and non-COVID patients. The current physical infrastructure, burdened with the COVID-19 onslaught, was unable to fulfil these needs. This led to a pressing need for alternative solutions for delivering not just outpatient consultations but also holistic health services including diagnostics and medicines.

2.3 Digital health innovations and start-ups in India

On 1 July 2015, the Government of India launched the Digital India campaign which laid foundation to strong digital infrastructure in the country

(Ministry of Electronics and Information Technology, 2019). In last 5 years, we have witnessed strong digital transformation in the country leading to rapid growth of e-commerce in India. Increase in mobile and internet penetration coupled with online transaction processing is leading to e-commerce boom in the country (Subathra *et al.*, 2019).

The COVID-19 crisis pushed the government to legalise telemedicine by revolutionising the practice of medicine (Agarwal *et al.*, 2020). As a result, during the lockdown, a significant number of patients switched to telemedicine and availed of doctor consultations from the comfort of their home (Mabiyan, 2020). The health informatics group, C-DAC, Mohali, India, has developed India's flagship telemedicine technology — eSanjeevani (esanjeevaniopd, 2021). eSanjeevani has completed more than 1.4 crore consultations till date (Ministry of Health and Family Welfare, 2021). In addition, during the lockdown, E-pharmacies served a whopping 6 million new customers at their doorstep (Mishra, 2020). The National Digital Health Mission's (NDHM) ambitious Health ID project (ANI, 2020) and digital health ecosystem extensively employ the use of health informatics (Ministry of Health and Family Welfare, 2019). The increased thrust on digitalisation in healthcare has created huge opportunities for start-ups in India. Start-ups like Medlife, Netmeds, Pharmaeasy and 1mg grabbed this opportunity and led to the foundation of the E-pharmacy business in India by launching their E-pharmacy platforms. The E-pharmacy business which currently contributes 1% (Sunny & Anand, 2019) will account for 15–20% of total pharma sales in the near future (Frost & Sullivan, 2019) and is expected to grow at CAGR of 33.95% during 2019–2024 (Business Wire, 2020). The COVID-19 pandemic has turned out to be a blessing in disguise for telemedicine and E-pharmacies. Big retail conglomerates like Amazon and Reliance have already sensed the opportunity and taken the first steps towards entering the market. Amazon has started its pilot testing of E-pharmacy in Bangalore (Ahmed, 2020), whereas Reliance has launched Jio Health, the telemedicine start-up, and acquired Netmeds, the E-pharmacy start-up (Sharma & Peermohamed, 2020). As of writing this, there are many start-ups such as Healthplix, Practo and Apollo which have launched their dedicated tele-health services.

3. Methodology for Developing Conceptual Framework

The authors of this study have adopted mixed methods involving two-step processes. First, a literature review was conducted using the keywords "Digital health ecosystems", "Health ecosystems", "Digital health systems", "E-health systems", "Health informatics" and "Health informatics in India". To identify articles, the authors used Web of Science and Google Scholar. After conducting a literature review, the authors used an auto-ethnographical approach (Kemppainen *et al.*, 2019) to arrive at a conceptual framework for typology of medical consumers and HDHSs.

The authors chose auto-ethnography as a method because it is unique and compelling. It enables the authors to work with insider knowledge and allows the authors to do and present qualitative work (Jones *et al.*, 2013; Rashid, 2015). This study builds on the authors' deeper insights about the topic of study (Myers, 1997) based on the authors' experience in the Indian health and retail pharma ecosystems.

Insights have been gathered from the authors' experience with the Indian health and retail pharma ecosystem comprising 33,000 Indian physicians, more than 15,000 brick-and-mortar pharmacies, 2000 pharmaceutical stockists, 40 carry and forwarding agents, leading E-pharmacies and organised retail pharma chains. In addition, the authors also have extensive experience of dealing with numerous medical consumers. Based on insights gathered over a period of 12 months, the authors have proposed a conceptual framework about the types of medical consumers and HDHSs.

4. Conceptual Framework for Types of Medical Consumers

The medical consumer is unique and different from a commodity consumer since the buying process for a patient is entirely different. Unlike a routine buying process, the need for a medicine for the patient is decided by his treating physician. Hence, the medicine buying process starts with a prescription from a treating physician and is refilled by the pharmacist (Figure 1).

Digital health innovations such as Telemedicine and E-pharmacies are now leading a major change in consumer behaviour. E-pharmacies are transforming the "medical consumer to the digital medical consumer".

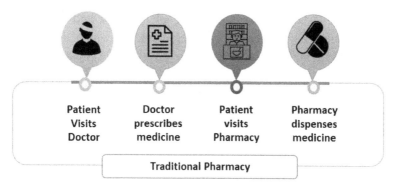

Figure 1. The prescription refilling process by offline pharmacy store for a medical consumer.

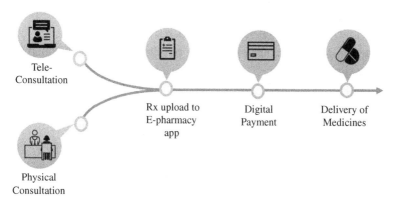

Figure 2. The consultation and prescription refilling process for a Digital Medical Consumer.

4.1 *Digital Medical Consumer (DMC)*

The recent legalisation of telemedicine is leading the way towards increasing the use of digitalisation for health services delivery. Telemedicine, coupled with E-pharmacies and increasing penetration of mobile phones and the internet, has led to the transformation of "the medical consumer to the digital medical consumer" (Figure 2).

The key behavioural changes for a Digital Medical Consumer (DMC) include the use of digital media for online consultation without the need to visit a clinic, online ordering of medicine from the comfort of one's home or office and electronic payments for the same.

The behavioural changes initiated by telemedicine and E-pharmacies are significant. The key benefits of telemedicine which also apply to E-pharmacies include reduced need to physically visit a clinic/store, reduction in the travel time and costs, increase in convenience, greater ease of access and reduced waiting time at doctor's clinic/store. Also, they do not disturb one's daily routine (Limor, 2018; Sarker *et al.*, 2019). Another change which E-pharmacies are ushering in is increasing the price sensitivity of the medical consumer.

4.2 Price-Sensitive Medical Consumer (PSMC)

Traditionally, once a medicine is prescribed by a physician, the local retail store will refill it at an MRP fixed by the government. Since, the pharmaceutical market is a price-regulated market (Motkuri & Mishra, 2020), discounts on MRPs are not practically possible. However, E-pharmacies are using discounts as well as lower cost of products as a mode of customer acquisition.

With reduced setup cost, higher bargaining power and direct purchases from pharma companies, E-pharmacies are offering discounts ranging from 10% to 20% on medicines. From a retail sales perspective, this is unconventional since the trade margins for retail pharmacies are capped at 16–20% (NPPA, 2018). Such high discounts for customer acquisition clearly disrupt the existing ecosystem as consumers tend to expect similar discounts from offline pharmacies as well. The organised pharmacies to an extent have the potential to match the E-pharmacies. However, this clearly impacts the viability of brick-and-mortar pharmacies. The ethical issues associated with such a practice of discounts in a price-regulated market are a separate topic of discussion.

Another way of increasing price sensitivity is by offering lower-priced products. The Indian market largely sells branded generic medicines having multiple brands from various companies. E-pharmacy mobile apps display the alternative brands priced lower. They also offer a valid method of substitution by modifying prescriptions with the help of registered medical practitioners. In contrast, the offline pharmacies with inherent limitations in terms of ability to offer discounts and inability to offer economical alternatives (primarily due to stringent regulations, limited digitalisation and the need for doctor's consent for substitution) cannot really compete with E-pharmacies on these accounts.

The emergence of the earlier two new classes of medical consumers will segment medical consumer classes into three categories, i.e., Traditional Medical Consumer (TMC), Digital Medical Consumer (DMC) and Price-Sensitive Medical Consumer (PSMC). The determinants for the buying decision-making process for each class of consumer are illustrated in Figure 3.

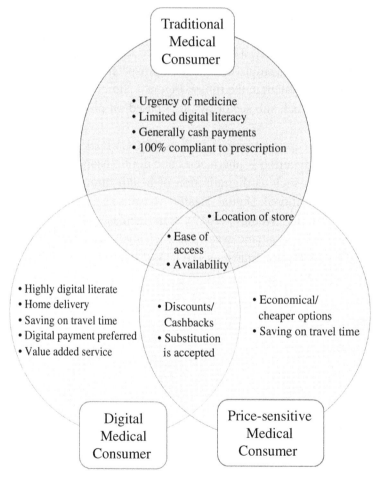

Figure 3. The determinants for the buying decision-making process for a Medical Consumer.

If we look at the key determinants for making buying decisions for each class of medical consumer, most of the determinants are unique and well differentiated from each other. Each medical consumer segment drives predominantly one sector of the retail pharma ecosystem, i.e., the traditional medical consumer drives the unorganised sector, the Price-Sensitive Medical Consumer is attracted towards the organised sector and E-pharmacies where he has a higher possibility of getting medicines at a lower cost, and the digital medical consumer is more likely to buy medicines online. There are exceptions to this categorisation. The two major exceptions are urgency of treatment and nature of disease as detailed further in the chapter.

This segmentation has a high significance since the percent change in these classes will determine the business prospects of sub-sectors of the retail pharma ecosystem in the future. Figure 4 shows the likely change in market share of each sub-sector by 2024 based on projected CAGRs for each sub-sector.

However, exceptional factors, such as the COVID-19 pandemic, regulatory changes favouring E-pharmacies and digital health services as well as policy drivers such as digitalisation of health through the Health ID project of the National Digital Health Mission (NDHM) (Ministry of Health and Family Welfare, 2019), can increase the penetration of E-pharmacies in a dramatic way. These changes will also give rise to Holistic Digital Health Start-ups (HDHSs), consisting of telemedicine

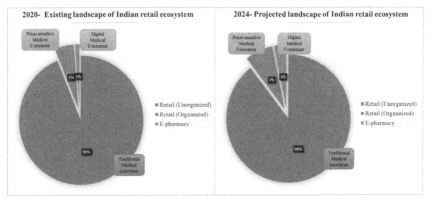

Figure 4. Projected MS% movement for sub-sectors of retail pharma.

and E-pharmacies as integral parts of the network, which will impact the way digital health ecosystems will work in the future.

5. Digital Health Ecosystems

Evolving diseases like COVID-19 have constantly highlighted the need for holistic and integrated health services. To deliver these health services, the current health systems are not sufficient since they lack a multi-disciplinary approach needed for management of patients (Serbanati *et al.*, 2010). Under these circumstances, health informatics can bridge the gap and provide holistic solutions including management of home recovery (Serbanati *et al.*, 2010). Across the world, multiple digital health service models have been postulated. These include mobile health (mHealth), electronic health (eHealth) and personalised health (pHealth) to name a few. The models aim to transform the way health services are provided (Ruotsalainen & Blobel, 2020).

5.1 *Definition of digital health ecosystem*

Hadzic & Chang (2010) define the digital ecosystem as follows:

> *"Dynamic and synergetic complex of digital communities consisting of inter- connected, interrelated, and interdependent DS situated in a DE that interact as a functional unit and are linked together through actions, information, and transaction (AIT) flows."*

Ruotsalainen & Blobel (2020) believe, "In Digital Health Ecosystem, health care and health information systems are highly dynamic and fully distributed. Thereby, health information is dynamically collected, used and distributed between its members (stakeholders)" (Ruotsalainen & Blobel, 2020).

In a nutshell, the purpose of a digital health ecosystem is to integrate multiple stakeholders under one roof in such a holistic manner that patient-centric services can be provided by multi-disciplinary teams. To achieve this purpose, health informatics will play the role of a catalyst. This will give rise to HDHSs.

5.2 Conceptual framework for Holistic Digital Health Start-ups (HDHSs)

Digital transformation has far-reaching implications on new value propositions, business model innovation, and the ability to seamlessly integrate all the stakeholders across ecosystems (Svadberg *et al.*, 2019). The authors postulate two possible HDHSs evolving in the near future.

5.2.1 Health ID-based HDHSs

Health ID is expected to be the central repository for healthcare records. This will also become the starting point for digital delivery of health services (Ministry of Health and Family Welfare, 2019). In the Health ID-based HDHSs, patients can consult a treating physician through either a teleconsultation or physical consultation using electronic health records. Health ID will capture the prescription of a treating physician in the form of an electronic medical record (EMR). The prescription thereafter can automatically be uploaded to the registered E-pharmacy of the patient's choice. Post invoice generation, the digital payments would be processed either through a cashless facility of insurance or through electronic payments. Subsequently, the medicines will be delivered at the patient's doorstep (Figure 5).

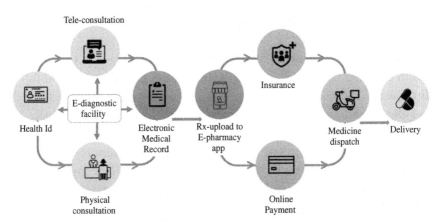

Figure 5. Health ID-based HDHSs.

5.2.2 *Corporate-driven HDHSs*

The private corporates operating either in the E-pharmacy business, tele-consultation services or the EMR industry are well placed to create corporate-driven HDHSs. While the corporate HDHSs evolve, we are likely to witness *vertical and horizontal acquisitions* of companies necessitated by corporate HDHSs (Figure 6).

The beauty of the HDHS platforms is that they work very well for diseases which do not require physical consultation or when the speed of delivery of medicine is not a concern, such as medicines for chronic diseases like diabetes. In such cases, certain percentage of patients will surely move to HDHS platforms since they are beneficial to the patients.

5.3 *The value proposition of HDHSs*

According to Meier (2013), digital transformation helps achieve cost savings, facilitates healthcare effectiveness and can optimise resource allocation. The push for digitalisation in health and the emergence of DMC along with telemedicine and E-pharmacies are transforming the healthcare sector, which we have never seen before. This transformation will impact the business of certain therapeutic segments faster than others. In this section, we have analysed the value proposition of HDHSs.

5.3.1 *HDHS evolution through the telemedicine window*

Consultation requirements can be classified on the basis of the nature of diseases: diseases which require physical consultation versus diseases

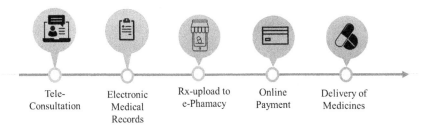

| Tele-Consultation | Electronic Medical Records | Rx-upload to e-Phamacy | Online Payment | Delivery of Medicines |

Figure 6.   Example of corporate HDHSs.

which can be managed using teleconsultation. This classification is primarily dependent on the nature and duration of the disease. Chronic diseases mainly include therapies relating to non-communicable diseases such as diabetes and hypertension, whereas acute therapies include anti-infectives and pain management therapies.

Chronic care diseases are generally long-lasting or in some cases they are lifelong, e.g., diabetes, and the medicine consumption in such cases is for a longer duration. This has significance because the annual burden due to the cost of medication for such diseases is high and the refilling of prescriptions is on a monthly basis. In India, almost 35% of households have one or more family members suffering from NCDs. Moreover, the out-of-pocket expenses on medications for NCDs are to the tune of 69% (Bhojani *et al.*, 2012). For diseases like diabetes, India is considered the capital of the world with the highest number of patients (Shashank *et al.*, 2007).

Telemedicine, which is legalised in India now, is highly suitable for patients with NCDs. The consultation for NCDs especially diabetes and hypertension can easily happen based on either lab reports or home monitoring of glucose or blood pressure. A digital medical consumer can easily book a sample collection online, lab reports are shared online followed by online consultations with a physician. It is imperative that what follows is online purchase of medicine. In addition, the benefit of discounts matters the most since the duration of treatment is long and cost of treatment is high. In addition, for diseases like COVID-19 where a patient is confined to home isolation one has no choice but to use digital health services.

On the other hand, unlike chronic therapy, acute care treatment is generally short term and limited till the cure of the disease, e.g., viral fever, where the duration of treatment generally lasts 5–7 days and the cost of the treatment is generally low; however, the urgency of treatment is very high. The same is true with the pain management segment. In addition, in these cases, physical consultation is largely necessary, ruling out teleconsultation. Hence, the first thing a patient requires is immediate availability of medicine. Moreover, in many cases, the shipping charges are higher than acute treatment and the time taken to deliver medicines is more than the entire duration of treatment. This makes E-pharmacies completely unviable for acute care therapy. Acute care also includes cases of surgical intervention and emergency including hospital stay, where the role of telemedicine and E-pharmacies becomes very minimal.

The prevalence of chronic diseases is almost 55%, which means the USD 280 billion healthcare industry offers huge opportunities for HDHSs which can offer comprehensive health services to this class of patients.

5.3.2 *HDHS evolution through the E-pharmacy window*

The pharmaceutical supply chain in India is a 4-level supply chain before medicines reach a patient. Pharmaceutical manufacturers supply medicines to stockists through the CFAs (clearing and forwarding agents). These stockists then supply the medicines to retailers (chemists) who eventually sell them to patients. The USD 18 billion turnover of the retail pharma market is calculated at PTR (price to retailer). The economics of supply are illustrated in Figure 7.

The likely vertical and horizontal integration in the E-pharmacy sector is threatening to disrupt the whole traditional supply chain. The possible future scenario is likely to give birth to an entirely different, probably shortened supply chain model. This model will be lean, involving direct

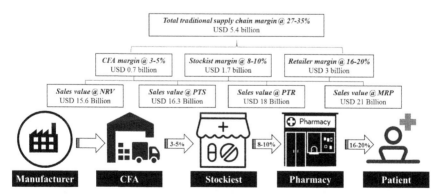

Figure 7.   Economics of traditional supply chain.

Note: NRV: net realised value, PTS: price to stockiest, PTR: price to retailer, MRP: maximum retail price.

supplies from manufacturers to E-pharmacies, reducing it to just one level of supply chain. This means the entire 35% supply chain margins will be available to E-pharmacies. This proves an important point that digital technologies can be instrumental in reducing a company's transaction costs and can help incentivise key stakeholders in the ecosystem (Valdez-De-Leon, 2019). In addition, volumes of sale will give E-pharmacies bargaining power to negotiate rates with manufacturers, which can result in additional discounts in the range of 5–7%, increasing their profits margins up to 40%. These margins will be double in contrast to the brick-and-mortar pharmacy trade margins of 16–20% (Figure 8).

These E-pharmacies with a strong value proposition can adopt multiple strategies for backward integration, which may include setting up one's own manufacturing unit, acquiring manufacturing units or contract manufacturing which will further increase their profitability. This in turn will provide E-pharmacies a strong platform to transform their business into holistic digital health start-ups. A few E-pharmacies like Pharm-easy have taken this route by adding e-laboratories to their service. In addition, they are contemplating the addition of telemedicine, thereby providing all the services under one roof.

HDHSs will offer three significant benefits to patients: affordability, availability and accessibility. As far as affordability is concerned, out-of-pocket expenses are a major barrier for availing health services and towards compliance of the prescribed medications. The impact of OOP

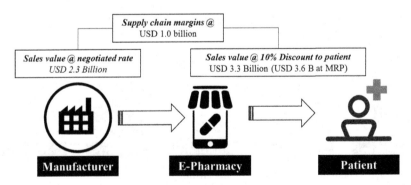

Figure 8.   Economics of E-pharmacy supply chain at estimated turnover of USD 3.6 billion (2024).

expenses of chronic diseases is much lower than acute diseases (New England Healthcare Institute, 2009). The scale of economies and higher margins of HDHSs can help start-ups acquire more consumers by offering discounts, cashbacks or other benefits such as free lab tests or free consultations. In the future, we may even see a comprehensive treatment package being rolled out for customer acquisition by HDHSs. Our analysis shows that HDHSs are likely to gain significantly from the chronic care segment.

6. Conclusion

The never seen before COVID-19 crisis has posed serious challenges for India. These include availability, accessibility and affordability of health services to everyone. Currently, the physical health infrastructure is being tested to its core. These problems require an innovative solution which digital health services can provide. Amid the COVID-19 pandemic, digitalisation across the healthcare industry has penetrated significantly in the form of telemedicine, E-diagnostics and E-Pharmacy. Internet-savvy citizens have embraced these newer technological platforms and this has led to the transformation of a medical consumer into some newer subsets, i.e., Digital Medical Consumer (DMC) and Price-Sensitive Medical Consumer (PSMC) along with the existing category of Traditional Medical Consumer (TMC).

The authors also anticipate the evolution of HDHSs as a result of the government push towards digitalisation in health, the government's willingness to create a digital health infrastructure and the emergence of digital medical consumers. Health informatics will play a significant role in transformation of the Indian health ecosystem and the evolution of the digital health ecosystem. Hence, the authors have proposed a conceptual framework for HDHSs which is ready to implement and can make a meaningful contribution towards supporting and delivering health.

Moreover, the authors believe these changes will have a significant impact on the economic value proposition of holistic digital health start-ups. This chapter has also tried to highlight the impact of HDHSs on chronic and acute therapy which will be really intriguing to see in the near future.

References

Abanmy, N. (2017). The extent of use of online pharmacies in Saudi Arabia. *Saudi Pharmaceutical Journal*, *25*(6), 891–899. https://doi.org/10.1016/j. jsps.2017.02.001.

Agarwal, N., Jain, P., Pathak, R., & Gupta, R. (2020). Telemedicine in India: A tool for transforming health care in the era of COVID-19 pandemic. *Journal of Education and Health Promotion*, *9*(1), 190. https://doi.org/10.4103/jehp. jehp_472_20.

Ahmed, Y. (2020). Amazon to deliver medicines through online pharmacy in Bengaluru. *India Today*. https://www.indiatoday.in/technology/news/story/ amazon-to-deliver-medicines-through-online-pharmacy-in-bengaluru-1711188-2020-08-14.

ANI (2020). PM Modi announces launch of National Digital Health Mission. *ETHealthworld.Com*. https://health.economictimes.indiatimes.com/news/ health-it/pm-modi-announces-launch-of-national-digital-health-mission/ 77558158.

Apollo Hospitals Enterprise Limited (2020). Annual report 2019–20. Apollo Hospitals Enterprise Limited. https://www.apollohospitals.com/corporate/ investor-relations/annual-reports.

Aziz, H. A. (2017). A review of the role of public health informatics in healthcare. *Journal of Taibah University Medical Sciences*, *12*(1), 78–81.

Bhojani, U., Thriveni, B. S., Devadasan, R., Munegowda, C. M., Devadasan, N., Kolsteren, P., & Criel, B. (2012). Out-of-pocket healthcare payments on chronic conditions impoverish urban poor in Bangalore, India. *BMC Public Health*, *12*(1), 1–13. https://doi.org/10.1186/1471-2458-12-990.

Business Wire (2020). Pharmacy retail market in India 2019. *Business Wire*. https://www.businesswire.com/news/home/20200221005348/en/Pharmacy-Retail-Market-in-India-2019---Featuring-Apollo-Pharmacies-Emami-Frank-Ross-Global-Healthline-Private-Medlife-Among-Others---ResearchAnd Markets.com.

Chetterje, P. (2020). Gaps in India's preparedness for COVID-19 control. *Lancet Infectious Diseases*, *20*(5), 544. doi:10.1016/S1473-3099(20)30300-5.

Desai, C. (2016). Online pharmacies: A boon or bane? *Indian Journal of Pharmacology*, *48*(6), 615. https://doi.org/10.4103/0253-7613.194865.

eSanjeevaniOPD (2021). Retrieved November 21, from https://esanjeevaniopd.in/.

Frost and Sullivan. (2019). In the spotlight: e-Pharmacy in India An Exponential Growth Opportunity. *Frost and Sullivan*. https://ww2.frost.com/wp-content/ uploads/2019/01/Frost-Sullivan-Outlook-on-e-pharmacy-market-in-India. pdf.

Hadzic, M. & Chang, E. (2010). Application of digital ecosystem design methodology within the health domain. *IEEE Transactions on Systems, Man, and Cybernetics-Part A: Systems and Humans, 40*(4), 779–788.

Halan, D. (2020). Impact of COVID-19 on online shopping in India. *ETRetail. Com.* https://retail.economictimes.indiatimes.com/re-tales/impact-of-covid-19-on-online-shopping-in-india/4115.

Herting, A. M. & Lennart Schmidt, A. (2020). A systematic analysis of how practitioners articulate business models across disruptive industries. *Technology Innovation Management Review, 10*(10), 29–42. https://doi.org/10.22215/timreview/1394.

IBEF (2020a). Healthcare industry in India. India Brand Equity Foundation. https://www.ibef.org/industry/healthcare-india.aspx.

IBEF (2020b). Indian pharmaceutical industry. India Brand Equity Foundation. https://www.ibef.org/industry/pharmaceutical-india.aspx.

Imhoff, M. (2001). Health informatics. *Intensive Care Med, 27*, 179–186.

Jadhav, R. (2020). 52% of India's allopathic doctors are practising in just 5 states. *Businessline.* https://www.thehindubusinessline.com/news/52-of-indias-allopathic-doctors-are-practising-in-just-5-states/article3122 7994.ece.

Jones, H. S., Adams, T. E., & Ellis, C. (2013). *Handbook of Autoethnography*, 1st ed. New York, USA: Routledge. https://doi.org/10.4324/978131542 7812.

Kastor, A. & Mohanty, S. K. (2018). Disease-specific out-of-pocket and catastrophic health expenditure on hospitalization in India: Do Indian households face distress health financing? *PLOS ONE, 13*(5), e0196106. https://doi.org/ 10.1371/journal.pone.0196106.

Kemppainen, L., Pikkarainen, M., Hurmelinna-Laukkanen, P., & Reponen, J. (2019). Data access in connected health innovation: Managerial orchestration challenges and solutions. *Technology Innovation Management Review, 9*(12), 43–55. https://doi.org/10.22215/timreview/1291.

Legaldocs (2018). How to start a medical store in India? Legaldocs. https://legaldocs.co.in/blog/how-to-start-a-medical-store-in-india.

Limor, W. (2018). Telemedicine trends to watch in 2018. telemedicine.arizona. edu. The University of Arizona. https://telemedicine.arizona.edu/blog/telemedicine-trends-watch-2018.

Luna, D., Almerares, A., Mayan, J. C., de Quirós, F. G. B., & Otero, C. (2014). Health informatics in developing countries: Going beyond pilot practices to sustainable implementations: A review of the current challenges. *Healthcare Informatics Research, 20*(1), 3–10.

Mabiyan, R. (2020). COVID-19 lockdown 2.0: Telemedicine in India to see continued growth. *ETHealthworld.Com.* https://health.economictimes.indiatimes.com/news/health-it/covid-19-lockdown-2-0-telemedicine-in-india-to-see-continued-growth/75172147.

Meier, C. (2013). A role for data. *American Journal of Preventive Medicine, 44*(1), S5–S11. https://doi.org/10.1016/j.amepre.2012.09.018.

Ministry of Electronics and Information Technology. (2019). India's trillion-dollar digital opportunity. *Ministry of Electronics and Information Technology.* https://www.meity.gov.in/writereaddata/files/india_trillion-dollar_digital_opportunity.pdf.

Ministry of Health and Family Welfare (Statistics Division) (2019). Rural health statistics. https://main.mohfw.gov.in/sites/default/files/Final%20RHS%20 2018-19_0.pdf.

Ministry of Health and Family Welfare (2021). https://pib.gov.in/Press ReleaseIframePage.aspx?PRID=1764724.

Ministry of Health and Family Welfare (2019). National digital health blueprint. https://ndhm.gov.in/home/ndhb.

Mishra, D. (2020). High sales, health focus make e-pharmacy hot. *The Times of India.* https://timesofindia.indiatimes.com/business/india-business/high-sales-health-focus-make-e-pharmacy-hot/articleshow/77709805.cms.

Motkuri, V. & Mishra, R. N. (2020). Pharmaceutical market and drug price policy in India. *Review of Development and Change, 25*(1), 30–53. https://doi.org/10.1177/0972266120929146.

Myers, M. D. (1997). Qualitative research in information systems. *MIS Quarterly, 21*(2), 241. https://doi.org/10.2307/249422.

New England Healthcare Institute. (2009). Thinking outside the pillbox. *New England Healthcare Institute.* https://www.nehi.net/writable/publication_files/file/pa_issue_brief_final.pdf.

NPPA. (2018). What margins are allowed to a Wholesaler and a retailer as per DPCO, 1995? *Official Website of National Pharmaceutical Pricing Authority, Ministry of Chemicals and Fertilizers, Government of India.* http://www.nppaindia.nic.in/en/faq/what-margins-are-allowed-to-a-wholesaler-and-a-retailer-as-per-dpco-1995/.

Oak, M. (2007). A review on barriers to implementing health informatics in developing countries. *Journal of Health Informatics in developing countries, 1*(1), 19–22.

Prachi, S. (2018). India's healthcare woes: Out-of-pocket medical expense pushed 55 million into poverty in 2017, says PHFI study. *Firstpost.* https://

www.firstpost.com/india/indias-healthcare-woes-out-of-pocket-medical-expenses-pushed-55-million-into-poverty-in-2017-says-phfi-study-4773741. html.

Rashid, M., Caine, V., & Goez, H. (2015). The encounters and challenges of ethnography as a methodology in health research. *International Journal of Qualitative Methods, 14*(5), 160940691562142. https://doi.org/10.1177/1609406915621421.

Ruotsalainen, P. & Blobel, B. (2020). Health information systems in the digital health ecosystem — Problems and solutions for ethics, trust and privacy. *International Journal of Environmental Research and Public Health, 17*(9), 3006.

Sarker, S. K., Bhas, G., Paul, R., Pal, H., Yusuf, M. A., & Eva, E. O. (2019). E-pharmacy utilization on the spectrum of digital pharmaceutical practices, patterns and challenges in Bangladesh. *Journal of Shaheed Suhrawardy Medical College, 11*(1), 43–47. https://doi.org/10.3329/jssmc.v11i1.43178.

Saurabh, P., Bhowmick, B., Amrita, & Biswas, D. (2012). Developmental impact analysis of an ICT-enabled scalable healthcare model in BRICS economies. *Technology Innovation Management Review, 2*(6), 25–31. https://doi.org/10.22215/timreview/565.

Scott, J. (2020). The economic, geopolitical and health impacts of COVID-19. World Economic Forum. Retrieved October 25, 2020 from https://www.weforum.org/agenda/2020/03/the-economic-geopolitical-and-health-conse-quences-of-covid-19/.

Serbanati, L. D., Ricci, F. L., Mercurio, G., & Vasilateanu, A. (2011). Steps towards a digital health ecosystem. *Journal of Biomedical Informatics, 44*(4), 621–636.

Sharma, S. & Peermohamed, A. (2020). Reliance retail acquires majority stake in Netmeds' parent for Rs 620 crore. *The Economic Times.* https://economictimes.indiatimes.com/small-biz/startups/newsbuzz/reliance-retail-acquires-majority-stake-in-netmeds-parent-for-rs-620-crore/articleshow/77625176.cms?from=mdr.

Shashank, J. & Rakesh, P. (2007). India — Diabetes capital of the world: Now heading towards hypertension. *The Journal of the Association of Physicians of India, 55*, 323–324. https://www.researchgate.net/publication/5995205_India_-_Diabetes_capital_of_the_world_Now_heading_towards_hypertension.

Srivastava, M., & Raina, M. (2020). Consumers' usage and adoption of e-pharmacy in India. *International Journal of Pharmaceutical and Healthcare*

Marketing, Vol. ahead-of-print (No. ahead-of-print). https://doi.org/10.1108/ IJPHM-01-2020-0006.

Statista Research Department (2020). Estimated number of public and private hospitals across India in 2019. *Statista.* https://www.statista.com/statistics/ 1128425/india-number-of-public-and-private-hospitals-estimated.

Subathra, C. & Selvanathan, S. (2019). Digitalisation in India (No. 978-93-87756-86–1). *Mayas Publication.* https://www.capeforumyoutrust.org/ assets/Publicationspdf/DIGITALISATION%20IN%20INDIA%20%20-%20 Jul%202019.pdf.

Sunny, S. & Anand, K. (2019). Current status of e-pharmacy in India: 2019 review. *Pharmatutor.* https://www.pharmatutor.org/articles/current-status-of-e-pharmacy-in-india-2019-review.

Svadberg, S., Holand, A., & Breunig, K. J. (2019). Beyond the hype: A bibliometric analysis deconstructing research on digitalization. *Technology Innovation Management Review, 9*(10), 38–50. https://doi.org/10.22215/timreview/1274.

Valdez-De-Leon, O. (2019). How to develop a digital ecosystem — A practical framework. *Technology Innovation Management Review, 9*(8), 43–54. https://doi.org/10.22215/timreview/1260.

Worldometer (2021). Retrieved May 4, 2021 from https://www.worldometers. info/coronavirus/.

Chapter 11

A Study of Perspectives on the Growth, Strategy and Branding in Indian MSMEs

Amol Randive[*,‡], Jayashree Vispute[*,§] and Shailendra Goswami[†,¶]

Vishwakarma University, Pune, Maharashtra, India
†Pushkaraj Group, Pune, Maharashtra, India
‡amol.randive@vupune.ac.in
§jayashree.vispute@vupune.ac.in
¶svg1091@gmail.com

Abstract

Growth of small firms into medium ones and medium-scale ones into large-scale enterprises is as important as creation of new ventures; but very few enterprises in the Indian economy grow vertically rather than horizontally due to external and internal factors (Raju, 2019). "Most firms are by definition, small: They start small, have a slim-to-fair chance of survival and if they do survive, they invariably remain small", concludes Fadahunsi (2012). The branding and strategy are essential for market success and sustainability of enterprises (ET Contributors, 2018).

The objectives of this study are (1) to understand how entrepreneurs perceive business growth; (2) to assess their strategic orientation in managing enterprises; and (3) to understand the role of branding in the growth of enterprises. Some of the growth-related aspects covered in this study are critical success factors for enterprise growth, challenges faced by Indian MSMEs and alternate Growth Models from all over the world. This is followed by the best practices in marketing and branding including entrepreneurial marketing, branding initiatives and digital marketing.

In order to comprehensively understand the perspectives, researchers have chosen qualitative methods. The literature largely includes 74 selected sources including peer-reviewed journals, government reports, and publications by renowned consulting firms. The real-life information is sourced using Focus Group Discussions, with 28 MSME owners as participants. The constructs used by previous researchers in various strategic orientation scales will be referred to better understand the orientation of enterprises.

This study provides insights on best practices in growth, strategy and branding as shared by the owner-managers and relevant literature from across the globe. Theoretical implications of the study include better identification of key variables in enterprises growth, effectiveness of alternate strategic orientations and value of branding initiatives. The practical implications of this study include more relevant inferences for Indian enterprises with respect to their growth strategies for MSME owner-managers.

Keywords: MSME growth, strategic orientation, entrepreneurial marketing, business strategies, innovation, branding initiatives and Indian MSMEs

1. Introduction

The growth of small firms serves as a critical measure of success and performance (Odoom, 2016), as firms create value as they grow (Vaz, 2021) and it is essential to further study the factors affecting growth of MSMEs (Vaz, 2021; Kamunge *et al.*, 2014). "MSME sector has come up as a dynamic and highly vibrant sector of the India's economy over the last five decades", as reported by the Ministry of MSMEs (2019); this sector is considered as the backbone of country's economy, as stated by Manikandan & Dhameja (2016). The three crucial functions are enhanced entrepreneurship, higher productivity and boosting employment (World Bank, 2004). Now, it is imperative that India's MSMEs demonstrate greater competitiveness (Banerjee, 2020). There are about 63.05 million micro industries, 0.33 million small and about 5000 medium enterprises in the country (Rastogi, 2019). According to Ayyagari *et al.* (2005), the term SME covers a wide range of definitions, measures and criteria across countries and organisations. The Reserve Bank of India also supports this view, as mentioned in the RBI Report (2019). The most common measures for scale of organisations are number of employees, sales turnover, profits and fixed assets. Across the globe, MSMEs are known by names like Small Businesses (USA, Germany), Small Firms, Small Enterprises, Small and Medium Industries (Korea), Small and Medium-sized Enterprises (SMEs), Small-Scale Industries (India, in the past), Township and Village Enterprises or TVEs (China), and Micro, Small and Medium Enterprises (EU, India, Japan).

Some of the characteristics of MSMEs are as follows: more than 90% of global enterprises are MSMEs (Sandhu & Azhar, 2019); small enterprises are not merely miniature versions of large firms (Burns, 2001); they are largely influenced by the immediate business environment (Krake, 2005); they constitute a heterogeneous group across the goods and service sector (Krake, 2005); these enterprises are known for entrepreneurial spirit and innovative nature (Sharma *et al.*, 2017); these contribute significantly to Asian economies (Asian Development Bank Institute, 2016); deregulation of economies is exposing such enterprises to increasing competition (UNIDO, 2017); these enterprises do not behave the same as large enterprises while responding to the environment (Resnick *et al.*, 2016); they differ from large enterprises with unique aspects like resource limitations, lack of funds, dependence on small number of customers and requirement of multi-skilled workforce (Forsman, 2008); they are perceived as high-risk enterprises (Raju, 2019); their size makes it more profitable to operate in a niche market which might not be that appealing for large players (Bjerke & Hultman, 2002); and their flexibility and closeness to customers are their biggest strengths (Kenny & Dyson, 1989).

Some of the drawbacks of MSMEs are as follows: MSMEs suffer from constraints induced by their size, called size-induced market failures (Asian Development Bank Institute, 2016); they struggle while moving through growth phases due to constraints in the local environment (Meyer & Meyer, 2017); they operate in a more challenging environment due to market failures (European Commission, 2015); they have several internal constraints like sociological, financial, human resource and technological challenges; they have to deal with issues like formalisation, access to knowledge, less competitiveness and marketing problems; unlike large firms, they have limited marketing funds (Weinrauch, 1991); general management is also one of the challenges of MSMEs (Huang & Brown, 1999); and some other challenges of MSMEs are poor infrastructure facilities, technological obsolescence, cumbersome regulatory practices and poor adaption to international trends (Banerjee, 2020).

Although half of the MSMEs have mentioned sales as the major challenge (A&A Business Consulting, 2019), plenty of India's local brands with greater impact have an international reputation and are therefore not considered small (Kapferer, 2002). It is widely accepted that marketing is a strategic tool for success and sustenance, yet a major weakness for MSMEs (Sudhakar *et al.*, 2017). MSMEs lack expertise in technology adoption, product development and marketing strategy (RBI, 2019). In these firms, emphasis is on product and search for low-cost marketing tactics (Spence & Essoussi, 2014). "Given the high failure rate of SMEs, it becomes vital to research the factors required to enable the SMEs to survive and indeed progress to the growth phase of the organisational life cycle", highlight Kamunge *et al.* (2014). Strategic thinking has implications on business performance (Blanchard, 2020). "In the absence of a unified theory of small business growth, models and approaches used to explain small business growth are fragmented and wide-ranging", asserts Fadahunsi (2012). There are diverse theories related to MSME growth given the lack of consensus on measures and factors of growth (Achtenhagen *et al.*, 2010).

According to Coad (2009), growth advantages of firms include satisfied employees with more challenging work and greater rewards, fulfilment for managers, lower production costs, deterred entry to competitors, spreading the risk, basis for security, sometimes growth is a more suitable metric of performance than profits, better alternatives for investment and avoiding taxes by investing profits. Disadvantages of growth include perceived loss of control by owner-managers as more people join, problems of coordination, risk of failure in new initiatives, risks of diversification, larger firms are less adaptable and less responsive, less motivating environment for employees in large firms, more routinised methods through professional managers, certain size thresholds in respective countries and loss of certain incentives. The different kinds of strategic orientations highlighted by Laukkanen *et al.* (2013) include entrepreneurial orientation, learning orientation, brand orientation and market orientation. "Strategic planning promotes forward-thinking, reduces the attention to operative details, and provides meaning for identifying and evaluating strategic alternatives that improve the performance of organizations", state Aguilera-Castro and Virgin-Ortiz (2016).

"The growth of small firms is a particularly erratic phenomenon", states Coad (2009). There is a need to define, measure and study business growth in a way that is relevant and meaningful for entrepreneurs-practitioners (Achtenhagen *et al.*, 2010). Hence, this study is an attempt to get closer to MSME sector reality based on literature review, Focus Group Discussions and Strategic Orientation assessment based on globally accepted scales. There are differences in the growth patterns of small firms (when compared with large firms) as follows: their entry rate is high across industries and also the failure rate in initial years (Coad, 2009); only a small portion of those are real innovators (Santarelli & Vivarelli, 2006); overconfidence and escape from unemployment are major reasons to start businesses (Coad, 2009); they enter at a small scale compared with incumbents (Bartelsman *et al.*, 2005); they tend to thrive in sub-markets that are not large enough (Penrose, 1959); competitive pressure is one of the major factors affecting their growth (Hay & Kamshad, 1994); survival of small firms depends on their growth; and they seem to have firm-specific productivity levels which can be limiting at times (Jovanovic, 1982).

2. Literature Review

2.1 *Growth*

Evidence-based reasons for long-term research on small businesses are as follows (Storey, 1994): (1) emphasis in small firms is on immediate solutions; (2) interests of business owners and society do not always coincide; (3) the small business sector is diverse, complex and evolving; (4) provides inputs for policymaking; and (5) provide researchers with the opportunity to make theoretical as well as empirical contributions. Most of the existing work on small business growth is based on the factor model (Fadahunsi, 2012); and contrary to common intuition, the same factors may not be responsible for business growth and survival (Fadahunsi, 2012).

Business growth and survival are two different aspects. In fact, the measures to assess both are different. Growth as the objective may not be applicable for all small and medium businesses, but survival is (Fadahunsi, 2012). "It has been argued that due to differences between industries, turnover offers a more neutral measure of growth that is especially useful when the analysis is not limited to a particular industry", state Helen *et al.* (2015). "In India, capital incentives were extended in relation to the size of the enterprise. Once the thresholds were crossed, enterprises were setting up either new enterprises or associated enterprises in order to milk the incentives. Thus, horizontal growth instead of vertical growth occurred perpetuating the small to think small, remain small and argue for small", states Raju (2019).

According to Churchill & Lewis (1983), key management factors in business growth are related to the company, such as financial resources, personnel resources, systems resources and business resources, and related to the owner, such as owner's goals, operational ability, managerial ability and strategic abilities. Vaz (2021), based on the extensive literature review of 165 articles, classified the determining factors for firm growth in three blocks: firm's internal factors, entrepreneur's idiosyncratic features and factors external to firm. "Sustained growth depends on how broadly you define your business — and how carefully you gauge your customers' needs. Every major industry was once a growth industry. But some that are now riding a wave of growth enthusiasm are very much in the shadow of decline. Others that are thought of as seasoned growth industries have actually stopped growing. In every case, the reason growth is threatened, slowed or stopped is not because the market is saturated", emphasises Levitt (1960). Blanchard (2020) summarises, "Research has also proven that by adopting a strategy, aims can be achieved and turnover increased".

Sales (or revenue) is the most commonly used measure of growth globally, followed by number of employees and then assets (Achtenhagen *et al.*, 2010). Other growth measures are growth willingness/growth intention, combination of earlier measures, growth strategies and value added. A comprehensive list of measures is as follows: absolute employee growth, absolute sales growth, employee growth rate, net profit margin, return on equity, return on assets, growth in firm value, sales from new customers, sales from new products/services and sales from new markets. The difference between size and growth was operationalised by Whetten (1987), as he notes "size is an absolute measure, whereas growth is a relative measure of size over time". Increase in amount of something, be it sales, turnover, profits, employees, plants, offices, etc., continues to dominate the entrepreneurship field (Achtenhagen *et al.*, 2010). Other perspectives on growth are qualitative, referring to process improvements, with or without tangible increase in quantity/size.

As written by Penrose in 1959, "Fundamentally dynamic vision of firms holds that firm growth is led by an internal momentum generated by learning-by-doing. Managers become more productive over time as they become accustomed to their tasks. Executive functions that initially posed problems because of their relative unfamiliarity soon become routinised. As managers gain experience, therefore, their administrative tasks require less attention and less energy. As a result, managerial resources are continually being released. This excess managerial talent can then be used to focus on value-creating growth opportunities". According to Marris's work published in 1963 and 1964, "The fundamental observation of the 'managerial' theory of the firm is that managers attach utility to the size of their firms. A manager's compensation, bonuses, and other perquisites are very often increasing with firm size. Furthermore, non-pecuniary incentives such as prestige, likelihood of promotion, social status, and power are also associated with firm size. As a result, firm size (and firm growth) are seen to be important factors in the 'managerial utility function', alongside the financial performance of the firm".

As per Hannan & Freeman's work on population ecology published in 1977, "The basic theoretical prediction pertaining to the growth of organisations is that these latter require resources which are specific to niches, and these niches have a particular 'carrying capacity'. If a firm has discovered a new niche with a rich resource pool, then this firm will be able to grow without hindrance. The number of firms in the niche will also grow, due to entry of new organisations. If the population grows to a level where the niche's resource pool is saturated, however, then competition between firms will limit the growth rates of firms".

2.2 Strategy

Some perspectives on firm growth view it as passion accumulation and absorption of opportunities, while others view it as intentional and strategic in nature (Coad, 2009).

Alternative growth strategies for small enterprises are as follows:

- Replication (grow simply by doing more of the same thing).
- Diversification (This relies on the managerial capacity and talent).
- Internal growth (wherein the firm grows organically).
- Growth by acquisition (most preferred while entering into new sector or market).

Growth strategies for strategic development according to the Ansoff Matrix (Ansoff, 1957) are as follows:

- Market penetration (increase sales of existing products in existing market).
- Market development (increase sales of existing products in unexplored market).
- Product development (launch of new products in existing market).
- Diversification (marketing of a completely new product in unexplored market).

Generic strategies for organisations as per Porter (1985) are as follows:

- Cost leadership (all or most market segments are targeted with the least price).
- Differentiation (all or most market segments are targeted with factors other than price).
- Focus (few or one market segment is targeted with focus on either cost or differentiation).

Market Expansion Strategies as listed by Ayal & Zif (1979) are as follows:

- Market diversification (implies fast penetration into a large number of markets).
- Market concentration (concentration of resources in few market and gradual expansion).

Key determinants of firm growth, as summarised by Coad (2009), in his work, "The Growth of Firms: A Survey of Theories and Empirical Evidence", are age, innovation, financial performance, relative productivity, ownership structure, legal status, management characteristics, human capital, nature of firm's activity, industry-specific factors and macroeconomic factors.

2.3 *Branding*

"Market orientation and brand orientation lead to enhanced market performance. Higher growth intention results into greater brand orientation", state Reijonen *et al.* (2014). Keller (1998) proposed that brand strategy is not just for large enterprises, and offered some contradictory suggestions for branding in small businesses. Benefits of branding for MSMEs include competitive differentiator, referral generation, staff motivation and recognition (Bassi, 2017). "SMEs' owner-managers tend to simplify the use of the brand instruments and synthesise the various brand procedures", states Tavares (2015). "Branding can assist SMEs to ensure sustained growth and ultimately its survival, however many struggles to integrate it into other daily business operations and build a reputable brand", mention Cant *et al.* (2013). Some of the popular Brand Development Models relevant for MSMEs are Krake's Brand Development Model for SME; "Readiness-Initiatives" Matrix proposed by Banerjee & Dasgupta (2009); SME Branding Conceptual Framework by Raki & Shakur (2018); and the five phases of SME brand-building by Centeno *et al.* (2013). The top ten branding challenges as identified by Aaker (2015) are "to treat brands as assets; have a compelling vision; create new subcategories; generate breakthrough brand building; achieve integrated marketing communications; sort out a digital strategy; build the brand internally; maintain brand relevance; create a brand-portfolio strategy yielding synergy and clarity; and leverage brand assets to enable growth". Hence, it is important to deliberate on the need for comprehensive understanding of alternate perspectives of entrepreneurs in branding.

Dumitriu *et al.* (2019) state, "Among some of the main components of digital marketing that after their implementation may result in a customer action that ultimately can get profitable for an SME are: Search Engine Marketing (SEM) and Search Engine Optimisation (SEO), Content Marketing (CM), Social Media Marketing (SMM), Pay-per-click (PPC), with the most used tools being Google AdWords (recently rebranded as Google Ads) and Social Networks Ads, Pay-per-sale (PPS), Affiliate Marketing (AM) and E-mail marketing (EM)". The Internet offers a vast number of opportunities (Bresciani & Eppler, 2010), and social media offers plenty of services (Srinivasan *et al.*, 2016). It is important to leverage on the online attention received by such enterprises (ET Contributors, 2018). In the emerging market setting, social media can be a great strategic tool (Odoom *et al.*, 2017), and digital marketing impact is measurable (Jarvinen *et al.*, 2012). According to Tiago & Verissimo (2014), the benefits of digital firms for enterprises are as follows: "Improves information gathering and feedback, user-friendly tool, increases knowledge, promotes internal and external relationships, supports decision making process, increases productivity, and better outcome measurement". However, there is a fear of loss of existing customers who are not online (Kithinji, 2014).

3. Research Methodology

The objectives of the study, fulfilled through primary and secondary data analysis, mainly cover entrepreneurs' perception of business growth, their strategic orientation as they manage ventures, the perceived role of branding initiatives in success, influencing factors in the Indian context and best practices.

This study is based on the qualitative methods. Overall, it is exploratory and descriptive in nature. The data used in the study include both secondary as well as primary data. The coverage of the literature is global in nature, whereas the primary data are mainly from enterprises based out of Pune, India.

3.1 *Comprehensive literature review*

The literature review part of the study included 74 sources selected by the researchers. The literature review method followed here is as follows: (1) selecting key words and search terms; (2) browsing titles and abstracts to select relevant articles; (3) coding articles; and (4) identifying emerging themes in the literature. The presentation of literature in this study is of a thematic nature. The literature coverage is as follows:

Source type: As far as type of source is concerned, publications/sources include around 52% journal papers, 14% journal reports, 15% books, 10% reports and 9% other sources like articles in a periodical and websites.

Publication year: The earliest publication considered in this study is from 1952 and the latest is from 2021. 17 of these sources were published in or before 2000, while 17 were published between 2001 and 2010, 14 published between 2011 and 2015 and 26 published between 2016 and 2021.

Geography: Around 20% sources are focused on India, while another 20% are of a global nature. Other regions and countries include Asia, Bangladesh, Canada, Europe, Finland, Hungary, Ghana, Kenya, Malaysia, Nairobi, the Netherlands, Pakistan, Portugal, Romania, South Africa, South Carolina, Switzerland, the UK and the USA.

3.2 *Systematic conduction of Focus Group Discussions (FGDs)*

In order to uncover attitudes and assumptions, well-organised Focus Group Discussions (FGDs) were conducted with around 10 business owners in each group. The guidelines provided by Richard A. Krueger (2002) regarding setting the venue, setting ground rules, leading the group and wrapping up the discussion were followed. The questions included introductory questions, probing questions, follow-up questions and exit questions on the theme. The researchers had defined FGD statements/questions to be presented as per the plan for 90 min. The questions included perspectives on the current state of MSMEs across different sectors in India; comments on the role of branding in growth of enterprises;

marketing-branding in small and medium enterprises versus large enterprises; take on promotion of brands/products versus promotion enterprise/organisation; criteria to measure business growth; factors influencing branding initiatives of business enterprises; best practices in MSME branding; viewpoints on the relevance, use and RoI of digital marketing for MSMEs; and remarks on how MSME brands can be managed better.

3.3 *Use of strategic orientation scales*

The Brand Orientation measure scale is adopted from studies by Odoom *et al.* (2018), Muhonen *et al.* (2017) and Helen *et al.* (2015); Customer Orientation scale and Competitor Orientation scale from the study by Khan *et al.* (2016); and Entrepreneurial Orientation scale from the study by Helen *et al.* (2015).

3.4 *Key factors in research on MSMEs*

Key factors highlighted in Odoom *et al.* (2018), Berthon *et al.* (2008) and Odoom *et al.* (2017) are as follows: years in business, sectors in business, firm ownership, number of employees, annual revenue, the nature of products on offer and use of digital marketing tools.

4. Analysis: Based on Literature Review (Tables 1–3)

Table 1.   Determining factors in firm growth

Entrepreneur	Internal	External
1. Motivation	1. Vision and mission	1. Political
2. Education	2. Objective	2. Economic
3. Experience	3. Strategic planning	3. Sociocultural
4. Age	4. Age	4. Technological
5. Risk propensity	5. Size	
6. Optimism and self-confidence	6. Sector	
7. Gender and race	7. Location	
8. Personal and professional networks	8. Legal form	
9. Number of founders	9. Human resources	
	10. Financial resources	
	11. Organisational structure	

Source: Authors' elaboration based on work of Vaz (2021).

Table 2. Growth models (phases) for enterprises

Authors	Focus	Growth Phases	
Churchill & Lewis (1983)	Growth stages and drivers	I.	Existence — growth through leadership
		II.	Survival — growth through direction
		III.	Success — growth through delegation
		IV.	Take-off — growth through coordination
		V.	Resource maturity — growth through collaboration
Joseph W. McGuire	Economic development	I.	Traditional small company
		II.	Planning for growth
		III.	Take-off or departure from existing conditions
		IV.	Drive to professional management
		V.	Mass production marked by a "diffusion of objectives and an interest in the welfare of society"
Lawrence L. Steinmetz	Business survival	I.	Direct supervision
		II.	Supervised supervision
		III.	Indirect control
		IV.	Divisional organisation
Roland Christensen and Bruce R. Scott	Development of organisational complexity	I.	One-unit management with no specialised organisational parts
		II.	One-unit management with functional parts such as marketing and finance
		III.	Multiple operating units, such as divisions, that act on their own behalf in the marketplace
Larry E. Greiner	Corporate evolution	I.	Growth through creativity
		II.	Growth through direction
		III.	Growth through delegation
		IV.	Growth through coordination
		V.	Growth through collaboration

Source: Authors' elaboration.

5. Data Analysis

5.1 *Profile of Focus Group Discussion participants/enterprises*

- *Type of business*: Both manufacturing and services.
- *Number of employees*: 2 to 10 (53%), 11 to 50 (28%), 51 to 200 (15%) and 201 to 500 (5%).

Table 3. Prominent characteristics of MSMEs w.r.t. marketing and branding

Theme	Point of View
Comparison with large enterprises	a. Conventional principles cannot be fully applied in MSME context (Berthon *et al.*, 2008). b. Widely used academic definitions related to marketing are not always useful for SMEs (Resnick *et al.*, 2016). c. Big difference in the marketing expertise and financial resources (Resnick *et al.*, 2016).
Growth and strategy	d. Key factors for growth and survival of enterprises are strategic positioning and marketing (Walsh & Lipinski, 2009). e. Getting through various growth phases, SME owner-managers experiment with diverse marketing techniques becoming good at accommodating those practices (Carson & Gilmore, 2000). f. Many MSMEs have a not-so-clear strategy related to effective sales promotion as they lack knowledge and resources for it (RBI, 2019).
Resources and approach	g. Marketing is at the core of successful MSMEs and largely depends on the owner's ability to market their products and services (Rabie *et al.*, 2015). h. Limited marketplace impact and lack of the specialist expertise are other challenges for MSMEs (Carson, 1985). i. "Can be seen as a somewhat unnecessary luxury due to the lack of resources, time and the need for short term decisions", state Kenny & Dyson (1989). j. "Intuition and the need of finding solutions are more evident in small firms than scientific marketing models", mention Bjerke & Hultman (2002).
Strengths and differentiators	k. "SME marketing in practice is thought to be largely done though networking; a combination of transaction, relationship, interaction and network marketing; through the use of Internet marketing or e-commerce", state Banerjee & Dasgupta (2009). l. "SMEs strong points include — flexibility, speed of reaction and the eye for (market) opportunities", states Krake (2005). m. "Brand owners take centre stage in the starting and developing stages of brand building as they are involved in the creation and developing of each one of the brand identities dimensions and brand activities involved in the process", state Centeno *et al.* (2013).

Source: Authors' elaboration.

- *Average annual turnover for last 3 years in crores*: Less than 1 (29%), 1 to 5 (53%), 6 to 10 (9%) and 11 to 50 (9%).
- *Years since establishment*: 2 to 5 (19%), 6 to 10 (52%), 11 to 20 (19%) and 21 to 40 (10%).
- *Customers by geography*: Equal number of enterprises having customers spread across the globe, nation-wide and within the state of Maharashtra, India.
- *Customer types*: Industrial/Corporate (48%), Multiple segments (29%), Retail and Household (19%), and All types (4%).
- *Registration status*: Partnership (10%), Private Limited (48%), Sole Proprietorship (38%) and other (4%).
- *Entrepreneurial experience in years*: 1 to 10 (53%), 11 to 20 (43%) and 21 to 40 (4%).
- *Education profile of respondents*: Graduation (48%) and postgraduation (52%).

5.2 *Strategic orientation of enterprises*

Strategic orientation of enterprises is measured using a scale. The scale used is strongly disagree (1) to strongly agree (7).

The MSMEs that participated in the focus group discussions have greater customer orientation and also brand orientation. They seem to have fairly good entrepreneurial orientation as well. However, their competitor orientation is less in degree and is reflected in the average scope as mentioned in Table 4.

Table 4.   Strategic orientation of enterprises

Strategic Orientation	Average out of 7
Brand orientation	5.79
Customer orientation	5.99
Competitor orientation	4.29
Entrepreneurial orientation	5.52

Source: Prepared by authors based on responses of entrepreneurs.

5.3 Perspectives as shared by the owner-managers

5.3.1 Perspectives on growth

While expressing this concern about succession, one of the participants said, "Succession planning is a challenge, as kids travel abroad or to better places". Motives of founding members also play a role in growth over time. One of the participants said, "Some people start business out of compulsion like pressure from family, need for additional income, or unemployment. While others start with a plan".

Several viewpoints discussed in the FGDs are listed as follows:

* Digitisation and automation are also crucial for industry 4.0, and in turn for scale-up and growth.
* Succession to next generation of leadership is considered as one of the critical issues for these enterprises.
* Being satisfied and content is not enough and not okay. If you do not grow, you might fail.
* Companies that are doing well need to invest in structure and processes.
* Entrepreneurs should be in a position to come out of business — to do something else or to do something better.
* Financial management and accounting are a major concern and weakness.
* In some enterprises, growth focus is missing.
* Inner fire of the entrepreneur, capabilities of the team and vision to think big make a difference.
* Survival becomes easy with growth.

While discussing the role of intent, one of the participants said, "Some organizations decide to remain small and remain so happily, may be being happy is their aim". One of the participants threw some light on the aspect of limitation of technical entrepreneur and stated that "entrepreneurs who are technically sound, tend to spend more time on product and production, but seems to be averse for financials and accounting".

5.3.2 *Perspectives on strategy*

"Change is inevitable, irrespective of size", said one of the participants while emphasising the need for strategy and changes. Stressing on the need for sustainability planning, one of the participants said, "Businesses should plan for sustainability right from the beginning". While discussing growth limiting factors, one of the participants said, "Many business owners have tendency to keep themselves busy in either sales or delivery. Need to invest time and money for improvement". The following are some perspectives on strategy:

- Mindset, toolset and skillset are critical success factors for business success.
- Entrepreneurs should institutionalise success or what has worked for them (replicability).
- Emphasis should be on market presence and market relevance.
- Not taking risk is the riskiest thing.
- Digitalisation is playing a role in the growth of MSMEs. Digitisation begins with capturing and storing right data. The next step is analysing it.

5.3.3 *Perspectives on branding initiatives*

While highlighting the lack of brand orientation among Small and Medium Enterprises, one of the participants said, "Branding has been largely ignored by MSMEs. Need to improve branding awareness among entrepreneurs. Need to look at brand as investment and not cost". The following are some perspectives on branding initiatives:

- Mostly, websites do not depict what is done currently because of no content update.
- Entrepreneurs get impatient about results of branding.
- There is limited PR effort as they are busy with routine and internal matters.
- Trends are important. Differentiators promote brands.
- A brand, once established, helps in numerous ways.

- Brand value also comes with risk and responsibility.
- The brand story has to be inside out driven by vision and values. Clarity and focus help.
- Keeping aside budget for branding helps.
- Some traditional ad methods are still relevant.
- Branding is applicable for all enterprises irrespective of their newness.

5.3.4 *Perspectives on how marketing-branding in small and medium enterprises differs from that of large enterprises*

- Large enterprises understand the difference between marketing and branding. Many of the MSMEs lack this clarity.
- MSMEs do not have to worry about the budget. Reputation and credibility matter.
- It is not just about spending on promotion; customer experience, quality and positioning matter.
- Choice of medium is critical.
- Large enterprises understand and focus on that uniqueness. Their plans are customer and market specific and not generic ones.
- The investment on branding depends on project requirements and funding scenario. Budget need not be the starting point.
- Large enterprises perceive a brand as an investment.
- A brand is made in the customers' mind and market, not in the office or factory.
- Branding should be outward looking and innovation matters.
- Some participants believe branding is more important to large players.
- Because of lack of delegation of work and sometimes lack of a capable team, entrepreneurs spend less time on branding and marketing.

5.3.5 *Perspectives on promotion of brands/products versus promotion enterprise/organisation*

- Some participants believe in starting with a product and consider it to be a gradual process. One said that starting big and branding from the beginning help. For some companies, company brand drives things. Many of them believed that company sustenance depends on product or series of products. Participants believe that the service sector scenario if different as they are dealing with more intangibles.

- One of the participants said, "Product has a fixed life, but company lasts longer", while giving more importance to organisation branding. While another member emphasised, "Product brand matters the most".

5.3.6 Perspectives on how growth can be measured better

- Some of the common criteria covered here include turnover, customer retention, repeat business by clients, customer satisfaction, market penetration, new customers and customer feedback.
- The participants mentioned new age criteria like search ranking, profit per client, customer referrals, customer reviews, social media followers and lifestyle improvement.
- Some of the interesting and futuristic criteria identified by participants include scalability, structure effectiveness, systems maturity, happiness of employees, responsiveness to market needs and societal impact.

5.3.7 Perspectives on factors that influence branding initiatives of enterprises

- Organisational factors discussed by the participants are as follows: values, growth ambitions, priorities and assumptions.
- Entrepreneur-related factors include personality, involvement in operations, passion or lack of it, and awareness about branding.
- Execution-related factors covered here are target audience, past experience with branding initiatives, identifying creation issues and timing of branding investments.
- Participants also mentioned external factors that influence branding.

5.3.8 Highlight of the focus group discussions

One of the participants summarised five common factors for the success of existing Indian small- and medium-scale firms that have witnessed growth:

1. *Vision*: Vision enables scouting for ideas; a larger scale and a bigger size make people think differently; they operate like a big enterprise,

even if they are small; they are always planning and preparing for a larger scale; vision need not be explicit or expressed, but it is always there at the back of the mind; and such entrepreneurs have a mental map to move forward.

2. *Process driven*: They work in a structured way; they are method driven, ready to scale up; they assume the same business functions and systems are essential irrespective of the business scale; and they are conscious of what they are doing and the repercussions on the whole thing.

3. *Superior business talent*: These entrepreneurs have "level 3 capability". Level 1 is about managing technology, level 2 is about managing people and level 3 is about managing environment, stakeholders and external factors.

4. *Governance*: Control becomes difficult with scale; governing a business is more important than building one; and the management control system plays a big role.

5. *Business idealism*: They are idealists; they have conviction about their work; they are concerned about the impact of their work, more than mere money and success; and their inner fire drives them.

6. Findings

- The factors related to the entrepreneur (such as passion, motive, vision and capabilities) and organisation (such as digitisation, succession planning, structure and financial management) are considered relatively more important for business growth.
- As far as strategic orientation of enterprises in concerned, customer orientation is the top most followed by brand orientation, entrepreneurial orientation and competitor orientation.
- Some of the new-age growth measures/criteria are search ranking, profit per client, customer referrals, customer reviews, social media followers and lifestyle improvement.
- Entrepreneurs seem to be relying on replicability (repeating the success to new markets and new products) as a growth strategy for the scale-up.
- When compared with large enterprises, MSMEs are assumed to have disadvantages like budget constraints, team capabilities and market limitations.

- Branding is not mainstream for most of the enterprises as it is not looked at as an investment and long-term activity, unlike large enterprises.
- The founders' vision, positive intent, institutionalised processes and team capabilities are important critical success factors for small and medium enterprises.
- One of the common things in discussions and research is lack of awareness, be it about schemes, tools or growth avenues.

7. Conclusion

The challenges seem to be different for different kinds of enterprises depending on the industry, sector, stage in the life cycle, market scenario and internal environment. The intent of enterprises/entrepreneurs to grow and the follow-up actions to build capabilities are crucial. With the evolving business environment, growth dynamics and strategic options are also evolving for enterprises. The contextual decisions seem to be more relevant and rewarding, both in the literature review and focus group discussions. Small and medium enterprises could benefit more from entrepreneurship-related guidance and coaching. A study of branding from an economics perspective will allow practitioners to benefit from the pros of the oligopoly market structure. In the long run, to a larger extent, branding is an attempt to establish oligopoly. Monopoly is difficult to achieve and perfect competition has more limitations. The enterprises seem to be more biased towards digital tools and social media branding. However, some have expressed caution w.r.t. limitations of the same, both in the literature and focus group discussion. The critical success factors are different for businesses depending on a variety of factors like industry/sector, stage of enterprise in the life cycle, external environment, market scenario, geographic presence and other internal dimensions. The strategies for small and medium enterprises need to be unique given their uniqueness when compared with large enterprises, as well as their content based on key factors such as entrepreneur (variables relating to the founders), enterprise (enterprise-related internal factors) and environment (macro-environment dimensions). The results of branding for a particular enterprise are influenced by the approach, objectives, investment, tools used and overall brand management. Considering all this, the diverse perspectives on each of the matters at hand, i.e., growth, strategy and branding, seem to be the reality of such a diverse MSME sector in India.

8. Implications

The implications of the research are as follows: (i) Unified theory on small business growth is likely to remain outside reach, as mentioned by Dobbs & Hamilton (2007). (ii) There seems to be an opportunity to build sector-specific theories, by limiting the variables and having more focus on relevant dynamics.

The implications for the practitioners are as follows: (i) Although it is not ideal to consider all the best things from other sectors, it will be helpful to understand best practices and adapt appropriately. (ii) Branding can be practised at several levels and these levels can coexist, like personal brand of entrepreneur, product brand, enterprise brand and product category brand. (iii) It is essential to clearly define what growth means to a particular entrepreneur/enterprise, industry/sector and product/services before jumping to strategy formulation.

9. Scope for Further Research

1. There is opportunity to evolve frameworks applicable for diverse industry sectors for measuring business growth, as supported by Fadahunsi (2012).
2. Most of the current work is of a descriptive nature and there is an opportunity to look at predictive models on small firm growth.
3. Considering the diverse perspectives on growth, there seems to scope for further research on the right size or optimal size for enterprise.

References

A&A Business Consulting (2019). Nationwise India SME Survey 2019 — Impact of current economic challenges on SMEs. Retrieved April 11, 2020 from https://www.aaconsulting.co.in/survey-report/survey-report-format.pdf.

Aaker, D. (2015). *Aaker on Branding: 20 Principles That Drive Success.* New Delhi: SAGE Publications.

Achtenhagen, L., Naldi, L., & Melin, L. (2010). Business growth — Do practitioners and scholars really talk about the same thing? *Entrepreneurship Theory and Practice, 34*, 289–316.

Aguilera-Castro, A. & Virgen-Ortiz, V. (2016). Model for developing strategies specific to SME business growth. *Entramado, 12*(2), 30–40.

Ansoff, H. I. (1957). Strategies for diversification. *Harvard Business Review, 35*(5), 113–124.

Asian Development Bank Institute (2016). SMEs in developing Asia — New approaches to overcoming market failures. Asian Development Bank Institute, Tokyo. Retrieved April 11, 2020 from https://www.adb.org/sites/default/files/publication/214476/adbi-smes-developing-asia.pdf.

Ayyagari, M., Beck, T., & Demirgüç-Kunt, A. (2005). Small and medium enterprises across the globe. World Bank, Draft Paper.

Banerjee, C. (2020). Redefining MSMEs will give the sector a boost. Retrieved April 11, 2020 from https://www.thehindubusinessline.com/opinion/redefining-msmes-will-give-the-sector-a-boost/article30505802.ece.

Bartelsman, E., Scarpetta, S., & Schivardi, F. (2005). Comparative analysis of firm demographics and survival: Evidence from micro-level sources in OECD countries. *Industrial and Corporate Change, 14*(3), 365–391.

Bassi, P. (2017). Role of branding in SMEs and their challenges in India. *Biz and Bytes, 8*(1), 110–121.

Berthon, P., Ewing, M., & Napoli, J. (2008). Brand management in small to medium-sized enterprises. *Journal of Small Business Management, 46*(1), 27–45.

Bjerke, B. & Hultman, C. M. (2002). *Entrepreneurial Marketing: The Growth of Small Firms in the New Economic Era.* Cheltenham: Edward Elgar Publishing Ltd.

Blanchard, K. (2020). Innovation and strategy: Does it make a difference! A linear study of micro & SMEs. *International Journal of Innovation Studies, 4*(4), 105–115.

Bresciani, S. & Eppler, M. (2010). Brand new ventures? Insights on start-ups branding practices. *Journal of Product and Brand Management, 19*(5), 356.

Burns, P. (2001). *Entrepreneurship and Small Business: Start-up, Growth and Maturity*, 4th ed. UK: Red Globe Press.

Cant, M. C., Wiis, J. A., & Hung, Y. T. (2013). The importance of branding for South African SMEs: An exploratory study. *Corporate Ownership and Control, 11*(1), 35–44.

Carson, D. & Gilmore A. (2000). Marketing at the interface: Not 'what' but 'how'. *Journal of Marketing Theory and Practice, 8*(2), 1–8.

Centeno, E., Hart, S., & Dinnie, K. (2013). The five phases of SME brand-building. *Journal of Brand Management, 20*, 445–457.

Churchill, N. C. & Lewis, V. L. (1983). The five stages of small business growth. *Entrepreneurial Management, 61*, 30–50.

Coad, A. (2009). The growth of firms: A survey of theories and empirical evidence. *New Perspectives on the Modern Corporation.* UK: Edward Elgar Publishing Limited.

Dobbs, M. & Hamilton, R. T. (2007). Small business growth: Recent evidence and new directions. *International Journal of Entrepreneurial Behaviour and Research, 13*, 296–322.

Dumitriu, D., Militaru, G., Corina Deselnicu, D., Niculescu, A., & Popescu, M. A.-M. (2019). A Perspective over modern SMEs: Managing brand equity, growth and sustainability through digital marketing tools and techniques. *Sustainability, 11*, 2111.

ET Contributors (2018). Small in size, large in ambition: Marketing strategies to help build a brand. *The Economic Times.* https://economictimes.indiatimes.com/small-biz/marketing-branding/marketing/small-in-size-large-in-ambition-marketing-strategies-to-help-build-a-brand/articleshow/65382354.cms?from=mdr.

European Commission (2015). User guide to the SME definition. Retrieved April 11, 2020 from https://op.europa.eu/en/publication-detail/-/publication/79c0ce87-f4dc-11e6-8a35-01aa75ed71a1.

Fadahunsi, A. (2012). The growth of small businesses: Towards a research agenda. *American Journal of Economics and Business Administration, 4*(1), 105–115.

Forsman, H. (2008). Business development success in SMEs: A case study approach. *Journal of Small Business and Enterprise Development, 15*(3), 606–622.

Hannan, M. T. & Freeman, J. H. (1977). The population ecology of organizations. *American Journal of Sociology, 82*(5), 929–964.

Hay, M. & Kamshad, K. M. (1994). Small firm growth: Intentions, implementation and impediments. *Business Strategy Review, 5*, 49–68.

Helen, R., Saku, H., Gábor, N., Tommi, L., & Mika, G. (2015). The impact of entrepreneurial orientation on B2B branding and business growth in emerging markets. *Industrial Marketing Management, 51*, 35–46. doi: 10.1016/j.indmarman.2015.04.016.

Huang, X. & Brown, A. (1999). An analysis and classification of problems in small business. *International Small Business Journal, 18*(1), 73–85.

Jovanovic, B. (1982). Selection and the evolution of industry. *Econometrica, 50*(3), 649–670.

Kamunge, M. S., Njeru, A., & Tirimba, O. I. (2014). Factors affecting the perfor-mance of small and micro enterprises in Limuru Town Market of Kiambu County, Kenya. *International Journal of Scientific and Research Publications*, *4*(12), 1–20.

Kapferer, J. N. (2002). Is there really no hope for local brands? *Journal of Brand Management*, *9*(3), 163–170.

Keller, K. L. (1998). *Strategic Brand Management: Building, Measuring, and Managing Brand Equity*. Upper Saddle River: Prentice Hall.

Kenny, B. & Dyson, K. (1989). *Marketing in Small Businesses*. Routledge: New York.

Khan, F. & Adnan, K. A. (2016). Brand orientation of small enterprises: A study based on apparels industry in Khulna City. *International Journal of Managing Value and Supply Chains (IJMVSC)*, *7*(1), 55–71.

Kithinji, L. W. (2014). Internet marketing and performance of small and medium enterprises in Nairobi County. School of Business, University of Nairobi, Masters Project.

Krake, F. B. G. J. M. (2005). Successful brand management in SMEs: A new theory and practical hints. *Journal of Product & Brand Management*, *14*(4), 228–238.

Krueger, R. A. (2002). *Designing and Conducting Focus Group Interviews*. United States: University of Minnesota.

Laukkanen, T., Nagy, G., Hirnoven, S., Reijonen, H., & Pasanen, M. (2013). The effect of strategic orientations on business performance in SMEs. *International Marketing Review*, *30*(6), 510–535.

Levitt, T. (1960 July–August). Marketing myopia. *Harvard Business Review*, *38*, 45–56.

Manikandan, S. & Dhameja, H. (2016). Micro, small and medium enterprises with special reference to start-ups. *Chavara IJBR*, *1*(1), 1–27.

Meyer, D. & Meyer, N. (2017). Management of small and medium enterprise (SME) development: An analysis of stumbling blocks in a developing region. *Polish Journal of Management Studies*, *16*(1), 127–141.

Ministry of Micro, Small and Medium Enterprises (2019). Annual report 2018–19. Retrieved April 11, 2020 from https://msme.gov.in/relatedlinks/annual-report-ministry-micro-small-and-medium-enterprises.

Muhonen, T., Hirvonen, S., & Laukkanen, T. (2017). SME brand identity: Its components, and performance effects. *Journal of Product & Brand Management*, *26*(1), 52–67.

Odoom, R. & Mensah, P. (2018). Brand orientation and brand performance in SMEs: The moderating effects of social media and innovation capabilities. *Management Research Review*. *42*(1), 155–171.

Odoom, R., Anning-Dorson, T., & Acheampong, G. (2017). Antecedents of social media usage and performance benefits in small- and medium-sized enterprises (SMEs). *Journal of Enterprise Information Management, 30*(3), 387–399.

Odoom, R., Narteh, B., & Boateng, R. (2016). Branding in small- and medium-sized enterprises (SMEs) — Current issues and research avenues. *Qualitative Marketing Research, 20*(1), 68–69.

Penrose, E. (1959). *The Theory of the Growth of the Firm.* Oxford: Basil Blackwell.

Porter, M. E. (1985). *Competitive Advantage. Creating and Sustaining Superior Performance.* New York: Free Press.

Rabie, C., Cant, M. C., & Wiid, J. A. (2015). Small and medium enterprise development: Do traditional marketing functions have a role to play? *Problems and Perspectives in Management, 13*(4), 79–84.

Raju, B. Y. (2019). *The Story of Indian MSMEs: Despair to Dawn of Hope.* India: Konark Publishers.

Raki, S. & Shakur, M. M. A. (2018). Brand management in Small and Medium Enterprises (SMEs) from stakeholder theory perspective. *International Journal of Academic Research in Business and Social Sciences, 8*(7), 392–409.

Rastogi, V. (2019). Micro, small, and medium enterprises in India — An explainer. *India Briefing,* September 4. Retrieved February 27, 2020 from http://www.asiabriefing.com/personnel/vasundhara-rastog.html.

Reserve Bank of India (2019). Report of the expert committee on micro, small and medium enterprises. Retrieved April 11, 2020 from https://www.rbi.org.in/Scripts/PublicationReportDetails.aspx?UrlPage=&ID=924.

Resnick, S. M., Cheng, R., Simpson, M., & Laurenco, F. (2016). Marketing in SMEs: A "4Ps" self-branding model. *International Journal of Entrepreneurial Behaviour and Research, 22*(1), 155–174.

Sandhu, M. S. & Azhar, T. M. (2019). Barriers to branding in SMEs: An exploration at surgical industry of Sialkot, Pakistan. *Paradigms, 13*(1), 134–142.

Santarelli, E. & Vivarelli, M. (2006). Entrepreneurship and the process of firms entry, survival and growth. *Industrial and Corporate Change, 16*(3), 455–488.

Spence, M. & Essoussi, L. H. (2014). SME brand building and management: An exploratory study. *European Journal of Marketing, 44*(7/8), 1037–1054.

Storey, D. (1994). *Understanding the Small Business Sector.* London: Routledge, Taylor & Francis Group.

Sudhakar, B. D., Nagarjuna, K., & Arokiara, D. (2017). Marketing assistance and digital branding — An insight for technology up-gradation for MSME's. *International Journal of Management Studies & Research, 5*(1), 180–185. SSRN: https://ssrn.com/abstract=3304456.

Tavares, V. M. (2015). Brand management in SMEs: Conceptualization of differences and research agenda. *European Journal of Applied Business and Management, 1*(1), 128–153.

Tiago, M. T. P. M. B. & Veríssimo, J. M. C. (2014). Digital marketing and social media: Why bother? *Business Horizons, 57*, 703–708.

UNIDO (2007). Approaches to SMEs networking for market access. Retrieved April 11, 2020 from https://www.unido.org/sites/default/files/2008-07/NETWORKING_ENG_0.pdf.

Vandana, S., Hetal, B., & Aja, S. (2017, March 21). Brand building challenges for MSME. SSRN: https://ssrn.com/abstract=3391702 or http://dx.doi.org/10.2139/ssrn.3391702.

Vaz, R. (2021). Firm growth: A review of the empirical literature. *Revista Galega de Economía, 30*(2), 7190.

Walsh, M. F. & Lipinski, J. (2009). The role of the marketing function in small and medium sized enterprises. *Journal of Small Business and Enterprise Development, 16*(4), 569–585.

Weinrauch, J. D. (1991). Dealing with limited financial resources: A marketing challenge for small business. *Journal of Small Business Management, 29*(4), 44–54.

Whetten, D. A. (1987). Organizational growth and decline processes. *Annual Review of Sociology, 13*, 335–358.

World Bank (2004). *"SME", World Bank Group Review of Small Business Activities*. Washington, DC: World Bank.

https://doi.org/10.1142/9789811269554_0012

Chapter 12

Factors Influencing Social Media Adoption by MSMEs: Using the UTAUT Model

Piali Haldar

Lexicon Management Institute of Leadership and Excellence,
Pune, Maharashtra, India
pialihaldar@gmail.com

Abstract

The purpose of this chapter is to identify the factors influencing Social Media (SM) adoption by Micro, Small and Medium Enterprises (MSMEs) to uphold their business using Unified Theory of Acceptance and Use of Technology Theory (UTAUT). The factors that influence the MSMEs to adopt SM are performance expectancy, effort expectancy, social influence and facilitating conditions. Data were collected through an online survey conducted in the National Capital Regions in India. A total of 338 participants who were owners or managers of business units provided useable responses. The data are collected using non-probability sampling. Data analysis was done using SPSS and AMOS. The findings of this research established that the UTAUT theory explains 63.3% of the variance towards intention to adopt SM in the context of MSMEs. The result of the study recognised that the variables such as performance expectancy, effort expectancy, social influence and facilitating conditions had positive and significant effects on intention to adopt SM apps among the owners and managers. Based on finding and results, theoretical and practical implications are provided for owner or managers of MSMEs.

Keywords: MSMEs, social media, UTAUT, India

1. Introduction

MSMEs are the driving force of our economic growth; they were highly affected by the pandemic crisis, but the business scenario is changing continuously and the country is moving towards a new normal. The penetration of social media (SM) has increased drastically in the post-pandemic era. The MSMEs are using SM to remain connected with customers, retailers, distributors and suppliers. The beauty of SM is that it is free; each user is a creator as well as user of information and ideas (Obar & Wildman, 2015). Consequently, SM has emerged as an effective marketing tool for MSMEs for improving the performance of an enterprise. According to Gama (2011), SM has come out as popular tool used by MSMEs for technical support for improving marketing performance because it is less expensive than traditional media. Previous research has established that MSMEs use SM for many reasons like marketing, internal and external communication, advertising, sales promotion, problem-solving, decision-making, customer relationship management, human resource management, social networks and internet marketing (Ainin, 2015; Surya *et al.*, 2020). Previous research has also established that SM has a significant effect on MSMEs in areas of performance (Ainin *et al.*, 2015; Musa *et al.*, 2016; Odoom *et al.*, 2017), knowledge management (Crammond, 2017), recruitment (L'Écuyer, 2019), knowledge creation and innovation (Papa *et al.*, 2018).

There have been some studies conducted on SMEs in developed countries such as Ireland (Durwin *et al.*, 2013), USA (Gavino *et al.*, 2018; Trainor, 2014; Nuseir, 2018) and the UAE (Ahmad *et al.*, 2018; AlSharji *et al.*, 2018), while very few studies have been conducted in developing countries such as Malaysia (Ainin *et al.*, 2015; Musa, 2016; Dahnil, 2014), Indonesia (Sarosa, 2012; Rozikin *et al.*, 2019) and India (Singh & Kalia, 2021). No one has used the Unified Theory of Acceptance and Use of Technology (UTAUT) model for predicting SM adoption among owners or managers in India. There are very few studies available on MSMEs' intention to adopt SM for business purposes. There is an urgent need to understand the adoption behaviours of owners and managers of MSMEs because in the post-pandemic era, the use of SM is growing steadily in the field of education, brand promotion and peer-to-peer communication. Thus, the purpose of this study is to fulfil the gap in this field of research. This paper aims to identify the factors influencing the adoption of SM by owners and managers of MSMEs with the UTAUT Model. The UTAUT theory considers that four factors, performance expectancy, effort expectancy, social influence and facilitating conditions, influence the adoption of SM.

For the current study, a widely accepted theoretical research framework, UTAUT Model, is proposed to understand the owners' and managers' intention to use SM, because the UTAUT theory was developed in an organisational context with four constructs: performance expectancy, social influence, effort expectancy and facilitating conditions.

2. Literature Review

UTAUT (Venkatesh *et al.*, 2003) was derived from eight of the most important technology acceptance theories: Innovative Diffusion Theory (IDT), Theory of Reasoned Action (TRA), the Model of PC Utilisation (MPCU), Theory of Planned Behaviour (TPB), Social Cognitive Theory (SCT), Technology Acceptance Model (TAM), Motivational Model (MM) and Combined TAN-TPB (C-TAM-TPB). The UTAUT model was proposed with four constructs to assess people's technology acceptance — performance expectancy, effort expectancy, social influence and facilitating conditions — and the original study explained 69% variance for behavioural intention to use technology. Thus, the UTAUT model will investigate the owners' and managers' intention to adopt SM.

Some recent studies use the UTAUT model to understand individuals' intentions to adopt mobile banking (Yu, 2012; Purwanto & Loisa, 2020), the e-learning system (Bellaaj *et al.*, 2015; Handoko, 2020), interactive whiteboards (Wong *et al.*, 2013), E-governance services (Alshehri *et al.*, 2012), electronic voting machines (Chauhan *et al.*, 2018), learning management systems (Moodle) (Raman *et al.*, 2014), blending learning (Khechine *et al.*, 2014), internet banking (Rahi *et al.*, 2019, 2018; Foon & Afah, 2010), MOOC (Wan *et al.*, 2020), information and communication (ICT) (Attuquayefio & Addo, 2014), open educational resources (OER) (Padhi, 2018), SM (Mandal & McQueen, 2012), mobile learning (Almaiah *et al.*, 2019), digital libraries (Orji, 2010) and electronic placement tests (Tan, 2013).

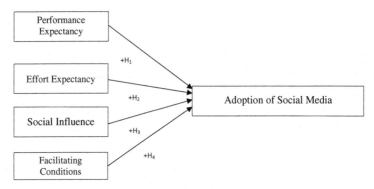

Figure 1.   Research framework of the study.
Source: Author's work.

Using the UTAUT theory, this paper develops a research framework to study the use of SM by owner and mangers in MSMEs. The underlying research model is presented in Figure 1.

2.1 *Performance expectancy*

Performance expectancy is defined as "the degree to which using a technology will provide benefits to consumers in performing certain activities" (Venkatesh *et al.*, 2012), which is the strongest predictor of behavioural intention (Venkatesh *et al.*, 2003). Performance expectancy is measured using similar constructs like perceived usefulness, extrinsic motivation and relative advantage from the Technology Acceptance Model (TAM), Motivational Model (MM) and Innovation Diffusion Theory (IDT), respectively. The MSMEs will use SM apps if they find them useful; they will also use SM for communication. Performance expectancy was used in previous studies to measure performance expectancy's positive effect on intention to use SM (Syaifullah *et al.*, 2021; Amril & Sari, 2019) in the context of MSMEs.

2.2 *Effort expectancy*

Effort expectancy is "the degree of ease associated with consumers' use of technology" (Venkatesh *et al.*, 2012). Effort expectancy is the concept supported by TAM and IDT, where perceived ease of use and ease of use are described in TAM and IDT, respectively. SM is designed to make peer-to-peer, business-to-business and business-to-consumer communication cost effective anytime, anywhere. The MSMEs will use SM if they find it easy to learn. If the users do not find it easy to learn, they will not devote time and effort to learn and there is a high chance that the intention to use SM will be low and they will suspend the use of SM. Effort expectancy was used in previous studies to measure effort expectancy's positive effect (Syaifullah *et al.*, 2021) and negative effect (Amril & Sari, 2019) on intention to use SM in the context of MSMEs.

2.3 *Social influence*

Social influence is considered to be the degree to which individuals perceive that others important to them believe one should use a technology (Venkatesh *et al.*, 2003). This construct is adopted from Ajzen's Theory of Planned Behaviour, where social influence is used to examine the influence of friends, relatives and family members as social norms. Previous studies measure the positive relationship between social influence and behavioural intention in the context of SM adoption in MSMEs (Amril & Sari, 2019).

2.4 *Facilitating condition*

Facilitating condition refers to the extent to which the technology provides an environment that either facilitates or hinders acceptance of any technology (Venkatesh *et al.*, 2003). Facilitating conditions include necessary resources as well as actual behaviour, like internet connectivity, compatible device (smartphone) as well as proper training, knowledge and skills for using the technology. Previous studies in different settings clearly established a positive relationship between facilitating conditions and behavioural intention to use SM in the context of MSMEs (Syaifullah *et al.*, 2021) and a negative effect as well (Amril & Sari, 2019).

Based on the literature, the following hypotheses were proposed:

H1. Performance expectancy has positive influencing SM adoption among owners and managers of MSMEs.

H2. Effort expectancy has positive influencing SM adoption among owners and managers of MSMEs.

H3. Social influence has positive influencing SM adoption among owners and managers of MSMEs.

H4. Facilitating condition has positive influencing SM adoption among owners and managers of MSMEs.

3. Research Methods

The UTAUT model has been used in different fields of research. However, there is hardly any study which has used the UTAUT model to study the use of SM in the field of MSMEs. For the current study, we have used the UTAUT theory and on the basis of the UTAUT theory, a

Table 1.   Descriptive statistics of respondents' characteristics.

Measure	Value	Frequency	Percentage
Gender	Male	227	66.8
	Female	111	33.2
	Total	338	100.0
Age	21–30	86	25.4
	31–40	81	24.0
	41–50	104	30.8
	51 and above	67	19.8
	Total	388	100.0
Qualification	Undergraduate	110	32.5
	Graduate	145	42.9
	PG	83	24.6
	Total	338	100.0
Occupation	Owner	181	53.6
	Manager	157	46.4
	Total	338	100.0

structured questionnaire was developed for studying the relationship between independent and dependent variables. The survey was conducted using a structured questionnaire. The opening question of the questionnaire was a screening question seeking to explore whether the respondent has used any SM apps in the past one month. Hence, the screening question helped in gathering data only from actual users of SM apps. Further, the statements for measuring performance expectancy (PE), effort expectancy (EE), social influence (SI) and facilitating conditions (FC) were adapted from Venkatesh (2003). In total, the questionnaire consisted of 16 statements. All the statements have been used earlier in different contexts, and to make the questionnaire contextual, the questions were modified. Each item of the questionnaire was measured on a five-point Likert scale ranging from 1 (strongly agree) to 5 (strongly disagree). Data were collected from 338 respondents through online survey methods using Google forms. Further, to maintain the anonymity of the respondents, limited demographic information such as gender, age, educational qualification and occupation was asked (Table 1). The data analysis method in this research was conducted with the help of SPSS and AMOS software.

4. Findings and Discussion

4.1 *Evaluation of the measurement model*

Both confirmatory factor analysis (CFA) and structural equation modelling (SEM) have been applied on the proposed research framework. The results of reliability, convergent and discriminant validity were ensured to proceed further. Table 2 illustrates that the Cronbach alpha value of each construct is above the threshold limit of .7 (Hair *et al.*, 2015) and composite reliability which measures internal consistency of the construct also depicts good values ($\geq$.7 for each construct, Hair *et al.*, 2015).

Table 3 depicts the convergent and validity measures and the correlation matrix. The values of AVE were greater than .5, which ensures the convergent validity of the items within a construct, and all the values of MSV and ASV were less than AVE, implying discriminant validity among the constructs.

Table 2.   Reliability measures.

Statements	Std. Loading[a]	Alpha Val.	CR
Performance Expectancy	.718	.716	
PE1	.631**		
PE2	.685**		
PE3	.644**		
PE4	.722[n.a.]		
Effort Expectancy		.825	.811
EE1	.826***		
EE2	.717***		
EE3	.732[n.a.]		
Social Influence		.751	.756
SI1	.782***		
SI2	.844***		
SI3	.646[n.a.]		
Facilitating Conditions		.701	.754
FC1	.804***		
FC2	.732**		
FC3	.812[n.a.]		
Intention to Use SM		.730	.745
ASM1	.811[n.a.]		
ASM2	.792***		
ASM3	.732***		

Note: [a]significant at $p \leq 0.05**$, $p \leq 0.001***$.
n.a. — not applicable.
Source: Author's work.

Further, the variance inflation factor (VIF) values were also obtained for each construct. The VIF values ranged from 1.81 to 1.97, which were below the threshold of 2, indicating that there is no multi-collinearity issue. Furthermore, Table 4 shows the measurement model estimates which were well within the desirable limits of values suggested by Hair *et al.* (2015).

Table 3.   Measures of validity and correlation matrix.

	AVE	MSV	ASV	PE	EE	SI	FC	ASM
PE	0.637	0.371	0.272	1.000				
EE	0.624	0.369	0.283	0.518	1.000			
SI	0.679	0.388	0.252	0.536	0.506	1.000		
FC	0.602	0.365	0.253	0.194	0.216	0.232	1.000	
ASM	0.625	0.361	0.322	0.684	0.361	0.454	0.244	1.000

Source: Author's work.

Table 4.   Measurement model estimates.

Model	$\chi2$	d.f.	$\chi2$/d.f.	GFI	TLI	CFI	REMSEA
	619.20	215	2.880	.895	.813	.816	.058

Source: Author's work.

Table 5.   Structural model estimates.

Model	$\chi2$	d.f.	$\chi2$/d.f.	GFI	TLI	CFI	REMSEA
	13.572	4	3.393	.911	.915	.898	.033

Source: Author's work.

4.2 *Evaluation of the structural model*

4.2.1 *Establishing the model fit*

The relationships have been established between four independent variables, that is, PE, EE, SI, and FC and dependent variable SMA using AMOS 21. Table 5 shows that the output of the analysis suggesting the good model fit as all the indices were falling within the prescribed limits.

4.3 *Hypothesis testing*

After achieving the model fit, the next step was to test the hypothesised theoretical relationships. The structural model with standardised regression weight is depicted in Figure 2. PE has positive influencing SM

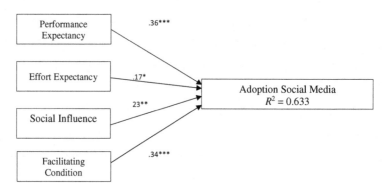

Figure 2.   Research model.

Source: Author's work.

Table 6.   Result of hypothesis testing.

Hypothesis	Standardised Coefficient (β)	*p*-Value	Results
H1. PE ---> Adoption	.36***	.001	Accepted
H2. EE ---> Adoption	.17*	.023	Accepted
H3. SI ---> Adoption	.23**	.049	Accepted
H4. FC ---> Adoption	.34***	.001	Accepted

Note: Significant at $p < 0.001$***, $p < 0.05$**, $p < 0.01$*.

Source: Author's work.

adoption among owners and managers of MSMEs ($\beta = .36$, $p < 0.001$), hence accepting H1. Similarly, EE ($\beta = .17$, $p < 0.01$), SI ($\beta = .23$, $p < 0.05$) and FC ($\beta = .34$, $p < 0.001$) have positive influencing SM adoption among owners and managers of MSMEs, resulting in acceptance of H2, H3 and H4, respectively (Table 6). In sum, all four hypotheses framed for the study have been accepted. Figure 2 also shows that altogether all dependent variables accepted in the proposed research framework explain the 63.2% ($R^2 = .632$) adoption of SM among owners and managers of MSMEs.

5. Discussion and Conclusion

In the present study, we have investigated the influence of PE, EE, SI and FC on adoption of SM apps such as WhatsApp, Facebook, Twitter and

Instagram among owners and managers of MSMEs. The results exhibit that PE, EE, SI and FC have significant positive influencing SM adoption among owners and managers of MSMEs. Further, the results of the current study reveal that PE is the strongest predictor which influences owners and managers of MSMEs to adopt SM.

The significant influence of PE is in sync with the previous studies' measures of performance expectancy's positive effect on intention to use SM (Syaifullah *et al.*, 2021; Amril & Sari, 2019) in the context of MSMEs. Individuals use SM because they feel that it saves their time in communication by providing information anytime, anywhere and connects them with stakeholders easily. It helps them share information, make payments and make better decisions.

The present study reveals a positive but weak relationship of PE with the intention to use SM perhaps because the managers and owners are using SM for different purposes and they are well versed with the functioning. They feel that SM is easy to use and they have attained technological self-efficacy. Hence, the results of the current study are in line with previous studies suggesting the contribution of EE in predicting the use of SM (Syaifullah *et al.*, 2021; Amril & Sari, 2019).

This study has also revealed that SI is an important factor that influences the managers and owners to use SM. First, they find SM useful for many reasons and they form a habit of using it. Verplanken *et al.* (1998) also stated that when we experience something useful or beneficial, there is a possibility to develop habitual pattern towards that phenomenon. Second, nowadays, we are living in an app economy and people are using different types of apps on a regular basis; hence, they look forward to using different apps including transport apps. Third, the usage of apps has a negligible cost and they are freely and easily downloadable. Further, these apps do not require much space in the phone. Lastly, people perceive that apps are easy to use and save a lot of surfing time by directly providing the required information. Also, apps save all the necessary information and the search history too. Therefore, apps work really fast compared to any other digital platform that provides information. There can be several reasons for this result.

This study validates collaboration as a significant predictor and suggests that commuters tend to get influenced by their peer groups, friends and people close to them to use transport apps. Thus, the behaviour of commuters is largely influenced by the endorsement of their peer groups, i.e., friends and family members. Previous studies also supported that people are influenced by the suggestions, recommendations and opinions of the people whom they think they should follow, thus a shared goal is a key element of collaboration (Wood & Gray, 1991; Bedwell *et al.*, 2012).

6. Conclusion and Implications

The present study identified four important dimensions that affect intention of the managers and owners of MSMEs to adopt SM. MSMEs contribute 37.5% to the GDP in India and 46% to export. In India, there are seventeen million people involved in MSMEs, which is approximately 41% of India's working population (KPMG Report, 2017). Only 2% of MSMEs are digitally enabled and are actively using digital technologies (KPMG, 2017).

The purpose of this study is to predict the factors that influence the adoption of SM among the managers and owners of MSMEs with the UTAUT theory approach. The findings of the study revealed that the model was able to explain 63.3% of the variance in behavioural intention. The result showed that variables such as performance expectancy, effort expectancy, social influence and facilitating conditions had a positive and significant effect on managers' and owners' intention to use SM. The study established that managers and owners of MSMEs find SM useful as it helps them in many ways. First, they can use SM for marketing and promoting their business. They also use SM for branding, market research, customer relationship management, service provision and sales promotions (Alves, 2016). Second, SM encompasses all the tools that allow MSMEs to interact with the customers (Järvinen *et al.*, 2012). Lastly, it allows the creation and exchange of user-generated content (Kaplan & Haenlein, 2009). Thus, MSMEs should promote intensive use of SM for marketing and business purposes.

To conclude, the study on factors influencing the intention of managers and owners of MSMEs to use SM will help policymakers, MSMEs and consultants to design policies and products to inspire the managers and owners of MSMEs to use SM, which in turn will enhance the performance and profits of MSMEs. There is no doubt that proliferation of SM use among MSMEs in India is far that of other developing countries.

7. Limitation and Future Research

Some limitations concerning the generalisation of the present study need to be addressed. First, this study is limited to MSMEs located in Delhi and NCR only; it would be better to see a replica of the proposed model in different parts of India and may be in other developing countries. Second, the intention to adopt SM seems to be beneficial for MSMEs as well as for the economy. The present study did not consider any factor like social security, perceived risk or physiological barrier which may affect the adoption of SM negatively. Third, it is important to research each and every app separately to understand how it can help the managers and owners of MSMEs and how it can make it more beneficial for them in the future. Fourth, SM has opened up a new paradigm for managers and owners of MSMEs and everyone directly or indirectly associated with MSMEs. Lastly, future researchers may use a longitudinal study to compare the commuters' behavioural changes towards usage of transport apps.

References

Ahmad, S. Z., Ahmad, N., & Abu Bakar, A. R. (2018). Reflections of entrepreneurs of small and medium-sized enterprises concerning the adoption of social media and its impact on performance outcomes: Evidence from the UAE. *Telematics and Informatics*, *35*(1), 6–17.

Ainin, S., Parveen, F., Moghavvemi, S., Jaafar, N. I., & Mohd Shuib, N. L. (2015). Factors influencing the use of social media by SMEs and its performance outcomes. *Industrial Management & Data Systems*, *115*(3), 570–588.

Almaiah, M. A., Alamri, M. M., & Al-Rahmi, W. (2019). Applying the UTAUT model to explain the students' acceptance of mobile learning system in higher education. *IEEE Access*, *7*, 174673–174686.

AlSharji, A., Ahmad, S. Z., & Bakar, A. R. A. (2018). Understanding social media adoption in SMEs. *Journal of Entrepreneurship in Emerging Economies*, *10*(2), 302–328.

Alshehri, M., Drew, S., Alhussain, T., & Alghamdi, R. (2012). The effects of website quality on adoption of e-government service: An empirical study applying UTAUT model using SEM. In *Conference Proceeding 23rd Australasian Conference On Information Systems*, December 3–5, 2012, Geelong 1–13.

Amril, A. & Sari, L. N. (2019). The level of information technology adoption and its factors in micro, small, and medium enterprises in Jambi City, Indonesia. *Journal Perspektif Pembiayaan dan Pembangunan Daerah, 6*(5), 559–572.

Bellaaj, M., Zekri, I., & Albugami, M. (2015). The continued use of e-learning system: An empirical investigation using UTAUT model at the University of Tabuk. *Journal of Theoretical & Applied Information Technology, 72*(3), 464–474.

Chauhan, S., Jaiswal, M., & Kar, A. K. (2018). The acceptance of electronic voting machines in India: A UTAUT approach. *Electronic Government, an International Journal, 14*(3), 255–275.

Crammond, R., Omeihe, K. O., Murray, A., & Ledger, K. (2018). Managing knowledge through social media. *Baltic Journal of Management, 13*(3), 303–328.

Dahnil, M. I., Marzuki, K. M., Langgat, J., & Fabeil, N. F. (2014). Factors influencing SMEs adoption of social media marketing. *Procedia — Social and Behavioral Sciences, 148*, 119–126.

Durkin, M., McGowan, P., & McKeown, N. (2013). Exploring social media adoption in small to medium-sized enterprises in Ireland. *Journal of Small Business and Enterprise Development, 20*(4), 716–734.

Foon, Y. S. & Fah, B. C. Y. (2011). Internet banking adoption in Kuala Lumpur: An application of UTAUT model. *International Journal of Business and Management, 6*(4), 161.

Gama, P. D. A. (2011). An expanded model of marketing performance. *Marketing Intelligence & Planning, 29*(7), 643–661.

Gavino, M. C., Williams, D. E., Jacobson, D., & Smith, I. (2019). Latino entrepreneurs and social media adoption: Personal and business social network platforms. *Management Research Review, 42*(4), 469–494.

Hair, J. F., Black, W. C., Babin, B. J., Anderson, R. E., & Tatham, R. L. (2015). *Multivariate Data Analysis.* New Delhi: Pearson Education.

Handoko, B. L. (2019). Application of UTAUT theory in higher education online learning. In *Proceedings of the 2019 10th International Conference on E-business, Management and Economics,* (pp. 259–264).

Khechine, H., Lakhal, S., Pascot, D., & Bytha, A. (2014). UTAUT model for blended learning: The role of gender and age in the intention to use webinars. *Interdisciplinary Journal of E-Learning and Learning Objects, 10*(1), 33–52.

L'Écuyer, F. & Pelletier, C. (2019). Exploration of social media capabilities for recruitment in Smes: A multiple case study. *HRM 4.0 For Human-Centered Organizations (Advanced Series in Management)*, 23(1), (pp. 221–239). Emerald Publishing Limited, Bingley.

Mandal, D. & McQueen, R. J. (2012). Extending UTAUT to explain social media adoption by microbusinesses. *International Journal of Managing Information Technology, 4*(4), 1.

Musa, H., Ab Rahim, N., Azmi, F. R., Shibghatullah, A. S., & Othman, N. A. (2016). Social media marketing and online small and medium enterprises performance: Perspective of Malaysian small and medium enterprises. *International Review of Management and Marketing, 6*(7), 1–5.

Nuseir, M. T. (2018). Digital media impact on SMEs performance in the UAE. *Academy of Entrepreneurship Journal, 24*(2), 1–13.

Obar J. A. & Wildman S. S. (2015) Social media definition and the governance challenge: An introduction to the special issue. *SSRN Electronic Journal*. doi: 10.2139/ssrn.2647377.

Odoom, R., Anning-Dorson, T., & Acheampong, G. (2017). Antecedents of social media usage and performance benefits in small- and medium-sized enterprises (SMEs). *Journal of Enterprise Information Management, 30*(3), 383–399.

Orji, R. O. (2010). Impact of gender and nationality on acceptance of a digital library: An empirical validation of nationality based UTAUT using SEM. *Journal of Emerging Trends in Computing and Information Sciences, 1*(2), 68–79.

Padhi, N. (2018). Acceptance and usability of OER in India: An investigation using UTAUT model. *Open Praxis, 10*(1), 55–65.

Papa, A., Santoro, G., Tirabeni, L., & Monge, F. (2018). Social media as tool for facilitating knowledge creation and innovation in small and medium enterprises. *Baltic Journal of Management, 13*(3), 329–344.

Purwanto, E. & Loisa, J. (2020). The intention and use behaviour of the mobile banking system in Indonesia: UTAUT model. *Technology Reports of Kansai University, 62*(6), 2757–2767.

Rahi, S., Ghani, M., Alnaser, F., & Ngah, A. (2018). Investigating the role of unified theory of acceptance and use of technology (UTAUT) in internet banking adoption context. *Management Science Letters, 8*(3), 173–186.

Rahi, S., Mansour, M. M. O., Alghizzawi, M., & Alnaser, F. M. (2019). Integration of UTAUT model in internet banking adoption context: The mediating role of performance expectancy and effort expectancy. *Journal of Research in Interactive Marketing, 13*(3), 411–435.

Raman, A., Don, Y., Khalid, R., & Rizuan, M. (2014). Usage of learning management system (Moodle) among postgraduate students: UTAUT model. *Asian Social Science, 10*(14), 186–192.

Rozikin, A. Z., Indartono, S., & Sugiharsono, S. (2019). The use social media and employee performance in MSMEs development: Glass noodle home industry Manjung Indonesia. *Jurnal Economia, 15*(2), 221–231.

Sarosa, S. (2012). Adoption of social media networks by Indonesian SME: A Case Study. *Procedia Economics and Finance, 4*, 244–254.

Singh, T. & Kalia, P. (2021). MSME owner/manager perceptions towards the adoption of E-marketing activities in India. In *Recent Developments in Individual and Organizational Adoption of ICTs* (pp. 43–59). IGI Global.

Surya, A. P., Muna, N., Indriani, F. (2020). Improving brand and marketing performance of SMEs through social media usage: An empirical research. *International Journal of Psychosocial Rehabilitation, 24*(6), 1846–1859.

Syaifullah, J., Syaifudin, M., Sukendar, M. U., & Junaedi, J. (2021). Social media marketing and business performance of MSMEs during the COVID-19 pandemic. *The Journal of Asian Finance, Economics, and Business, 8*(2), 523–531.

Tan, P. J. B. (2013). Students' adoptions and attitudes towards electronic placement tests: A UTAUT analysis. *American Journal of Computer Technology and Application, 1*(1), 14–23.

Trainor, K. J., Andzulis, J., Rapp, A., & Agnihotri, R. (2014). Social media technology usage and customer relationship performance: A capabilities-based examination of social CRM. *Journal of Business Research, 67*(6), 1201–1208.

Venkatesh, V., Morris, M. G., Davis, G. B., & Davis, F. D. (2003). User acceptance of information technology: Toward a unified view. *MIS Quarterly, 27*(3), 425–478.

Venkatesh, V., Thong, J. Y., & Xu, X. (2012). Consumer acceptance and use of information technology: Extending the unified theory of acceptance and use of technology. *MIS Quarterly, 36*(1), 157–178.

Wan, L., Xie, S., & Shu, A. (2020). Toward an understanding of university students' continued intention to use MOOCs: When UTAUT model meets TTF model. *SAGE Open, 10*(3), doi: 10.1177/2158244020941858.

Wong, K. T., Teo, T., & Russo, S. (2013). Interactive whiteboard acceptance: Applicability of the UTAUT model to student teachers. *The Asia-Pacific Education Researcher, 22*(1), 1–10.

Yu, C. S. (2012). Factors affecting individuals to adopt mobile banking: Empirical evidence from the UTAUT model. *Journal of Electronic Commerce Research*, *13*(2), 104.

Appendix

MSME classification based on capital invested.

MSME Classification	Manufacturing Service
Micro Investment ≤10 lakhs rupees	Investment ≤25 lakhs rupees
Small Investment >10 lakhs but <2 crore rupees	Investment >25 lakhs but <5 crore rupees
Medium Investment >2 crores but <5 crore rupees	Investment >5 crores but <10 crore rupees

Source: Ministry of Micro, Small and Medium Enterprises, Government of India.

Chapter 13

Free and Open-Source Software as an Innovation Stimulus for SMEs: An Indian Perspective

Ruchi Jain* and **Ruchika Jeswal**[†]

Amity School of Business, Amity University, Uttar Pradesh, India
*rjain@amity.edu
†ruchikajeswal@gmail.com

Abstract

The business value chain is increasingly dominated by software ranging from managing transportation to backend processes. Technology-based intermediaries are playing crucial roles in the development of an emerging economy like India. The automated tools implied are majorly software based and plying with the data. Now, the hardware is seen as a commodity and software is used as a differentiation plank for competitive positioning. In such a scenario, the Micro, Small and Medium Enterprises are finding it difficult to survive with the costing of proprietary software by the international giants like SAP, Microsoft or Oracle. Thus, they are opting for open systems of innovation made possible by usage of Free and Open-Source Software (FOSS). The collaborative innovation models offered by FOSS in emerging areas like Artificial intelligence and Machine learning are leaving no reaction time for proprietary software. Free-to-use source code with all the possibilities of creative contribution by communities can help the nation control the technology stacks crucial for the national information infrastructure. With such strong socioeconomic reasons, it is the appropriate time for the SMEs to think of open source as "freedom" instead of "free" in the Indian ecosystem. All the stakeholders involved should play their part to prove

FOSS as a road of salvation along with the government with the prime responsibility of developing the requisite infrastructure.

Keywords: Free and open-source software, disruptive technologies, emerging economies, business processes

1. Introduction

The transforming ecosystem in India is providing a lot of avenues to emerging entrepreneurs and their innovative ideas. Information Technology (IT) based start-ups are specially leading the bandwagon with the creation of capabilities for growth and new solutions, both at home and abroad. The young entrepreneurs of India who belonged to a digitally enabled middle class are craving growth and change. They are eager to adopt the new developmental approaches to cater the best value to their clients, providing the best technological solution for their business problems. In the modern internet economy, Free and Open-Source Software (FOSS) displays "decentralised voluntarism" where programmers and researchers are constructing intellectual edifices of astounding complexity.

In an emerging economy and price-sensitive country like India where pirated copies of proprietary software are freely available, FOSS paves the road to salvation for Micro, Small and Medium Enterprises (MSMEs), though they are combatting the bedecked proprietary software by international giants like SAP, Microsoft or Oracle.

The chapter focuses on the clear-sighted bets on the growth of FOSS available for the MSMEs. It also proposes FOSS as the plan for the commoditisation of currently locked-down technologies owned by the tech giants.

2. Genesis of Free and Open-Source Software

The seed of origin of FOSS is rooted in hackers' ethics and culture from the 1960s. Hackers were inspired by the desire to create technical splendours above all other goals (Coleman, 2012). These hackers gave considerable weightage to sharing information and collaboration, which played a crucial role in the evolution of the internet and its potential for innovation (Castells, 2003). The initiative of free information was propagated further, thus causing accelerated advancement of the hacker's concept (Levy, 1985). Richard Stallman in 1985 created a computer system against proprietary software. This system was entirely based upon free software and hoped to feed the aspirations of the sharing community. The action led to the development of Free Software foundation, thus taking up the baton of the "free information" revolution further.

As a milestone in the journey of a free computer system, Linux was conceptualised in 1991 by Linus Torvalds (Finland). He called for contributors to develop Linux as an ever-evolving FOSS product, which was further fortified by his leadership style.

3. Free and Open-Source Software (FOSS)

3.1 *The theoretical concept*

Under licensed technology, Intellectual Property Rights (IPR) in the form of copyrights and patents guard software and their source codes. The access to the source code is restricted and closely guarded in Closed Source Software (CSS) or Proprietary Software.

Contrary to the idea of "Copyright", the free software concept is based on the "Copyleft", which never restricts the usage and sharing of the information (Couture, 2021). To unleash the restrictions imposed by thriving commercial software, the FOSS is deployed. It is software with source code open or available to the public for use and modifications. There exist four freedoms in such software (Figure 1):

- The freedom to use the programme for any purpose (freedom 0).
- With access to the source code, the freedom to study the working of it (freedom 1).
- The freedom to replicate or make copies for collaboration (freedom 2).
- The freedom to improve or modify the versions (freedom 3).

With such freedom, the development pattern of Linux was appreciated and termed as "bazaar" where open ideas got pooled in and the best ideas picked to make the software better without any ethical concern

Figure 1.   Four types of freedoms in FOSS

(Raymond, 2001). It increased the participation of open contributors with free-to-access source code with more of creativity and less ethical dilemma.

In 1998, in order to compete with Microsoft, Netscape published its source code with the intention of riding the free software movement bandwagon (William, 2002). The result was Firefox, which is one of the popular browsers now. This commercialisation of the concept shifted the focus from being "Free Software" to "Open Source", which was widely accepted in business parlance.

So, the FOSS concept is grounded in the principal of sharing, and the source code of such software is created as a collaborative effort of individual developers and contributing communities. They are inspired by the idea of providing creative inputs and efforts for making the source code and software better than the previous versions.

(a) **Performance parameters of FOSS**

As common perception relates FOSS with no costing, there are strong apprehensions about the performance of such a product. Considering that,

Table 1.   Performance parameters of FOSS.

S. No.	Parameter	Functional Utility of Parameter
1	Adaptability	• Number of downloads. • Number of users/well-known users. • Awards. • Modularity, by-products, etc.
2	Activity	• Progress made by the developers. • Number of bugs reported & fixed. • New features, discussions, etc.
3	Longevity	• How long the OSS solution has been in use.
4	License	• Well-defined conditions for the contribution of code. • Flexibility without restrictions to implement alternative formats. • Integration between the proprietary solution and other systems, etc.
5	Fork-ability	• Based on open model. • Protection against proprietary forks.
6	Services	• Quality of support. • Capacity building. • Consulting from community. • Industry and other paid models.
7	Documentation	• User manuals and tutorials. • Developer documentation.
8	Security	• Responding to vulnerabilities.
9	Functionality	• Testing against functional, essential and desirable requirements.
10	Integration	• Standards. • Modularity. • Collaboration.
11	Nature of the Trust	• Level of democracy of management. • Impact on types of distributions.
12	Skill Set	• Available in the user. • Available in partner-company. • Available in developer.

Source: Compiled from http://egovstandards.gov.in.

the Government of India has defined the performance parameters which can be expected from FOSS (Table 1).

(b) **A list of CSS vis-à-vis their FOSS alternatives**
FOSS is seen as the facilitator in plugging the digital divide and creating communities that believe in open-source products and freedom of knowledge (Raisinghani, 2003). It is widely available in almost all the formats like ERPs (Adempiere, ERP next, Open bravo), Operating systems (Linux, Ubuntu), Internet Browsers like Mozilla Firefox and Content Management Systems (Joomla). A comparison between CSS and FOSS products is provided in Table 2.

4. Innovation and FOSS

(a) **Mainstream Open Innovation system**
Innovation techniques adopted by a company are defined by the validated concept of "absorptive capacity" (Cohen & Levithal, 1989). Innovation insights can be absorbed from competitors, customers and inter-organisational networks, thus creating a conducive ecosystem of innovation. The open system of innovation is propagated over and above the closed system of innovation by Chesbrough (2003). The foremost advantage is accumulation of better ideas by external knowledge sources. Better value can be created by integrating external ideas with internal knowledge and a proportion of this value can be claimed easily by the organisation. Three archetype processes were identified, i.e., Outside-in process, inside-out process and coupled process for enrichment of open innovation (Gassmen & Enkel, 2004) (Figure 2). The outside-in process realises the difference in the presence of knowledge creation and innovation, and thus encourages flow of information from outside to inside the company, whereas the company can use external channels for commercialising its own ideas through inside-out process. The third, coupled process, is the foundation used by FOSS as it is an integration of the two and harnesses the benefits of both the processes for innovation. FOSS also satiates the innovative and creative instincts of the contributors and provides the dynamic framework, which can be customised and extended as per the requirement.

Table 2.   CSS vis-à-vis their FOSS alternatives.

S. No.	Domain	CSS	OSS
1	Enterprise Resource Planning (ERP)	Oracle ERP, SAP ERP, Microsoft Dynamics	ADempiere, Ofbiz, Dolibarr, ERPNext, WebERP, Opentaps
2	Operating Systems (OS)	Microsoft Window, Mac OS, iOS	GNU/Linux, Android, Ubuntu
3	Internet Browser	Internet Explorer, Safari	Mozilla Firefox, Chromium
4	Content Management Systems (CMS)	Morello, Sharepoint	Joomla, WordPress, Drupal
5	Office Suites	Microsoft Office	Open Office
6	Web Server	Microsoft IIS, Google server	Apache, Nginx
7	Cloud Infrastructure	Amazon web services, Microsoft Azure, VMWare	OpenStack, Eucalyptus
8	Virtualisation	VMWare	VirtualBox, Xen, LinuxKVM
9	Database	SQL Server, Oracle, DB2	MYSQL, PostgreSQL
10	Big Data	Google BigTable, Intersystem's Cache	Hadoop, MongoDB, Hbase, Spark, Redis NoSQL
11	Application Servers	BEA Weblogic, IBM Websphere	Apache Tomcat, JBoss
12	IDE/Development	Visual Studio, ASP. Net	Eclipse, PHP
13	Scientific Solutions	MATLAB, Mathematica	Scilab, Octave, SageMath
14	Data Analysis	SPSS, SAS, Stata	R
15	HTML/CSS Editor	Dreamweaver	BlueGriffon, SeaMonkey, Aloha
16	Graphic Program	Adobe Photoshop, AutoCAD	GIMP, FreeCAD, LibreCAD
17	Publishing	Microsoft Publisher	Scribus
18	Media Player	Window Media Player	VLC, Miro
19	GIS	ArcView, ArcWeb and ArcGIS	Grass GIS, Quantum GIS
20	Spatial Database	Oracle Spatial, Sybase	PostGIS
21	Digital Repository	Dlib, AutoLib, Soul, Alice	Dspace, Eprint, Koha

Source: https://www.ripublication.com/ijaer18/ijaerv13n16_44.pdf.

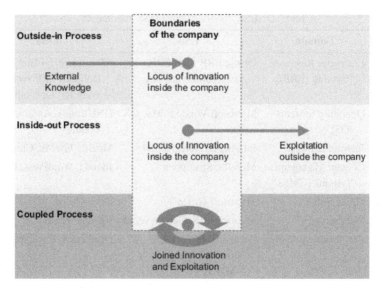

Figure 2.   Archetype process of open innovation (Gassmen & Enkel, 2004).

(b) **Emerging economies harnessing FOSS potential**

Emerging economies are characterised by restricted availability of resources. Hence, the innovation in such economies circumvents the traditional methods and becomes dependent on specific methods more implied in their ecosystem (Ulijn & Brown, 2004). FOSS is a popular source of innovation in the IT sector (Dravis, 2003). The infused dynamism of FOSS creates the requisite developmental ecosystem and framework upon which the ICT sector can build up its edifices to move further. The inherent properties of FOSS like low investment required and brief development cycle majorly remove the anticipated entry barriers and make it suitable to be adopted by SMEs from emerging economies (Wong, 2004). FOSS provides creative stimulation to the engineers of the developed countries and also creates joint learning avenues with the IT-based organisations of these resource-restricted nations (Tapia & Maldonado, 2009). Considering it to be full of potential, the governments of countries like India are investing in creating an ecosystem for SMEs to adopt FOSS as part of their innovative products and services (Hoe, 2006).

FOSS requires immense team work of the contributors with the help of Internet, which is considered as a bottom-up innovation approach and

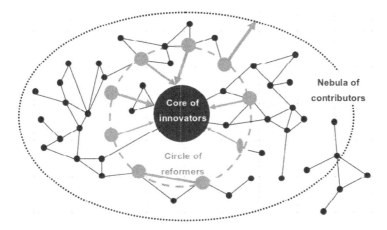

Figure 3.   Bottom-up innovation in free software development (Cardon, 2005).

termed as organisational coherence (Cardon, 2005). The contributing leaders are referred to as the "core of innovators" as they propagate the original idea and creatives, followed by the "circle of reformers" who select the best of the contributing ideas. The outermost layer comprises the "nebula of contributors" who generate ideas to satisfy their creative instincts (Figure 3).

5. Micro, Small and Medium Enterprises (MSMEs) in India

MSMEs are considered to be the engine of growth for an economy. Their contribution to the Indian GDP has shown unparalleled growth in the last few years. The number of Indians employed in MSMEs in the financial year 2021 across India amounts to a whopping 110 million (*Source*: Statistica). The share of MSME Gross Value Added (GVA) in All India Gross Domestic Product at current prices (2011–2012) for the years 2018–2019 and 2019–2020 was 30.5% and 30.0%, respectively.

Indian MSME analysis shows a distinct growth in the last few years. The number of MSMEs increased in India by a CAGR of 18.5% from 2019 to 2020. The land disbursal to the MSME has increased by 40% in the financial year 2020.

The government is also promoting SMEs by providing various schemes like KVIC, Coir Board, NSIC, NI-MSME and MGIRI. The government is also establishing various initiatives for the welfare of SMEs such as the Special Credit Linked Special subsidy launched in November 2021 to help enterprises in various service sectors meet technology requirements. The government has also doubled the budget allocation for MSMEs for the year 2022.

As per an economic Survey, the growth of MSMEs not only creates profits for their promoters but also contributes to job creation and productivity in the economy. So, the policy should be such that it enables MSMEs to grow by unshackling them. To unshackle MSMEs and thereby enable them to grow, various incentives would have to be made with necessary hand-holding for a period of 10 years.

All this points to the fact that the MSME sector plays a major role in the socioeconomic development of the country. The importance of this sector grew as its contribution to the GDP of the country increased. The sector's contribution can never be undermined as it has been instrumental in bringing about entrepreneurial development in the country, especially in the semi-urban and rural areas of India. But MSMEs lack in various aspects, especially in terms of technology adoption.

Technology adoption and MSME: Technology in its various forms can act as a boon for MSMEs. It has led to a transformation in the global economy in terms of doing business. It also plays an essential role in escalating the profitability of organisations. The benefits of IT to MSME are less explored. It can increase MSMEs' efficiency, reduce costs and expand market reach, at both the domestic and international levels. As the MSME sector plays an important role in the nation's economy, the sector benefits individual MSMEs, collectively delivering positive results, leading to employment creation, revenue generation and overall business competitiveness. Often, MSMEs hesitate to adopt the latest technology due to their lack of understanding and knowledge of selecting the correct technology solutions. Such issues can be resolved by creating more awareness among MSME entrepreneurs and providing solutions like FOSS.

(a) **MSME harnessing FOSS potential**

Information Technology is an accelerator that brings growth and flexibility to business activities. Adoption of FOSS can easily fulfil the supporting role played by IT in day-to-day operations of Smes with minimal financial resources. These Smes can adopt the FOSS environment for webservers, hosting web applications, heavy internet usage, email messaging, file servers used for storage by employees, backup servers and databases along with Enterprise Resource Planning solutions. The fact that this open system can be freely accessed, used or modified by anyone helps Smes remain competitive and increases their chances of survival.

Several IT-based Smes are also designing their business proposition based on FOSS and related systems. New business models are emerging based upon the innovative and potent ideas about economies, finance and collaboration. Some the Indian MSMEs designed their business model around FOSS and are now ascending the value chain. Some of the established names are Calibre (e-book management), Frappe Technologies (ERPNext), Zerodha (a financial service company), Bagisto (an e-commerce platform) and Hasura (a GraphQL engine on Postgres). Former Red Hatters have also started companies like Ashnik, Unotech and Vinca Cybertech that are built around FOSS services.

Popular business models that use FOSS and are responsible for monetising the enterprises can be of various types. Companies like *Red Hat* use the "**Service Model**" which provides free downloads but charges commercially for technical support and training. The "**Open Core Model**" used by *MongoDB* and *MuleSoft* charges for add-ons and other supporting components. This is advanced further by "**Dual-licensing models**" in which a product is released with two licenses — a restrictive and permissive license as done by *MySQL*. On the other hand, the "**SAAS or subscription model**" is designed for monetising in the form of a subscription of the tools and service platform, e.g., *Compiere and salesforce*.

Till now, the approach of businesses has been very makeshift and highly opportunistic, which needs to be streamlined further. The Internet of Things, Big Data, Machine Learning, Artificial intelligence and cloud-based software like the latest technologies are available as FOSS systems. So, Smes in India must have a strategic and contemplative approach in adopting these. This requires appreciation of the collaborative development model of FOSS, engagement with the FOSS community, and comprehension of licenses and the factors that drive the leadership in FOSS expansion.

(b) **FOSS communities for supporting MSME**

In the modern Indian economy based on the internet, the FOSS system displays "decentralised voluntarism" where programmers and researchers are constructing intellectual edifices of astounding complexity. The verity that groups of people can make a community and contribute in creating or enriching software code gives rise to a lot of possibilities. The Internet has made it feasible to overcome geographical boundaries, making it available for everybody's consumption to increase the market reach of FOSS. It is now powering our smart devices like phones and smart watches. Along with it is used by corporates in their ERPs, operating systems, social media platforms and various IT based applications. FOSS is now considered to be the creation of public assets in India. These assets are enabling companies to produce new technologies without being dependent on costly proprietary offerings. Since 2018, there have been many projects initiated in India, namely, Hasura, Hoppscotch and Chatwoot, which also have significant communities contributing to their creation. From the Indian perspective, these communities can be segmented on various bases like organisation type, purpose of constitution and type of governance (Table 3).

(c) **Government of India creating the FOSS ecosystem**

With the penetration of Internet in India, FOSS is emerging as the natural choice of IT-based start-ups as one of the most feasible business models. Digital governance is also promoting such open-source platforms due to flexibility in usage along with all other benefits. Thus, creating a conducive IT ecosystem for nurturing FOSS with stakeholders like academic partners, providers and a contributing community along with the government is high on the agenda. Being an emerging economy, the Indian Government has taken lot of initiatives to foster a conducive environment of harnessing the potential of FOSS, especially for those who are resource restrained (Table 4).

Table 3. Segmentation of FOSS communities.

S. No.	FOSS Community Type	Functionality	Example
		Based on Organisation Type	
1	FOSS Groups	Regional- and national-level interest groups across India working for FOSS.	• FOSS India Foundation • FOSS@Amrita • PyLadies Delhi
2	Individual Volunteers for FOSS	Individuals contributing time and efforts for ecosystem and mobilisation of FOSS systems.	• Aruna Sankanarayanan (MIT Media Labs, Massachusetts) • Cherry G Mathews (CEO, QikPik) • Vaishali Thakkar (Freelance Linux Kernel Engineer)
3	FOSS Non-profit Organisations	Facilitates grassroots implementation, arranges funds and promotes FOSS products, recommends government policies & ecosystem.	• Centre for Internet and Society • FOSS United Foundation • Mozilla Foundation • E-Governments Foundation
		Based on Purpose of Constitution	
4	Single-Project Communities	They may originate as the idea of an individual, as a part of an enterprise or academia.	• ERP next • Tensor Flow • Python
5	Domain-Specific Communities	They may be communities around a FOSS project. Can be in form of an Umbrella organisation.	• Open Bioinformatics Foundation • Apache software foundation • The Linux Foundation
6	FOSS Communities for Alternative Reasons	They can be meant for advocacy, legal aid. Can be regional or user groups as entity.	• Centre for Internet and Society • Free software foundation of India • Django girls
		Based on Type of Governance	
7	The Benevolent Dictator Model	They have project founders as the final decision-maker in case of disputes or arguments.	• Clojure153 • Linux
8	Apache Software Foundation Governance Model	In it, a Board of Directors is elected to set corporate policy and appoint Project Management Committees.	• Apache Software Foundation
9	Debian Governance Model	The community selects a leader from within, along with officers for administrative and technical profiles.	• Open Invention network

Source: Compiled by authors from https://civicdatalab.in/work/foss/stateoffoss/.

Table 4.   Initiatives by GOI for developing the FOSS ecosystem.

S. No.	Organisation	Initiatives Undertaken
1	National Resource Centre for Free & Open-Source Software	• Established for R&D and awareness creation. • Support and adoption of FOSS in the country.
2	Bharat Operating System (BOSS) Solutions	• GNU/Linux-based localised Operating System. • Supports 18 Indian languages. • Certified by Linux Foundation. • Meet stringent demands of e-governance.
3	Edu-BOSS	• Fully featured educational variant of BOSS. • Ore-installed with educational applications, games, paint and graphic tools, typing tutor.
4	BOSS Server	• Useful for hosting website and internal servers. • Lightweight version of Debian-based GNU/Linux. • Designed for hosting web server, proxy server, mail server, etc.
5	Megh Doot	• Indigenously developed cloud suite to offer cloud services.
6	Swar-Suchak	• Voice-enabled information retrieval system in multiple languages. • Integrates mobile telephone network with automatic speech recognition system.
7	GEM	• Input mechanism uses gestures to give input. • By mouse, touchpad, joystick, etc.
8	Anumaan	• Text entry system to aid people with motor disabilities. • Integrated with Linux desktop and stand-alone tool.
9	ALViC	• Technology solutions developed for differently abled people. • To make computer usage easier and affordable.
10	Creative Computing@ School	• Educational e-journal for CBSE. • Share educational pedagogical experience by teachers.
11	Integrated Library Management System	• Automation solution for public, academic and digital video libraries. • Comprehensive functionality successfully integrating Koha & D Space.

Source: Compiled by authors from https://www.meity.gov.in/content/major-foss-initiatives.

6. Challenges in Implementing FOSS in India for MSMEs

FOSS is creating a sensation in India, especially in technology-based businesses. With IT and electronics companies aggressively adopting FOSS, sectors like SMEs, retail and BFSI are slowly choosing the benefits of open innovation. Although India is adopting FOSS, there still exists a lot of scope to harness the latent potential. India is taking long strides to adopt FOSS, but the Indian ecosystem is still facing a lot of challenges. Some of them can be explained as follows:

(1) **Low awareness of the FOSS ecosystem:** Although FOSS in India is growing at a faster rate than in the past, it will take some time to mature, as awareness of the potential of FOSS is yet to be realised by masses.

(2) **Low involvement of stakeholders:** A FOSS ecosystem consists of various stakeholders — educational institutions like schools and colleges, the government, FOSS solution providers, consumers and the FOSS community. The awareness towards FOSS has considerably increased, but only in the case of consumers. Poor community participation, lack of proper business model, lack of well-established governance models in leveraging FOSS and a lack of India-based ISVs have hindered the ecosystem.

(3) **Lack of structured FOSS community:** The Indian FOSS community is in the nascent stage, and technology-based companies, developers and other stakeholders are still developing the culture of giving back to the community. This is due to the socioeconomic context of our engineers, which prevents them from contributing to the development of the FOSS ecosystem.

(4) **Lack of organisational support:** NASSCOM and CII, which play a major role in defining the technology policy in India, must come out in the open in favour of FOSS. Companies should take a firm stand in not only using FOSS but also contributing back to the community.

(5) **Fewer initiatives by IT sector:** IT companies need to give back to the community. They need to understand the need to participate in leveraging FOSS software both internally and externally. IT companies need to sponsor user groups and communities developing FOSS

software. Business models need to be developed around FOSS to make the ecosystem sustainable.

(6) **Inadequate consumer demand:** It is crucial to generate demand and increase the market size. Only having a developer community is not enough. Demand and supply dynamics need to be in sync. Therefore, an aggressive consumption trend is required to be developed for the growth of the FOSS ecosystem.

(7) **Strong advocacy on shortcomings:** Awareness levels towards the FOSS ecosystem are still low. Appropriate advocacy is required to be developed towards FOSS and its ecosystem to build customer confidence related to the usage of FOSS. Such an ecosystem can be developed when companies that use FOSS credit it when advertising their products.

(8) **Restricted role of government:** The government's role is restricted in the development of FOSS. They need to play an important role in adoption, appreciation and contribution to make India emerge as a FOSS hub. India needs to become a large consumer and create a supportive environment through the right policies for FOSS companies to grow.

(9) **Limited awareness of educational institutes:** Educational institutes play a crucial role as facilitators, as the use of FOSS in classrooms/production applications helps in raising awareness, creates demands for FOSS products and processes, and develops the right talent pool.

(10) **Unempathetic FOSS vendors:** FOSS solution providers can also promote FOSS by creating a unified message about what it stands for and the benefits it offers to the consumers. The FOSS vendors must take a holistic approach of creating awareness, interest, desire and action among the consumers by hand-holding them towards achieving requisite results.

7. Conclusion

FOSS has been one of the most inspiring developments in the last 20 years. FOSS has been able to infuse innovation by being a part of technology-based offerings, right from a smartwatch to the sophisticated AI-based

ERP. It is bound to play a very important role in the growth of MSMEs. Apart from being available free of cost, FOSS also satiates the innovative and creative instincts of the contributors and provides the dynamic framework, which can be customised and extended as per the requirement. With the penetration of the internet in India, FOSS is emerging as the natural choice for IT-based start-ups as one of the most feasible business models. The digital India campaign by Indian government is also promoting such open-source platforms due to flexibility in usage along with all other benefits.

FOSS has variety of challenges but can be overcome by the active involvement of various stakeholders like individual volunteers and consultants, FOSS groups, schools, higher educational and research institutes, tech enterprises and governments. For the FOSS environment to thrive, there is a need for all players to be invested, to work together, to co-create and to contribute. FOSS is considered a tool for freedom, power, inclusion and collaboration. It has also tackled digital inclusion challenges by working on localising FOSS to Indian languages. India is set to become a vibrant hub for FOSS innovations with stimulating opportunity for MSMEs. Thus, creating a conducive IT ecosystem for nurturing FOSS with stakeholders and the government is high on agenda. Such an ecosystem will lead to the establishment of technological dialogues and the creation of universally accessible resources that are developed by communities for the benefit of society at large.

References

Adoption of free and open source software in India (2019). https://www. ripublication.com/ijaer18/ijaerv13n16_44.pdf.

Can-india-ever-become-a-global-foss-hub (2019). https://www.mindtree.com/ sites/default/files/2017-10/306%20mindtree-thought-posts-can-india-ever-become-a-global-foss-hub_0.pdf.

Cardon, D. (2005). Innovation by usage. In A. Ambrosi, V. Peugeot, & D. Pimienta (Eds.), *Word Matters. Multicultural Perspectives on Information Societies*. Caen: C&F Editions.

Castells, M. (2003). *The Internet Galaxy: Reflections on the Internet, Business, and Society*. Oxford: Oxford University Press. https://doi.org/10.1093/acpro f:oso/9780199255771.001.0001.

Coleman, G. (2012). *Coding Freedom: The Ethics and Aesthetics of Hacking.* Princeton: Princeton University Press.

De, R. (2019). Economic impact of free and open source software — A study in India. https://icfoss.in/doc/ICFOSS_economic-impact-free(v3).pdf.

Dhir, S. & Dhir, S. (2017). Adoption of open-source software versus proprietary software: An exploratory study. *Strategic Change, 26*(4), 363–371. doi: 10.1002/jsc.2137.

Dravis, P. (2003). *Open Source Software. Perspectives for Development.* Washington: Global Information and Communication Technologies Department, The World Bank.

Framework for adoption of FOSS in e-governance systems (2019). http://egovstandards.gov.in/sites/default/files/Framework%20for%20Adoption%20of%20Open%20Source%20Software%20in%20e-Governance%20Systems.pdf.

Ghose, D., Naskar, S., Shabbiruddin, & Roy, A. (2019). An open source software. *International Journal of Open Source Software and Processes, 10*(1), 49–68. doi: 10.4018/ijossp.2019010104.

Hoe, N. (2006). *Breaking Barriers: The Potential of Free and Open Source Software for Sustainable Human Development.* New Delhi: UNDP and Elsevier.

Levy, S. (1985). *Hackers Heroes of the Computer Revolution.* New York: Dell. https://www.indiabudget.gov.in/budget2019-20/economicsurvey/doc/vol1chapter/echap03_vol1.pdf.

Industry performance: 2018–19 and what lies ahead (2019). http://nipp.tech/storage/app/file/210219_085554.pdf.

IT & ITeS industry in India: Market size, opportunities, growth…IBEF (2019). https://www.ibef.org/industry/information-technology-india.aspx.

Kumar, R., Kumar, S., & Tiwari, S. K. (2018). Adoption of free and open source software in India. *Int. J. Appl. Eng. Res, 13*(16), 12725–12731.

Nourishing dwarfs to become giants: Reorienting policies for MSME growth. In *Economic Survey 2018–19*, Vol. 1. Ministry of Finance (July 2019).

Open source vs. proprietary software pros and cons (2019). http://www.optimusinfo.com/downloads/white-paper/open-source-vs-proprietary-software-pros-and-cons.pdf.

Raymond, E. S. (2001). *The Cathedral and the Bazaar.* Sebastopol, CA: O'Reilly Media, Inc.

Singh, A., Bansal, R., & Jha, N. (2015). Open source software vs. proprietary software. *International Journal of Computer Applications, 114*(18), 26–31. doi: 10.5120/20080-2132.

Stallman, R., Lessig, L., & Gay, J. (2002). *Free Software, Free Society: Selected Essays of Richard M. Stallman*. Boston, MA: Gnu Press Free Software Foundation.

Taher (2012). Open source movement in India with special reference to digital library software: Problems and prospects. *Journal of Knowledge & Communication Management*, 2(2), 178. doi: 10.5958/j.2277-7946.2.2.014.

Tapia, A. & Maldonado, E. (2009). An ICT skills cascade: Government-mandated open source policy as a potential driver for ICT skills transfer. *Information Technologies and International Development*, 5(2), 31–51.

Ulijn, J. & Brown, T. (2004). Innovation, entrepreneurship and culture, a matter of interaction between technology, progress and economic growth? In T. Brown & J. Ulinj (Eds.), *Innovation, Entrepreneurship and Culture*. Massachusetts: Edward Elgar Publishing.

West, J. (2003). How open is open enough? *Research Policy*, 32(7), 1259–1285. doi: 10.1016/s0048-7333(03)00052-0.

West, J. & Gallagher, S. (2006). Challenges of open innovation: The paradox of firm investment in open-source software. *R&D Management*, 36(3), 319–331. doi: 10.1111/j.1467-9310.2006.00436.x.

Williams, S. (2002). *Free As in Freedom: Richard Stallman's Crusade for Free Software* (1st ed.). Sebastopol, CA: Farnham: O'Reilly Media.

Wong, K. (2004). *Free/Open Source Software: Government Policy*. New Delhi: UNDP Asia Pacific Development Information Program in Co-operation with Elsevier.

https://doi.org/10.1142/9789811269554_0014

Chapter 14

With Love for Loved Ones (WLFLO): A Start-Up Creating Value and Opportunities

Supriya Singh[*], **Punit Saurabh**[†], **Pradeep Kautish**[‡]
and Girish R. Kulkarni[§]

Institute of Management, Nirma University, Ahmedabad, Gujarat, India
[*]*supriya.singh@nirmauni.ac.in*
[†]*punit@nirmauni.ac.in*
[‡]*pradeep.kautish@nirmauni.ac.in*
[§]*girish.kulkarni@nirmauni.ac.in*

Case Highlights

1. The business model is designed to address complex challenges of today's human society.
2. Naturally aligned with 7 SDGs out of 17 SDGs of the United Nations.
3. Envisions making India the global capital for eco-friendly bags.
4. Statistical models and projections indicate that WLFLO has the potential to create 5 lakh livelihood opportunities in rural and urban parts of India.
5. Strengthening rural economy and increasing country's exports.
6. Reviving traditional craft businesses of India, promoting local culture.

1. Introduction

It was a casual break from routine work for Devender Singh. Coincidently he visited a small unit producing eco-friendly bags out of Jute in the suburbs of Kolkata with his friend. He was amazed by the artistic talent of poor workers stitching the bags in a small unorganised room. Out of curiosity, he started talking to the workers and found that around 15 to 17 of the workers were living in two small cramped rooms away from their native villages somewhere near Sundarbans (West Bengal) in order to earn their livelihood. He figured out that their expenses had doubled due to their distant stay away from their homes, due to lack of opportunity in their own villages because of which they were forced to migrate for jobs. Here, they could not stay with their family and were forced to earn and maintain two kitchens at a time (one at the native village and the other at the current residence). This increased the cost of living for each family and created the issue of centralisation for the cities due to over-crowding. When they are staying away from their families, they are not able to transfer any values to their kids, and this way the social fabric gets degraded. While interacting with the workers, he casually asked them the following: "If you find an opportunity in your own village, will you work there?" They all showed a keen interest and said "YES" in a fraction of a second. Devender thought, it is the time that the village must be the centre of development wherein the manufacturers have to be in the village providing opportunities to the rural workforce. This was the mindset behind the current social venture of Mr. Devender Singh.

2. Background

Devender hails from a Punjabi family settled in Kolkata (West Bengal). His father is a self-made businessman who worked in the labour-intensive electrical gadget repairing business in the collieries in the Asansol, Dhanbad and Raniganj belt of West Bengal; hence, his father always wanted him to become an electrical engineer. But Devender's interest drove him towards computers which he finally chose as a career. He was always fascinated about the opportunities that can be unlocked by computers, so he became an engineer in computer science after completing his B.Tech. from Asansol Engineering College. As he is the son of an entrepreneur, Devender had witnessed all the struggle and hard work which an entrepreneur has to go through.

When he was in his final semester, he expressed to a couple of his classmates that he planned to set up a software company and asked them to join him. One of them took him to a corner of the class and said, "Yahan bolo nahi toh log waha par pagal kahenge". (Whatever you want to say, say it here, people of the class will call you a fool.) So, that was the kind of reaction he used to receive from people around when he expressed his thoughts of being an entrepreneur. But that never bogged him down, as Devender's positive attitude gave him more strength to prove that "yes I can achieve it". He uses a very good line to motivate himself: "When a school dropout like Bill Gates can become the epitome of success then why can't engineers like me can".

3. Experience

Towards the end of his graduation term, he expressed his willingness to open his own company in front of his father. But as he had already been selected to join Wipro through college placements, he had to join the company as his family did not want him to get burdened with such a huge risk in the initial days of his career.; they wished for him to live a secured life. Now, Devender was in the corporate culture. He learned how the corporate sector functions, team building, people's perspectives, leadership skills, etc. He was doing well in his job.

During his days at Wipro, he received a letter from DSIR, under the DST Department of Technology, with approval and sanction for a grant for a project that he had proposed to the Government of India, which was beneficial for Indian universities. The project was for a handheld device which was called "MPAS", Mobile Presence Authentication System, that could take the fingerprints of professors and students and transfer them to a central server for authentication and matching with the existing fingerprint database and send out the result. He started working on the project under the guidance and support provided by IIT Kharagpur and CDAC Kolkata.

He gained corporate exposure and was leading a well-salaried life, but he wanted to add value to the lives of others through something which would touch lives for the better. He says, "Fear actually creates a dent in the potential of an individual so fear is the biggest retarding post. One has to overcome the fears with logical thinking and rational approach; once we are able to overcome the fears we keep things with the right perspective, so overcoming the fear is very important". He fought with his inner dilemma of leaving the job or not and figured out that "he had nothing to lose" as he will be gaining more experience, meeting new people and if he fails he can start working somewhere once again. He always had the vision to start his own software company which worked on disruptive platforms; therefore, he decided to quit his 9-to-6 MNC job and started his entrepreneurial journey by incorporating VBS Technologies Pvt. Ltd. along with a small team of software developers.

4. Entrepreneurial Journey

It was his first step in the arena of entrepreneurship and a blank slate, a completely white canvas for him. "It's very easy to walk on the path that is known to us but it takes a lot of courage to walk on a path which is not taken by anyone". So, he hoped that he would be able to figure out the goal so that the people who would be following him find it easier. People have their own skill sets, likes and specific inclinations, so according to those parameters, it is the entrepreneur's duty to create value for one and all within the ecosystem. There were many challenges in front of him as a budding entrepreneur.

4.1 *Challenges faced by Devender Singh as an upcoming entrepreneur*

Social issues: Persuading his family to jump into one's own business after living a salaried life.

No funds: To start a software venture, one need not have deep pockets or funds, as all you need is a laptop and internet connection. But to complete the daily working capital requirements, you need a regular flow of funds.

Market understanding: One should know the "pain points" of the people and how to address those pain points; only then will you make some money. In the initial phase, it is difficult to trace clients and grab deals.

Team building: This has always been a crucial ingredient for successful entrepreneurship. So team building was a big challenge — when there are different people in your team, they have a different thought process and different ways of looking at things, so managing different personalities, putting them together to achieve the common task, was something which was very taxing at times.

Team management: Difference of opinions and the **negative attitude of people** were very challenging at times which led to huge losses — loss of time, loss of money, loss of businesses, clients, etc.

Failed projects: An employee's mistake and a client's problems have both given Devender some tough times.

There were many more challenges, but the above-mentioned ones were learning points for him and taught him how one should maintain all the details about those who are engaged in a project and keep the interest levels high. Devender faced all the challenges and proudly worked on numerous software projects for private companies like AAA global ventures, Dr. Lauren Coeil as well as various government departments like the Haldia Development Authority West Bengal and a few district magistrates of Bengal.

As an entrepreneur, he always believed that it is his dharma to create value and opportunities for people around him. He was well aware of the challenges that the world was facing like unemployment, women's disenfranchisement, environment degrading and lack of cleanliness, and tool it as his moral responsibility to contribute his bit to society which could only be possible by being a social entrepreneur. He thought of a venture, a model through which multiple issues can be addressed with one stroke.

4.2 Birth of WLFLO

Devender Singh started WLFLO handicraft LLP in August 2016. It is an organisation making eco-friendly bags and other merchandise. He started operations in June 2016 and slowly added natural fibres like bamboo fibre and cotton. WLFLO manufactures world-class, eco-friendly and hand-crafted jute products.

When he started the company he did not have any idea about the industry. He wanted to make products which would evoke a warm feeling for both the receiver and the giver. So, he thought of handcrafted products made in villages. Initially, he thought of woollen clothes like shawls and sweaters made by grandparents with love, affection and warmth for their kids because these days such things seem to be invisible. He wanted to create products with love so that is where the name comes from, WLFLO — "With Love For Loved Ones". But later, he ended up with handcrafted jute merchandise. The story of his motivation to take up this business has been elaborated at the beginning of this chapter. The first milestone set by Devender was to set up his own unit which was accomplished in 2017 after research of 5 to 6 months at the unit set up in December 2016. Then, he started training people because he wanted people from the differently abled community to experience this, so he established a production cum training centre. The second milestone was to have a group of people who will manufacture products there and another group of people who will be trained there. In the first year, WLFLO did not earn any revenue as it was preparing for its facilities, training people, making designs, structuring the company, struggling with orders, etc. Then, after the second year, the revenue was approximately 13 lakhs, and in 2018 it was about Rs. 19 lakh.

WLFLO deals with some of the most crucial challenges that mankind is facing. In the year 2016, the United Nations came up with 17 sustainable development goals and the WLFLO model is already addressing 7 on the list. On the one hand, it is creating eco-friendly alternatives for conscious global citizens and, on the other hand, it is addressing some complex issues like strengthening the rural economy, creating employment opportunities in rural India, skilling women and men from rural socioeconomic backgrounds and bringing differently abled people into the mainstream of the society. For WLFLO, Devender interviewed 34 differently abled individuals in the first batch. As it was very important to align them with the ethos and values of WLFLO, he selected 7 candidates who were inducted and trained while also getting paid for 3 months of training. He made sure that all the workers were happy working for WLFLO. The objective of this training was to ensure that they have the sense of ownership. When the workers found out that they were being paid during training, it gave them hope and motivation. The initial investment to start this social venture was managed from Devender's personal savings. It was a self-realisation and an aspiration to produce something which is trendy as well as eco-friendly, which is the core idea behind this venture.

4.3 Business model of WLFLO

4.3.1 Business model of competitor bag makers

There are many bag-making units in our country that undertake the whole course of production under one roof. These units bring all factors under one roof and structure the process using minimum activity time for maximum production with the help of advanced machinery. Engaging lakhs of people in this format is something which would take great resources. One needs to hire so many people, needs to ensure that there is a continuous flow of orders, quality has to be maintained, etc. This model already exists, but it is not addressing social problems. This could not give employment to the rural population in their own village or neighbourhood.

WLFLO is working on a quadruple bottom line of People, Planet, Profit and Culture. There are 4 units of production which are in operation right now, the first unit in Laohati, second in Rairachi, third in Dakkhindari and fourth in the Minakha police station area, which is 110 km away from Kolkata Airport. WLFLO is focusing on packaging materials. WLFLO has few people on its payroll and three people managing each of the units. These are supervisory roles that ensure the production is optimum and is carried out in the best possible way (Figure A.1).

What is WLFLO doing that is **different**?

WLFLO has hired one master craftsman and a couple of more people in the production team who are responsible for providing training and taking care of production. In the production side, they have created employment opportunities for more than 100 people as of now. WLFLO is different from its competitors as it is not keeping people on its payroll because it cannot increase the overhead of the company, but it is creating a platform where it gives the people associated with WLFLO training, direct orders, raw materials and necessary infrastructure. So, the trained people are using this platform to earn their livelihood.

WLFLO employs rural and differently abled people only. It provides paid training to rural people, and for any person who was trained by WLFLO, there are 2 ways ahead: (1) monthly company payroll and (2) micro entrepreneur

(1) Monthly payroll basis

The industry does not encourage people to become a bag maker on monthly salary basis. People who manufacture the bags are reluctant to be on monthly salary because that will limit their remuneration to a certain limit. Whatever amount of bags they stitch, say 50 bags a day or 100 bags a day, they are going to get the same amount. So, the trend which is prevailing in this industry is a per job or per unit basis. The industry has set up a price for every bag, and every manufacturing unit pays almost the same amount per unit. The workers prefer to undertake jobs on a unit basis. WLFLO is following the trends prevalent in the market and has both kinds of people.

(2) Micro entrepreneur

WLFLO creates micro entrepreneurs by giving an opportunity to the labourers to become small entrepreneurs. Here, the workers are registered with the company as active members.

WLFLO has come up with its **COE, "Centre of Excellence"**, unit for eco-friendly products. The raw material is first brought to the COE and, according to the order, the cutting process is done followed by the printing process. Then, the processed raw material is piled up and sent to other units where it is distributed to the people associated with WLFLO. For example, if Ajay is a beneficiary of WLFLO who is trained to make eco-friendly bags out of jute, he will have his profile ready on the software. Ajay will find customers or market requirements for WLFLO products, he comes and gives his card (proof of registration with the company) to the centre head, who authenticates Ajay's proficiency and capability on the basis of the checklist that was made during his training time. After exhibiting the necessary skill set, Ajay is capable of making these bags, so the material will not go waste. Therefore, according to his skill set, Ajay gets a sanction for a finite unit of bags, say 200 bags, in his name. Now, Ajay takes the raw material for the bags to the stitching centre present in the same campus. He need not have his own manufacturing machine; he can show his card and get a machine allotted to him and start working. This creates a sense of ownership as he takes the trouble to generate the order, manage raw material, manufacture, check the quality, deliver the goods, etc. He is no longer a mere worker; he is a micro entrepreneur. He gets to know that it is not an easy process. He becomes more responsible with this activity (Figure A.2).

The following products are manufactured: (1) Card holders, (2) Files and folders, (3) Laptop bags, (4) Shopping bags with jute packaging and (5) Customised gift items as per client's design and demand. Devender wants to create multiple WLFLO centres in different districts of the country with the capacity for 100 installed machines so that around 200 people from rural communities, especially women and the differently abled, can get employment in each district, which is obviously not an easy task. This is what he has envisioned for the structure of WLFLO.

When he started, he had around 2 machines and today he has 53 machines. When the company started, it made just 100–200 bags a day, but now it has a production capacity of 12,000 units per day.

4.4 *Marketing*

Once the first lot of products came out, they were displayed to prospective buyers and thereafter Devender started marketing these products. He did not hire people for marketing in the initial phase due to insufficient funds, so he personally took care of that. Slowly, he started receiving queries from different corporates due to word-of-mouth marketing. Therefore, he gradually hired people who have prior experience of working with a social venture. The intent behind this was to make a like-minded team that has an inclination towards society and wants to solve social issues.

The initial products were designed by Devender himself. He took care of the production, quality control, purchases, etc., making it a one-man army. He studied the entire industry minutely and figured out various cost centres. For example, today if any shopkeeper in Ahmedabad wants to buy 2000 bags at the market price of Rs. 70 per bag, then it is a Rs. 140,000 order. Now conventionally, that person will go to the market and buy these bags and use them. If that person directly approaches WLFLO for 200 bags, he will get the best rates as he is directly dealing with manufacturers and hence the mediators and marketers do not earn out of this.

As the business expanded, Devender realised the need of hiring a new team of dedicated people to take care of different aspects of the business. Marketing of the main products was very crucial, and WLFLO opened a few channels for the same. The first marketing channel was their website www.wlflo.com. To sell their products through other web links, they partnered with the world's largest online retail platform, Amazon.

For the growth of institutional sales, WLFLO approached IIM Calcutta, Calcutta Innovation Park, Iskon. All of them liked the concept, found the price point competitive, liked few of the products and placed orders with WLFLO. Then, WLFLO approached many corporate houses like hyper exchange, conferences in various corners of the country, a few colleges and schools, all of whom also started purchasing the products — this was the second channel of marketing. Then, WLFLO started exporting these products by getting in touch with fashion designers in different important cities of fashion like New York and Paris. Devender came across a fashion designer from New York who displayed these products in the "New York Fashion Week" September 2017. A good network of satisfied customers, supporting well-wishers, colleagues and friends constantly helps Devender with new references and publicity of business.

When we talk about corporates and hand-packaging materials, in many cases we see that the gifts that are being given to the clients, customers or employees are wrapped in plastic paper. WLFLO has options of reusable beautifully designed handmade jute pouches, which gives an aesthetic value, with some pictures or messages that the corporates wish to convey; this means an urbanised design, aesthetic values and optimum ROI for the investor.

4.5 *Growth of social enterprise*

Every business survives because of its customers; if the customer is happy, the business does well. WLFLO did not intend to sell only emotions,

Devendra wants people to opt for WLFLO's products considering their quality and not just for sake of some charity. Sympathy can help you fetch clients only once, but if you are making quality products, pricing it competitively, that is the very foundation of a sustainable business. Right from day 1, Devender made it a policy to deliver high-quality products at the best possible prices. The WLFLO model, which is a distributed model, ensures that the overheads are lower; for a unit to have everything under one roof, its overheads will go up, but this WLFLO model helps reduce the overheads as it helps to reduce the cost. WLFLO transfers this benefit to its customers, which is the reason why it is able to price these products on such a competitive level. It procures material in bulk directly from mills at the best price. Then it goes for cutting printed in one place. Lastly, the processed material is sent to distinct centres at various locations for the final sewing. So now, the person who used to travel, for e.g., 10 km earlier can just reach the comfortable WLFLO centre in his own locality and will be able to stitch his bag. Here, that person is saving about 2 h a day. So, in those 2 h a day, the production goes up and cost of material comes down. In the end, WLFLO will be able to sell at a better price point than other competitors. WLFLO has become India's most low-cost jute bag manufacturer because of this model.

4.5.1 *Social value creation*

WLFLO wants to create a positive impact on society by helping people with disabilities and from economically weaker sections in the villages. Talking about an incident of hiring, Devender said, "Initially when I was hiring and interviewing, in first batch I inducted and skilled 7 out of 34 differently abled people and offered them training. I came across candidates who told me, 'Sir hum training karke Kya Karenge humare paas bahut certificate hai, aap Hamein kuch kaam dijiye' (Sir what shall we do with this training, we have a lot of certificates of training, just give us some job). I found a need to survival in all of them but it was very important for me to align them with the ethos and values of WLFLO. So, I insisted that they go for a 3-month training and paid them for the training on a monthly basis. When they found that they were being paid for their training, it created a hope and motivated them to work".

The main objective of WLFLO is to provide some eco-friendly alternatives to the world. When anyone buys a bag, it is used for a couple of months or years but when the bag is discarded, it becomes burden on this planet till eternity as those bags are not biodegradable. To fight this issue, WLFLO created eco-friendly, beautifully designed, urbanised, handcrafted, world-class quality bags that were competitively priced. WLFLO is trying to take it to all kinds of consumers.

WLFLO provides great support to the jute industry by producing jute products. It sources jute directly from mills for a better rate. For cotton bags, the grey fabric is sourced from Vidarbha (Maharashtra) region farmers, and Ichhankaranji, Kherol and Malegaon also. On the one hand, WLFLO is creating eco-friendly alternatives for conscious global citizens and, on the other hand, it is addressing some complex issues like strengthening the rural economy, creating employment opportunities in rural India, skilling women and men from rural socioeconomic backgrounds, bringing differently abled people into the mainstream of society, providing sustainable livelihood, reducing poverty, gender equality, good jobs and economic growth, reduced inequality, responsible consumption and climate action.

4.6 Issues/challenges faced

Connectivity to the city: The city is the mainland where the manufactured products will be bought and sold; so, a unit cannot be set up in a village hundreds of kilometres away from the city. Hence, a problem arose to choose the best fitted place where skilled people can be found along with proper connectivity with mainland Kolkata. In the initial phase, Devender chose a place which was moderate distance from Kolkata city, so that it becomes easy for him to manage. He had planned a village unit with around 4 machines and to help this unit, 3 more units were opened in the suburbs of Kolkata. The strategic viewpoint was to support the village unit by the other 3 units on the outskirts of Kolkata.

Balancing constant demand and supply: To settle down and sustain the company, it was very important for Devender to manage a certain level of demand and supply of handicraft products. There was a need for a platform which would provide the company with continuous work. So, he set up one unit near Kolkata Airport; since this was very close to the city, he could invite people, the prospects, to see how their order is going to bring a positive change to the lives of people.

Make people believe in WLFLO's agenda: There exist so many bogus social ventures and NGOs which make fools of people by showing fraudulent works. Therefore, in the initial phase, it was very crucial for Devender to make the prospective clients believe that their purchasing power can bring about a positive change. Slowly and gradually, he was successful in making the clients trust over the product's quality standards and competitive pricing by carrying out exhibitions on various platforms. Besides that, since the bags were made by a social venture, buyers felt their contribution will be going a long way towards addressing some complex issues of our society. So conscious buyers, conscious companies and organisations started placing orders with WLFLFO; once he started receiving orders, it became easy for Devender to manage the facility that he had opened.

Expansion: Devender found an opportunity to take care of 1200 weavers in the Shantipur Solia region of Bengal — these are saree weavers who wanted to collaborate with WLFLO and wanted Devender to take care of their production and marketing, but unfortunately WLFLO does not possess such facilities and infrastructure as of now.

Supply chain and scaling up: Scaling up was a tough call to make as Devender could not automate all manual work. The core business idea talks about handcrafted goods made by rural and differently abled people. If automated, the manpower employed will lose their jobs. Hence, Devender chose of a path with slow growth so that the purpose of the business could be solved. Right now, the supply chain is a big issue for WLFLO. WLFLO wishes to take care of the entire supply chain right from the farmer and that is only possible when they are scaling up or when they put in more funds. Starting a social venture is not fund intensive, but scaling up requires huge funds.

Lack of funds: Devender spent all his savings and diverted everything to WLFLO. He sold some gold and added to the WLFO fund. His family supported him and acted as a pillar for him. The idea of WLFLO was inspired by the "Startup India", "Make In India", "Skill India" and "Swachh Bharat" campaigns by the Government of India. Devender managed to run his venture on his own saving. The income generated by the venture was very limited in value, but he never applied for any sort of funding programmes by the Government of India or any other organisation. He wants to create earning opportunities for 500 people, and with a speed of making 200 bags per person in one day, he aims to sell 100,000 bags per day. To fulfil this WLFLO needs multiple centres and huge capital. The company intends to procure cotton directly from farmers, but as there is a lot of processing required like weaving and other things, a big in-house facility and infrastructure are required along with the requisite funds. The need of the hour is for further scaling up of the business to other states of the country and it is very important for Devender to grab good-value external funding.

Dealing with unprofessionalism: This type of industry is full of skilled unprofessionals. That is, the manpower is highly skilled but the professional attitude is missing. Here comes the question of how to manage the grassroots talent, their problems, emotions, etc. WLFLO makes only eco-friendly alternatives out of natural fibres like jute, cotton, bamboo fibre and canvas. To make the rural and uneducated people realise the importance of eco-friendly products was not an easy task. Hence, Devender organised an orientation programme for them with an agenda to make them realise that their part of the journey is not an isolated task; they are doing something good for themselves, their families, society, the country and for mankind on the whole.

Right workforce: Working for a social venture is something which requires a different mindset at times; so, having people who have such an inclination towards society is very important. WLFLO is facing issues in finding like-minded people, who are willing to step forward and invest their time to be a part of this journey.

Technological advancement: Right now, the processes of WLFLO are done manually with less technological support. It hampers the pace and growth of work, and WLFLO wishes to reach out to 100,000 people in next 5 years, but that is only possible with the help of right software infrastructure, which Devender is trying to build (Figure A.3).

4.7 *Future goals*

WLFLO wants to build an artificial intelligence-based (AI-based) application which can sense or calculate demand and supply on a real-time basis. For example, the entire European market is in need of eco-friendly bags, and who would make these bags? People in India, Bangladesh, China and Nepal would make these bags. Now, when we talk about people making a bag, it is a labour-intensive job, so to manage people, it becomes very challenging at times. The WLFLO artificial intelligence platform has got 2 important aspects. Part 1 is called JOB, "Job Order Bank", meaning collating orders from different sources like from Ahmedabad to Delhi, from Canada, from London, and from the United Nations. All the orders will get collated or collected here. And before you commit to a customer, you need to know whether you will be able to deliver it as per the customer's demand. So to do this in a real-time basis, WLFLO creates an application which will use artificial intelligence to figure out whether it has that capacity or not. With this, WLFLO will come up with realistic forecasting as it does not want to rely on unrealistic figures. This is the demand side. When it comes to the supply side, each of the WLFLO centres is already training people, who are preparing a database, and this database has very important parameters like the proficiency level of each worker, for example, it can happen that a person has experience of 13 months, but he can only handle pressure of a certain complexity when it comes to making a particular type of bag. Periodically, the WLFLO system will test these people, rank these people, so that the system has updated information about the available skill set, so that WLFLO can reach out to half a million people through such a database within 3 years of time.

As WLFLO is making eco-friendly bags, Devender is looking forward to taking care of 1,200 saree weavers in the Shantipur Solia region of Bengal. He wants to collaborate with them and they want him to take care of their production and marketing, but he does not have such a band width as of now, but with expansion he wants to expand to other products like sarees. In Banaras, weavers are leaving their traditional jobs. Although there is demand, these people are leaving their jobs because of the unorganised nature of these jobs. If such jobs were to be organised, it will generate due importance and remuneration that these people deserve. The exploitation will lessen and there will be a transparent system that will be established.

By expanding WLFLO's reach, Devender Singh started a programme called GLORY, "Growth and Livelihood Opportunities for Rural Youth". It is a platform for cognizant individuals and organisations to co-create sustainable livelihood opportunities and unleash the rural potential. It is step towards instituting an ecosystem of growth for musicians, small farmers, artisans, weavers, craftsmen, self-help groups, painters and cooperatives by facilitating skill enhancement, quality infrastructure and accessible market links. Through an integrated approach of "Collective Production and Marketing" that is a mix of online and offline strategies, GLORY reduces the time, effort and overheads of all the above arts and crafts people. It increases the competitiveness of rural producers (price and quality-wise) with access to wider markets.

Case Questions

Q.1 Being from a family business background, Devender did not join his own family business. What can be the reasons?

Q.2 Was it a wise decision for Devender Singh to enter into social entrepreneurship from a software business background? Justify your perspective.

Q.3 What according to you can Devender do differently for his business model?

Appendix

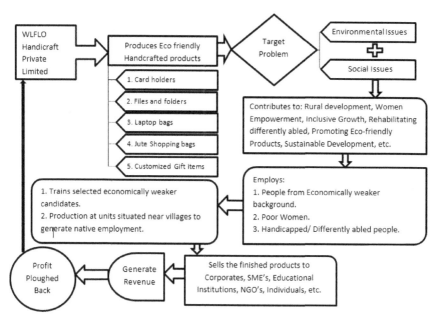

Figure A.1.   Business flow analysis of WLFLO.

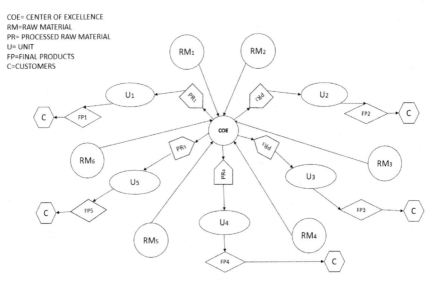

COE= CENTER OF EXCELLENCE
RM=RAW MATERIAL
PR= PROCESSED RAW MATERIAL
U= UNIT
FP=FINAL PRODUCTS
C=CUSTOMERS

Figure A.2.   Network model of WLFLO.

Key Partners:	Key Activities:	Value Propositions:	Customer Relationship:	Customer Segments:
1. Machine manufacturers. 2. Small scale units for ancillary products. 3. Jute Factories 4. Cotton Farmers. 5. Logistic Partners.	1. Hiring and Training 2. Product Designing 3. Stitching 4. Marketing on right platform 5. Packaging 6. Customized Delivery	1. Ecofriendly product 2. Trendy handlooms 3. Support to handicapped and socially excluded class.	1. Online 2. In Person 3. Events 4. Referrals	1. Academic/ Student buyers 2. Corporate clients 3. Fashion Lovers
	Key Resources: 1. Office Space 2. Center of Excellence 3. Raw material 4. Machinery 5. Basic infrastructure 6. Network of Skilled Team 7. Logistic Channel		**Channels:** 1. Networking 2. Public Speaking 3. PR 4. Trade Shows 5. Third Party Contactors	

Cost Structures:	Revenue Streams:
1. Infrastructure Development 2. Manufacturing 3. Online Platform 4. Wages and Salaries 5. Maintenance Cost 6. Raw material Cost 7. Marketing and Branding	1. Per Unit Sales 2. Bulk Sales 3. Customized Orders

Figure A.3.   Business model canvas of WLFLO.

WLFLO website

WLFLO products

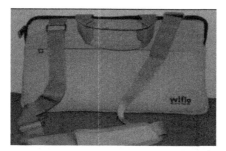

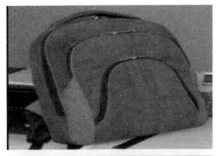

WLFLO's GLORY ("Growth & Livelihood Opportunities for Rural Youth") Programme:

for

" G L O R Y   O F   H U M A N I T Y "

" G L O R Y   O F   B H A R A T "

https://doi.org/10.1142/9789811269554_0015

Chapter 15

Systematic Literature Review on Retention in Entrepreneurial Firms: A Step Towards Sustainable Development

Shivangi Saxena[*] and Divya Goel[†]

Jaypee Institute of Information Technology, Noida, Uttar Pradesh, India
*shivangisaxena.research@gmail.com
†divyagoel.jmi@gmail.com

Abstract

Entrepreneurial firms, which include the new-age start-ups and an emerging era of Small and Medium Enterprises (SMEs), have a central role to play in the economic growth of a country. Moreover, they have a central role in the economy and are imperative for employment generation and boosting technological advancement. It is well established that the management of established large-sized firms is significantly different from the challenges faced in the management of the small-sized entrepreneurial firms. Also, out of the numerous factors that influence the growth of SMEs and start-ups, one of the key differentiating factors is the leadership and the team/people that drive organisational growth. It has been seen that attracting, hiring and retaining key employees has always been challenging for any organisation, but in the case of small-scale entrepreneurial firms, it is even more daunting. In the context of this, the objective of the present chapter is to develop a framework for understanding the factors that affect employee retention in entrepreneurial firms using a systematic literature review. This chapter is an effort to find evidence from the past that indicates the factors affecting the employee retention in entrepreneurial firms. The findings from this study suggested that the HR policies can play the major role in retention practices.

315

Keywords: Entrepreneurial firms, employee retention, systematic literature review, employee, employer, human resource policies, ethics, organisational image

1. Introduction

In today's scenario, we will see that the planning for a start-up is not difficult, but sustaining the start-up in the market is rather a big deal. Many entrepreneurs come to the industry every year but only a few of them sustain (Agarwal *et al.*, 2004; Urban & Joubert, 2017; Moayedfar & Madani, 2019). There must be different reasons for the success of the few and the failure of the rest. The variables affecting the sustainability can be the knowledge of the founder, funds, government policies, working environment and the most important could be the employees working in the firm (Andonova & Zuleta, 2007; Urban & Joubert, 2017; Green, 2019). These days, much effort is being taken by the government and academicians in the development of individuals as entrepreneurs (Bamberger *et al.*, 1990; Carpentier *et al.*, 2019).

Institutions are setting up incubation centres to develop business acumen and initiate the seed of business development in millennials. Government agencies are helping new start-ups by providing them soft loans and other timely help (Carpentier *et al.*, 2019; Bilal *et al.*, 2016).

Even the big established brands like Tata, Future Group and Infosys are helping new-age entrepreneurs as venture capitalists. The amount of trust shown by these big firms is boosting the morale of the new entrepreneurs. Indian products have always made their way to international markets (Dana, 2000; Urbancová & Hudáková, 2017).

The EDP programmes held by the government and universities at different levels play a key role in developing market sentiments for the founder of the start-ups. These start-ups help in the creation of job opportunities as well as the economic development of the country (Aldrich, 1990).

As it is said, employees are the real asset of a company, so they play an important role in the development and the rise of any organisation. As observed from the literature available and the practices in the start-up industry, it is seen that for any start-up, it is difficult to attract employees and even more difficult to retain them (Bamberger *et al.*, 1990; Block *et al.*, 2018; Ahammad *et al.*, 2020).

2. Literature Review

From the literature available, it has been observed that retention of employees is a major problem faced by entrepreneurial firms. Management of talent was always a key issue in any organisation and when it comes to entrepreneurial firms (Cardon & Stevens, 2004; Ahammad *et al.*, 2020), it becomes even more complex. Entrepreneurship development is a topic that carries great importance in today's scenario. Entrepreneurship plays a very important role in economic development. Entrepreneurs act as catalytic agents in the process of industrialisation and economic growth. Joseph Schumpeter states that the rate of economic progress of a nation depends upon its rate of innovation, which in turn depends upon the distribution of entrepreneurial talent in the population (Dabic *et al.*, 2011; Urbancová & Hudáková, 2017). Technological progress alone cannot lead to economic development unless technological breakthroughs are put to economic use by entrepreneurs. It is the entrepreneur who organises and puts to use capital, labour and technology in the best possible manner for the setting up of his enterprise. Previous studies on employee turnover have suggested the importance of taking a macro perspective in studying human resource retention.

In the past, it has been argued that an effective human resource management strategy should balance the cost of replacing employees who leave against the cost of retaining those who stay (Barrick & Zimmermen, 2009; Green, 2019). Since it is generally more expensive to replace highly productive employees than to replace weak performers, a cost-effective human resource management strategy will attempt to minimise turnover among string performers.

2.1 *Retention*

Retention as a term can be understood as the state of remaining in the same place. When it comes to employee retention, it can be termed as the organisation's ability to retain its workforce (Glen, 2006). The efforts and the strategies adopted by the organisation to keep their workforce with them can also be the explanation for employee retention. Basic talent management is a key factor in any of the organisation.

While talking about employee retention in any organisation, one should not forget the difference between the low-performing employee and a high performer. In this way, the organisational efforts should be in the direction of retaining the valuable and high-performing employees (Kwoon & Yoo, 2011; Moayedfar & Madani, 2019). Employee turnover is always an issue for any organisation and when it comes to entrepreneurial firms, this is an even bigger issue.

Referring to Pareto's Law, we get a clear picture that 80% of the companies' work output is dependent on 20% of its dedicated and talented pool of employees (Dr. Joseph Juran). And so, when it comes to employee retention, it is these 20% employees those are needed to be retained in the organisation. Assessment as in itself is not a very easy task to be done. While assessing the performing employees or we can say the real gems in the organisation, there must be some clear boundaries of assessment. The keys factors that should be kept in mind while assessing the employees in any organisation are as follows:

(A) Identification of the key duty sets: This question itself contains a higher level of understanding and importance. Before assessing an employee in the organisation, it is rather important to understand the clear sets of duties that any organisation is expecting from its employees because each organisation can have their own curated definition of what constitutes value and therefore identifying talent from scratch involves defining "value creation" and then assessing the talent in the employee accordingly.

Talking in terms of entrepreneurial firms, the vital few can be the employees who are acting as the pillars to the organisation and can seamlessly work for the betterment of the organisation. This category of employees can be seen with few differentiating characteristics:

Interpersonal (easy to work with), which clearly indicated that how well versed an employee is to work with the colleagues.

Competency (academically and technically sound) is a very important factor in today's racing world.

Keen Learners (always ready to learn new things and adapt) are always appreciated in the organisations.

Motivated (self-motivated people) employees always deliver their best in the organisation.

(B) The ways to access the talent: Most managers in entrepreneurial firms adopt the strategy of seeing and identifying talent. In entrepreneurial firms, there are a limited number of employees, thus they do not have a systematic HR department, resulting in the assessment purely based on the managers' discretion. After hiring the right people in the first place, employee engagement is the key to talent retention. Studies show that a high level of employee engagement is beneficial for all because there is a positive correlation between employee engagement and good organisational outcomes.

Employee retention can be a crucial factor for many companies to survive in this hyper-competitive era. Attrition in any organisation incurs cost in terms of recruitment, hiring and training of new employees. If organisations formulate the right strategy to retain their top talent, they can save cost and can develop sustainable competitive advantage.

2.2 Retention strategies

The most important factor in front of any entrepreneurial firm is the retention of employees, and more importantly the retention of employees valuable to the organisation. Many retention strategies have been studied till date and explained in different management books, but the task is to identify which strategy will work best on your organisation. These effective employee retention strategies should be a part of the Human Resource module. Some of the retention strategies are discussed in the following:

2.2.1 Hiring right

The first and the key point is hiring the right people. While hiring, keep in mind to ask different questions related to their expectation from the workplace, their motivation, their tasks, their aspirations and other questions that help the interviewers analyse the personality of the candidate

(Kwoon & Yoo, 2011). This will not only tell you a lot about the person but also give you a fair idea if his passion for work will align with your organisation. Thus, the best fits are easy to retain in the organisations.

2.2.2 *Work environment*

The work environment in any organisation plays an important role in the employees' work satisfaction, leading to employee engagement and then to retention. When the organisation has strong ethics and cultural values, the employee has a feeling of association with the organisation and people feel like they belong there; this condition leads to satisfaction of employees.

2.2.3 *Competent workforce*

When an employee works in any organisation, the work equation with the other team members and the managers plays a key role in job satisfaction. An employee rarely quits a job; rather, he quits the boss, the working culture and the environment of the organisation. The upper level should always be supportive and understanding towards the subordinates as they represent the organisation to the employees (Morrell *et al.*, 2001). So, in any organisation, the middle management (managers) should be trained in technical as well as interpersonal skills.

2.2.4 *Training and development*

Continuous learning is the desire of every employee. When people join any organisation, they seek opportunities for training and learning new things, to enhance their skill set. Providing a platform to the employees for training can help increase employee loyalty and, thus, in reducing attrition.

2.2.5 *Work–life balance*

In today's scenario, work–life balance is the factor that plays an important role in the performance of the employee. When an organisation stops thinking about the employee's personal life and always expects 100% output from them, there is an imbalance in the work–life for the employee.

This situation often results in quitting. Thus, the organisational approach should not be in wanting people to hold these grudges and quitting.

2.2.6 *Rewards and recognition*

Every individual likes to be appreciated for the work they are doing. When an organisation fails to appreciate the employees for their hard work, dissatisfaction is created in the employee's mind, which further converts into job dissatisfaction and then to quitting the job. As an organisation, it is very important to recognise work in a timely manner and pay rewards in terms of incentives to the employees. This keeps the employees motivated and reduces the rate of attrition.

2.2.7 *Bond with the employees*

In case of formal communication in any organisation, it is often observed that people talk what is expected out of their designations. This makes the workplace a stereotyped place where people come, work and go back home. Enthusiasm that can do wonders on workplace and ironically it goes missing in today's scenario. An organisation can remove this barrier of boredom by bonding with its employees informally. HR departments can organise a family day type of function which encourages even the families to be a part of the setup.

2.2.8 *Feedback and communication*

We all know that employees need feedback to improve and to do their best work — both positive and constructive advice. Positive feedback should be given regularly to motivate employees and to give them the determination they need to do their best work. But constructive and corrective feedback is also important, particularly when there is an urgent issue that needs to be aborted.

2.2.9 *Exit interview*

There may be a number of reasons for different individuals to leave the organisation. From an organisation's point of view, it is important to understand the real reason behind any employee leaving the job. At the time of leaving, the employees are not under any sort of pressure and so they are more honest and clearer in explaining the details of quitting. This may help the organisation understand if the problem lies in the system or if it is some other factor that is responsible for attrition.

2.3 Benefits of retention

Retention strategies if adopted properly bring many benefits to the organisation and some of them are stated as follows:

1. Existing employees' skills, talent and values are known to the organisation. The employees that are in the organisation for a longer period are the real assets to the organisation as their skills, interests and motivation are well understood over the duration.
2. Existing employees' cultural fit is another plus point for any organisation as the employee fits well into the organisation's culture and thus they benefit from each other. Performance and attitude are more factors that are associated with the existing employee's understandability to the organisation.
3. Existing employees' aspirations and expectations are clear to the organisation. When an employee is with the organisation for a longer period, his/her expectations and aspirations are well known to the organisation and vice versa the organisation's expectation is also known to the employee; this in turn helps both in achieving the organisational and personal goals.
4. Employees' adjustment with the company's climate and environment is also very fruitful for mutual benefit of both the employee and the company. An organisation's climate always affects the productivity of the employees in any organisation, and when the employee is best fitted in the organisation's climate the productivity is high.
5. As for the cost of recruitment and training, when any organisation brings an employee to the company, it includes the cost of recruitment and then the training cost. If an employee is retained in the company, both costs will not be incurred again.

6. Even the employee's family members get adjusted to the company's environment. Every organisation has a different style of working and different sets of expectations with the employee, and when an employee is in the organisation for a longer period, even the family of the employee gets adjusted to the culture, resulting in an increase in productivity.

2.4 *Research framework*

The research framework as shown in Figure 1 is divided into three sections: talent attraction, retention strategies and talent retention. Retention from the core is dependent on many factors, and talent attraction is one major factor among them. There should be a clear reason for talent to join any organisation as it may affect the retention of the talent. There are other factors like the employee's own attitude, the employer, the HR policies, the organisation and some other external factors that affect the retention of employees in any entrepreneurial firm. Before developing any retention model, all these factors must be kept in mind and, taking into consideration all this, a model for employee retention in entrepreneurial firms can be developed.

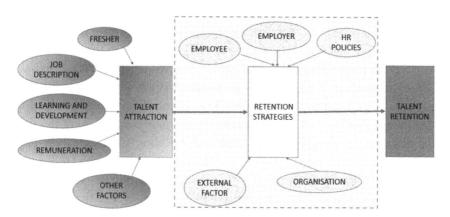

Figure 1.   Employee attraction to retention (integrated view).

3. Methodology

This literature review is done with an intention to analyse previous research work, find the research gaps and develop the scope for further research. Relatively less turnover research has focused specifically on how an employee decides to remain with an organisation and what determines this attachment. Retention processes should be studied along with quitting processes (Das & Baruah, 2013). Managing and retaining promising employees is an important fundamental way to achieve competitive advantage among organisations (Walker, 2001). Descriptive research can be defined as the research that systematically analyses any situation or problem. It is basically a type of conclusive research. It helps in the study of different associated variables by classifying the degree of their association and, thus, helps in making predictions. This process involves the searching, filtering and classification of research papers. Eight of the prominent databases — Elsevier, Emerald, Google Scholar, Springer, Taylor and Francis, Science Direct, ProQuest and IGI Global — were searched to find 102 research papers. The combination of key words used to identify the relevant research papers was as follows: "HR Practices", "Organisation Culture", "HR Policies" and "Employee Attraction", keeping "Entrepreneurial Firms" and "Employee Retention" common. The papers taken into account for this research were published on or before December 2018.

The initial search resulted in a total of 102 hits, which were then further sorted. The step-by-step sorting included manual screening of titles in the first step to remove irrelevant papers. This resulted in the segregation of research papers, elimination of duplicates, whitepapers, ACM digital, conference papers, book chapters, proceeding papers and opinion articles. In the next step, the papers were closely examined by reading the abstract and then the full text and after doing this, the papers that did not discuss the concepts of entrepreneurial firms and retention were removed. The authors were left with only 19 peer-reviewed papers. This indicated the scope for the study in the field of retention, specifically based on the entrepreneurial firms. From the above review of papers, five major factors that affect the retention of employees in the entrepreneurial firms came into the light.

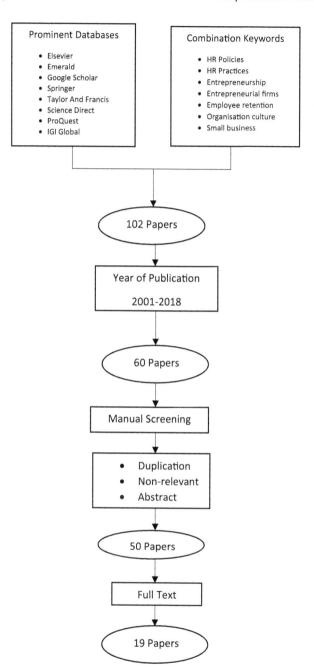

Figure 2. Depiction of the flow of research methodology that the authors adopted.

4. Discussion

Table 1 depicts that employee, employer, HR policies, organisation and external factors are the five major factors that affect employee retention in the entrepreneurial firms in the service industry. Strong HR policies are major factors that may contribute to the retention of employees in entrepreneurial firms. The HR policies in any organisation help in connecting

Table 1. Table classification.

Authors \\ Factors	Employee	Employer	HR Policies	Organisation	External Factors
Sauermann (2017)				✓	
Bartram (2005)			✓		
Dabic, Creido, & Romeromartenez (2011)	✓		✓		
Glen (2006)		✓	✓		
Cho, Gary, & Mclean (2009)			✓		
Cardon, Christopher, & Stevens (2004)		✓	✓		
Anderson (2000)			✓		
Barrick & Zimmermen (2009)			✓		
Clarke & Wilkinson (2001)			✓		
Hausknecht, Rodda, & Howard (2009)			✓		
Perrin (2016)			✓		
Kinyili, Karanja, & Namusonge (2015)	✓		✓		
Das & Barua (2013)	✓		✓		✓
Onteri (2013)	✓	✓	✓	✓	
Kwon & Yoo (2011)	✓		✓	✓	
Monsen & Boss (2009)			✓	✓	
Kickul (2001)		✓	✓		✓
Kaur (2017)	✓	✓	✓	✓	✓
Messmer (2002)		✓	✓		

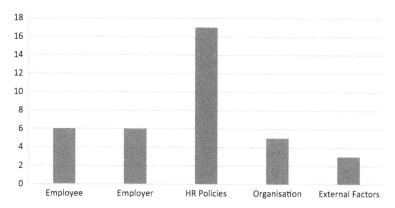

Figure 3.   Graphical representation.

the employees with the organisation. Thus, if the connection is strong, then the employee will be an integral part of the organisation.

Figure 3 represents that the most important factor among the five factors is the HR policies of the organisation. The next important factors ranked are employee and employer. External factors affect retention the least. With the increasing encouragement of the modern Make-in-India concept, entrepreneurial firms are coming up with great pace and serving society with more employment options. While retention plays important role in the firms, the factors affecting retention must be studied in depth.

This chapter also explores various research gaps identified after conducting an intensive literature review. Some of the gaps are discussed in detail in the following. This discussion is supported by previous research work and interviews with experts.

Discussion A: Retention strategies for entrepreneurial firms.
There is a dearth of retention strategies for entrepreneurial firms. Retention strategies only focusing on employee retention of these firms are much needed in today's scenario. Retention of employees plays a vital role in the performance of any organisation. Even the success stories of any organisation cannot be done without a dedicated workforce who bonds with the organisation.

Discussion B: In-depth analysis of higher attrition rate needs to be done for entrepreneurial firms.
Attrition rate is higher in entrepreneurial firms and this issue must be dealt with great care. Attrition rate must be analysed deeply in these organisations. As discussed in the research papers, the factors affecting the attrition rate in entrepreneurial firms are discussed. As depicted in Figure 3, the factor that affects attrition most is HR policies in any organisation. The next two important factors are employee and the employer. The factor that least affects the attrition rate is external factor.

Most of the research papers studied have emphasised that HR policies of any organisation affect the retention. However, there is a dearth of studies clearly depicting how these policies can be made to increase the retention of employees in entrepreneurial firms.

Discussion C: HR policies as the major contributor in the retention.
The HR policy of any organisation is the connection between the employee and the organisation. The stronger the connection, the better the retention. Employees directly get affected by the HR policies of the organisation and if the policies made mutually benefit both employees and employer, they may act as the major contributing factor in retention.

Most of the research papers agreed with the importance of HR policies in different ways in any organisation. However, there is no direct study done targeting entrepreneurial firms.

Discussion D: Employee satisfaction in the entrepreneurial firms can be analysed as the factor to employee retention.
Employee satisfaction may directly affect employee retention as satisfied employees tend to be more loyal to the organisation. The satisfaction of the employees can be studied in different forms and there may be another set of factors working behind the satisfaction of the employee, specifying employee satisfaction in entrepreneurial firms. Further research should be done on employee satisfaction leading to retention.

5. Conclusion

Entrepreneurship development is a topic that carries great importance in today's scenario. Entrepreneurship plays a very important role in economic development. Entrepreneurs act as catalytic agents in the process of industrialisation and economic growth. Joseph Schumpeter states that the rate of economic progress of a nation depends upon its rate of innovation, which in turn depends upon the distribution of entrepreneurial talent in the population. Technological progress alone cannot lead to economic development unless technological breakthroughs are put to economic use by entrepreneurs. It is the entrepreneur who organises and puts to use capital, labour and technology in the best possible manner for the setting up of his enterprise.

But at the same time, despite giving so much to the social and economic growth of the region, entrepreneurs face the problem of talent retention in their firms. The employee in these firms joins the young firms, learns from there and moves to another established brand. This concept of ladder-climbing makes the growth of entrepreneurial firm slow. As it takes time to train the employee, when the employee gets the required training and moves to another brand, it leaves the founder with no option but to hire and train again. This chapter is an effort to shed some light on the solving of these problems for entrepreneurs.

Retention in entrepreneurial firms is different from that of established firms. While the baseline factors remain the same, the process differs. Established firms, for instance, have a brand image, set processes of work, ample training and development procedures, job stability, learning and development opportunities, remuneration and rewards. On the other hand, entrepreneurial firms hire trained and multitasking people because, with their limited resources, they cannot spend much on training. They can showcase their robust style of working to give ample amount of exposure to the employee for greater learning. Retention in entrepreneurial firms can be improved by giving challenging jobs and opportunities to employees to become the face of the organisation, along with involvement in decision-making, vision matching and transparency of the processes.

References

Agarwal, R., Echambadi, R., Franco, A. M., & Sarkar, M. B. (2004). Knowledge transfer through inheritance: Spin-out generation, development, and survival. *Academy of Management Journal, 47*(4), 501–522.

Ahammad, M. F., Glaister, K. W., & Gomes, E. (2020). Strategic agility and human resource management. *Human Resource Management Review*, *30*(1), 100700.

Aldrich, H. E. (1990). Using an ecological perspective to study organizational founding rates. *Entrepreneurship Theory and Practice*, *14*(3), 7–24.

Anderson, P. & Pulich, M. (2000). Retaining good employees in tough times. *The Health Care Manager*, *19*(1), 50–58.

Andonova, V. & Zuleta, H. (2007). The effect of enforcement on human resources practices: A case study in rural Colombia. *International Journal of Manpower*, *28*(5), 344–353.

Atkinson, A. B. & Stiglitz, J. E. (1969). A new view of technological change. *The Economic Journal*, *79*(315), 573–578.

Bamberger, P., Bacharach, S., & Dyer, L. (1989). Human resources management and organizational effectiveness: High technology entrepreneurial startup firms in Israel. *Human Resource Management*, *28*(3), 349–366.

Bamberger, P., Dyer, L., & Bacharach, S. B. (1990). Human resource planning in high technology entrepreneurial startups. *Human Resource Planning*, *13*(1), 37–44.

Barrett, R. & Mayson, S. (2007). Human resource management in growing small firms. *Journal of Small Business and Enterprise Development*, *14*(2), 307–320.

Barrick, M. R. & Zimmerman, R. D. (2009). Hiring for retention and performance. *Human Resource Management*, *48*(2), 183–206.

Bartram, T. (2005). Small firms, big ideas: The adoption of human resource management in Australian small firms. *Asia Pacific Journal of Human Resources*, *43*(1), 137–154.

Bilal, A. R., Khan, A. A., & Akoorie, M. E. M. (2016). Constraints to growth: A cross country analysis of Chinese, Indian and Pakistani SMEs. *Chinese Management Studies*, *10*(2), 365–386.

Block, J. H., Fisch, C. O., & Van Praag, M. (2018). Quantity and quality of jobs by entrepreneurial firms. *Oxford Review of Economic Policy*, *34*(4), 565–583.

Cardon, M. S. & Stevens, C. E. (2004). Managing human resources in small organizations: What do we know? *Human Resource Management Review*, *14*(3), 295–323.

Cardon, M. S. (2003). Contingent labor as an enabler of entrepreneurial growth. *Human Resource Management*, *42*(4), 357–373.

Carpentier, M., Van Hoye, G., & Weijters, B. (2019). Attracting applicants through the organization's social media page: Signaling employer brand personality. *Journal of Vocational Behavior*, *115*, 103326.

Cho, Y. & McLean, G. N. (2009). Successful IT start-ups' HRD practices: Four cases in South Korea. *Journal of European Industrial Training, 33*(2), 125–141.

Dabić, M., Ortiz-De-Urbina-Criado, M., & Romero-Martínez, A. M. (2011). Human resource management in entrepreneurial firms: A literature review. *International Journal of Manpower, 32*(1), 14–33.

Dana, L.-P. (2000). Creating entrepreneurs in India. *Journal of Small Business Management, 38*(1), 86.

Das, B. L. & Baruah, M. (2013). Employee retention: A review of literature. *Journal of Business and Management, 14*(2), 8–16.

Glen, C. (2006). Key skills retention and motivation: The war for talent still rages and retention is the high ground. *Industrial and Commercial Training, 38*(1), 37–45.

Green, K. (2019). *Competitive People Strategy: How to Attract, Develop and Retain the Staff You Need for Business Success.* Great Britain and United States: Kogan Page Publishers.

Hausknecht, J. P., Rodda, J., & Howard, M. J. (2009). Targeted employee retention: Performance-based and job-related differences in reported reasons for staying. *Human Resource Management, 48*(2), 269–288.

Hayton, J. C. (2005). Promoting corporate entrepreneurship through human resource management practices: A review of empirical research. *Human Resource Management Review, 15*(1), 21–41.

Kickul, J. (2001). Promises made, promises broken: An exploration of employee attraction and retention practices in small business. *Journal of Small Business Management, 39*(4), 320–335.

Kinyili, J. M., Karanja, K., & Namusonge, G. S. (2015). Role of remuneration and career advancement practices on the retention of employees in organizations: Evidence from research. *International Journal of Advanced Research in Management and Social Sciences, 4*(7), 254–279.

Kwon, H. D. & Yoo, O. S. (2017). Retention of capable new employees under uncertainty: Impact of strategic interactions. *IISE Transactions, 49*(10), 927–941.

Moayedfar, R. & Madani, C. M. (2019). African immigrant entrepreneurs in South Africa: Exploring their economic contributions. *Entrepreneurial Business and Economics Review, 7*(4), 57–72.

Monsen, E. & Wayne Boss, R. (2009). The impact of strategic entrepreneurship inside the organization: Examining job stress and employee retention. *Entrepreneurship Theory and Practice, 33*(1), 71–104.

Morrell, K., Loan-Clarke, J., & Wilkinson, A. (2001). Unweaving leaving: The use of models in the management of employee turnover. *International Journal of Management Reviews, 3*(3), 219–244.

Perrin, R. (2016). Retaining older employees is a smart business move. *Strategic HR Review, 15*(6), 246–249.

Rust, R. T., Stewart, G. L., Miller, H., & Pielack, D. (1996). The satisfaction and retention of frontline employees: A customer satisfaction measurement approach. *International Journal of Service Industry Management, 7*(5), 62–80.

Sauermann, H. (2018). Fire in the belly? Employee motives and innovative performance in start-ups versus established firms. *Strategic Entrepreneurship Journal, 12*(4), 423–454.

Urban, B. & Joubert, G. C. D. S. (2017). Multidimensional and comparative study on intellectual capital and organisational performance. *Journal of Business Economics and Management, 18*(1), 84–99.

Urbancová, H. & Hudáková, M. (2017). Benefits of employer brand and the supporting trends. *Economics & Sociology, 10*(4), 41–50.

https://doi.org/10.1142/9789811269554_0016

Chapter 16

Entrepreneurial Leadership and Designing Industry 4.0 Business Models: Towards an Innovative and Sustainable Future for India

Slimane Ed-Dafali[*,¶], Muhammad Mohiuddin[†,‖],
Md Samim Al Azad[‡,] and Aidin Salamzadeh[§,††]**

*Department of Management, National School of Commerce and Management,
Chouaib Doukkali University, Morocco
†Department of Management, Faculty of Business Administration,
Laval University, Canada
‡School of Business, North South University, Bangladesh
§Faculty of Management, University of Tehran, Iran
¶ed-dafali.s@ucd.ac.ma
‖muhammad.mohiuddin@fsa.ulaval.ca
**samim.azad@northsouth.edu
††salamzadeh@ut.ac.ir

Abstract

Business Models of the Industry 4.0 era have received limited attention from researchers. Transformational leadership is needed to innovate, design and build business models in the era of disruptive Industry 4.0. Based on an extensive literature review, this paper leads to an in-depth understanding of the pathway between the business model innovation (BMI) and Industry 4.0 through entrepreneurial leadership. The study develops a new business model framework to manage and shape the scale, speed and complexity of technological and innovative changes based on efficiency-centred and novelty-centred business model designs. Entrepreneurial leadership 4.0 is required to deal with the challenges of the latest technological advances. The traditional business model requires redesigning its processes and structure by balancing digital competencies, managerial traits and business skills. The current research contributes to business model literature by developing leadership 4.0 to reengineer and redesign BMI.

Keywords: Business model innovation, Industry 4.0, entrepreneurship, sustainability, research agenda

1. Introduction

The success of Industry 4.0 adoption requires a new leadership mindset with multi-dimensional skills, competencies and understanding of advanced digital business platforms and their transformational implications, which can be called leadership 4.0. Beyond the purely technical aspects of Industry 4.0, leadership 4.0's effectiveness is virtually equivalent to effective entrepreneurial leadership in the context of digitalisation, automation, robotisation and machine learning. The leadership 4.0 paradigm is needed as the business landscape is transforming rapidly. Entrepreneurial leadership is defined as leadership that creates visionary scenarios that are used to assemble and mobilise a "supporting cast" of participants who become committed by the vision to the discovery and exploitation of strategic value creation (Gupta *et al.*, 2004; Palalić *et al.*, 2017). In addition to the impact on innovation performance (Fontana & Musa, 2017; Rehman *et al.*, 2021), recent studies have highlighted the importance of entrepreneurial leadership in implementing Industry 4.0 technologies (Tortorella *et al.*, 2021). Other studies have reported an increased need to better understand leadership characteristics and skills in the era of Industry 4.0 (Guzmán *et al.*, 2020). The Indian markets, unique in some ways (Dana, 2000), have also been prone to such changes in recent years. It has raised a hot debate about creating a sustainable future for India (Safar *et al.*, 2020; Singh *et al.*, 2021).

The connection between Industry 4.0 and relevant business models has been implicitly investigated in the Indian context (Nascimento *et al.*, 2018). Recent empirical evidence suggests that entrepreneurial leadership significantly influences the adoption of Industry 4.0 business models (Cucculelli *et al.*, 2021). Industry 4.0 business model innovations are needed to cope with the changing business ecosystem. Manufacturing firms need to engage in more efficient business model designs, by transforming their BM from the traditional "make-and-sell" BM into a "sense-and-act" BM (Köbnick *et al.*, 2020). As business models reflect the company's strategic choices (Zott & Amit, 2008), As business models reflect the company's strategic choices (Zott & Amit, 2008), any proposed process redesign needs to be managed by entrepreneurial leaders or managers. From the business model innovation perspective, entrepreneurial leaders continually need to coordinate and balance digital competencies, managerial traits and managerial skills to deal with the latest technological advancement challenges (Chanut-Guieu *et al.*, 2019). We are interested in how entrepreneurial leadership can influence the design of Industry 4.0 business models. The plan-do-check-act (PDCA) method was applied to facilitate the design implementation of business model innovation structures and processes through entrepreneurial leadership and according to the Industry 4.0 challenges (Gurău *et al.*, 2015). This method aims at providing a probabilistic approach to redesign business models with their different stages and structures and map the potential challenges of how an organisation creates, delivers and captures value within the Industry 4.0 environment.

This paper aims to support better business decision-making and provide options for leaders in reengineering and redesigning their business models through leadership 4.0 effectiveness. In what follows, we shall first discuss the theoretical background of entrepreneurial leadership and the fourth industrial revolution. In the second section, we will illustrate how emerging technology and the digital era affect the business model innovation process by redesigning and reengineering its processes and structure. Through an extensive literature review, we will define the type of entrepreneurial leadership needed to design the Industry 4.0 business models.

2. Entrepreneurship and Industry 4.0 in India

The fourth industrial revolution, also called Industry 4.0, was initially introduced in Germany by transforming industrial sectors to a new height by integrating advanced technological development in digitalisation and automation and is being expanded across the world. Indeed, technology use has helped revolutionise important aspects of an organisation's various functions (Mohiuddin *et al.*, 2022). Therefore, Industry 4.0 has been introduced to create a high-tech competitive advantage (de Man & Strandhagen, 2017). Because it can be conceptualised as an industrial upgradation of a production system (Frank *et al.*, 2019), it is essential to define the structure and methodology of the implementation guidelines for Industry 4.0 for successful implementation in the industry (Gökalp *et al.*, 2017). Schwab (2016), the founder and executive chairman of the World Economic Forum, argued that Industry 4.0 would fundamentally alter the way we live, work and relate to one another. The fourth industrial revolution will ultimately lay the foundation for adopting new business models (Rüßmann *et al.*, 2015), which can disrupt the existing way of doing business (Rao & Prasad, 2018). Industry 4.0 can also change all business processes, including products and services, business models and markets, work environment and skills development (Pereira & Romero, 2017). In this sense, the Industry 4.0 trend is mainly related to adding value to the manufacturing process (technology-push) (Frank *et al.*, 2019). A clearer understanding of the role of Industry 4.0 on the overall corporate strategy will help firms understand better how to develop business models and strategise the "make or buy" decision on Industry 4.0 technology (Agrawal *et al.*, 2018). Recent evidence suggests that enterprises use business model approaches to design digital value creation concepts (Goerzig & Bauernhansl, 2018). Importantly, Filser *et al.* (2021) argued that entrepreneurship and BM design play an important role in the BMI core literature. Nevertheless, both entrepreneurship and business model are not clearly and unambiguously defined. A business model is described as "a concise representation of how an interrelated set of decision variables in the areas of venture strategy, architecture, and economics are addressed to create sustainable competitive advantage in defined markets" (Morris *et al.*, 2005, p. 727). A business model lets us simplify complex realities (Stähler, 2002) of doing business by which a company can sustain itself (Rappa, 2000). It creates value that lies beneath the actual processes (Petrovic *et al.*, 2001). In order to generate profitable and sustainable revenue streams (Dubosson-Torbay *et al.*, 2002), it develops effective customer interaction, asset configuration and knowledge leverage (Venkatraman & Henderson, 1998) and sets of actors, activities and collaborations (Rajala & Westerlund, 2005). Also, entrepreneurship is viewed as a concrete solution to generating competitive advantage and technological growth in all types of firms that are oriented towards leadership and excellence in the new global economy (Gupta *et al.*, 2004). Technological innovation and entrepreneurship lie at the heart of the fourth industrial revolution because of technological innovation's critical role in the entrepreneurial processes. Within Industry 4.0, entrepreneurs can drive both evolutionary and revolutionary innovations (Kruger & Steyn, 2021; Pereira *et al.*, 2021). They are essential ingredients in designing a successful business model innovation through Industry 4.0. This chapter defines the Industry 4.0 business model innovation as the conceptualisation and implementation of Industry 4.0 business models (Dana *et al.*, 2022a, 2022b). Today's leaders must simultaneously embrace both exploratory and exploitative innovation activities to catch the opportunity of value creation, capture and delivery associated with Industry 4.0 through business model innovation. However, it is also crucial to consider the embeddedness of entrepreneurial innovations within their sociocultural context to fully meet the needs of Industry 4.0. Also, entrepreneurs need to innovate and respond to change quickly to new business opportunities by using creativity, design thinking skills and technological solutions. Both firms and the education system should take advantage of opportunities to develop technological entrepreneurship aimed at enhancing technological empowerment and employment among students and employees as a foundation to advance new technologies and acquire skills and competencies necessary for Industry 4.0 (Hosseini *et al.*, 2022a, 2022b). In the modern world of technological complexity, new skills are urgently required, especially in dealing with these technological advances in which disruptive innovation played a catalyst role in generating economic and social change. Leadership 4.0 is becoming increasingly vital as technological capability that motivates creativity and innovative work by encouraging team members to try new approaches to team tasks and by setting an example of trust, as well as by using a common vision for developing the process of technological entrepreneurship. We argue that the discourse of entrepreneurial leadership in the modern world of Industry 4.0 is crucial for both technological exploration and exploitation. At the venture-level activities, Chalmers *et al.* (2020) assume that leveraging large datasets and algorithms of artificial intelligence could be turned towards entrepreneurial opportunity identification and exploitation. In this context, companies should develop their ability to explore new business opportunities through Industry 4.0. It is important to note that opportunity is a central concept within entrepreneurship. Entrepreneurs can improve their leadership by building solid intellectual capital, psychological capital, social capital and mentoring entrepreneurial teams for a common organisation goal. They can also develop their leadership style that can enable them to seize the entrepreneurial opportunity that could be marketed profitably. The reality today is that digital leadership is urgently needed to support the digital transition within Industry 4.0, particularly when it helps entrepreneurs to improve their entrepreneurial and strategic decision-making. In the context of technology firms, Martín-Rojas *et al.* (2013) found that top management support for technology and technological skills and technological distinctive competencies is a strategic issue for corporate entrepreneurship and to achieve a competitive advantage (Tajpour *et al.*, 2022). Beyond the traditional entrepreneurial skills, Onar *et al.* (2018) suggest that new business thinking, collaboration with different parties and communication with various stakeholders are essential skills for leadership 4.0. They indicate that e-learning technologies such as gamification, virtual labs and learning analytics should be considered in university programmes. To successfully implement Industry 4.0, firms must deliver valuable products and services efficiently and effectively to meet customer expectations promptly and successfully compete in the current competitive environment. Such an environment involves managing and shaping the scale, speed and complexity of the technological and innovative changes, as well as organisational, managerial and leadership challenges associated with this 4th industrial revolution.

Like many similar countries, entrepreneurial activities are related to Industry 4.0 waves in India. Thus, people need more relevant skills to face new threats and opportunities (Sangwan & Herrmann, 2020). The future of work and enterprising communities will also change accordingly (Mehta & Awasthi, 2019). In a seminal study, Madasala (2018) explored the opportunities and challenges of Industry 4.0 for entrepreneurship development in India. This study provides a big picture of what might happen in the near future. Besides, Hajoary & Akhilesh (2021) propose a framework to access the readiness and maturity of Industry 4.0 in some societies, including India.

3. Emerging Technologies and Business Model Innovation in India

Today's firms and entrepreneurial ventures are increasingly faced with new structural challenges in a new era, such as standardisation in Industry 4.0, balancing human and automation, technological uncertainty and technological complexity, as well as regulatory changes and lack of specialist staff and those due to increasing and globalising competition, which often require managers to significantly redesign their business models to overcome these new environmental conditions and also organisations can quickly cope with technological challenges in order to gain competitive advantage (Salamzadeh, 2018). An effective business model innovation bridges the gap between technological opportunities, organisational capabilities and technological requirements. Many studies have been undertaken to assess the relationship between technology innovation and business models or the change in business models (George & Bock, 2011). Previous studies have revealed the lack of research on Business model innovation through Industry 4.0 (Arnold *et al.*, 2016; Müller, 2019). Recent advances have shown that the potential of both efficiency-centred and novelty-centred business models through Industry 4.0 needs to be considered (Müller *et al.*, 2021). When designing Industry 4.0 Business Models, entrepreneurs then need to identify products or service improvements to guarantee effective integration between activities (Kruger & Steyn, 2021). Industry 4.0 Business Models create new opportunities to compete by redesigning or reengineering the business model and its processes and structure. Importantly, a better business model will often beat a better idea or technology (Chesbrough, 2007). Though scalability and growth disproportionately reward stakeholders, igniting many investigations to radically redesign business processes and structures, the fourth industrial revolution may improve the flexibility, speed, productivity and quality of the production process (Rüßmann *et al.*, 2015). Industry 4.0 adoption requires a radical business model innovation of manufacturing companies (Frank *et al.*, 2019; Müller *et al.*, 2018; Müller *et al.*, 2021). From the business model innovation perspective, Industry 4.0 is viewed as a new industrial maturity stage of product firms, based on the connectivity provided by the industrial Internet of Things (IoT), where companies' products and processes are interconnected and integrated to achieve higher value for both customers and the companies' internal processes (Frank *et al.*, 2019). This may create value for industrial activities and enable access to new markets through IoT solutions, business analytics, blockchain and other emerging technologies. A high-value proprietary technology is the only way to provide value for both customer and internal business processes and to design more sustainable business models. This capability of directly tying internal process quality to meet external customers may keep business models successful. It will be necessary for industrial firms, technological solution innovators and software providers to recognise and understand how sociocultural contexts interact in changing world.

In an innovation context and a changing world, the transition to this new technology will make it possible to move to an industry and production units, mobilising digital technology and guaranteeing the optimisation of business processes by an appropriate change by creating, delivering and capturing sustainable value through business model innovation of an Industry 4.0 solution that better meet customers' changing requirements and adopts the new manufacturing paradigm (Jayashree *et al.*, 2021; Mohiuddin *et al.*, 2019). The business model provides a coherent framework that takes technological characteristics and potentials as inputs and converts them through customers and markets into economic outputs. The business model is conceived as a focusing device that mediates between technology development and economic value creation (Chesbrough & Rosenbloom, 2002). It has elements of both strategy and operational effectiveness (Morris *et al.*, 2005). For example, Filser *et al.* (2021) conducted a bibliometric citation analysis of 30 core articles referenced in 380 business model innovation publications. They identified four core literature streams: value creation through BMI, strategic BM concepts, design of the BM and its connection to entrepreneurship, and interrelation of BM and strategy. Through bibliometric analysis, they highlight that leadership and experimentation with technology contribute to value creation within the BM design through product and technology innovation. More recently, scholars have begun to address leadership issues in the context of Industry 4.0. Prior studies have recognised the role of leadership in Industry 4.0 (Cucculelli *et al.*, 2021; Guzmán *et al.*, 2020; Tetik, 2020).

India is a land of emerging technologies, many of which have been implemented through innovative business models. Such emerging technologies led to major societal changes, and Indian entrepreneurs have developed disruptive business models to exploit entrepreneurial opportunities (Hagl & Duane, 2020; Lindgren, 2020). The range of business model innovations is vast as Indian entrepreneurs exploit entrepreneurial activities at the bottom of the pyramid and wealthy classes. New technologies have also facilitated such business model innovations (Sengupta *et al.*, 2021).

4. Entrepreneurial Leadership in Designing Industry 4.0 Business Models

It is a long-held view that entrepreneurial top management teams are responsible for motivating and leading their employees and setting stretching goals. The design of Industry 4.0 business models requires leadership and the development of an appropriate people and skills strategy that matches the roadmap of the BM transition (Köbnick *et al.*, 2020). A good leader must take advantage of the best employee motivation ideas to foster acceptance of Industry 4.0 business models and reinforce employees' engagement towards higher operational performance levels. Until recently, empirical evidence suggested that family leadership has a significant positive influence on the adoption of Industry 4.0 business models, but only in terms of family ownership (Cucculelli *et al.*, 2021). The successful implementation of Industry 4.0 technologies requires top management's cognitive and leadership capabilities (Agrawal *et al.*, 2018). It requires leaders to have a global mindset. Because Industry 4.0 requires new challenges and new ways of doing things, developing novel business model designs is of prime importance (Frank *et al.*, 2019; Müller *et al.*, 2018, 2021). Novelty and efficiency are the appropriate contingency factors to consider while redesigning the business model

(Zott & Amit, 2008). Thus, they are the corresponding themes (on the business model level) for product differentiation and cost leadership (on the product market strategy level). Consequently, this new business model requires radical redesigning of its processes and structure and a new organisational culture that integrates both efficiency-centred and novelty-centred business model designs. In the fourth industrial revolution paradigm, there is more to this than a simple switch of focus. In fact, it is about which and how technologies could make substantial changes in our perspective towards change in doing business. Under the digital business strategy, these changes may enhance the ability to create personalised customer value at the cost of mass production (Goerzig & Bauernhansl, 2018). It may lead to cost-efficient manufacturing systems based on economies of scale. Such business models will bring new opportunities for relevant companies. Usually a firm must make a choice between them or it will become stuck in the middle (Porter, 1998, p. 17). Leaders may obtain the desired Business Model Innovation for Industry 4.0 through employees' involvement, leadership 4.0 effectiveness and management commitment. The transition to Industry 4.0 from a traditional organisation requires a substantial change at a system level and support from the leaders to innovate, design and build business models. In a consumer-centred economy, the industrial paradigm of leadership 4.0 must help design new business models to overcome strains imposed by growing social, economic, technological and ecological considerations. It is not about the hierarchical view of leadership. Thus, leaders must engage in technological leadership 4.0 to enhance the firm's capabilities in a realistic, standardised and repeatable way. Digital leadership is defined as a combination of the leadership style of transformation leadership and the use of digital technology (Mihardjo & Sasmoko, 2019) for an emerging digital marketplace. Good leadership also includes matching the appropriate level of Managerial Skills with technological competencies, leading to efficient technology adoption. Digital leadership is embedded within the competencies and capabilities to help employees achieve their career goals and aspirations to rightly leverage core Industry 4.0 technologies and adapt technological skills development for competitive advantage. In new models of organisational architecture, entrepreneurial leaders must learn to balance digital competencies, managerial traits and managerial skills in dealing with the latest technological advances and challenges critical to gaining and sustaining a competitive advantage. For that, the business leaders also have the challenges of identifying Business Model chances and risks of Industry 4.0. Leaders now also need to develop the competencies of their employees to effectively develop, adopt and govern Industry 4.0 technologies. Entrepreneurial leadership is assumed to create an effective 4.0 business model design for value creation. Following the PDCA cycle enables us to facilitate the processes of value creation through transforming and redesigning traditional business models in the era of Industry 4.0. The PDCA cycle is considered to be one of the most commonly used tools for implementing continuous improvement of a business's products or processes, including business models.

Summarised in Figure 1, the Industry 4.0 Business Model can be designed through entrepreneurial leadership following four sequential but iterative steps: (i) **Plan** is to set stretching goals based on customer and internal process requirements and the targeted business model innovation. This phase aims to prototype the selected value proposition to satisfy customers' present and future needs and provide greater support in solving their problems. Different tools and methods may be used to facilitate the design of business models and assist innovative and disruptive technologies. (ii) **Do** is to implement the improved Business Model plan. This stage is related to improvements and restructurings in the Business Model process and structures. The phase requires integrating new and existing tools to implement and experiment with the actual business model innovation. (iii) **Check** is to test the performance of the business model through appropriate criteria, and assessment performance regarding the challenges of Industry 4.0 to help firms bridge the design implementation gap in Industry 4.0 business model innovation. (iv) **Act** is to revise and adjust the business model according to Industry 4.0 challenges. This stage implies that successful business models are established as the standard, and unsuccessful business models are redesigned and restructured.

An innovative product may be a feat of engineering. Today, innovation may generate value when designing and engineering the six subcomponents that characterise a business model: value proposition, target market, value chain, value capture (cost structure and revenue streams), value network or ecosystem, and competitive strategy. In a world of

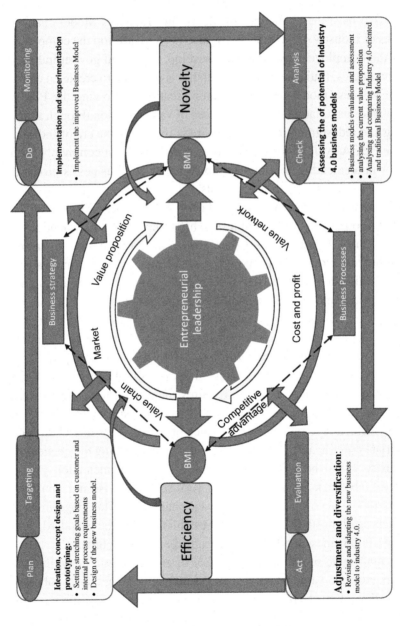

Figure 1.   The proposed framework of the role of entrepreneurial leadership in designing Industry 4.0 business models

Source: Authors' elaboration.

technological change that disrupts existing ways of doing business, a new business model framework for managing change is necessary (see Table 1). As a co-creation method of value, the design thinking method can be used to support firms to efficiently improve the ideation process. Therefore, artificial intelligence (AI) solutions and machine learning have shown great potential in enhancing design thinking practice and in capturing value from innovation. Among the many challenges faced by the Industry 4.0 adoption process, engagement of technologically adept leadership 4.0 within the entrepreneurial innovation ecosystem is fundamental. The design-thinking approach requires concrete leadership actions with sufficient ability to reach clear collective commitments and risk acceptance as well as strategic agility, each of which can enhance a firm's ability to transform and renew its business model in the most valuable way (Doz & Kosonen, 2010). Specifically, with regard to BM design, Filser *et al.* (2021) argued that the core of designing a new BM lies in understanding customer desires, customer assessments, their behaviour and competitors, which goes beyond traditional market research, and leadership 4.0 needs to have attributes to lead in a new industrial 4.0 business ecosystem and satisfy the client's needs and demand in the new context.

For instance, the appropriate leadership 4.0 can decide the firm's value proposition and competitive strategic positioning. It will ultimately be responsible for redesigning its business models through leadership 4.0 and ultimately drives increased profitability. Industry 4.0 is expected to influence value proposition since the technology makes it possible to offer new opportunities for value creation and create new business models by balancing new product quality and innovativeness. Industry 4.0 will also solve some of the challenges facing the world today, such as resource and energy efficiency, urban production and demographic change (Kagermann *et al.*, 2013). Charismatic business leaders may encourage employees to share knowledge between them and to accomplish challenging goals or achieve a common vision or objectives, and capture knowledge from customers by developing a sense of community, co-creating individualised value propositions and communicating with customers through multiple channels. Effective leadership may be quite effective without relying on influence or using authority through creating an organisational climate and a culture of openness that supports and encourages creativity. A leader

Table 1. An explorative theoretical framework for Industry 4.0 business model

Leadership level

Entrepreneurial competencies: Balancing digital competencies, managerial traits and business skills.

Entrepreneurial leadership 4.0: Shared leadership, cognition, communication, ethical leadership, network leadership style, power, innovation leadership, digital culture and digital competence.

Business level

Key partners
- Customers
- Suppliers
- Manufactories
- Ecosystem members
- Public partners
- Co-creators
- Business partners
- Third-party data providers
- Data sharing partners

Key activities
- Additive manufacturing
- Technological integration
- Insourcing/outsourcing options
- Logistics

Key resources
- Smart Human Resources 4.0
- Smart manufactories
- Resource efficiency
- Technological capabilities
- Automated machine tools
- Robotic automation
- Predictive analytics tools
- Shared data infrastructure

Value proposition
- Superior customer value
- Product or service offering
- Differentiation of product or service
- Supporting decision-making and problem-solving
- Collaborative transactions
- Based on crowdsourcing and other open innovation
- Customised and individualised value propositions
- Achieving mass customisation
- Closed-loop production value chain
- Resource and energy efficiency
- Online value co-creation

Customer relationship
- Smart product-service system
- Co-creators of value

Channels
- Online shop
- Direct selling
- Bricks and clicks
- M2M communication
- Wired and wireless network
- AI-based chatbot
- Social media platforms
- Flexible logistics systems

Customers segment
- B to B / B to C/ Multi-sided markets
- Existing customer segment
- New customer segment
- Changing customer behaviour
- Industry 4.0 solution providers

Revenue streams
- New payment models (e.g., pay-per-use payment models)
- Revenues from Big Data analytics
- Subscription-based revenue
- Lifelong service contracts and premium
- Revenue sharing
- Cybersecurity-related services

Cost structure
- Material, machine, production and labour costs
- Cost leadership strategy
- Costs of data storage
- Third-party license fees
- Cost of data acquisition

Addressing sustainability
- Addressing the design and implementation of Industry 4.0 business models through efficiency, sufficiency and consistency strategies for sustainable practices.
- Addressing all three pillars of sustainability — economic, social and environmental.
- Taking into account the efficient allocation of resources.

Source: Authors' elaboration.

creates a conducive climate that allows employees to think freely or outside the box. Entrepreneurial leadership characteristics and skills are clearly needed in today's businesses and must be mapped to the areas where dizzying digital transformation will add value to businesses. The recent industrial advances and the technological developments profiled by the Industry 4.0 paradigm create radically new ways to interact with customers. Charismatic business leaders might create a shared vision in which technological innovation ecosystems oriented to shared value creation are supported and encourage both team learning and knowledge sharing. The latter will facilitate complex problem-solving and find new ways and methods to improve consumer commitment and attachment. It will ultimately lead to successful business model innovation. Crowdsourcing and other open innovation mechanisms may increase the involvement of committed followers in the decision-making process. Business intelligence and the Internet of Things enable and support collaborative value creation that is oriented towards ecosystems (Salamzadeh *et al.*, 2023a, 2023b). Under new demands and conditions, companies in the Industry 4.0 era need to offer cost-efficient production, scalable and more agile provisioning and lean delivery processes to enable new business models aiming to fulfil customer needs to match supply with demand of individual requirements and enable more elasticity and flexibility in production. Since the business model determines the complexity of delivery processes (Meier *et al.*, 2010), it is derived from the digital business strategy, which helps to make the strategy more explicit (Goerzig & Bauernhansl, 2018). In terms of financial components, i.e., the cost structure and revenue streams, Müller (2019) argued that Industry 4.0 can have a transformative impact on revenue streams through automation and may create new payment models such as pay-per-use payment models. They state that revenue streams are named predominantly by the providers of Industry 4.0-based solutions. Furthermore, Industry 4.0 will lead to great changes by opening new revenue streams. In Industry 4.0, firms use continuous revenue models with subscription-based, lifelong service contracts as part of the value capture component (Weking *et al.*, 2018), where risks and revenues are eventually distributed among the interactive partners (Gaiardelli *et al.*, 2021) by supporting determined value creation and delivery mechanisms. Fundamentally, technological advances and applications have led to the introduction of new innovative solutions and may eventually develop new cost structures essential for creating and sustaining a competitive advantage and identifying competitively superior resources. In their study on business models and product market strategy, Zott & Amit (2008) point out that novelty-centric business models contribute to the firms' performance if they are coupled either with a differentiation or cost leadership strategy. This strategy implies lower prices charged to customers, as well as lower input and production costs (Porter, 1998). In terms of sustainability, Industry 4.0 business model innovation requires specific value creation strategies and sustained joint efforts to developing better new products, because both technical and business risks may be shared between suppliers and customers. Therefore, this business model must provide leverage for integrating sustainability considerations. In Industry 4.0, it is the design of business models that incorporates efficiency, sufficiency and consistency strategies to address sustainability (de Man & Strandhagen, 2017). This requires vision and the ability to adapt ethical leadership, because ethical business development contributes towards enhancing corporate social responsibility and environmental management systems in an Industry 4.0 context (Kazancoglu *et al.*, 2021). Analogous to the definition of the sustainable business models as a modification of the conventional business model concept, highlighted by Geissdoerfer *et al.* (2018), we can state that Industry 4.0 sustainable business models could be brilliantly thought out by either (1) incorporating concepts, principles or goals that aim at sustainability or (2) integrating sustainability into their value proposition, value creation and delivery activities, and/or value capture mechanisms. For the successful and sustainable implementation of Industry 4.0, it is critical to rely on appreciating socio-technical features and aspects to design a sustainable architecture for integration in Industry 4.0 (Sony & Naik, 2020). In such an agile process leading to open business models, customers are involved in the co-creation process. Additionally, Industry 4.0 requires new leadership skills and sufficient authority with the knowledge to fully implement a firm's activities depending on the environment changes and requirements. The integration of design thinking may enhance the sustainable business modelling process while integrating a value mapping process (Geissdoerfer *et al.*, 2016). In addition to cost containment, an increase in competitiveness and customer requests has been suggested to improve motivations towards Industry 4.0 investments (Bravi & Murmura, 2021). Thus, new and disruptive business models required for Industry 4.0 technologies (Kagermann *et al.*, 2013) allow businesses to sell the functionality and accessibility of products instead of only selling tangible products (Stock & Seliger, 2016). In Industry 4.0, the main purpose is the emergence of digital manufacturing, or smart factory (Barreto *et al.*, 2017), and new and disruptive business models are highly driven by the use of smart data to offer new services (Stock & Seliger, 2016). With the arrival of Industry 4.0, business modelling has been changing in the last few years because value chains have become more responsive (Pereira & Romero, 2017), and robotic systems have become faster viable economic alternatives to human labour (Strange & Zucchella, 2017). A smart factory requires the synergy of the skills of robots and humans to increase productivity and quality, utilising, mutually, the capabilities of humans and industrial automation devices (Evjemo *et al.*, 2020). While the prospects of smart factory adoption seem good, HR departments across different organisations require Smart Human Resources 4.0 implementation by changing both organisational structure and leadership style (Sivathanu & Pillai, 2018). Smart data arise from big data analytics and predictive analytics tools to predict customers' needs and wants. The factory process will become embedded with Cyber-Physical Systems, allowing manufacturers to seamlessly and instantly share data with many people in real time, quicker than ever. Therefore, companies should understand how they could push leadership to optimally use technologies and related data (Gaiardelli *et al.*, 2021). The infusion of Industry 4.0 in the value chain will lead to potentially deep changes. These changes imply "A move from centralised to decentralised supply chains, where consumer goods manufacturers can implement a 'hybrid' approach with a focus on localisation and accessibility or develop a fully personalised model where the consumer effectively takes over the productive activities of the manufacturer" (Bogers *et al.*, 2016, p. 225). This will naturally give rise to the opportunity to implement new business models supported by additive manufacturing technologies to effectively create value and capture part of that value by leveraging automation, digitisation and increased connectivity across the entire spectrum of manufacturing value chain processes to increase operational efficiency and to proliferate innovative practices for companies. Companies using additive manufacturing technologies can significantly increase the effort and quality of price calculations for their products (Schröder *et al.*, 2015). According to Gibson *et al.* (2015), there are four different categories of drivers of production costs associated with additive manufacturing: cost of the machine, production costs, material costs and labour costs. The sum of these cost drivers represented the total unit cost. Industry 4.0 enables effective maintenance through e-maintenance and smart maintenance strategies (Sezer *et al.*, 2018), enabling predictive maintenance and monitoring through low-cost devices. Using Industry 4.0 capabilities, corporations could engage in a cost leadership strategy to sell a large number of products at lower prices (Agrawal *et al.*, 2018). The move from traditional maintenance approaches to predictive maintenance approaches is not about the destination — it is about the journey. This is important because there is the need for a clear vision and strategy to optimally use the power of technologies related to Industry 4.0. The reason behind this is that if there is no effective leadership in an organisation, no changes will be made (Atkinson & Mackenzie, 2015). Furthermore, it is also important to point out that leaders should motivate and encourage the organisation's employees to act as entrepreneurial leaders, as well as allowing them to make the direction of technological progress in a desirable way.

5. Conclusion

Entrepreneurs are in need of leadership 4.0. This chapter aimed to investigate the importance of entrepreneurial leadership in redesigning and reengineering business model innovation in the era of Industry 4.0. This paper provides options for leaders in reengineering and redesigning their business models through leadership 4.0. Based on previous studies, we can declare that environmental management and technological innovation are crucial factors for business model innovation through Industry 4.0. The PDCA cycle can be considered for business model improvement as a continuous process widely used in management and manufacturing. In the era of the Industry 4.0 paradigm, both managers and experts can adopt a transformational approach to Industry 4.0 by redesigning existing business models or developing new ones. Through the evolution of business models under the impact of technology innovation, it would make sense to consider the consumer acceptance of the Industry 4.0 business model. However, some products that may be potentially interesting high-value-added valorisation pathways in digital technology require upscaling facilities from a technological perspective. It is noteworthy that top leadership and employees' involvement matters. This new manufacturing paradigm would entail a change in mindset, leadership style, focus and creating, delivering and capturing sustainable value through business model innovation of Industry 4.0 solutions. Based on an extensive literature review, we believe that the concept of business model innovation can create a new pathway to socio-technical aspects such as leadership when implementing Industry 4.0 technologies, addressing recent calls to enhance relevance within the field (Tortorella *et al.*, 2021). Thus, we can conclude that the appropriate leadership 4.0 will decide about the firm's value proposition and competitive strategic positioning and will ultimately be responsible for redesigning its business models through entrepreneurial leadership 4.0.

The Indian ecosystem is full of evidence related to entrepreneurial leadership in designing Industry 4.0 business models. Such an approach could move India towards an innovative and sustainable future (Chheda & Banga, 2013; Díaz, 2020). Future researchers could focus more deeply on various aspects of entrepreneurial leadership and how it could be used for business model innovation. Besides, such a relationship is poorly studied in emerging economies where Industry 4.0 is becoming a mainstream trend.

References

Agrawal, A., Schaefer, S., & Funke, T. (2018). Incorporating Industry 4.0 in corporate strategy analysing the impacts of Industry 4.0 in modern business environments (pp. 161–176). Washington, United States: IGI Global.

Arnold, C., Kiel, D., & Voigt, K.-I. (2016). How the industrial internet of things changes business models in different manufacturing industries. *International Journal of Innovation Management*, 20(8), 1640015.

Atkinson, P. & Mackenzie, R. (2015). Without leadership there is no change. *Management Services*, 59(2), 42–47.

Barreto, L., Amaral, A., & Pereira, T. (2017). Industry 4.0 implications in logistics: An overview. *Procedia Manufacturing, 13*, 1245–1252.

Bogers, M., Hadar, R., & Bilberg, A. (2016). Additive manufacturing for consumer-centric business models: Implications for supply chains in consumer goods manufacturing. *Technological Forecasting and Social Change, 102*, 225–239. https://doi.org/10.1016/j.techfore.2015.07.024.

Bravi, L. & Murmura, F. (2021). Industry 4.0 enabling technologies as a tool for the development of a competitive strategy in Italian manufacturing companies. *Journal of Engineering and Technology Management, 60*, 101629. https://doi.org/10.1016/j.jengtecman.2021.101629.

Chalmers, D., MacKenzie, N. G., & Carter, S. (2021). Artificial intelligence and entrepreneurship: Implications for venture creation in the fourth industrial revolution. *Entrepreneurship Theory and Practice, 45*(5), 1028–1053.

Chesbrough, H. (2007). Business model innovation: It's not just about technology anymore. *Strategy & Leadership, 35*(6), 12–17.

Chesbrough, H. & Rosenbloom, R. S. (2002). The role of the business model in capturing value from innovation: Evidence from Xerox Corporation's technology spin-off companies. *Industrial and Corporate Change, 11*(3), 529–555.

Cucculelli, M., Dileo, I., & Pini, M. (2022). Filling the void of family leadership: institutional support to business model changes in the Italian Industry 4.0 experience. *The Journal of Technology Transfer, 47*(1), 213–241.

Chheda, K. & Banga, C. (2013). Impact of entrepreneurial leadership on performance of small and medium enterprises in India. *Journal of Asia Entrepreneurship and Sustainability, 9*(2), 34.

Dana, L.-P. (2000). Creating entrepreneurs in India. *Journal of Small Business Management, 38*(1), 86–91.

Dana, L.-P., Salamzadeh, A., Hadizadeh, M., Heydari, G., & Shamsoddin, S. (2022a). Urban entrepreneurship and sustainable businesses in smart cities: Exploring the role of digital technologies. *Sustainable Technology and Entrepreneurship, 1*(2), 100016.

Dana, L.-P., Salamzadeh, A., Mortazavi, S., & Hadizadeh, M. (2022b). Investigating the impact of international markets and new digital technologies on business innovation in emerging markets. *Sustainability, 14*(2), 983.

de Man, J. C. & Strandhagen, J. O. (2017). An Industry 4.0 research agenda for sustainable business models. *Procedia Cirp, 63*, 721–726.

Díaz, E. R. (2020). Entrepreneurial leadership in Indian and Mexican graduate students. *Latin American Business Review, 21*(3), 307–326.

Doz, Y. L. & Kosonen, M. (2010). Embedding strategic agility: A leadership agenda for accelerating business model renewal. *Long Range Planning, 43*(2–3), 370–382.

Dubosson-Torbay, M., Osterwalder, A., & Pigneur, Y. (2002). E-business model design, classification, and measurements. *Thunderbird International Business Review, 44*(1), 5–23.

Evjemo, L. D., Gjerstad, T., Grøtli, E. I., & Sziebig, G. (2020). Trends in smart manufacturing: Role of humans and industrial robots in smart factories. *Current Robotics Reports, 1*(2), 35–41.

Filser, M., Kraus, S., Breier, M., Nenova, I., & Puumalainen, K. (2021). Business model innovation: Identifying foundations and trajectories. *Business Strategy and the Environment, 30*(2), 891–907.

Fontana, A. & Musa, S. (2017). The impact of entrepreneurial leadership on innovation management and its measurement validation. *International Journal of Innovation Science, 9*(1), 2–19.

Frank, A. G., Mendes, G. H., Ayala, N. F., & Ghezzi, A. (2019). Servitization and Industry 4.0 convergence in the digital transformation of product firms: A business model innovation perspective. *Technological Forecasting and Social Change, 141*, 341–351.

Gaiardelli, P., Pezzotta, G., Rondini, A., Romero, D., Jarrahi, F., Bertoni, M., ... & Cavalieri, S. (2021). Product-service systems evolution in the era of Industry 4.0. *Service Business, 15*(1), 177–207.

Geissdoerfer, M., Bocken, N. M., & Hultink, E. J. (2016). Design thinking to enhance the sustainable business modelling process — A workshop based on a value mapping process. *Journal of Cleaner Production, 135*, 1218–1232.

Geissdoerfer, M., Vladimirova, D., & Evans, S. (2018). Sustainable business model innovation: A review. *Journal of Cleaner Production, 198*, 401–416. https://doi.org/10.1016/j.jclepro.2018.06.240.

George, G. & Bock, A. J. (2011). The business model in practice and its implications for entrepreneurship research. *Entrepreneurship Theory and Practice, 35*(1), 83–111.

Gibson, I., Rosen, D., & Stucker, B. (2015). *Additive Manufacturing Technologies: 3D Printing, Rapid Prototyping, and Direct Digital Manufacturing.* New York: Springer Verlag.

Goerzig, D. & Bauernhansl, T. (2018). Enterprise architectures for the digital transformation in small and medium-sized enterprises. *Procedia Cirp, 67*, 540–545.

Gökalp, E., Şener, U., & Eren, P. E. (2017, October). Development of an assessment model for industry 4.0: Industry 4.0-MM. In *International Conference on Software Process Improvement and Capability Determination* (pp. 128–142). Cham: Springer.

Gupta, V., MacMillan, I. C., & Surie, G. (2004). Entrepreneurial leadership: Developing and measuring a cross-cultural construct. *Journal of Business Venturing, 19*(2), 241–260.

Gurău, C., Lasch, F., & Dana, L.-P. (2015). Sources of entrepreneurial value creation: A business model approach. *International Journal of Entrepreneurship and Small Business, 25*(2), 192–207.

Guzmán, V. E., Muschard, B., Gerolamo, M., Kohl, H., & Rozenfeld, H. (2020). Characteristics and skills of leadership in the context of Industry 4.0. *Procedia Manufacturing, 43*, 543–550.

Hagl, R. & Duane, A. (2020). Exploring how augmented reality and virtual reality technologies impact business model innovation in technology companies in Germany. In Jung, T., tom Dieck, M. C., & Rauschnabel, P. A. (Eds.), *Augmented Reality and Virtual Reality* (pp. 75–84). Cham: Springer.

Hajoary, P. K., & Akhilesh, K. B. (2021). Conceptual framework to assess the maturity and readiness towards Industry 4.0. In Chakrabarti, A., & Arora, M. (Eds.), *Industry 4.0 and Advanced Manufacturing* (pp. 13–23). Springer, Singapore.

Hosseini, E., Ardckani, S. S., Sabokro, M., & Salamzadeh, A. (2022a). The study of knowledge employee voice among the knowledge-based companies: The case of an emerging economy. *Revista de Gestão, 29*(2), 117–138. https://doi.org/10.1108/REGE-03-2021-0037.

Hosseini, E., Tajpour, M., Salamzadeh, A., & Ahmadi, A. (2022). Team Performance and the Development of Iranian Digital Start-ups: The Mediating Role of Employee Voice. In Dana, L.-P., Sharma, N., & Singh, V. K. (Eds.), *Managing Human Resources in SMEs and Start-ups: International Challenges and Solutions* (pp. 109–140). Singapore: World Scientific Publishing.

Kagermann, H., Wahlster, W., & Helbig, J. (2013). Securing the future of German manufacturing industry: Recommendations for implementing the strategic initiative INDUSTRIE 4.0. *Final Report of the Industry, 4*, 1–21.

Kazancoglu, Y., Sezer, M. D., Ozkan-Ozen, Y. D., Mangla, S. K., & Kumar, A. (2021). Industry 4.0 impacts on responsible environmental and societal management in the family business. *Technological Forecasting and Social Change, 173*, 121108.

Köbnick, P., Velu, C., & McFarlane, D. (2020). Preparing for Industry 4.0: Digital business model innovation in the food and beverage industry. *International Journal of Mechatronics and Manufacturing Systems, 13*(1), 59–89.

Kruger, S. & Steyn, A. A. (2021). A conceptual model of entrepreneurial competencies needed to utilise technologies of Industry 4.0. *The International Journal of Entrepreneurship and Innovation, 22*(1), 56–67.

Lindgren, P. (2020). Multi business model innovation in a world of smart cities with future wireless technologies. *Wireless Personal Communications, 113*(3), 1423–1435.

Madasala, A. R. (2018). Exploring the opportunities and challenges of Industry 4.0 for entrepreneurship development in India. *International Journal of Management, IT and Engineering, 8*(9), 306–314.

Martín-Rojas, R., García-Morales, V. J., & Bolívar-Ramos, M. T. (2013). Influence of technological support, skills and competencies, and learning on corporate entrepreneurship in European technology firms. *Technovation, 33*(12), 417–430.

Mehta, B. S. & Awasthi, I. C. (2019). Industry 4.0 and future of work in India. *FIIB Business Review, 8*(1), 9–16.

Meier, H., Roy, R., & Seliger, G. (2010). Industrial product-service systems — IPS2. *CIRP Annals, 59*(2), 607–627.

Mihardjo, L. W. W. , & Sasmoko, S. (2019). Digital Transformation: Digital Leadership Role in Developing Business Model Innovation Mediated by Co-Creation Strategy for Telecommunication Incumbent Firms. In Orlando, B. (Ed.), *Strategy and Behaviors in the Digital Economy*. IntechOpen, Germany. https://doi.org/10.5772/intechopen.82517

Mohiuddin, M., Azad, M. S. A., Ahmed, S., Ed-Dafali, S., & Reza, M. N. H. (2022). Evolution of Industry 4.0 and its implications for international business. In J. W. M. Mohiuddin, M. S. A. Azad, & S. Ahmed (Eds.), *Global Trade in the Emerging Business Environment*. Germany: IntechOpen.

Morris, M., Schindehutte, M., & Allen, J. (2005). The entrepreneur's business model: Toward a unified perspective. *Journal of Business Research, 58*(6), 726–735.

Müller, J. M. (2019). Business model innovation in small-and medium-sized enterprises: Strategies for industry 4.0 providers and users. *Journal of Manufacturing Technology Management, 30*(8), 1127–1142.

Müller, J. M., Buliga, O., & Voigt, K.-I. (2018). Fortune favors the prepared: How SMEs approach business model innovations in Industry 4.0. *Technological Forecasting and Social Change, 132*, 2–17.

Müller, J. M., Buliga, O., & Voigt, K.-I. (2021). The role of absorptive capacity and innovation strategy in the design of industry 4.0 business models — A comparison between SMEs and large enterprises. *European Management Journal, 39*(3), 333–343.

Nascimento, D. L. M., Alencastro, V., Quelhas, O. L. G., Caiado, R. G. G., Garza-Reyes, J. A., Rocha-Lona, L., & Tortorella, G. (2018). Exploring Industry 4.0 technologies to enable circular economy practices in a manufacturing context: A business model proposal. *Journal of Manufacturing Technology Management, 30*(3), 607–627.

Onar, S. C., Ustundag, A., Kadaifci, Ç., & Oztaysi, B. (2018). The changing role of engineering education in Industry 4.0 era Industry. In de Fuentes García-Romero, J. M. *4.0: Managing the Digital Transformation* (pp. 137–151). Cham: Springer.

Pereira, J., Braga, V., Correia, A., & Salamzadeh, A. (2021). Unboxing organisational complexity: How does it affect business performance during the COVID-19 pandemic? *Journal of Entrepreneurship and Public Policy, 10*(3), 424–444. https://doi.org/10.1108/JEPP-06-2021-0070.

Pereira, A. C. & Romero, F. (2017). A review of the meanings and the implications of the Industry 4.0 concept. *Procedia Manufacturing, 13*, 1206–1214.

Petrovic, O., Kittl, C., & Teksten, R. D. (2001). Developing business models for ebusiness. https://dx.doi.org/10.2139/ssrn.1658505.

Porter, M. E. (1998). *Competitive Advantage: Creating and Sustaining Superior Performance*. United States: Free Press.

Rajala, R. & Westerlund, M. (2005). Business models: A new perspective on knowledge-intensive services in the software industry. *BLED 2005 Proceedings*, Slovenia, June 6–8. http://aisel.aisnet.org/bled2005/10.

Rao, S. K. & Prasad, R. (2018). Impact of 5G technologies on Industry 4.0. *Wireless Personal Communications, 100*(1), 145–159.

Rappa, M. (2000). Managing the digital enterprise. http://digitalenterprise.org/index. html.

Rehman, K. U., Aslam, F., Mata, M. N., Martins, J. M., Abreu, A., Morão Lourenço, A., & Mariam, S. (2021). Impact of entrepreneurial leadership on product innovation performance: Intervening effect of absorptive capacity, intra-firm networks, and design thinking. *Sustainability, 13*(13), 7054.

Rüßmann, M., Lorenz, M., Gerbert, P., Waldner, M., Justus, J., Engel, P., & Harnisch, M. (2015). Industry 4.0: The future of productivity and growth in manufacturing industries. *Boston Consulting Group, 9*(1), 54–89.

Safar, L., Sopko, J., Dancakova, D., & Woschank, M. (2020). Industry 4.0 — Awareness in South India. *Sustainability*, *12*(8), 3207.

Salamzadeh, A. (2018). Start-up boom in an emerging market: A niche market approach. In Khajeheian, D., Friedrichsen, M., & Mödinger, W. (Eds.), *Competitiveness in Emerging Markets* (pp. 233–243). Cham: Springer.

Salamzadeh, A., Nalakam Paramba, J., & Karuthedath, S. (2023a). The evolution of business incubation practices over the years: A bibliometric analysis. *International Journal of Entrepreneurship and Small Business*, *48*(1), 1–21.

Salamzadeh, A., Nalakam Paramba, J., Karuthedath, S., & Dheer, R. (2023b). Determinants of startup performance: An empirical analysis of startups from Kerala, India. *International Journal of Entrepreneurship and Small Business*, *48*(2), 12–32.

Sangwan, K. S. & Herrmann, C. (2020). Enhancing future skills and entrepreneurship. In *3rd Indo-German Conference on Sustainability in Engineering* (p. 292). Cham: Springer Nature.

Schröder, M., Falk, B., & Schmitt, R. (2015). Evaluation of cost structures of additive manufacturing processes using a new business model. *Procedia Cirp*, *30*, 311–316.

Sengupta, T., Narayanamurthy, G., Hota, P. K., Sarker, T., & Dey, S. (2021). Conditional acceptance of digitised business model innovation at the BoP: A stakeholder analysis of eKutir in India. *Technological Forecasting and Social Change*, *170*, 120857.

Sezer, E., Romero, D., Guedea, F., Macchi, M., & Emmanouilidis, C. (2018, June). An industry 4.0-enabled low cost predictive maintenance approach for smes. In *2018 IEEE International Conference on Engineering, Technology and Innovation* (ICE/ITMC) (pp. 1–8). IEEE (pp. 1–8), Stuttgart, Germany, doi: 10.1109/ICE.2018.8436307.

Singh, G., Bhardwaj, G., Singh, S. V., Chaturvedi, P., Kumar, V., & Gupta, S. (2021, November). Industry 4.0: The industrial revolution and future landscape in Indian market. In *2021 International Conference on Technological Advancements and Innovations (ICTAI)* (pp. 500–505). IEEE. Tashkent, Uzbekistan.

Sivathanu, B. & Pillai, R. (2018). Smart HR 4.0 — How Industry 4.0 is disrupting HR. *Human Resource Management International Digest*, *26*(4), 7–11.

Sony, M. & Naik, S. (2020). Industry 4.0 integration with socio-technical systems theory: A systematic review and proposed theoretical model. *Technology in Society*, *61*, 101248.

Stähler, P. (2002). Business models as an unit of analysis for strategising. Paper presented at the International Workshop on Business Models, Lausanne, Switzerland.

Stock, T. & Seliger, G. (2016). Opportunities of sustainable manufacturing in Industry 4.0. *Procedia Cirp, 40*, 536–541.

Strange, R. & Zucchella, A. (2017). Industry 4.0, global value chains and international business. *Multinational Business Review, 25*(3), 174–184.

Tajpour, M., Salamzadeh, A., Ramadani, V., Palalić, R., & Hosseini, E. (2022). Knowledge sharing and achieving competitive advantage in international environments: The case of Iranian digital start-ups. In Jafari-Sadeghi, V., Dana, L-P. (Eds.), *International Entrepreneurship in Emerging Markets* (pp. 206–224). Routledge.

Tetik, S. (2020). Strategic leadership in perspective of Industry 4.0. In *Agile Business Leadership Methods for Industry 4.0. Emerald Publishing Limited* (pp. 193–207). Bingley. https://doi.org/10.1108/978-1-80043-380-920201012.

Tortorella, G., Miorando, R., Caiado, R., Nascimento, D., & Portioli Staudacher, A. (2021). The mediating effect of employees' involvement on the relationship between Industry 4.0 and operational performance improvement. *Total Quality Management & Business Excellence, 32*(1–2), 119–133.

Venkatraman, N. & Henderson, J. C. (1998). Real strategies for virtual organising. *Sloan Management Review, 40*(1), 33–48.

Weking, J., Stocker, M., Kowalkiewicz, M., Bohm, M., & Krcmar, H. (2018). Archetypes for industry 4.0 business model innovations. In Bush, A, Grover, V, & Schiller, S (Eds.), *Proceedings of the 24th Americas conference on information systems (AMCIS)* (pp. 1–10). Association for Information Systems (AIS). https://aisel.aisnet.org/.

Zott, C. & Amit, R. (2008). The fit between product market strategy and business model: Implications for firm performance. *Strategic Management Journal, 29*(1), 1–26.

Index

A
adaptability, 104
adaptable, 104
added advantage, 102
artificial intelligence (AI), 41

B
bags, 300–301
Big data, 44
Blockchain, 43
boosting, 95
boosts employees, 96
branding initiatives, 235–238,
   243–245, 247–248
brand orientation, 231, 235, 238, 241,
   243, 246
business development, 93, 103
business environment, 94
businesses, 2, 92–94, 96, 99, 105
business growth, 92, 96
business leaders, 128
business models, 333
business opportunities, 96

business performance, 103,
   105–106
business problems, opportunities and
   threats, 96
business success, 96, 103

C
capitalise, 105
challenges, 19–20, 22–29, 33–34, 91,
   93–94
challenging times, 105
changing environment, 96
communication, 103
communication skills, 92
competencies, 92, 151–168
competition, 90–94
competitive, 94
competitive advantage, 94, 102
competitive edge, 100–101
competitive environment, 105
competitors, 94, 101, 104
confidence, 92, 94–95
convincing the clients, 103

COVID-19, 6–8, 125, 128, 144, 204–206, 208–209, 214–215, 218, 221
creativity, 92–93
creativity and innovation, 94
critical, 93
critical thinking skills, 103
cryptocurrency Bitcoin, 43
culture, 106
customer, 104
cyberattacks, 46

D
data analytics, 42
delivering quality, 103
developing countries, 129
digital, 203–206, 208–211, 214–215, 217–218, 220–221
digital expansion, 104
digital health ecosystem, 204–206, 209–210, 215, 221
digitalisation, 49, 204, 207, 209, 211, 213–214, 217, 221, 336
digital leadership, 342
digital literacy, 104
digital medical consumer, 204, 210–211, 214, 218
digital payment, 44
digital revolution, 38

E
ease of doing business, 14
E-business platforms, 102
eco-friendly, 293–294, 298, 304, 306–307
e-commerce, 45
economic, 90
economic development, 126
economic growth, 90, 126

economy, 92
EdTech, 178–181, 185–191, 194–196
education, 106
effective leadership skills, 94
efficiency, 93, 96
embeddedness, 337
emerging economies, 273–274, 280, 284
employee retention, 317, 323, 324, 326–328
employees, 93–96, 103, 106, 318–322, 326–328
employer, 326–328
employment creation, 126
empower, 106
empowering employees, 96, 105
empowerment, 96
enterprises, 9
entrepreneurial, 89–90, 94, 99, 105, 329
entrepreneurial competencies, 89, 105
entrepreneurial firms, 317–319, 323–324, 326–329
entrepreneurial leadership, 126, 334
entrepreneurial opportunity, 338
entrepreneurial orientation, 103–105, 116
entrepreneurial processes, 337
entrepreneurial roles, 126
entrepreneurial skills, 90, 92, 96, 99, 103, 105
entrepreneurial teams, 338
entrepreneurs, 14, 19–21, 23–29, 33–34, 90, 92–94, 103–105, 300–301
entrepreneurship, 2, 16, 106, 296
environment, 95, 104, 297

EO, 116–117, 119–121
E-pharmacies, 204–205, 209–215,
    217–220
ethics, 320
expansion, 103
export performance, 58

F
family business, 308
family support, 126
financial management skills, 103
financial resources, 104
firm's performance, 105
first mover, 102
flexible, 104
foster, 96
free and open-source software
    (FOSS), 274–276, 278, 280,
    283–284, 287, 289

G
GDP, 2
grow, 104–105
growing SMEs, 89
growth, 94, 103, 106

H
health, 203–211, 214–215, 218–221
healthcare, 6
health informatics, 205–210, 215,
    221
high-quality, 99
holistic digital health start-ups, 204,
    206, 214, 220–221
HR policies, 323, 326, 328
HR practices, 324
human resource management,
    317
human resource module, 319

I
India, 2, 4, 6–8, 10
Indian start-ups, 13, 16
industry, 104
Industry 4.0, 42, 333, 345
initiative, 95, 105
innovation, 38, 91–94, 96, 104–106,
    151–153, 155–156, 158–159,
    165–168, 206, 216, 288–289
innovative solutions, 92
Internet of Things (IoT), 41
intrapreneurial, 94, 106
issues, 19–22, 24–29, 32–34

J
JP, 97
JP Rafts, 97

K
knowledge, 104

L
leader, 95–96, 103
leadership, 92, 94, 96, 105–106
leadership and entrepreneurial
    skills, 96
leadership inspires, 96
leadership skills, 89–90, 94, 105
learning, 151, 153–154, 158–159,
    162, 165–166, 179–181, 183–185,
    189–195

M
machine learning, 44
Make in India, 16
manage, 89, 93, 105
management, 94
managing business, 93
marketing, 104

market leader, 105
measures, 19–20, 22, 24, 27–28, 30, 34
medical, 204–207, 210–214, 221
medium-sized businesses, 128
MICMAC, 76
micro-environment, 101
micro, small and medium enterprises (MSMEs), 2–3, 6, 9, 57, 90, 228–230, 235, 237–238, 240–241, 243–244, 246, 255–256, 258–260, 264–267
micro, small and medium levels, 90
mobile cloud computing, 40
modified total interpretive structural modelling (m-TISM), 60
MSME sector, 228, 231, 248
m-TISM, 67

N
networking, 92, 151, 157, 164, 165

O
opportunities, 92, 103–105
organisation, 104, 323

P
performance, 94–96
productivity, 96
profitability, 96, 105
prompt in meeting, 103
prudent spending, 103–104
purchase behaviour, 43

Q
qualitative research, 125
quality, 98
quality products, 99

R
recognition, 151
reliability, 103
resource, 91–92, 101, 151, 153–154, 156–158, 160, 162–163, 165
resource-based view (RBV), 57
resource management, 93
retention, 317, 319–320, 322–324, 326–329
retention strategies, 319, 327
risk-taking capacity, 104
robotics, 44
RP Inc, 97, 99, 102–103, 105
rural, 299–300, 305

S
SaaS start-up, 3
scanning, 104
skills, 92, 94, 96
small and medium enterprises (SMEs), 2, 16, 19–24, 34, 90–94, 105–106, 116, 119–121, 151–168
small and medium firms, 91
small businesses, 4, 8, 125, 229, 231, 235
small entrepreneurs, 94
SME ecosystem, 16
SME leaders, 105–106
SMEs and start-ups, 41
SMEs' entrepreneurial and leadership, 106
social media (SM), 255–262, 264–267
start-up ecosystem, 11
start-ups, 3, 10, 13–14, 16, 179, 186, 188–189, 191, 194–196, 205, 209, 221

strategic orientation, 203, 231, 236, 238, 241, 246
sustain, 94
sustainable, 93
sustainable growth, 151, 154–157, 161, 165

T
technical skills, 91, 104
technology, 178–181, 183–185, 188–196
telemedicine, 204–205, 209–212, 214, 217–221
timely investment, 103
training programmes, 106
transformational leadership, 333

U
unicorns, 13

Unified Theory of Acceptance and Use of Technology Theory (UTAUT), 255, 257–258, 260, 266
uniqueness, 102

V
VRIO, 101
VRIO analysis, 100–101

W
With Love for Loved Ones (WLFLO), 298, 300, 302, 304, 307
women entrepreneurial leaders, 126, 127
women entrepreneurs, 125–126, 128, 142–143, 145
women entrepreneurship, 126, 128
women leaders, 126

Printed in the United States
by Baker & Taylor Publisher Services